D1558869

Bandits, Eunuchs, and the Son of Heaven

Bandits, Eunuchs, and the Son of Heaven

Rebellion and the Economy of Violence in Mid-Ming China

David Robinson, 1965-

University of Hawai'i Press
Honolulu

Library of Congress Cataloging-in-Publication Data

Robinson, David M.
  Bandits, eunuchs, and the son of heaven : rebellion and the economy
of violence in mid-Ming China / David Robinson.
      p. cm.
  Includes bibliographical references and index.
  ISBN 0–8248–2391–5 (cloth : alk. paper)
  1. Insurgency—China.   2. China—Politics and government—1368–1644.
3. China—Social conditions—960–1644.   I. Title: Rebellion and the economy
of violence in mid-Ming China.   II. Title.

JC328.5   .R63 2001
951'.026—dc21   2001035135

Designed by Santos Barbasa

Printed by The Maple-Vail Book Manufacturing Group

To the memory of
James Peter Geiss

Contents

Acknowledgments

I would like to express my sincere thanks to the ever helpful staffs at the Gest Library of Princeton University, the collections in Kyoto University and its affiliated Institute for Research in Humanities, the Harvard-Yenching Library, the Beijing University Library, and the Beijing Capital Library.

Generous funding over the years has made my research and writing possible. Fellowships from Princeton University freed me from pecuniary worries during my graduate years. Foreign Language Area Studies fellowships made possible a year of language training at the Inter-University Center in Yokohama and a month of fieldwork in Hebei Province. A short postgraduate fellowship from Princeton University allowed me to begin revision of an unwieldy dissertation, while Colgate University's Research Council provided funds for traveling to sites and collections in the United States, Japan, and the People's Republic of China, thus enabling me to finish the bulk of the manuscript for this book. With the support of a postdoctoral fellowship from the American Council of Learned Societies, in 2000, I returned to Kyoto University and its stimulating research environment, where I completed the finishing touches.

As critical as access to documents and funding have been, without the guidance and encouragement of teachers and colleagues, this book would not have been possible. I would like to thank William Atwell, Roger Des Forges, Fuma Susumu, James Geiss, Martin Heijdra, Frederick Mote, Susan Naquin, Willard Peterson, Sugiyama Masaaki, and members of the Colgate University History Department for sharing their expertise and enthusiasm over the years. Finally, the erudite comments of the University of Hawai'i's anonymous readers saved me from many embarrassing mistakes, while the expert editing of Patricia Crosby and Jane Taylor contributed greatly to whatever coherence and clarity I may have achieved in the end.

1
Introduction
The Economy of Violence

With a lunge and a mighty kick, the slight sixteen-year-old boy sent the leather ball hurtling skyward. Uttering a cry of admiration, a strapping young Mongol dressed in a red riding tunic scrambled to keep the ball aloft. Among those who watched the athletic play was a small knot of sturdy men whose sharp eyes darted back and forth between the boy and a dark man elegantly dressed in a red silk gown embroidered with an image of a dragon across the chest. Amid his exertions, the boy frequently turned to the dark man with commentary on the game and what appeared to be sardonic barbs directed at mutual acquaintances.

This scene from one spring afternoon in 1509 is one of the most remarkable in China's long and colorful history. The boy was Wuzong, the tenth emperor of the Ming dynasty (1368–1644). He was supreme ruler of the world's largest, richest, and most populous empire at the time. And to more than a quarter of the globe's population, he also was the Son of Heaven, the one and only person who could mediate between Heaven and Earth and whose proper behavior was inextricably bound up with the harmonious functioning of the cosmos. His kickball companion was a member of the elite imperial bodyguard, whose numbers the young ruler had expanded greatly and in whose company he spent most of his waking hours, much to the distress of his civil officials, who insisted that the young emperor concentrate on weighty matters of state. The ball game occurred in a place called the Leopard Quarter, which served both as Wuzong's private residence and as the center of the emperor's alternate, unofficial government, which often bypassed the well-established civil bureaucracy. The dark man in red silk was Zhang Zhong (Zhang the Loyal), a palace eunuch who acted as the emperor's personal servant and boon companion, as well as a military leader and influential political figure.

What makes the scene remarkable is the identity of the small knot of sharp-eyed men watching this imperial amusement. They all hailed from a medium-sized county called Wenan, about a day's ride south of the capital. Wenan, not coincidentally, was also the home of the eunuch Zhang, their neighbor who had introduced them into one of the most exclusive and securely guarded places in all the world, an inner sanctum where even the highest-ranking state ministers seldom trod. Zhang's neighbors were men of many talents, but they have come down in the imperial records of the Ming court as little more than bandits and rebels.

Explaining this extraordinary meeting in the heart of the Forbidden City between the Son of Heaven, in principal the absolute and paramount ruler of China, and a group of toughs from the lower levels of Ming society requires consideration of the economy of violence during the Ming. Illicit violence was an integral element of Ming society, intimately linked to social dynamics, political life, military institutions, and economic development. Nearly everyone in China—from statesmen and military commanders to local officials and concerned social thinkers, from lineage heads and traveling merchants to farmers, transport workers, and peddlers in the street—grappled with the question of how to use, regulate, or respond to violence in their lives.

"Economy of violence" refers to the administration or management of concerns and resources related to violence in society—when and why people resort to violence, licit or illicit, and how such actions are perceived.[1] A complete analysis of the economy of violence in China during the late imperial period would have to be broad, multilayered, and minutely sensitive to variations of time, place, gender, class, religion, ethnicity, and intellectual orientation. In its broadest sense, the economy of violence intersects with a great range of interconnecting phenomena. The role of martial arts, martial ethos, and military institutions in late imperial society forms an important if still little-explored facet of China's economy of violence. Violence in theater, literature,[2] and the visual arts provides valuable insight into the economy of violence, as does the role of physical and symbolic violence in religious practice, doctrine, and imagery.[3] The economy of violence intersects with studies of the family related to the occurrence, motivation, and reception of wife-beating, husband-beating, and child abuse, as well as acceptable levels of corporal punishment in family discipline.[4] Also relevant are issues of violence, both physical and psychological, in formal and informal penal systems—such as the use of the cangue, public beatings, and executions. Important, too, are popular concepts of honor, justice, and vengeance in various parts of China during different historical periods. One would also need to examine views of the origins, significance, and management of violence.

Much research remains to be done before a truly integrative analysis of China's economy of violence becomes possible. This study contributes to our understanding of the economy of violence during the late imperial period through analysis of a constellation of issues related to banditry and rebellion in the capital region during the middle Ming period, roughly 1450 to 1525. I focus on the middle Ming and the capital region because the specifics of time and place profoundly shape the contours of violence. By the middle Ming, the dynasty was mature and stable; the chaos of the founding years in the late fourteenth century was safely past, and the turmoil of the dynasty's final years lay in the distant future. Beijing was China's political center and the empire's largest city; the surrounding capital region was home to an enormous concentration of military garrisons intended to protect the emperor and his court. This was the most closely regulated and, one might surmise, the most secure region of the entire empire. Yet even here, at the very heart of the body politic, violence was an integral element of local order; in unexpected ways, it linked the lowest levels of society with the most exalted.

Banditry and rebellion confronted the imperial state with an armed challenge and thus demanded attention from the dynasty. The resulting documentary record, while replete with biases and omissions, provides historians with a greater degree of detail than is available for many other facets of the economy of violence during this period. Thus, the first reason for selecting banditry and rebellion as objects of study is a relatively rich vein of extant documents.

The second, and ultimately more important, reason for examining banditry, rebellion, and related issues is that they reveal much about Chinese society during the Ming period.[5] An ongoing, lower-level threat to the dynasty, banditry sheds light on such enduring features of life in the capital region as the interplay among geography, economics, administrative systems, and illicit violence, the complex ways men of force were tied to local officials and capital elites, and the strategies used by the imperial state alternately to eradicate, disband, or co-opt men who were perceived as likely to turn to banditry, or worse.

Rebellion posed one of the greatest threats to a dynasty, by openly challenging the authority and rule of the imperial house and undermining the regime's legitimacy. According to Confucian orthodoxy, rebellion signaled a failure of imperial government, whether through moral laxity of the emperor and his officials, misguided government policies, or some combination of the two. Heaven's favor and the support of the people were at risk, and thus the cosmological and moral underpinnings of the dynasty were called into doubt. Such a crisis prompted conscientious officials to publicly review many existing policies, to point out the emperor's failings, and to propose correctives. Rebellion thus provides a rare opportunity to view contemporary policy evaluation when officials believed it really mattered.

Banditry and rebellion also posed more mundane security threats to the dynasty. From the interruption of the flow of silver and grain to the capital to physical damage inflicted on local yamen offices and records, from deadly assaults on imperial officials to the disruption of agricultural production and widespread human privation, banditry and rebellion alarmed, even terrified, a wide range of social groups in the Ming. Imperial officials and private observers took up well-established social practices that normally were so taken for granted that few people believed they deserved special note. Like disruptions from a geological fault, banditry—and more especially rebellion—were abrupt, violent forces that suddenly exposed layers of Ming society normally hidden from the modern historian.

We know a great deal more about the political, moral, and ideological elements of Ming social order than we do about the role and regulation of violence and coercion.[6] Several excellent studies have examined efforts by the Ming central government to shape social behavior and mores through education, ideology, religion, rites, sumptuary regulations, and law codes.[7] Others have focused on the place of local elites in the social order, portraying them variously as public-spirited mediators between the interests of the central government and local communities or as self-interested players who sought to dominate local society and use their connections at court to gain special privileges.[8] These researches have enormously advanced our understanding of the workings of late imperial society, yet the place of violence in the social order of Ming China remains largely unexplored.

Most Western scholarship that touches on violence during the Ming period has discussed it in the context of the chaos attendant upon dynastic foundings and collapses or as a transient consequence of severe short-term socioeconomic dislocations.[9] Most studies have limited the discussion of violence to the tumultuous rise of the dynasty in the late fourteenth century and its collapse in the early seventeenth century.[10] Scholarly inquiry that bears on the question of violence during the middle period of the dynasty has centered on the outbreak of piracy along the southeastern coast during the mid-sixteenth century. These studies generally argue that piracy and its attendant violence were by-products of specific historical conditions: Ming prohibitions against a highly lucrative international trade, tense relations between maritime traders and local elites, political and military changes that occurred in coastal regions of Japan, and ongoing tensions between the central government and the interests of what one scholar has aptly coined the "coastal periphery."[11] Relatively little attention has been paid to the ongoing violence in the inland areas.

Although such tumultuous periods as dynastic change may give rise to aberrant conditions, these conditions reveal much about ongoing but less well-documented social patterns.[12] James Tong's groundbreaking *Disorder under Heaven* did much to dispel the mistaken notion that Ming China was a bucolic paradise and showed that violence was an enduring facet of social life. Tong's statistical analysis demonstrated that for any given year during the dynasty, armed conflict might be found in at least one region of the empire and that some areas of China were notorious for their perennial violence and truculent populations.[13] Yet even Tong's magisterial work leaves much untouched. His analysis remains predicated on the assumption that violence was in some sense an aberration—the product of poor rulers, of distance from centers of political and military power, or of domestic unrest produced by international conflicts.[14] This study argues, in contrast, that violence was fully integrated into Ming life, during good times and bad.

Recent Japanese, Korean, and Chinese scholarship has begun to uncover a poorly understood but fascinating segment of Ming society, where violence pervaded everyday life. Beggars, vagabonds, enforcers, pettifoggers, pickpockets, robbers, bandits, and petty government clerks populated this fluid world.[15] "Fighters guilds" (*dahang*) in the thriving southeastern cities of Hangzhou, Suzhou, and Songjiang offered a variety of services during the late Ming. For a fee, their members would bully, beat, maim, or even kill as directed. They could be brutally direct, surrounding their victim on a crowded city street and pummeling him senseless. More subtle but no less dreaded was their reputed delayed "death touch": strikes to critical pressure points on their victim's body that left no observable mark and whose deadly efficacy would become manifest only weeks or even months later.[16] Brothels, gambling dens, confidence games, extortion, and blackmail also figured in the netherworld of late imperial China. Even such macabre practices as the use of corpses to extort hush money or to frame enemies were prevalent enough to be addressed both in vernacular literature and legal codes.[17]

Songshi, or "pettifoggers," comprised another prominent group in late imperial society. Most officials and literati during the late imperial period damned the pettifoggers for encouraging unnecessary litigation, for hoodwinking simple commoners with promise of easy gain, for colluding with government clerks at the expense of both the state and the people, and for making use of local toughs and private eyes to dig up (or make up) dirt on local officials and men of status.[18]

The pettifoggers, though, were not social parasites. Often drawn from the ranks of the lowest examination degree holders, students, and those who had failed the civil service exams, the pettifoggers provided critical services in a society that was surprisingly litigious. They prepared for their clients legal documents that satisfied the demanding technical and stylistic requirements of the magistrate's court. They handled anfractuous negotiations over the service fees or bribes with the men who oversaw criminal and civil investigations—yamen clerks. If a client was dissatisfied with the court's decision, the pettifoggers offered guidance about how to appeal the decision to higher courts. All this took place despite the fact that by law, the pettifoggers were not permitted into the courtroom. Their very existence was repeatedly (which suggests ineffectively) prohibited by government officials.[19] The generalization that legal action was anathema to most Chinese simply does not bear scrutiny for many areas of the empire. Many county yamens commonly processed between ten thousand and twenty thousand pages of court documents each year. During the course of their lives, most people, either by themselves or as family members, became involved in at least one legal case.[20]

The most systematic and fruitful attempts to incorporate the role of violence into our understanding of social order during the late imperial period have been studies based on developments along the southeast coast (southern Fujian and eastern Guangdong Provinces) during the subsequent Qing period (1644–1911). Violence there was closely linked to lineage structure, demographics, geography, ethnicity, economics, and brotherhood associations during the eighteenth and nineteenth centuries.[21] Violence formed an enduring feature in local society throughout much of southeastern China, inextricably interwoven into the fabric of the social order.[22] Fierce lineage-based feuds grew out of particularly harsh local conditions in southern Fujian and eastern Guangdong, where limited arable land, intense commercial competition, weak state control, and strong lineage organizations (whose development was largely the result of the factors noted above) made violence an everyday concern.

The violence often acquired a life of its own. Feuds were open-ended and deeply etched into patterns of daily life, influencing notions of honor and justified vengeance. Violence initiated by lineage heads often slipped beyond their control. Mercenaries who sold their services and had a strong interest in the continuation, even escalation, of violence often came to dominate lineage conflicts. In a very real sense, violence developed into a local industry, providing opportunities to indigent men, ambitious bravos, elites who used local muscle to protect commercial interests, and grasping local clerks who solicited bribes to suppress damaging evidence or ensure advantageous judicial decisions. Scholars have likewise sought to explain the relationship among violent conflict, population growth, and the changing value of land,[23] and the causes and perceptions of banditry, theft, and criminality in the Southeast during the eighteenth and early nineteenth centuries.[24]

All these studies convincingly show that violence was fully integrated into nearly all aspects of life in the Southeast during the Qing period, influenced by and in turn affecting economics, demographics, state-society relations, organized crime, lineage solidarity, land relations, and social organization. These studies are correct when they insist that limited and ineffective state presence greatly contributed to the brutal tenor of life in the Southeast during the Qing, which prompted men to turn to powerful lineages and mutual-aid associations for protection.

Yet, as this study will demonstrate, violence was by no means exclusive to the periphery. Intricate and often delicate sets of connections bound bandits, military personnel, men of force, and capital elites during the Ming period. Chinese economies of violence varied greatly according to time and place. As recent work on religious variety has demonstrated the importance of regional variation, the study of violence must be equally sensitive to local differences.

That it is still necessary to point out either the pervasiveness or regional variation of violence in China suggests certain fundamental differences in our understanding of early modern Europe and China during those centuries. Most general descriptions of fifteenth- and sixteenth-century western Europe include violence as a prominent characteristic of the age.[25] J. R. Hale wrote of "an undercurrent of violence in all levels of society" and a "society brutalized by a habitual exposure to and indifference toward cruelty."[26] Fernand Braudel drew attention to the "endless subterranean revolution which marked the whole of the sixteenth century and then the whole of the seventeenth century,"[27] the "agile, cruel, everyday war"[28] of banditry in the Mediterranean during the latter half of the sixteenth century, and the fact that "human life was not valued highly in the sixteenth century."[29] Commenting on late-fifteenth-century Parma, Italy, Jacob Burckhardt wrote, "Burglary, the demolition of houses, public assassination and murders, were events of everyday occurrence."[30] The generally violent tenor of the times is often linked to the increasing frequency, intensity, and technical sophistication of warfare in Europe.[31]

Ironically, it was through the greater power occasioned by the demands of intensified warfare that the central state in such countries as France and England came to monopolize violence.[32] Although the question has stirred intense debate, many have argued that the growing power of the central state exercised a salutary influence on interpersonal violence. In a classic essay, Lawrence Stone argued that levels of violence in England fell steadily during these centuries.[33] Although many have objected to Stone's methodology and conclusions, what is of note here is that scholars of early modern European history have addressed this issue as a matter of course.[34]

Violence has also been considered in relation to important political and social change elsewhere in the early modern world. Scholars have drawn causal links between banditry and state power in the Ottoman Empire during the sixteenth and seventeenth centuries. Many have explained the existence of large, well-organized bandit groups as a sign of Ottoman decline and the result of growing decentralization of power. In contrast, Karen Barkey has more recently argued that in fact the state successfully manipulated these bandit groups as part of efforts at state consolidation. In either case, negotiations between the state and these notorious bandit chiefs figured prominently in contemporary chronicles, were openly acknowledged by government officials (even the sultan), and have played an important part in modern narratives of sixteenth- and seventeenth-century Ottoman history.[35] Violence, assassination, escalating warfare, and growing militarization transformed Japan during the latter half of the fifteenth and the majority of the sixteenth century, before Oda Nobunaga, Hideyoshi Toyotomi, and Tokugawa Ieyasu gradually established political and military hegemony, ushering in the establishment of the *pax Tokugawa* in the early seventeenth century.[36]

In stark contrast, until very recently scholars of Chinese history have evinced little interest in violence during this period. Part of the reason may be that state-building is not a particularly relevant issue for China during these centuries. China enjoyed a well-established tradition of a strong centralized government staffed by a professional bureaucracy recruited through a taxing series of civil service examinations. Again, unlike Europe, scholars generally have taken it for granted that the Chinese state had long monopolized violence, and that overall levels of violence were low. R. Bin Wong has recently argued that while the late imperial Chinese state did rely on coercion, far more important were its efforts to maintain control through extensive commitments to education, morals, and material well-being.[37]

Wong is correct to emphasize the distinctively broad moral and educational ambitions of the Chinese imperial state, but one suspects that modern scholars, influenced by the insistence of lofty Confucian rhetoric (both in imperially compiled sources and in privately written records), have been too quick to dismiss violence and crime as adventitious. Prescriptive descriptions of society by Chinese literati and officials have influenced our understandings of Ming society through their constant refrain of social harmony, moral cultivation, the civilizing effects of education, and the people's innate good and obedient nature. These should be understood not as a reflection of social reality but as evidence of social ideals. Coercive force by the government and illicit violence in society were a very real part of everyday life in Ming China.

The initial observations of early European visitors contributed greatly to enduring European perceptions of traditional China as ordered, civil, and harmonious, and may explain in part the a priori dismissal of the entire issue of violence. Held captive by Chinese authorities in Canton for nearly a decade during the 1520s and 1530s, several Portuguese adventurers with diplomatic credentials desperately attempted to call attention to their plight by writing letters to Portuguese authorities in India and Portugal.[38] As a way to secure their liberation, the imprisoned diplomats encouraged the Portuguese colonization of southern China. One of the captives, Vasco Calvo, peppered his correspondences with assurances of the profitability and ease of China's colonization: "Another India would be won, and of as great profit."[39] "It was more difficult to take Goa than it will be to take these cities and subjects, by reason of the people's being very weak to a large extent, and they have no loyalty towards king nor father or mother; they go only with him who can do most."[40] "This is the most suitable race and country of any in the whole world to be subjugated."[41]

To allay any potential qualms about the difficulty of invading Canton, the letters portrayed the Chinese as docile, timid, and unskilled in war. Routinely abused by government officials, "The people is so docile and fearful that they dare not speak."[42] "The Chinese are full of much cowardice, and hence they come to be presumptuous, arrogant, cruel."[43] Calvo informed his Portuguese readers, "Arms were all but unknown among the people." He claimed that "they [the common people] have nothing in the way of sword or arrow. . . . From the time they are born until they die they take nothing in their hand but a knife without a point to cut their food."[44] The Portuguese remarked, "None of the people may carry arms except they do it under pain of death. The men of arms may not carry them at home when they have done their duty, the mandarins give them [i.e., weapons] so long as they serve under them: when this is finished they are collected at the house of the mandarin."[45] Calvo jeered that the imperial armies were less competent than children, and, "It is a mere mockery to talk of men of arms in this country of China."[46] "There is not a Malabar [southwestern coastal region in India] that could not fight with forty of these men and kill them all," Calvo observed derisively, "because they are just like women; they have no stomach, simply outcries."[47]

Writing late in the sixteenth century, Italian Jesuit Matteo Ricci, a far more informed and insightful observer than Calvo, echoed many of his claims. "No one is permitted to carry arms within city limits," Ricci noted, "not even soldiers or officers, military prefects or magistrates, unless one be en route to war or on the way to drill or to a military school."[48] After acknowledging in passing that travelers might carry metal daggers "on a journey as protection against robbers," Ricci wrote, "Fighting and violence among the people are practically unheard of, save what might be concluded by hair pulling and scratching, and there is no requiting of injuries by wounds and deaths."[49]

Accustomed to the higher levels of daily violence of western Europe, some Portuguese adventurers were further inured to bloodshed, cruelty, and physical coercion during their attempts to colonize Asia. Others, like the authors of the Canton letters, intentionally understated the martial abilities of the Chinese to encourage Portuguese colonization. Although few would accuse the Catholic missionary Matteo Ricci of being violent, his standards for acceptable levels of personal violence were formed in central Italy, an Italy which at the time was "completely overrun with delinquents, vagabonds, and beggars"[50] and "a brigand's paradise."[51] In the words of one scholar, "Ricci's childhood world of Macerata was encircled by war and suffused with violence."[52] Thus, China's failure to impress Europeans as a violent place or culture should not imply that violence and crime were absent; they simply paled in comparison with current European standards. To put contemporary European standards in perspective, among the very few people in the world who struck the European observers as meriting praise for their martial qualities were the Japanese samurai warriors engaged in an unprecedentedly vicious, long, and bloody civil war during the sixteenth century.[53]

The generally favorable writings of Matteo Ricci and later Jesuits strongly influenced European images of China, but they were challenged periodically by criticisms of the Central Kingdom. Inspired in part by Jesuit writings, such writers as Voltaire and others were drawn to certain ideals of Chinese culture and politics: its strong civil tradition, the ascendancy of men of merit and learning, the secular natural philosophy of "Confucianism," and its promise of harmony and social order. In contrast, others were much more critical, often stressing the dominance of China's despotic emperors, who maintained their rule through merciless oppression and sheer terror. In the nineteenth century, the themes of China's stagnation, timelessness, rampant corruption, and unhealthy insularity gained new currency.[54]

What is important for our purposes here is that the presumption of China as a formidably ordered empire with a subservient and generally docile population persisted and became pervasive. Writing in the late seventeenth century, mathematician Gottfried Wilhelm Leibniz praised the Chinese because they "also yield to us in military science, not so much out of ignorance as by deliberation. For they despise everything which creates or nourishes ferocity in men, and almost in emulation of the higher teachings of Christ, they are averse to war." He further noted, "It is difficult to describe how beautifully all the laws of the Chinese, in contrast to those of other people, are directed to the achievement of public tranquillity and the establishment of social order, so that men shall be disrupted in their relations as little as possible."[55] Montesquieu, who was generally critical of China and its government, countered that "China is a despotic state whose principle is fear" and drew attention to the terrible "chains" with which the state armed itself to keep the populace in check.[56] Despite countless reports of banditry, rebellion, and savage brutality from a China in the throes of civil chaos and more recently the Great Proletarian Cultural Revolution, the image of an ordered and docile populace persists.[57]

Banditry and rebellion in China hold relevance for larger questions about state and society relations in the early modern world. Extending more than 1,200 miles from the Great Wall in the north to semitropical rice lands in the south and more than 1,000 miles from the Pacific Ocean in the east to the desolate, wind-swept province of Shaanxi to the west, the Ming empire in 1500 was the greatest of its day. With an estimated population greater than 155 million at the turn of the sixteenth century[58] (compared with approximately 60 million for all of Europe[59] and 30–35 million for the Ottoman Empire),[60] it was the most populous empire in the world. During the late fifteenth and early sixteenth centuries, its dynastic capital, Beijing,[61] had a population of between 800,000 and one million;[62] at least four other cities had populations above 500,000, while

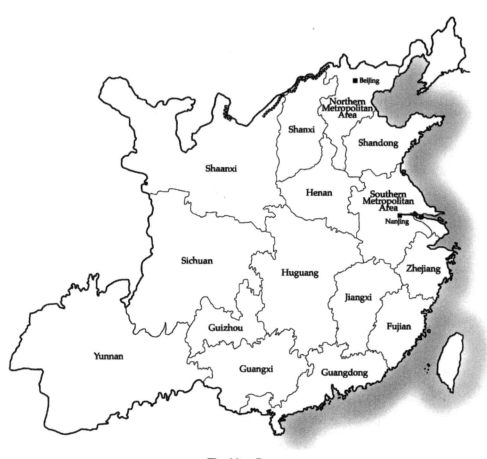

The Ming Empire

another four or five hovered in the range of 300,000.[63] Venice, with a population of 115,000, was Beijing's nearest rival, while the capital of the Ottoman Empire, Constantinople, had a population of 70,000 in the late fifteenth century (which rapidly grew to 400,000 in the next century).[64] Finally, there was China's large and powerful economy. After a mid-fifteenth-century lull, the Ming economy grew vigorously through most of the sixteenth century.[65] Commenting on the global economy during the early modern period, Andre Gunder Frank has recently pointed out, "the entire world economic order was—literally—Sinocentric."[66]

Most germane to the question of violence and its relationship to state-society relations is the fact that the Ming boasted one of the largest and most sophisticated governments in the world. From his palace in Beijing, the emperor oversaw a bureaucracy composed of more than 20,000 men and a subbureaucracy several hundred times that size.[67] They staffed the central government and the 1,200 or so prefectural, subprefectural, and county seats spread across the empire.[68] Although of limited scale and efficiency by twenty-first-century standards, the Chinese bureaucracy deeply impressed many European observers of the late sixteenth century. The Augustinian monk Juan González de Mendoza wrote in his influential 1585 work on China, "This mightie kingdome is one of the best ruled and gouerned of any that is at this time knowen in all the world."[69]

This study, then, examines the role of illicit armed violence in the social order of the world's most populous country and explores how the largest, most sophisticated, and prestigious central government of the day sought to regulate violence. As a non-Western country, China raises important theoretical questions about the relation between the emergence of strong centralized governments and violence. Such scholars as Max Weber, Norbert Elias, Anthony Giddons, and Charles Tilly have emphasized the monopoly or virtual monopoly over violence in the development of strong centralized states in early modern Europe. In contrast, Karen Barkey, in her study of banditry and state formation in the Ottoman Empire, has contrasted western European patterns of state formation with those of China (her remarks are based primarily on conditions during the Qing), Russia, and the Ottoman Empire. She argues that the latter three were often more likely to negotiate rather than destroy threats to the state. This study finds ample support for her characterization of the late imperial Chinese state. Large, strong, and centralized by contemporary world standards, China nonetheless maintained an extensive range of strategies to deal with illicit violence.[70]

One noteworthy facet of the late imperial Chinese state's attitude toward violence was the firm belief that all segments of society could be integrated into the body politic. In apparent contrast to early modern Western Europe, the Chinese state saw no need to identify certain groups or classes as "the other" to define an acceptable society or to bolster uncertain authority.[71] Through an ever-shifting mix of physical coercion, education, moral suasion, negotiation, and co-option, it was held that even the most recalcitrant elements could be transformed into useful members of the wider community.[72]

An example from one of China's best-known vernacular novels, *Journey to the West*, aptly demonstrates some of these concerns and beliefs. Sun Wukong, often known as Monkey or the Monkey King, has appealed to generations of Chinese of all ages and has been featured in plays, movies, and cartoons. Possessed of supernatural powers, Monkey begins the novel as an arrogant, petty potentate who wreaks havoc throughout Heaven and Earth. The forceful and deceptive hand of Guanyin, a powerful Buddhist deity, finally restrains Monkey by placing an iron ring on his head; the ring causes excruciating pain whenever he behaves improperly. In this way, Monkey gradually is transformed into an invaluable, but not markedly less violent, guardian for a sacred enterprise—securing Buddhist texts from India.

The novel lends itself to many interpretations, but here we may use it as a metaphor for the regulating power of state authority.[73] Simple extirpation of trouble-makers might on occasion be unavoidable, but the ideal course of action always entailed redirecting violent forces to the advantage of the state and the society. Monkey became only slightly less violent in the employ of Buddhism than he had been in his earlier career; but he now directed his violence toward acceptable, even laudable, ends. In this respect, the transformation of Monkey's character stands as a metaphor for the far-reaching and powerful transformative capacity of imperial authority—a capacity based no less on coercive force than on moral suasion or "virtue."

Structure and Event

This study is in two parts. The first part analyzes the causes and enduring structures of violence and social order in the capital region during the period 1450 to 1525; the second part describes in detail a historical instance of banditry, rebellion, and its consequences that transpired from 1509 to 1525, until now all but unexamined in English. These two parts are intended to complement and supplement each other in several ways. Part 1 examines structural features of society in the capital region, which, while subject to change, constituted relatively stable patterns of social organization. Part 2 explores in depth an event that, while an outgrowth of the structural patterns discussed in part 1, was a product of a specific time and set of circumstances.

Between 1509 and 1513, Ming China experienced some of the most widespread and intense social unrest of the dynasty. Nearly all corners of the empire witnessed large-scale military clashes between powerful outlaw bands and a wide variety of local garrisons, imperial regulars, elite Capital Garrison troops, Mongol regiments, Shaolin Temple warrior monks, private militias, aboriginal Wolf Troops, and veteran soldiers from the northern borders. The largest of these rebellions, the 1510

Rebellion (often dubbed the Rebellion of Liu the Sixth and Liu the Seventh in Chinese and Japanese studies) developed on the North China plain and eventually spread to nearly half of Ming China's thirteen provinces and two metropolitan areas.[74]

Late in July 1509, the imperial court specially appointed two high-ranking officials to suppress the dangerously widespread brigandage afflicting much of North China. Both officials won special permission to maintain their own private military retainers during their tour of duty. As summer turned to fall, China's emperor, the Military Ancestor, began publicly to express frustration with local officials, whom he believed had covered up the true extent of banditry and who had failed to effectively check its spread. In February 1510, however, the emperor did praise the efforts of one prominent official who had implemented harsh policies combining terror, intimidation, and tight social controls. In April 1510, this same official successfully petitioned the court to call up special Mongol regiments from prefectures south of Beijing to meet the growing danger of powerful outlaw bands.

Later that month, the emperor responded to what he perceived as the fundamental causes of North China's turmoil. He ordered his officials to ritually purify themselves for nine days to atone for the long drought and dust storms that afflicted North China. The Martial Ancestor also dispatched an official to offer sacrifices and report to the deities of Heaven and Earth, of grain and soil, and of mountains and rivers. Coupled with these measures designed to restore cosmic harmony, the emperor announced extensive pardons for a wide range of offenders in an effort to lessen social strife and resentment.

Thus, widespread drought, imminent threat of harvest failure, and increasingly virulent banditry provided the potential for widescale rebellion. It was court intrigue in Beijing, however, that sparked the powder keg. During the spring of 1510, bitter struggle for political dominance between two leading palace eunuchs upset established patronage networks that had linked eunuchs to leading men of force from counties south of Beijing. Such men as Zhang Mao and his subordinates, like Liu the Sixth, Liu the Seventh, and Tiger Yang, who had enjoyed intimate ties with leading palace eunuchs and local officials, were now declared enemies of the state. During the closing months of 1510, a vindictive campaign of extirpation provoked the Liu brothers and Tiger Yang into a series of flagrant attacks on government offices and storehouses.

The government's military campaign against the Liu brothers and other rebel leaders in North China changed dramatically over the first eight months of 1511. It began uncertainly and without any apparent sense of urgency. During the early months of 1511, the Liu brothers avoided pitched battles with imperial forces, preferring instead to bribe army officers south of the capital to turn a blind eye to their presence. By March, however, perhaps responding to pressure from their superiors, these same army officers were beginning to push conflicts to the brink. Elsewhere in North China, highly mobile bandit groups attacked imperial warehouses, freed prisoners from local government compounds, and abducted officials. It is critical to remember that although their names eventually grew synonymous with the rebellion, up to this point, the Liu brothers and Tiger Yang represented only a fraction of the outlaw armies that roamed North China. They were not even the most prominent. During the spring of 1511, the Ming court responded by organizing a one-thousand-man force drawn from the elite capital garrisons, mobilized regulars from local garrisons in Shandong and the Northern Metropolitan Area, and collected extra levies to cover rising military costs.

By mid-April 1511, the unrest had grown to sufficient proportions that one of the most senior statesmen at the Ming court felt the need to address the causes of and proper response to the problem in a long and detailed policy paper. Based on his senior recommendations, the court appointed a pair of high-ranking civil and military officials to oversee the campaign against the bandits. Partly because of the limited resources initially placed at their disposal, rather than adopt an aggressive military stance, these two men attempted to negotiate the surrender of the Liu brothers and Tiger Yang, who had grown to be the most prominent rebel leaders in North China. The imperial court eventually grew impatient with the inconclusive negotiations; in August 1511, the two supervising officials were recalled to the capital, taken into custody, and interrogated. One, broken and disgraced, died in an imperial prison cell. New, presumably more aggressive men replaced them.

The government facilitated a more militant approach by greatly increasing troop levels, funding, and discretionary powers. In fact, the court grew so frustrated with the incompetence of imperial regulars and the capital garrisons, the empire's putative elite forces, that in mid-August 1511, it approved calls to transfer battle-tested troops from the northern border to serve in the campaign against the bandit-rebels. This decision marked an important departure from conventional policy. Valued for their fighting prowess against the Mongols and Jurchens, China's chief rivals to the north, the border troops were also seen as a potential threat to the central government and thus generally were kept

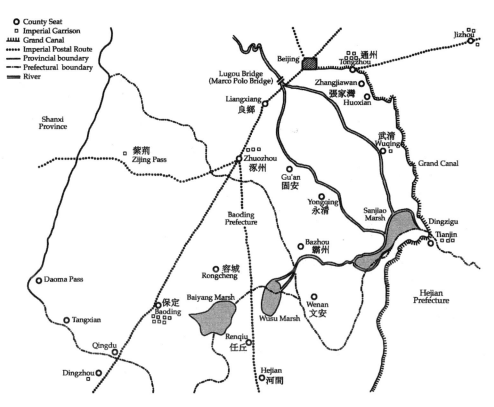

O County Seat
□ Imperial Garrison
ᴜᴜᴜ Grand Canal
••••• Imperial Postal Route
——— Provincial boundary
—··— Prefectural boundary
▬▬ River

The Capital Region during the Mid-Ming Period

far from the capital. Their deployment against domestic challengers reflects both the bandits' growing strength and the government's rising worries.

During these first eight months of 1511, bandit armies grew to the proportions of true rebellion. They attacked government offices and fought imperial troops not only in the Northern Metropolitan Area and Shandong but throughout Henan, northern Huguang, and eastern Shanxi Provinces. Perhaps under the influence of Madman Zhao, a government student and member of the local elite from a county south of the capital forced to join the outlaws, the bandits began to articulate imperial ambitions.

From September 1511 to May 1512, the rebels posed their most acute military and political threat to the Ming dynasty. Of the dozens of smaller, nameless outlaw bands operating throughout North China, two major groups took loose form, one under the leadership of Tiger

Yang and Madman Zhao and a second under the command of the Liu brothers. Only loosely joined, the two groups campaigned north from the vicinity of Beijing south to the Yangzi River, west from the mountain passes between Shanxi Province and the Northern Metropolitan Area east to the coastal plains of Shandong. Although both groups moved almost constantly, the smaller band under the leadership of the Liu brothers was the more mobile. They successfully exploited the large supply of horses available in North China and their formidable cavalry skills to repeatedly defeat imperial armies. Forces under Tiger Yang, Madman Zhao, and others absorbed more local groups, grew less mobile, and adopted grander political rhetoric and forms. At their height, their followers reputedly numbered more than 130,000 men, who were organized into twenty-eight garrisons overseen by an embryonic bureaucracy.

Neither rebel group posed a serious threat to the dynasty's legitimacy. Nor did they take many pains to establish regularized political or economic control of the areas through which they passed. Their raiding, however, threw into clear relief the limitations of imperial control at the local level. Rebel forces repeatedly trounced local military garrisons, captured walled cities, and seized government offices for use as temporary headquarters. Local officials either resisted militarily, fled at the rebel's approach, or attempted to ensure their city's safety through large bribes of silver, gold, and livestock. For the duration of the rebellion, uncertainty reigned—neither rebel groups nor local government exercised lasting effective control. Everyone—county magistrates, jailers, landed elites, small-time criminals, ruffians, and common farmers—faced questions of loyalty, opportunity, and survival.

By late April 1512, unrelenting military pressure, constant movement, and several disastrous river crossings had greatly worn down Madman Zhao's forces. Before June was over, border troops, aboriginal forces, and capital garrison troops finally crushed Madman Zhao's army in a series of battles in northern Huguang, eastern Henan, and the Southern Metropolitan Area. Zhao fled disguised as a Buddhist monk until a massive manhunt brought him to imperial justice late in June.

In contrast, although a much diminished threat by May 1512, the Liu brothers continued to exploit weaknesses in Ming China's defenses. Pressured by imperial forces, the Liu brothers had abandoned their highly mobile mounted style of warfare on the North China plain. Instead, they seized large ships, which they used for raids along the Yangzi River and its dense system of tributaries. Local pirate groups lent their support to the Liu brothers, causing some observers to worry aloud about a new river-borne rebel league, which would imperil the Ming's secondary capital of Nanjing located on the Yangzi's southern bank. While the combined forces of the Liu brothers and their new allies raided with near total impunity up and down the length of the Yangzi, their time was drawing short. Ming imperial regulars, Mongol regiments, and troops from northern border garrisons began to take up positions along the Yangzi in June and July 1512.

Late in August 1512, these forces took advantage of a brutal typhoon that devastated the rebel fleet, which was caught exposed near the mouth of the Yangzi River. The final battle occurred at nearby Mount Wolf early in September, about 6 miles outside the prosperous city of Tongzhou on the northern bank of the Yangzi. There, imperial forces wiped out the remaining beleaguered rebels, bringing to an end China's largest rebellion of the sixteenth century.

The 1510 Rebellion should be understood not merely in terms of the excesses of an eccentric emperor and his abusive eunuchs, or peasant struggle against feudal oppression. It should be seen in the context of ongoing violence, banditry, and links among local elites, imperial officials, and men of force, conditions that existed during the reign of all emperors, competent or otherwise. Many details of social life in the capital region, inadvertently revealed during the course of the rebellion and the subsequent imperial investigations, provide valuable insight into the role of violence during more normal, but less well-documented, times.

Chapter 2 examines the social, economic, geographic, political, cultural, and military structures of the capital region. It analyzes the myriad ways the capital influenced the development of the surrounding region, including the massive court-ordered population relocations, the development of eunuchism in counties south of the capital, the presence of resettled Mongols, and the administrative ambiguities arising from the heavy concentration of imperial estates and military garrisons spread throughout the area. Chapter 2 draws attention to the fact that although the state exercised a pervasive influence in the capital region, it also created a multitude of jurisdictional interstices that often undermined state control.

Chapter 3 shows that throughout the mid-Ming period, banditry posed a serious, ongoing problem in the capital region. Drawing on local gazetteers, court annals, and most especially an incomparably rich compilation of court rulings, chapter 3 demonstrates that members of imperial garrisons frequently engaged in banditry, exploiting those administrative interstices introduced in chapter 2. It also documents the spatial patterns of brigandage and demonstrates that bandits targeted the entrepôt cities surrounding Beijing and the major transportation arteries leading to and from the capital, and concludes by examining the links between capital elites and local toughs.

Chapter 4 delineates the ways Chinese government officials, military officers, and local elites during the fifteenth century attempted to control volatile elements of the population by organizing them into various military organizations (both public and private). It argues that underlying these efforts was a belief that through proper organization and supervision, men of force could be turned to the interests of order and prevented from providing critical leadership roles in bandit and rebel groups. This chapter also examines the variety of weapons available in Ming society, as well as the state's attempts alternately to prohibit the manufacture, possession, and sale of certain weapons on the one hand, and to make effective use of privately held weapons to bolster social order on the other.

Chapter 5 provides a detailed case study of the complex patronage networks connecting local bandits, regional military commanders, ranking civil officials, palace eunuchs, and even the emperor of China. It examines the ties among these men and demonstrates how political rivalry among palace eunuchs in the capital in the years 1509–1511 disturbed patronage patterns in counties south of Beijing. The result was intensified pressure for suppressing banditry, frantic negotiations to find new patrons, and eventually the spark igniting a rebellion that quickly grew to national dimensions.

Chapter 6 tells the story of the 1510 Rebellion as it grew from small bands operating south of the capital to great rebel armies, which marched from the Pacific Ocean to the Taihang Mountains and from north of the capital to south of the Yangzi River. Particular attention is given to the changing nature and composition of the rebel forces as they moved out of the capital region, the rebellion's impact on local communities, and the evolving strategies of the imperial court to suppress the outbreak. The chapter concludes with an exploration of banditry, men of force, and social unrest in the decade after the rebellion, arguing that no fundamental structural changes occurred in the rebellion's wake.

Documentary and Terminological Concerns

Through each chapter runs a concern with men of force—that is, men who depended on the use or threat of violence, often but not exclusively illicit, to achieve their ends. "Men of violence" is a patently elastic category, which has no exact counterpart in Ming social groupings. It is related in varying degrees to such clearly pejorative terms as *"wulai"* (local tough), *"liumang"* (hooligan), *"youshou"* (loafer), *"xianshou"* (idler), *"wangming"* (desperado), *"guanggun"* (bare sticks), and *"wuji zhi tu"* (unregistered ones) on the one hand, and more ambiguous appellations, such as *"haojie"* (unfettered hero), *"haojun"* (unfettered hero), *"renxia"* (knight errant), and *"youxia"* (wandering knight errant), on the other.

Almost all these terms imply some degree of rootlessness or marginality. "The people" of China were all to engage in full-time agriculture, a morally positive vocation in the eyes both of government officials and of social thinkers. Since at least the Warring States period (ca. fifth to third century B.C.), Confucian and Legalist thinkers alike spoke of farming as the "root," and primary, while viewing commerce as the "branch," clearly secondary. Farmers produced the food and taxes on which society and the state depended. With fields, which needed regular care, farmers were tied to the land and thus were more easily subject to state registration and were more accessible for resource extraction (taxes, corvée labor, and various irregular surcharges and levees). While dynasties experimented periodically with promoting commerce and industry as a source of fiscal revenue, tax regimes remained fundamentally agrarian. Government authorities and lettered elites often harbored a strong bias against commoners who did not engage in agriculture.

The lexicon that evolved to describe these men who fell outside socially acceptable categories reveals much about contemporary attitudes. Many terms were pejorative and dismissive. They are redolent with images of odious insects that feed on human blood and life-giving agricultural crops. The names conjure up visions of morally suspect subjects constantly on the move because of natural disaster, fear of the law, or lack of industry. The terms were flexible and contextual, and although writers occasionally attempted to use them with precision, more often the nomenclature overlapped. It lumped together diseased urban vagrants, dissolute young dandies, hardened criminals, rural folk newly arrived in the city, and headstrong young men who clashed with officious clerks or village headmen. All were troublemakers, actual or potential; none were members of respectable society. At the same time, though, the sheer richness of the lexicon used to describe these men serves as a strong linguistic sign that "hooligans," "bare sticks," "local toughs," and various sorts of riffraff constituted a lasting and culturally significant feature of Chinese society.[75]

Some expressions carried varied connotations, as seen in the term "*haojie,*" which is found in the phrase *haojie zhi shi* (a man of *haojie*) in the fourth century B.C. Confucian classic *Mencius, IIIA,* where it meant "an outstanding scholar."[76] This meaning still had currency during the middle Ming period, when the famed scholar-general Wang Yangming (1472–1529) praised an influential disciple as a "*haojie zhi shi.*"[77] Given Wang's strong emphasis on action in life, it is possible that even here his use of the term may have included the connotation of unfettered hero or man of action.

The term "*haojie*" also referred to rebels and warlords who sought to establish dominance during the waning years of the Yuan dynasty. The Ming dynastic founder, Zhu Yuanzhang (1328–1398), frequently used the term with apparently neutral or even positive overtones. This usage may be explained in part by the fact that Zhu himself was among those who contested Yuan rule and sought to establish their own regimes. To cast them in a categorically bad light would have been to undermine his own legitimacy. Further, given the founder's repeated descriptions of himself as a man born of humble status who rose in the world through decisive action (and the favor of heaven), it seems reasonable to assume he valued the qualities of unfettered heroes.[78] In contrast to "*wulai*" or "*wangming,*" "*haojie*" and related terms connoted considerable power or influence. One eminent eighteenth-century historian (Zhao Yi) famously described the Ming founder as combining in his person the qualities of "a sage, an unfettered hero [*haojie*], and a bandit."[79]

First articulated by the renowned historian Sima Qian (active second century B.C.) in his classic *Records of the Historian,* "*xia,*" or the knight errant, and related compounds such as "*renxia,*" "*buxia,*" and "*youxia*" also exhibited considerable ambiguity.[80] A defining quality of *xia* was the willingness to right wrongs, regardless of the consequences. This penchant for direct action could entail violating the laws of the state and breaking with customary social practices. Sima Qian's crisply drawn portraits of *xia* included their violent and unconventional ways but also made clear the author's approval of their determination and personal efficacy, establishing *xia* as a cultural category of behavior and attitude that persists to the present day. During Ming times, admirers of the *xia* ideals could be found among highly educated young elites and unlettered farm boys, among influential statesmen and rebel leaders, aspiring scholars and professional criminals. We will return to the wide appeal of direct action, violence, and China's martial tradition in the conclusion of this study.

Before turning to the specifics of banditry, rebellion, and force in the capital region during the Ming, one final matter demands attention:

the sources used to reconstruct life in China during the fifteenth and sixteenth centuries. I have sifted through local gazetteers, commemorative writings, funerary inscriptions, and privately written chronicles, but the documentary backbone of this study remains such imperial records as court reports, memorials, official proclamations, administrative statutes, and court-sponsored narratives.

Chief among these imperial sources used in this study is the *Ming shilu* (hereafter referred to as the *Veritable Records of the Ming Dynasty*). The *Veritable Records* were imperial annals compiled for each reign of the dynasty. They provide daily, sometimes multiple, entries, composed of reports from officials in the field and in the capital ministries, as well as the comments of the emperor. They comprise the single most important set of documents for the study of the Ming period, especially the first half of the dynasty, and the information they contain often informed private literati jottings and locally compiled gazetteers.[81]

Available in a two-volume, 1,500-page photographic reprint, the *Huang Ming tiaofa shileizuan* (Classified compendium of the precedents of the August Ming, hereafter *Classified Compendium*) is a fifty-chapter (*juan*) compilation of regulations and provisions for the implementation of the Ming dynasty's law code, the *Ming lü* (Ming Code). Most of the cases are from the Chenghua (1465–1497) and Hongzhi (1488–1505) reigns. This is perhaps the single richest source for the social history of late-fifteenth-century China.[82] Although somewhat biased toward events that occurred in the Northern Metropolitan Area, the *Compendium* includes cases from across the empire, often in surprising detail for the period. These vivid details provide an invaluable point of entrance into the terra incognita of violence and crime during the Ming period.

Despite the great wealth of information that these and other imperially derived records provide, they pose serious historiographical questions. Officials in the employ of the court compiled documents according to the dictates of the imperial state. Routine bureaucratic reports and records often confined themselves to matters the state found most pressing: tax collection, the conscription of corvée labor, river and canal management, officials' performances, and the preservation of a modicum of social order. While contemporary field reports and court depositions often could contain a wealth of detailed information exceeding the narrow parameters noted above, as they wended their way through the bureaucratic pipeline[83] they were condensed and edited. Much to the chagrin of scholars today, those originals have largely been lost or destroyed. (Scholars who research China's last imperial dynasty, the Qing, work with a qualitatively different document base than those who work in earlier periods.) Far fewer remain of records by private scholars who held views that contrasted sharply with the aims and values of the state, almost none by commoners who dared cross the local landlord or county magistrate, much less those who might challenge the Son of Heaven and his awe-inspiring imperial apparatus.

In using these documents, the modern historian must remain aware not only of the often subtle personal and political biases that contributed to the particular rendering of individual incidents in such sources as the *Veritable Records*[84] but also the more general administrative strictures and rhetorical imperatives that informed and shaped those documents. The emperor, his officials, and the imperial state often appear as selflessly striving to benefit "the people." One might conclude that the state and memorialists observed the strictest standards of Confucian morality. Their proposals, whether it was dredging the Grand Canal, establishing a new county seat in the distant southwest, or negotiating with neighbors to the north of the Great Wall, often imparted a timeless quality through the use of seemingly unchanging moral or historical principles. Enough officials observed such rhetorical and administrative guidelines sufficiently long that they took on a life of their own. One senior Ming historian has gone so far as to suggest that the seductive power of this literary-moral rhetoric often overwhelmed officials; they gradually lost their ability to understand and discuss social reality around them without constant and misleading reference to this rhetoric.

While we may safely assume that the Ming state and individual officials retained their ability to differentiate between the realms of unadorned social reality and administrative ideals, the documents they left behind are sometimes staggeringly misleading. For instance, one might register considerable surprise to discover that military clashes on China's western border, dismissed in imperial records as little more than "incursions" or "raids" by insatiable and innately combative "barbarians" in western China, were actually part of a decades-long jihad launched by Muslim potentates in Turfan. Other times, the discordance arises from understatement or omission. A 1507 entry in the *Veritable Records of Wuzong* tersely notes that several "forts" in Sichuan requested permission to surrender to Ming authorities. They had "rebelled" sixteen years earlier in 1507 and had not submitted taxes or corvée services since then. The entry fails to note that these were not isolated military outposts but large and thriving agricultural communities, which had slipped outside imperial order for a decade and a half.[85] The entry also employs the term "surrender," implying that the groups voluntarily recognized the superior power and legitimacy of the Ming court—no mention is made of the extensive negotiations, the give-and-take, or the military threats that such arrangements inevitably entailed. Finally, the *Veritable Records* and various memorials submitted to the throne portray people who left their lands to begin anew somewhere else as greedy, grasping, small-minded blackguards who willfully abandoned their rightful place in society, or as pathetic, nearly mindless refugees who instinctively fled sites of natural disaster. Rhetorical conventions left little room to acknowledge people's true motivations or perceptions.

The court used interchangeably the terms "thieves," "bandits," and "rebel" to refer to nearly any group that used force to pursue goals the court considered inimical to its interests. Mongols of whom the court disapproved became "Tartar thieves," and Muslims active in southwestern and northwestern China were called "Muslim thieves." The court and memorialists often described small, poorly organized local toughs in the same terms they used to denote mighty rebel leaders who commanded great hosts. Imperial documents offer little distinction between groups enjoying widespread popular support and those seen by local communities as brutal and parasitic. Clearly, administrative interests and rhetorical demands often obscured social reality,[86] and as the following chapters make clear, such terms as "brigand" and "banditry" should seldom be taken at face value.

How then is the historian to reconcile the often yawning gap between imperial records, especially court chronicles, and social reality throughout the realm? The central protagonists of this study remain silent and elusive in the imperial records that form my documentary base. Men of force such as Liu the Sixth and Tiger Yang did not bequeath their memoirs to descendants. Supporters did not leap to their defense in pamphlets. They did not even make depositions to imperial inquisitors; they died in battle. What we know of them and their role in society must be gleaned from a historical record compiled by and for the imperial government, its local representatives, and a literati elite deeply vested in the imperial system.

In exploring this murky world of illicit armed violence during the fifteenth and sixteenth centuries, the historian faces a series of knotty methodological questions. Can one honestly claim to write about men and places when the majority of extant records comes not from those individuals and communities but instead from imperially generated documents? Isn't one constructing nothing more than a shadow history —the role of violence as reflected through the values, concerns, and self-serving rhetoric of an imperial system that shared little if anything in common with the purported objects of analysis? Would not common sense and intellectual integrity require the abandonment of such an obviously futile or, worse, fundamentally deceptive, enterprise at the outset?

That some two hundred pages of text still await the reader suggests that I have not answered these questions with a simple yes. All history requires imagination. Even the historian blessed with the richest body of documentary, visual, physical, or acoustic materials must still exercise his or her imagination. This transcends the already complex task of gathering, organizing, and selecting often challenging materials. Gaps and silences appear. Contradictions confront. Suspicions arise. Unspoken motivations must be plumbed, and misleading justifications must be evaluated. At many points, indeed often at the most critical junctures, the historian relies on his or her imagination and intuition to bridge these gaps, to extrapolate from the reassuring terra firma of the known and documented to the realm of the plausible, the probable. I have drawn on privately compiled sources whenever available, read imperial records with a healthy dose of skepticism and an awareness of their particular agendas and language, and sought to listen as much to what extant documents pass over in silence as to what they dwell on at length.

I have endeavored to read imaginatively between the lines of court documents and relate imperial discourse to the realities of local society. I am acutely aware of the danger of seduction by imperial rhetoric, in all its many forms. China was not a model of social harmony, where emperors and their officialdom were all benevolent and the people all content in their places, as imperial rhetoric was wont to maintain. Based on a careful reading of those documents, I offer here an analysis of a critical but until now completely unexplored facet of Ming China's economy of violence: a reconstruction of the structural components of banditry and rebellion in the shadow of Beijing during the fifteenth and sixteenth centuries, the careers of several well-known men of force, and the ways local elites, local administrators, and the central government attempted to regulate armed illicit violence in daily life.

2
The Capital Region

In 1500, Beijing and the surrounding area, the capital region, were simultaneously very old and very new. The region's chief topographical features had formed nearly one million years before, and finds of *Homo erectus* in the area date from 500,000 B.C. Agriculturists had practiced in the region for roughly ten thousand years, and important walled political centers had appeared in or close to Beijing since at least the sixth century B.C. More recently, the Khitan Liao dynasty (907–1115) had located its southern capital in present-day Beijing, the Jurchen Jin dynasty (1115–1234) had established their central capital there, and, most recently, the Mongol Yuan dynasty (1272–1368) had chosen the site for their capital, Dadu. Thus, by the fifteenth century, Beijing and the capital region constituted a core area of China, long settled and closely associated with centers of political power.

Yet, Beijing and the capital region were also very new in the fifteenth century. The founding emperor of the Ming dynasty (1368–1644) had situated his dynastic capital not in Beijing but in Nanjing to the south, closer to his power base and the economic center of the empire.[1] Relegated to the status of a military outpost and deprived of the economic and political resources that made possible the splendor that dazzled Western observers like Marco Polo, Beijing's glory quickly faded. When the third Ming emperor decided to make Beijing the main dynastic capital, early in the fifteenth century, it was not simply a matter of issuing an imperial decree or changing the city's name. Beijing's reconstruction was an enormous effort, which strained the empire's resources and required decades to complete.[2] Even the idea of Beijing as the capital was new to men of the Ming during the early decades of the fifteenth century. During the first half of the century, they self-consciously referred to it as the "northern capital" to distinguish it from the now secondary capital of the south, Nanjing. Only later would Beijing's position grow sufficiently established that writers would refer to it as simply "the capital."

Given the ritual and political centrality of Chinese capitals, the process of remaking Beijing into a capital city set in motion powerful political, economic, social, and military forces that would transform much of life in the surrounding region. During the first three reigns of the dynasty (1368–1424), in an effort to bolster defense, stabilize local society, and reinvigorate a suffering economy, the Ming state relocated more than one million people from around the empire to what became the Northern Metropolitan Area. Emperors granted large tracts of land throughout the region to imperial favorites. Among these favorites were eunuchs from counties south of Beijing fortunate enough to have secured positions in the imperial city. The Ming government attempted to organize Chinese society into hereditary households responsible for providing designated services to the state. As much as one-fifth of the Ming empire's hereditary military households were concentrated in the Northern Metropolitan Area to keep Beijing secure.

Despite Beijing's powerful influence over the Northern Metropolitan Area, the state's interests in the capital were not monolithic, and its authority in the area often gave rise to tensions at the local level. Emperors and their civil officials in Beijing frequently sparred over how imperial power should be allocated and exercised. This was particularly true during the reigns of emperors who refused to conform to the civil bureaucracy's expectations of how the Son of Heaven should govern. These tensions played out on the local level as magistrates and prefects came to terms with recipients of imperial largess and the considerable influence endowed by such favor.

Even within the imperial bureaucracy, jurisdictional conflicts arose. Jurisdiction over local military populations was anything but straightforward, and on occasion military officers openly threatened local civil officials with naked force. Even more thorny were matters involving Mongols settled in the area. Were they subject to regular military jurisdiction? Were they the responsibility of civil officials? Neither set of authorities was anxious to find out, and many officials either attempted to shift responsibility elsewhere or elected to turn a blind eye to problems. These murky lines of jurisdiction and competing spheres of influence were well suited to those who violated the laws of the empire. Thus, one might assume that the area around Beijing would be one of the most secure in the empire, when in fact armed, mounted brigands periodically plundered the region in broad daylight.

This chapter analyzes the capital region as it developed in the fifteenth and early sixteenth centuries. It examines the geography, demography, and economy of the area, as well as some important social, military, and political institutions that shaped the texture and tenor of life for the region's people. Only with a sense of these larger structural factors can we begin to understand the circumstances that led to that unlikely gathering of bandits, eunuchs, and the Son of Heaven in the emperor's private quarters one spring afternoon of 1509.

The Land

The capital region is located on the North China plain, which extends north to the Great Wall, west to the Taihang Mountains, and south to the banks of the Yellow River. As this region has been analyzed in some detail by several modern scholars, the following description will highlight only a few of the area's major characteristics.[3] First, the topography is extremely flat. Second, the area was prone to severe flooding, especially during the summer.[4] Having originated in the loess uplands west of the Taihang Mountains, most of the rivers on the North China plain carried huge amounts of silt. As silt built up in riverbeds, the rivers became more likely to flood. Extensive aboveground waterworks designed to prevent floods and direct water flow marked much of the capital region. When they broke, flooding was severe; huge swaths of the plains were inundated.

Third, much of the region was low lying, and marshes were common.[5] Contemporaries described Wenan County, home to many of the leaders of the 1510 Rebellion, as "the bottom of a cauldron" after the fact that it was low lying and subject to flooding.[6] One consequence of this with implications for agriculture was that the region's soil was often alkaline. The marshlands also served as bandit bases because they offered hideouts difficult to find and easy to defend. It is no accident that much of the action in China's most famous novel of bandits and violence, set in the twelfth century but probably reflecting conditions in the sixteenth century, *Shuihu zhuan* (appropriately entitled *Outlaws of the Marsh* in one translation), occurs in the marshy areas south of the capital and neighboring Shandong Province.[7]

Agriculturally, the Northern Metropolitan Area lies within what has been called the "wheat-kaoliang region." In Wenan, Bazhou, and other surrounding counties south of the capital, the principal grains grown in the early sixteenth century were millet, sorghum, barley, summer wheat, and buckwheat.[8] According to the 1629 edition of the *Wenan Gazetteer*, other crops included sesame, soybeans, mulberry, jujubes, plums, pears, apricots, apples, and grapes. As was common in much of the region, notably in the southern sections of the Northern Metropolitan Area, some cotton was grown, and silk or silk wadding were produced as cash crops, especially late in the dynasty.[9] Salt production figured prominently in the economy of neighboring Hejian Prefecture, especially during the latter half of the dynasty, with important production centers in Tianjin and Cangzhou.[10] Most peasants in the Northern Metropolitan Area farmed their own small plots of land, although many also worked for larger landowners in the region during harvest time.[11]

By the late fifteenth century, economic activity in North China was sufficient to support periodic markets and several commercial towns (zhen).[12] For instance, by the early seventeenth century, Wenan boasted one periodic market and seven commercial towns.[13] Neighboring Bazhou had thirteen periodic markets by the mid-sixteenth century if not earlier, as did Zhuozhou.[14] Potouzhen, a prosperous town in Hejian Prefecture along the Grand Canal, was a transfer point for regional trade as goods traveled to and from thriving Linqing, which in turn linked the North China plain with China's economic heartland, the Jiangnan region.[15]

There was considerable commercial variation within even the Northern Metropolitan Area, and during the Ming, Qing, and Republican periods, the northeast generally had far fewer periodic markets than the southern counties.[16] This greater prevalence of markets in the south may have been the result of the more widespread cultivation of cotton as a commercial crop in Shandong, Henan, and the southern portion of the capital region, a phenomenon that has led some scholars to argue that economically, the Northern Metropolitan Area lagged behind neighboring Shandong and Henan.[17]

Although Beijing's economy figured prominently in the region,[18] other important economic centers had also emerged in the Northern Metropolitan Area by the late fifteenth century. Situated on the Grand Canal with ready access to the sea, Tianjin developed rapidly during the fifteenth century as a key link in the grain transport system; three to four million piculs of grain passed through the city annually. Salt and fishing were also major economic activities.[19] Cangzhou was at the crossroads between Beijing and Shandong, a critical link in water and land transport networks. One of the empire's six salt distribution commissions was located here too, supplying Hebei, Henan, Shandong, and the strategic border defense areas of Xuanfu, Datong, and Jizhou to the north.[20] Linking Beijing to central China, Baoding served as an important military center. During the Ming, it was home to the Daning Regional Military Commission. Baoding supplied animal and agricultural products as well as handicrafts to Beijing.[21]

Finally, one must keep in mind the steady flow of wealth through

the capital region to Beijing. For most of the dynasty, roughly four million piculs of husked grain per year was shipped via the Grand Canal
to Beijing on the empire's fleet of more than 11,600 barges.[22] Military
supplies, silks, porcelain, produce, tax silver, metalware, medicinal
herbs, tribute goods, and all manner of merchandise poured into the
capital from neighboring counties, distant provinces, and beyond the
seas.[23] Such towns and cities as Tongzhou, Zhangjiawan, Hexiwu, and
Tianjin to the east, Lugou Bridge (Marco Polo Bridge) to the west, and
Liangxiang and Zhuozhou to the south were all important hubs leading to Beijing.[24] Put in terms of William Skinner's well-known concep-
tualization of China's eight macroregions, each with its own core and
periphery, this area constituted the core of the North China macro-
region.[25] Yet it was here that banditry was reported most regularly.

People

In the early sixteenth century, North China society was still relatively
new and surprisingly fluid. Torn by the devolution of central power
during the late Yuan period in the mid-fourteenth century, devastated
by the battles of the Yuan-Ming transitions, and ravaged by the civil
war of 1399–1402, the economically depressed and underpopulated capital region was rebuilt during the late fourteenth and early fifteenth centuries. As noted above, during the first three reigns of the dynasty, the
imperial Ming government relocated more than one million people to
the region.[26] To stimulate the local economy, ensure government revenue,
and encourage household registration, the government supplied grain
seed, agricultural tools, and plow animals. Seventy to 80 percent of the
troops relocated to the area were put to work on military agricultural
lands. The government also granted extensive tax exemptions, commonly for three years, but sometimes in perpetuity for marginal lands
brought under cultivation.[27]

The relative newness of society in the capital region is revealed in
village names. Close to half of today's village names date from the early
fifteenth century, when tens of thousands of families were uprooted and
forced to begin life anew in alien lands.[28] The efforts of Ming authorities
to integrate these waves of new residents into the household registration systems were not completely successful at the outset and grew
only more tenuous over time. The influx of outside families into individual communities created subtle social divisions and tensions. Descriptions of military units, often composed of these outsiders, reveal
that even a century after their relocation to the capital region, differences
in language, custom, and dress were still acutely and deeply felt.

Among those relocated were Hui Chinese and Mongols who sought their fortunes with the Ming dynasty. The Hui were (and still are) ethnically Han Chinese who practiced the Muslim faith and observed some social customs differing from the majority Han population. The "eight great surnames" of Hui were moved from Erlang gang, Shang-yuan County, Yingtian Prefecture (present-day Nanjing) to North China in 1404.[29] Four of these surnames were located to the west of the Grand Canal, while the remainder settled in Mengcun. Later, Hui from Nan-jing, Shanghai, Zhejiang, Jiangsu, Shandong, and Anhui increased the size of the Hui community in Mengcun.[30] Hui in Tongzhou, an entrepôt close to Beijing and important for its massive rice warehouses, were also relocated there during the Yongle period.[31] The Hui community in Mengcun Village near Cangzhou survives to this day and is known as the home of the martial art "The Eight Ultimates" (Bajiquan), just one of several styles of martial arts closely associated with the Hui, who had periodic recourse to violence in their relations with the Han Chinese majority.[32]

More significant both in numbers and strategic importance to the empire was the steady migration of Mongols into China during the first century of the Ming dynasty.[33] During the early years of the Ming, the Mongols north of the Great Wall were China's most pressing military threat, and China adopted a variety of policies designed to lessen the Mongol menace. One of these measures targeted the large numbers of Mongols who remained in China proper after the Yuan dynasty fell, in 1368. The Ming had three primary goals. The first was to reduce the possibility of collusion between "Ming Mongols" and their brethren north of the Great Wall. The second was to gain the political support of the Ming Mongols and to make use of the Mongols' considerable mili-tary skills. The third was to encourage further Mongol emigration to China as a way to undermine solidarity among steppe Mongols and to bolster Ming military strength.

To this end, the court bestowed generous treatment on these Ming Mongols. Settling many of them in and around the capital, the Ming government gave them lands, houses, and the goods needed to estab-lish homes. The court also incorporated them into the hereditary mili-tary household system of China.[34] The leading scholar on the subject has persuasively argued that the Mongols retained much of their lan-guage and culture well into the dynasty.[35] While in general these scat-tered communities of Mongols proved to be loyal and useful subjects, many officials and local residents remained skeptical of their motives, especially during periods of crisis.[36] Some of the Mongols also turned to banditry (see chapter 3).

Regional society retained its great fluidity throughout the fifteenth century as hundreds, if not thousands, of people continued to move within, to, and from the five provinces of North China. The main difference, however, was that whereas the imperial government had directed the majority of relocations during the late fourteenth and early fifteenth centuries, internal migration during the remainder of the century generally occurred without regard to the state's wishes. In fact, many of the relocations violated imperial law, as families attempted to escape natural disasters, crop failure, famine, taxes, and corvée service.[37] These massive population shifts sharply undermined government efforts to accurately register the people. The result was enormous challenges for many local governments, which were responsible for the timely delivery of tax grain to the central government, the extraction of corvée labor for public works projects, and the preservation of local security.

With the massive influx of people and a recovering economy, the population of the Northern Metropolitan Area expanded steadily through the fifteenth century. Although official Ming population figures cannot be taken at face value, they are suggestive.[38] The number of registered individuals for the Northern Metropolitan Area is as follows: 1.9 million in 1393, 3.4 million in 1491, and 4.3 million in 1578.[39] Bazhou, the subprefecture that oversaw Wenan, the home of many of the 1510 Rebellion leaders, was the second most populous subprefecture or county in Shuntian Prefecture,[40] with 52,463 people on the tax rolls.[41] Seventy-four percent of these households were referred to as commoners (min), 23 percent as military families, and 3 percent as "miscellaneous households."[42] According to the 1629 edition of the Wenan Gazetteer, the population of Wenan was 33,304 during the Chenghua reign (1465–1487) and 24,242 during the Jiajing reign (1522–1566).[43] The total population of neighboring Hejian Prefecture was more than 350,000.[44]

If the physical features and the approximate population of the Northern Metropolitan Area can be ascertained, the inner workings of local society in the region are less straightforward. What is clear, however, is that most who lived in such subprefectures and counties as Bazhou and Wenan were not affluent.[45] For purposes of tax assessment and corvée responsibilities, local populations were commonly divided into three ranks of households—upper, middle, and lower—each of which was again subdivided into upper, middle, and lower, for nine categories (the sandeng jiuze system). Nearly 70 percent of all households fell into the very lowest category, and lower households constituted almost 95 percent of all households.[46]

Who were the local elites who dominated society in the counties and villages around the capital? One small group consisted of those who held official degrees through success in the imperial examination system, by purchase (or contributions), or by imperial largess.[47] During the century and a half from the dynasty's founding to the turn of the sixteenth century, eighty-three men in Wenan secured the lowest class of official degrees.[48] The area produced thirty-three "provincial scholars" (juren) during those same years.[49] Only two men from Wenan are known to have passed the most prestigious examination of the empire, the "metropolitan scholar" (jinshi), one in 1457 and one in 1484.[50]

Contemporary sources are almost completely silent about the role of degree holders during the county's largest crisis of the sixteenth century, the 1510 Rebellion. Fewer than fifty of these degree holders were alive at the time,[51] and the four or five most prominent families of the late Ming were only beginning to register examination-system success by 1500.[52] What we know of the role of local elites in Wenan's reconstruction after the 1510 Rebellion is limited to a reference to the magistrate of Wenan enlisting the help of the "prominent elders" (qijiu) in rebuilding the city wall in 1514.[53] The solitary exception to this striking dearth of information about degree-holding elites in Wenan at the turn of the sixteenth century is the licentiate named Zhao Sui, who joined the rebels and rose to become one of their most prominent leaders (see chapter 6). The lack of information about degree holders suggests their incomplete dominance over local society. They shared power with such groups as described below, including imperial in-laws, men of force, eunuchs, and others with ties to imperial interests in Beijing.

Eunuchs comprised another noteworthy, and often influential, group in local society south of the capital.[54] Eunuchs had worked as servants in the imperial palace since the late fourteenth century,[55] and beginning in the early fifteenth century, their functions, numbers, and power increased. By the mid-fifteenth century, eunuchs were a well-established element of the Ming bureaucracy, serving in the capital and in the provinces in military and civil posts.[56] Numbers fluctuated, but early in the Zhengde reign, an estimated twelve thousand palace eunuchs served in Beijing.

The prefectures south of Beijing were important sources of eunuchs during the Ming, and several of the most prominent eunuchs of the early Zhengde reign were from this area.[57] Geographical proximity, similar varieties of spoken Mandarin, and shared social customs probably facilitated recruitment in these prefectures. Judging from what we know of practices during the later and more thoroughly documented Qing period, it is also likely that successful eunuchs from this area recruited in their native regions to bolster the ranks of their supporters in the palace, where competition was fierce and sometimes deadly.[58]

Successful eunuchs in Beijing, Zhang the Loyal, for example, often managed to translate their connections at court into local influence, as well as to secure military posts for male relatives. Like other local elites, they patronized Buddhist and Daoist temples, contributed to public works, such as bridges, and acted as power brokers.[59] The frequency with which well-known literati composed commemorative texts (for temples and other public works) and eulogies for eunuchs belies the tendency for literati to vilify eunuchs in other writings.[60]

Eunuchism afforded the chance for wealth, status, and some measure of security to families who otherwise faced grinding poverty. An official observed in 1507, "At this time, imperial favor extended to the nine generations of eunuchs who held power. Foolish people raced to castrate their sons and grandsons in hope of gaining wealth and status. As many as several hundred people from a single village did so. Although it was strictly prohibited, it did not stop them."[61] A 1513 report indicates that in Hejian Prefecture, poor parents with more than two sons had the others castrated and that although the Ministry of Rites gave posts to several thousand eunuchs annually, an even greater number were denied positions.[62] Frustrated, mutilated, and still poor, some of those denied employment in Beijing turned to begging and banditry. Shen Defu (1578–1618) wrote:

> North of Renqiu, Hejian, several dozen eunuchs hide among the ruins of [city?] walls. Whenever [they] encounter passing carts and horses, the weaker among them mass together to beg for money. The stronger ones take hold of the horses' reins and demand a pay-off. Occasionally, when two or three riders travel unaccompanied in desolate areas, [the eunuchs] pull them down from the saddle. Some grasp their throat, others grab their privates, and seize all that is in [the passerby's] money belt.[63] [The eunuchs] then leave in a commotion. When the person who has been robbed first regains consciousness, he is confused and does not know [what has happened]. When [I] arrived outside the capital walls, [it] was the same. Local magistrates consider this as ordinary and never prohibit [it]. It is the cruelest of the harms that merchants and travelers [suffer].[64]

Despite the woeful fate of most eunuchs, the wealth and status to be gained through service on behalf of the throne exerted an irresistible attraction for many in the capital region. One court official reported that during the Zhengde reign (1506–1521), more than 3,500 castrated men from the single prefecture of Shuntian had petitioned the throne for positions.[65] Given that in 1523 more than 900 eunuchs from Gu'an County, located south of the capital in Shuntian Prefecture, had requested posts in Beijing,[66] the figure of 3,500 for the entire reign seems very low. Eunuchism remained a feature of society in the capital region throughout the remainder of the sixteenth century and beyond.[67]

Another physical sign of imperial influence and power in the region was the number of widely scattered estates granted by the emperor.[68] According to a 1489 survey, nearly 168,000 acres (12,800 *qing*) were set aside for "imperial estates"; by 1514, the number had risen to more than half a million acres (37,595 *qing*).[69] The throne granted additional estates to the empress dowager, the heir apparent, the imperial princesses and in-laws, and to members of the merit aristocracy.[70] For example, the same 1489 report noted that more than 526,000 acres (33,000 *qing*) of land spread over 332 sites had been granted to imperial in-laws, eunuchs, and others. These lands together constituted an estimated 15 to 45 percent of the total acreage of the Northern Metropolitan Area.[71]

These lands influenced several facets of capital region society. First was the issue of revenue control. Civil officials generally opposed the expansion of the estates, contending that it entailed a serious loss of revenue to the state and represented a triumph of private interest over public good.[72] Failing the abolishment of these properties, civil bureaucrats argued that the peasants who worked on these holdings should be assessed at a fixed rate (generally, one-third of the harvest) and that local civil authorities should collect that revenue on behalf of the estate holders.[73] This far exceeded Ming China's normal land tax rate, which generally ranged between 5 and 10 percent.[74] The land grantees, however, pressed strongly for the right independently to determine rents and directly collect them. In many cases, estate holders prevailed.[75]

A second influence of these domains and their attendant personnel was the challenge to the authority of local officials (and more generally to the civil bureaucracy). Imperial estates were overseen by eunuchs, who in turn hired local managers.[76] To ensure rent collection, local managers often maintained an assortment of deserting soldiers, local toughs, and men who had managed to escape from the household registration system.[77] Local officials charged that these underlings abused the power and influence of their employers to perpetrate all manner of outrages against manor tenants, nearby residents, and on occasion authorities themselves, including annexing lands, extorting goods and money, establishing illegal toll stations, seizing livestock, raping women, and committing murder.[78] Feeling unequal to the challenge, many officials tacitly acknowledged the power of these de facto satraps. In the words of one contemporary official, "Commoners were at a loss as to what to do and local officials dared do nothing."[79]

Less of a challenge to local civil authorities but more of a burden to commoners in the Northern Metropolitan Area was the Ming dynasty's horse administration. The court established the horse administration to ensure a steady supply of battle-worthy horses to China's northern border defenses. Government-run horse markets along the border with Tibet and Mongolia secured a portion of this supply.[80] The second major source was domestically bred horses, which by the mid-fifteenth century were concentrated in the Northern Metropolitan Area. Selected by local officials on the basis of wealth (measured either by the size of household or the extent of their lands), "horse households" were responsible for breeding and maintaining horses. In a military emergency, these mounts were to be delivered to the capital garrisons in Beijing or sent to the northern border.

The Ming horse administration bears on the question of banditry in general and the 1510 Rebellion in particular in two ways. First, although generally considered far inferior to either Tibetan or Mongolian mounts (one sixteenth-century observer quipped that domestic horses "are like jackals, like wolves, like dogs"), tens of thousands of horses were spread through the capital region and parts of Shandong.[81] They comprised an important source of steeds for the mounted bandits (see chapter 3) and for the 1510 rebel forces.

Second, whether "horse households" actually raised horses themselves or, as became more common from the late fifteenth century onward, paid an annual fee in silver to the government to cover the cost of buying horses on the open market, they shouldered a considerable economic burden. Although the descriptions of these pitiable horse households penned by officials during the late fifteenth and early sixteenth centuries were often a rhetorical device to enhance the force of their various proposals and reforms, they had a basis in reality. Attempts to escape this particularly onerous corvée service were widespread, and attempts to sabotage the system were common.[82] But no evidence suggests that horse households were any more likely to participate in banditry or rebellion than other groups in the region.

Ming Military

Another prominent expression of the Ming state in the capital region was its attempt to guarantee a reliable source of troops and preserve social stability through a hereditary military system.[83] Following Yuan practices, Ming armies were drawn from hereditary military house-holds.[84] Each was responsible for producing one male for military service, who served as a soldier or officer, depending on the household.[85] To supply this "principal soldier" *(zhengjun)* with food, clothing, and incidentals while serving in the garrison, an additional male from the military household accompanied him to his post; they were called "supernumerary troops." In theory, both the principal soldier and the supernumerary troops accompanying him were exempt from taxes and corvée labor; in practice, though, supernumerary, and even principal troops, were often subject to a variety of corvée services.[86]

By 1500, the Ming military had declined sharply from the glory days of the late fourteenth and early fifteenth centuries.[87] Like the rest of the household registration system at the time, military registers were often outdated, inaccurate, and subject to falsification.[88] Desertion rates were high, as much as 50 percent, the result in part of soldiers' exploitation by their commanding officers.[89] Those who remained in the ranks more often than not were unfit for drill, much less combat. Yet for all these problems, the Ming military managed to preserve enough manpower and fighting skill to neutralize domestic challengers until the early seventeenth century.[90]

The military institutions of the Ming loomed large in the history of the capital region. At least one-quarter of the population in the capital region had direct links to various levels of military organization during the early fifteenth century. Approximately one-sixth of the empire's 493 units of guards were stationed in the capital or the capital region,[91] and one modern scholar has estimated that one-quarter of the Ming empire's troops were stationed in the Northern Metropolitan Area.[92]

Military forces in the region were stationed with either the elite capital garrisons in Beijing or with the various brigades and battalions garrisoned throughout the capital region.[93] Troop strength in the capital garrisons numbered on paper 380,000 men by late in the Zhengde period. However, inspection revealed that only 140,000 troops were actually present, and of those, only 20,000 were fit for service.[94]

In theory, approximately 5,600 soldiers manned each of the garrisons, but troop strength levels generally fell far below this number.[95] For example, according to the 1540 *Hejian Prefectural Gazetteer,* principal troops ranged from 4,906 to as few as 801 in the six garrisons in Hejian Prefecture.[96] The contrast with the ballooning ranks of the supernumerary troops *(yuding)* is striking. Tianjin Garrison alone could boast of more than 6,500, nearly twice the number of principal troops.[97] What to do with these supernumerary soldiers was an ongoing question for

China's officials of the fifteenth and sixteenth centuries. Recent studies show that for a variety of reasons, supernumerary soldiers increasingly were subject to regular military obligations and to work duty in various construction and transportation projects.[98]

In addition, soldiers from garrisons in the northern provinces of Shandong, Henan, Shanxi, Shaanxi, and the capital region itself reported to Beijing each spring and fall for drill.[99] The rotation system was intended to ensure rigorous training for provincial forces and to distribute more equitably the responsibility for defending the empire's capital. In 1426, 160,000 such troops rotated in and out of Beijing, although by the mid-Ming the figure had fallen by nearly half.[100] The large number of military personnel passing through the Northern Metropolitan Area on their way to and from Beijing often involved lapses in discipline, intimidation of civilian populations, and plundering by soldiers (see chapter 3).

Because the Ming military influenced such a great percentage of the population in the capital region, a few general observations about the conditions of the hereditary households are useful to understand the dynamics of local society. When a principal soldier reported to his designated garrison on the death, retirement, or desertion of the previous principal soldier from his household, he was required by law to take his wife and children, a practice designed to reduce the likelihood of flight back to his home, to tie him more firmly to his garrison, and to ensure the household's next generation of soldiers.[101] After reporting to the designated garrison unit, the principal soldier, with his wife and children, might live in the barracks, but it was just as likely in some regions that they would find lodging in private housing, sometimes at a considerable distance from the administrative offices of the garrison.[102] Soldiers assigned to the often widely scattered military agricultural lands tended to live cheek by jowl with local commoner populations.

Conditions for hereditary military households could be bleak.[103] According to an account by European observers late in the sixteenth century:

> There is probably no class of people in the country as degraded and lazy as the soldiers. Everyone under arms necessarily leads a miserable life because he is following his call not out of love for his country, nor from loyalty to the King, nor from any desire to acquire fame and honor, but solely as a subject laboring for an employer. . . . When they are not actually engaged in military activities, they are assigned to the lowest menial employments, such as carrying palanquins, tending pack animals, and other such servile occupations.[104]

In general, soldiers supplied their own clothing and gear.[105] Annual wages varied with rank, ranging from 1,000 piculs of grain for senior generals to 18 piculs for noncommissioned officers to 6 piculs for soldiers assigned to agricultural colonies; much of this was commuted to silver.[106] Extortion by commanding officers, payments to loan sharks, variations in market prices, and grain shortages diminished these wages.[107] Finally, military officers, as well as civil and eunuch officials, often forced their soldiers to work as servants or laborers.[108] As the number of supernumerary troops in the garrisons grew, they, too, were put to work on the agricultural colonies, were reduced to servants and construction laborers, or were pressed into active military service.[109]

Not all military households, however, were condemned to this exploitation and privation generation after generation.[110] In general, only certain branches of a military household actually shouldered the burden of supplying principal and supernumerary soldiers. Recent scholarship suggests that over time, those branches of a family that resided in the garrison and regularly served as soldiers grew distant from the original military household, which could be located far away.[111] For instance, in 1468, a centurion from Baoding Prefecture came to blows with his uncle when the centurion believed his uncle had shortchanged him on supplies. The centurion complained that although his uncle did not have to serve in the military and could devote himself to cultivating the family's ancestral fields, he still begrudged giving him supplies.[112] In an even more extreme case, a household member actively serving in the military returned to his ancestral home in another province to seek money for supplies. His relatives not only spurned his request, they actually burned the family's ancestral tablets, declaring that henceforth, relations between the branches of the family were at an end.[113]

Even those branches of the military households registered in garrisons engaged in a wide variety of economic activities,[114] which ranged from running small businesses, to acting as personal retainers, to engaging in brigandage. A single legal case involving a supernumerary soldier in Shanxi Province during the mid-1460s mentions in passing four supernumerary soldiers who sold noodles and sugar, ran an eatery, and hawked beef strips, one supernumerary officer (*sheyu*) who ran an eatery, a principal soldier with a restaurant, and another who sold straw.[115] One group of enterprising soldiers from the environs of Beijing carried on a brisk trade in Buddhist rosaries made from human cranial bones. Working with Tibetan monks in the capital, the soldiers exhumed graves in the area, strung the bones together, and sold them in the markets of Beijing, claiming that they were made in Tibet.[116]

After at least the late fifteenth century, another route to better food, clothing, and standing in the garrison communities both for principal and supernumerary soldiers was service as military retainers for military officers and civil officials.[117] One of the principal leaders of the 1510 Rebellion, Tiger Yang, worked as a military retainer for a censor responsible for eliminating banditry in North China (see chapter 5). As the underlings of imperial princes and eunuchs, members of military households appeared in many legal cases in the late fifteenth century.[118]

Local Security

When assessing opportunities for and local response to banditry and rebellion, one must bear in mind the resources devoted to providing security for the local society. The organization of these resources varied with time and region. The following description is based primarily on conditions in the capital region during the mid-Ming. For simplicity's sake, local security may be divided into three sometimes overlapping categories: military garrisons, local government forces, and private efforts.[119]

In principle, military garrisons were responsible for suppressing banditry in their jurisdictions. In reality, however, by no later than the mid-fifteenth century, they played only a minimal role in maintaining local order.[120] They contributed little to the suppression of the 1510 Rebellion or to defenses against the massive outbreak of piracy along the southeastern coast during the mid-sixteenth century. In fact, as we shall see, they often served as bases for enterprising soldier-bandits.

Of the three categories, security organized by local government was normally most important. This general rubric included such forces as the local militia (minbing) and the constabulary. Originally organized to offset the growing weakness of the Ming garrisons during the fifteenth century, militias acted primarily as local defense forces drawn from among the populace.[121] Militia members were either conscripted through corvée service or were hired as substitutes for a fee.[122] Groups of men from local militias may be further subdivided into those who served in various constabulary capacities and those who acted as "people's stalwarts" (minzhuang).[123] Local constabularies were based either in district, subprefectural, or prefectural yamens or local constabulary offices located at crossroads, fords, and other strategic points.[124] Although Ming constabularies were charged with "locating and apprehending bandits and interrogating scoundrels and cheats," contemporary observers often accused them of theft and robbery.[125]

This is not surprising, since local security forces and brigands were often drawn from the same pool of men. Consider the description of Bazhou's "Local Sons Soldiers" (zidibing), a variety of local government security forces, as found in the 1548 Bazhou Gazetteer—"those skilled in horse riding and archery selected from among the people."[126] These were precisely the same qualifications that capital-region highwaymen and 1510 Rebellion leaders possessed and sought in potential compatriots. Put another way, in this economy of violence, local officials competed with other potentially disruptive elements of the population for the services and loyalties of men of force through a negotiated process of recruitment, generous wages, preferential social status, and patronage (see chapter 4).

First recruited in large numbers in the wake of the Tumu debacle of 1449, people's stalwarts had become a standard feature of local defense forces in North China by the late fifteenth century.[127] In the districts of Hejian Prefecture, the putative number of people's stalwarts varied from 48 to 280; the mid-sixteenth-century Bazhou Gazetteer lists one hundred men.[128] It is difficult to say how many men actually were available for local defense. Questions of desertion and competence aside, the people's stalwarts were conscripted on the basis of population and taxes, and this corvée service was increasingly commuted to silver payments, with which local government was to hire replacements.[129] In periods of crisis, these men were thrown into local defenses, often under the leadership of nearby garrison commanders.

If local militia and the constabulary constituted the basic day-to-day security forces of most localities in the capital region, one further source of local defense must be considered here.[130] In times of crisis, retired officials or other members of the local elite could have a strong influence in local defense. For example, in 1510, a retired official sojourning in Cangzhou played a critical role in the week-long defense of that city, and later, in 1511, a retired censor in Yuzhou reportedly was able to assemble three thousand local men for battle.[131] While details are scarce, these local elites were often a driving force behind largely privately organized and financed militias, which on occasion were vastly more effective than either garrison regulars or normal county security personnel.[132] In general, however, the participation of local elites from the Northern Metropolitan Area in defense efforts during the 1510 Rebellion was not nearly as evident as it was in the rebellions of the late Yuan or late Ming dynasties.[133]

Beijing during the Ming was like a towering tree overshadowing everything on the North China plain. Other cities might grow, but they would always be lesser entities in the shadow of Beijing. The looming walls, material splendor, and teeming population of the capital city were like the luxuriant leaves and branches of the tree, obvious signs of the city's power and vibrancy.

Perhaps more important was the extensive root system, radiating outward from Beijing and irresistibly penetrating into almost every facet of society in the surrounding counties. As a tree's root system draws sustaining nourishment to its trunk and branches, the capital drew resources from the surrounding counties and prefectures. Men traveled to Beijing to perform such corvée labor service as warehouse guards, yamen runners, and construction workers. They supplied the city with food, fuel, and manpower. Women, too, served in the Forbidden Palace as milk-nurses, imperial consorts, washerwomen, and occasionally even empresses.[134]

Yet roots multiply and grow without regard to any neat order, and the sheer number of these roots guaranteed that they would become tangled. Civil and military jurisdictions overlapped. And as insects might insinuate themselves into the life-giving root system of a great tree, many men and women in the capital region attempted to attach themselves in some way to imperial interests, no matter how tenuous the connection. The following chapters show how far and deep the long roots of the capital reached into local society around Beijing.

3
Banditry during the Mid-Ming Period

By midsummer 1468, the clerk Shi Huizong had begun the last leg of a 1,000-mile journey from his hometown, Fuqing County, in the southeastern coastal province of Fujian, to Beijing. Shi, like hundreds of other clerks and assorted minor functionaries, was making an annual delivery of tax silver and other tribute items. However, misfortune struck when he reached Huoxian, a prosperous entrepôt along the Grand Canal less than 25 miles south of the capital. There, armed bandits seized the silver and his luggage, silks, and travel money. Shi's fate was not an isolated incident. Officials from the southern provinces of Zhejiang and Jiangxi complained that their residents were similarly robbed in the capital region while attempting to deliver taxes and tribute to Beijing. The officials took pains to point out that imperial troops from garrisons around the capital were often among the bandits.[1]

To students of early modern European history, the fact that such men as Shi could safely transport their cargo over nearly 1,000 miles, roughly the distance between Paris and Cracow, may seem striking. Safe passage over that long a distance suggests a strong central government with considerable political, economic, and military resources. For those who study China, the site of the robbery is perhaps more surprising. Surely, if Shi was to be robbed, it should have been in distant, mountainous Fujian, with its reputation for quick-tempered and unruly natives, not in the suburbs of the empire's capital.

Indeed, in his pioneering and widely cited *Disorder under Heaven: Collective Violence in the Ming Dynasty,* James Tong concluded that the overwhelming majority of outlaws were concentrated in southern China, far from the imperial capital.[2] Based on a statistical analysis of 130 prefectural gazetteers, Tong discovered only one instance of predatory banditry in the Northern Metropolitan Area during the first half of the dynasty.[3] Tong's findings accord well with several studies that have found banditry, in particular, and illicit violence, in general, to be largely phenomena of the periphery, activities that flourished in the absence of a strong state presence.[4]

To contemporary Ming observers, though, Shi's experience was anything but exceptional. Brigandage and gang violence were stubborn problems in the heart of the Ming empire. Mounted brigands, equipped with armor, bows, arrows, and swords, blocked roads in and around Beijing and its satellite cities during the mid-Ming. Armed gangs of unruly young men roamed the streets of the capital "with absolutely no fear" of the authorities. Travelers transporting goods along the Grand Canal, which linked the rich revenue-producing provinces of South China to the capital in Beijing, faced armed robbers, extortionists, and swindlers as they passed through the Northern Metropolitan Area.

The existence of such brigandage in the shadow of the capital deeply disturbed officials of the day and violated their expectations about imperial security. In the mind's eye of the well-known Hanlin academician and famous statecraft writer Qiu Jun (1420–1495), approaching Beijing should have been akin to arriving at an oasis or entering paradise. He sketched in his massive statecraft compilation *Daxue yanyibu* (1487) a description of the situation if proper security measures were implemented:

> The roads will be free from the worry of obstruction, and merchants and officials will be spared the concern of fearing travel. People from all directions, having traveled a difficult and hazardous road, will arrive in the vicinity of the capital, where they will lift their heads and raise their eyes to see the emperor's palace amid red clouds and purple mists—that is, they will have the joy of having ascended to the realm of the immortals.[5]

As the following sections will demonstrate, few travelers experienced the red clouds and purple mists of the capital as a realm of the immortals, unless it resulted from the aftereffects of a sharp blow to the head suffered while being robbed. After having described the brigandage rampant throughout Hejian and Baoding Prefectures, one minister of war exclaimed late in the fifteenth century, "When travelers arrive in these regions, they are terrified and fearful as if they had entered enemy territory. During a time of peace should the capital region be like this?"[6] Another minister of war wrote in 1470, "If even in the imperial capital and the capital region bandits are as [brazen] as this, will bandits in other remote regions have any further worry [about prosecution]?"[7] In 1516, a regional inspector used a medical metaphor to describe the situation. The people of the prefectures south of the capital were like the blood and vital essence *(qi)*, which nourished and protected the heart of Ming China, Beijing. He warned darkly, however, of the spreading banditry in these prefectures soon reaching the "heart" of the empire, with presumably dire consequences.[8] The statements of the three officials reveal fears about the spread of banditry to Beijing itself, the expectation that of all places, the capital should be well ordered, and the realization that provinces more distant from the capital were even less subject to imperial control.

A brief explanation of some key terms and important sources: The terms "brigandage" and "banditry" are here used interchangeably and as rough translations of the Chinese terms *"dao," "zei," "daozei," "xiang-mazei,"* and *"qiangdao."* Both very old words, the two base terms, *dao* and *zei,* had acquired several meanings and usages by the Ming dynasty;[9] for our purposes, it is sufficient to note that banditry in the Ming context was one variety of "robbery by force" punishable by death.[10] This chapter generally focuses on mounted bandits, the variety most prevalent in North China.

Gangs and Banditry in Mid-Ming Beijing

As noted in the previous chapter, Beijing changed dramatically over the course of the fifteenth century. Its population soared from approximately 300,000 to nearly one million as imperial in-laws, officials, military personnel, laborers, artisans, prostitutes, chiefs, students, scholars, doctors, monks, beggars, and thieves from around the empire sought their fortunes in the new capital. As urban life grew more vibrant and complex, crime and violence escalated. In response, the Ming court steadily expanded security forces, and by the early sixteenth century, a full complement of institutions devoted to maintaining order in the capital had evolved: the Bandit Apprehension Garrison, the Imperial Guard, the Ward's Office, and the Ward-Inspecting Censors of the Five Ward. Police substations dotted the city, while foot and mounted constables and military personnel patrolled Beijing's broad promenades and twisting lanes.[11] These were supplemented by neighborhood patrols drawn from the civilian population of the city.[12]

Despite the growing resources devoted to capital security during the fifteenth and early sixteenth centuries, police authorities in mid-Ming Beijing faced many daunting challenges. Contemporary officials frequently observed that the capital's newly large, mobile, and complex population was not properly registered with local authorities.[13] Even those duly registered permanent inhabitants of the city often proved

immune to close supervision or prosecution. An unusually large pro-
portion of Beijing's residents were either government officials, related
to the imperial family by blood or marriage, or, as past recipients of
imperial largesse, members of the Ming's merit aristocracy. Many used
their privileged social and political connections to avoid criminal prosecution. Finally, the enormous military population in and around Beijing (nearly 400,000 men were on the payroll) furnished a ready supply
of soldiers who exploited jurisdictional interstices between military
and civilian authorities to engage in various levels of criminal activity.[14]
Even when not involved in criminal activities, military personnel posed
a potential threat to order in the capital. For instance, one morning in
February 1489, one of the capital's gates opened late. In their rush to
enter the city, a group of soldiers reporting to duty trampled to death
seventeen people.[15]

Government reports blamed much of the crime in Beijing on the
"unregistered ones" *(wuji zhi tu),* a phrase synonymous in many officials' minds with the criminal element. Late in 1464, for example, it was
reported that gangs of "unregistered men" and soldiers had taken to
thrashing people on the streets of Beijing and Nanjing.[16] Another frequent complaint involved the considerable numbers of poorly supervised, laxly disciplined, and violent soldiers who resided in the capital.
Proposed solutions to these problems included increased patrols, door-
to-door inspections for criminals and unregistered residents, stricter enforcement of household registration, mutual responsibility organizations,
pardons and rewards for criminals who surrendered themselves to
authorities, rewards for people who either captured criminals or provided information that led to their arrest, and penalties for officials who
failed to rigorously implement security measures.[17]

Gangs made up predominately of young men called "bare sticks"
(guanggun) and "urban toughs" *(lahu)* appear frequently in the reports
on crime in Beijing and its satellite cities during the mid-Ming period.[18]
The term "urban toughs" appears occasionally early in the fifteenth century, and by the end of the century it was used regularly.[19] Their activities were varied. For instance, in 1479, groups of urban toughs in Tongzhou beat commoners, pilfered merchandise from markets during the
day, and stole livestock at night.[20] Later that year, groups of unruly men
in Tongzhou beat passersby in the street and committed robbery. Many
were said to have been repeat offenders, who had no fear of the authorities.[21] Intergang rivalries contributed to levels of urban violence in Beijing during the waning years of the dynasty.[22]

Ming officials explained the relation between gangs and crime in several ways. In December 1480, the minister of war argued that robbery in the capital resulted from gangs of young men from Beijing and of criminals absconding from other regions who resettled in the capital. He noted that they stole goods in markets, opened gambling dens,[23] and, when low on funds, pawned their goods in pawnshops (yinzibu). The minister claimed that when pressed by authorities, these gangs would flee Beijing and turn to banditry in the suburbs.[24] In a commemorative essay penned for an officer in the Imperial Guard about to set out on patrol south of Beijing, one literati echoed this perception. "At year's end," he wrote, "the scoundrels of the capital region have expended all their income on food, drink, and gambling. Their thoughts turn with increasing desperation to robbery and theft. When the cold northern winds kick up dust, they leap upon their mounts and rush into the surrounding boulevard, arrows whistling."[25] In 1485, it was reported that gangs carried arms, ran gambling dens, "dominated" (bachi) markets, settled scores for others, preyed on men delivering tax grain and silver to Beijing from other regions, and maintained close connections to brothels.[26]

This linkage of gangs and brothels was a truism for many Ming authorities. Beijing was home to an enormous sex industry, catering to clients from all social statuses. Although a portion of this trade was legally registered and taxed (the euphemistic "Cosmetic Tax"), much was not, especially the more squalid brothels staffed by poverty-stricken girls that sprang up just outside the city walls.[27] As might be expected, the bandits' relations with brothels were not always harmonious. A 1457 report noted that "wandering heroes" (youxia) cursed and whipped prostitutes who refused their demands, although whether these were strictly sexual demands is not made clear.[28] Stolen goods were often deposited in houses of prostitution for temporary safekeeping, a practice that took advantage of the Ming policy of not holding brothels responsible for the criminal actions of their clients.[29]

One response of authorities to reports of urban toughs was to round up the usual suspects by arresting all "idlers" in the city: men gathered in groups who "showed no sense of shame," who were not transporting goods, or who otherwise failed to account for their presence in the capital. Depending on their offenses, those found guilty were beaten with bamboo rods, forced to wear the cangue, or exiled to distant borders.[30]

Although extant records tell us little about the family backgrounds, criminal records, or motives of individual urban toughs, a brief look at urban tough Zhang Ben may be helpful. Zhang, probably registered as a commoner since no other status is indicated, had been arrested three times by 1479 and faced the possibility of execution by strangulation for his offenses, beginning with his theft of two mules in 1476. He was apprehended, interrogated, and sentenced to internal exile on the frontier, where he was to serve as a "soldier's helper," one who would work to maintain an imperial regular. Zhang Ben escaped, though, and in 1478 he was again arrested in Tongzhou after stealing two more mules. Once again, he managed to escape from prison, and he and two supernumerary soldiers burglarized a home, making off with twenty-eight bolts of cotton fabric and 4,500 copper coins. When the local constable attempted to arrest them, the three resisted. They finally were taken into custody, and because of their repeated offenses, were sentenced to one month in a cangue, a broad heavy wooden board worn around the neck like a portable pillory.[31]

Soldiers and other local toughs fleeing the hereditary military system frequently found patrons in powerful members of the elite. Influential families could provide protection to men for whom they had a use. While most were put to work as laborers or servants, some were used as hired muscle.[32] One contemporary observed of a "local bully" (tuhao) who lived outside the walls of Beijing, "With his wealth he was able to make people exert themselves to the utmost; all the vagabonds (wulai) of the capital flocked to him."[33] A June 1504 report by the Ministry of Justice accused "influential families" in Beijing of seizing lands from commoners, forcing merchants to sell goods at artificially low prices, beating people to death, harboring bandits, and taking a portion of their loot.[34] Most irksome for officials at the Ministry of Justice was that these families regularly used their political influence to deflect any possible legal repercussions in those rare cases where a victim dared bring charges. In July, the Ministry issued a prohibition against the abuses committed by the "housemen" of imperial in-laws and members of the nobility of merit.[35] Managers of imperial estates scattered throughout the capital region often took advantage of a measure of immunity based on their ties to palace eunuchs and imperial in-laws to harbor "criminals" and toughs.

The exploits of the retainers and servants in the household of the Duke of Dingguo (Xu Yongning) illustrate how these patron-client relations worked. Huang Xi and nearly a dozen other men "commended" themselves to the household of the Duke of Dingguo early in 1493. All were members of military guards in Beijing and held positions ranging from chiliarch to supernumerary soldier. In January 1494, one Li Qi approached Huang and his companions about settling a score with an acquaintance. They agreed to help and, armed with iron horse stirrups and other weapons, made their way to the Eastern Watchtower, Dong-cheng Corner, outside the Chongwen Gate in southeastern Beijing, to seek their prey. Not finding him at home, they pummeled his friend, knocking out two of his teeth.

Two weeks later, they went to the house of a salt merchant near Chongwen Gate and attempted to extort money from him, saying that the Duke of Dingguo had dispatched them to collect a debt. When the merchant protested that he had never borrowed money from the duke, Huang and the others took him to Yongfu Temple, where they bound and beat him. Under duress, Wang falsely admitted to having borrowed money, whereupon he was escorted back to his home and was forced to put on a banquet for Huang and his compatriots. He also gave them 5,900 copper cash.

Early in April 1494, Huang and the other retainers accompanied a son of the Duke of Dingguo outside Chongwen Gate, where they made a show of force, traveling with their horses arranged in military for-mation along one of the city's broad promenades. When they spied a supernumerary officer who had failed to show proper deference by dis-mounting from his horse, Huang and the others "roughed him up," kicking him to the ground and striking him in the face with horse whips. He was brought before the duke's son; after pleading for his release, the supernumerary officer was set free.

Finally, Huang and his comrades agreed to collect a debt of 2.3 taels of silver on behalf of a noodle maker. (A tael weight of silver was about 2.5 ounces; a skilled laborer in 1500 earned approximately 2 ounces of silver a month.) Arriving at the debtor's home, they claimed that they had been sent by the Duke of Dingguo to take him into custody for failure to pay the debt. Terrified, he begged them to mediate on his behalf, and presented a banquet for them. They left after having ex-tracted 3 taels, enough to cover the debt and secure a little something for themselves.[36]

In this patron-client relationship, both Huang Xi and the duke's son attempted to maximize their advantages. The duke's son used Huang and his companions to bolster his image as a man to be reckoned with in Beijing. What other unreported services he may have required of Huang is difficult to say. Ming officials commonly complained that in-fluential families took a percentage of criminals' loot. Huang used the duke's name and influence to intimidate his victims and to avoid pros-ecution—at least temporarily.

Although in this instance the duke's son and his "muscle" may have secured some advantage, these relationships were ripe with potential for conflict. The duke's son may have turned a blind eye to Huang's exploits, but it is reasonable to assume he may not have been entirely satisfied that Huang perpetrated many of his offenses in the name of the duke's family without his blessing. Judging from the examples cited above, the duke's son did not benefit from all of Huang's activities. In fact, he ran the risk of tarnishing his reputation among residents in Beijing and of attracting the unwanted attention of the law, which in fact finally did occur.[37] Even though the duke's son possessed superior wealth, status, and political influence, he was still unable to command the absolute obedience of his retainers. In other words, his clients were not merely his minions—they relied on their patron's influence to further his ends, as well as their own. They did not always do so with his knowledge and approval, or to his benefit, a point that officials of the day emphasized to Beijing's elites. One early-sixteenth-century memorialist phrased the problem in the following terms: "Only two or three parts in ten of the [stolen] goods make their way into the patron's hands, while eight or nine parts of ten line private pockets [i.e., their subordinates]. [Moreover] all of the people's resentment and officials' indictments are directed against the patron. What advantage, pray tell, do titled nobles and imperial-in-laws gain from association with such men?"[38]

Besides urban gangs and men of force who attached themselves to capital elites, throughout the 1450s bandits threatened security in Beijing and its environs.[39] In a May 1468 edict, the emperor indignantly wrote the following:

> Recently, banditry in and around the capital has become rampant. Openly riding their horses in gangs of several dozen, at night they set fires, brandish [their] weapons, and plunder residents' goods. During the day, [they] intercept the carts of those people who pass by, seizing their donkeys and mules. They even go so far as to take people's lives. Even though there are intendants charged with apprehending bandits, imperial soldiers from the warden's offices of the five wards, and patrolmen, they do not really try to capture the bandits; so that [now] they are totally unrestrained by fear and act outrageously.[40]

The official charged with eradicating these highwaymen complained that foot patrols were unable to pursue the mounted outlaws. He also noted that local authorities knew many of the brigands were soldiers, and were making only perfunctory attempts to apprehend the outlaws.[41]

One of the most common varieties of highwaymen was known as

"whistling-arrow bandits" (*xiangmazei,* frequently abbreviated to *xiang-ma),* so named for the brigands' practice of attaching bells to their mounts or using whistling arrows when they raided.[42] A December 1480 report claimed that whistling-arrow bandits traveled in bands, wore armor, and blocked roads around Beijing.[43] In 1485, mounted bandits raided in broad daylight in and around Beijing,[44] while in 1473 they had plundered in slightly more distant suburbs to the east, west, and south.[45] Mounted brigands equipped with armor were also active in Tongzhou, blocking roads and seizing goods.[46]

Mounted banditry continued to be a high-profile crime in the capital region during the first quarter of the sixteenth century, with major outbreaks in 1509–1510, 1518, and 1521.[47] Brigandage in and around the capital was further reported in 1522, 1523, and 1528.[48]

If brigands were drawn to Beijing proper, they were also active in and around the capital's satellite cities. Located at the northern terminus of the Grand Canal, a dozen miles east of Beijing, Tongzhou was a thriving city during the Ming. Here, goods were unloaded and transported by cart to Beijing. In addition to its many specialized markets and periodic markets, Tongzhou boasted of inns "everywhere."[49] Part of Tongzhou's vibrancy resulted from its critical imperial rice granaries, which supplied the capital. The wealth passing through prosperous Tongzhou attracted the attention of more than the imperial in-laws and influential eunuchs, who used their imperial connections to engage in illegal economic activities and to intimidate potential competitors. It also drew bandits and *lahu.*[50]

Because of the city's strategic importance, a "grand defender" was appointed to maintain order in Tongzhou. He was responsible for overseeing the training of thousands of imperial troops from the Tongzhou and Wuqing garrisons stationed in the city, for the maintenance of the city walls and moat, for ensuring the smooth flow of grain and tribute items bound for Beijing, for repairing bridges, and for keeping waterways in order. Other duties included preventing powerful interests from exploiting the soldiers of his jurisdiction, and working with the regional inspector to keep soldiers from abusing the civilian population.[51]

The man who held the post for much of the last half of the fifteenth century, Chen Kui, developed a reputation for harsh measures against banditry and was rewarded on numerous occasions for his success.[52] Yet even he was sometimes powerless against the highwaymen. For instance, in May 1466, banditry rendered the roads to Beijing impassable, severing the capital's rice supply and sending grain prices spiraling. The court responded by specially dispatching a regional military commissioner and a censor from the capital to patrol from Tongzhou south to Linqing.[53] In the end, even the redoubtable grand defender of Tongzhou, Chen Kui, was cashiered for not controlling the highwaymen.[54] The post remained as challenging for the remainder of the century and into the next. In 1513, the salary of the circuit intendant of Tongzhou was suspended because he had failed to put down banditry, and in 1515, he was demoted for giving a free hand to brigands.[55]

The surprisingly prominent banditry around the capital owed something to the limited resources allocated to security.[56] For example, in theory the grand defender of Tongzhou commanded four garrison units—more than 22,000 troops. But by the mid-sixteenth century, after losses through desertion, death, or illness, and most important, soldiers put to work on construction projects, fewer than 10 percent of this number were actually available for defending the city.[57] A few dozen men might be held responsible for the security of the busy main routes leading to Beijing. It is not known how many troops actually patrolled the region, but if other manpower figures during the Ming are any indication, the total force was probably smaller than the prescribed levels established by the central government in Beijing. The editors of the 1549 *Tongzhou Gazetteer* bemoaned the military weakness of the area.[58] Others believed that only the addition of a new subprefecture could eliminate the administrative vacuum and attendant banditry along the more than 60-mile stretch south from Tongzhou to just north of Jinghai.[59]

Less than 16 miles to the southwest of Beijing and located on several important overland routes that terminated in Beijing, Liangxiang also attracted its share of mounted bandits. When the problem grew severe, in 1488, imperial military personnel were dispatched: four commanders, chiliarchs, and centurions from the capital each commanded thirty skilled cavalry troops who were to patrol trouble spots around Liangxiang.[60] If the late Ming vernacular tale "The Story of A Braggart" is any indication, the area had a national reputation for brigandage in the Ming. In this story, set in the Jiajing reign (1522–1566), the protagonist, a former imperial constable of formidable martial skills, is warned against traveling alone between Liangxiang and Maozhou to the south. Rampant banditry simply made the trip too hazardous.[61]

Bandits controlled much of the countryside near Maozhou, a small but thriving commercial center near the border of Baoding and Hejian Prefectures south of Beijing. According to one late-Ming historian, local magistrates adopted a laissez-faire attitude toward the outlaws, while prominent families from nearby Renqiu County maintained close relations with them. Maozhou, too, was situated on overland trade routes and hosted an annual temple fair at the Medicine King Temple held early in the fourth lunar month. The fair attracted merchants from much of North China and large numbers of aristocratic families, military elites, eunuchs, bravos, and famous courtesans from Beijing. The excitement of the Medicine King Temple Fair also attracted less savory members of the capital region.[62]

Banditry was reported in other areas on the major routes to Beijing from the south and west, like Zhuozhou, Zhangjiawan, and Hexiwu. As with Tongzhou and Liangxiang, this brigandage resulted almost certainly in part because of the constant stream of goods and silver making its way north to Beijing along these official routes. With the wealth that private traders and imperial grain transport boats brought to its busy docks, Zhangjiawan became a flourishing town during the Ming dynasty.[63] Called by one Ming observer "the foremost town east of the capital," Hexiwu was described as "an important stage on the road to the capital, [where] boats swarmed like ants in the harbor, while the creak of carts and the hoof-beats of horses never ceased from dawn till dusk."[64]

Although the survival of the Ming court depended on the Grand Canal for the timely shipment of grain, silver, and a large variety of other goods, banditry and other forms of criminal activity commonly occurred along its length. Travelers frequently encountered gangs of young toughs and beggars, who reportedly beat people, extorted goods, swindled merchants, and even seized grain shipments from soldiers delivering rice to the capital.[65]

Constables were assigned to patrol the Grand Canal and to man checkpoints where papers were to be inspected. Many officials, however, complained that inspection was lax, often nonexistent, and that local police authorities and garrison officers simply ignored the many abuses taking place along the Grand Canal.[66] Indeed, some constables and their associates were not above indulging in robbery when circumstances permitted.[67] They were joined by local residents of towns along the canal, transport workers, and "the poor" from other regions who had been drawn to prosperous areas like Beijing and Linqing, a major commercial city on the Grand Canal in Shandong.[68]

A 1471 report gives some feeling for the difficulties in transporting goods to the capital. When the Grand Canal froze during the winter months, those delivering grain and goods from the south were forced to resort to overland delivery. In such areas as Dingzigu, near modern-day Tianjin, transport workers using false names and registration papers would agree to move the goods to Beijing. When they arrived at a pre-arranged spot, these transport workers would call out to their hidden companions, who pounced on the cart in groups of as many as a dozen, relieving the owner of all his belongings. Local officials claimed to be helpless; the culprits' false names and registrations rendered them untraceable.[69]

Solutions to security problems along the Grand Canal ranged from the administrative to the military. The report above recommended that local military households be registered with local elders (laoren) and security leaders (zongjia) and further that transport workers inform authorities about the number of horses and goods they were to deliver. He also suggested that carts travel in groups of ten; if one cart were robbed, the remaining nine were to be culpable for the losses.[70] Later in the fifteenth century, the famed statecraft writer Qiu Jun proposed that during the months when the Grand Canal froze and overland trans-portation was necessary, goods were to be moved in caravans of at least five carts, each cart under the protection of three mounted soldiers drawn from two special units of four hundred men assigned specially to the task. The cart owners were to supply provisions for the men and their horses. Qiu also proposed that troops who ordinarily would have reported to Beijing for annual training exercises were instead to man security posts along the Grand Canal from the capital all the way south to Xuzhou, in present-day northern Jiangsu.[71] Despite all these efforts, banditry along the Grand Canal between Tianjin and Tongzhou contin-ued into the sixteenth century.[72]

Banditry and the Ming Military

The massive concentration of military garrisons throughout the capital region profoundly influenced many facets of society there, including banditry and violence. Sufficient numbers of principal and supernu-merary troops served in garrisons of the Northern Metropolitan Area to ensure a pool of men with a modicum of military training and ready access to the weapons of the day. Driven by often dire economic straits, many soldiers were not above using force to supplement their incomes. Seizing on jurisdictional ambiguities between military and civilian ad-ministrators, some soldiers periodically raided, while maintaining their status in the military camps where they served. Minimizing their dis-ruptive influence constituted a major concern for local civil authorities.

Many military and commoner agricultural colonies in the Northern Metropolitan Area developed a reputation for unruliness. The mag-istrate of Weixian, Guangping Prefecture, successfully requested the relocation of military colonists in his jurisdiction because they "bothered the people and were difficult to govern."[73] In his discussion of the descendants of colonists who had been relocated to Cheng'an, Guangping Prefecture, early in the fifteenth century, one official wrote that they were "reputed to be unruly," avoided corvée service, and were given to the pursuit of archery, horsemanship, and falconry.[74] The editors of the early-sixteenth-century *Baoding Prefectural Gazetteer* remarked that troops stationed in the counties of Qingdu, Rongcheng, and Tangxian were "fierce," "held authorities in contempt," and seldom paid all their taxes.[75] For at least one mid-sixteenth-century observer, the military camps and colonies were culturally suspect as well, preserving what he vaguely called "Mongol customs" long after the fall of the Yuan dynasty.[76]

That these troops often lived in close proximity with commoners worried officials for several reasons. The well-known advocate of statecraft theory Qiu Jun (1420–1495) noted with concern in the late fifteenth century that troops in Beijing were scattered through the twisting lanes of the capital, and some lived dozens of *li* (1 *li* equals approximately .3 mile) outside the city walls. He worried that they could not be called to arms quickly in a crisis and that household registration was in shambles.[77] To the east, in Tongzhou, one commentator wrote wistfully of the esprit de corps that troops might enjoy had they actually lived together in military barracks. With the illegal sale of military agricultural lands, guard barracks grew dilapidated, and troops' homes became interspersed among the commoner population.[78] This was one facet of a much larger phenomenon—the widespread transfer into private hands of such tax-free government lands as imperial pasturage and military training fields. In this case, the result presumably was the disappearance of densely settled military communities.

If some commentators regretted the demise of these military communities, others were certain that the military households in Hebei had a distinctly deleterious influence on local society. For instance, a 1485 report noted the following:

In those areas of Baoding, Hejian, and such prefectures, military lands are interspersed [with regular land]; banditry occurs as a matter of course. Compared with other areas, [they, i.e., the bandits] are in fact far more numerous; that is, insofar as in these areas the civilian and military populace engage not in agriculture [but] solely in highway robbery. The horses, mules, cattle, and such stolen by the men are sometimes bought [by the local people] at half price and sometimes

[they] are enticed [by profit] to harbor the stolen loot. [Such people] are called "receivers" or "bootleg buyers."[79]

Early in the sixteenth century, another observer wrote:

In the areas of Gu'an, Yongqing, Bazhou, and Wenan south of the capital, [men of] the capital garrison and military colonists live scattered [among civilians]. [They are by] nature arrogant and violent. [They] are fond of horsemanship and archery. [They] regularly block the roads and seize [travelers'] valuables, then scatter so they cannot be caught. People call them "whistling-arrow bandits" [xiangmazei].[80]

Although these authors clearly believed such military communities were a source of social disorder, the passages also suggest that bandits enjoyed at least a measure of local support. A widespread network to dispose of stolen livestock linked much of North China; it is certain that more than just the men who stole the animals profited from this illicit trade.[81] Furthermore, the brigands' propensity to seek refuge in military colonies and to disappear into the countryside was contingent on locals' reticence to inform officials of the outlaws' presence. Perhaps it was the fact that the bandits specialized in robbing travelers along the major routes to and from Beijing that made this tolerance possible. The threat of bandit retribution, too, no doubt figured in the local population's silence. Details are lacking, but incidents from 1469 suggest the violence that bandits could inflict on civilian populations. A group of twenty-two men led by a soldier of the Anterior Daning Guard roamed between Dongba and Xiba, near Beijing, destroying homes, seizing goods, and mutilating those who incurred their wrath. They reportedly cut off the hands and feet of their victims at the slightest provocation.[82]

Garrison officers were responsible for maintaining control over military personnel in their units, while civil officials oversaw the rest of the population.[83] While in theory this division of authority and responsibility between civil and military authorities was straightforward, in actual practice, questions of jurisdiction were common. Members of hereditary military households frequently lived interspersed among commoner populations and engaged in occupations that were often indistinguishable from those of civilian households. As registration records grew less reliable during the fifteenth century, questions of jurisdictional responsibility between military and civil authorities over individual households increased.

Debate over jurisdictional borders was especially acute when military colonies were located at considerable distances from military authorities. As noted above, military colonies developed reputations for unruly, often illegal, behavior, and local civil officials attempted to extend their supervisory controls over military households. These attempts reflected a desire both to eliminate banditry among military populations and to prevent the spread of these practices to neighboring commoner households, for which the local civil official was responsible. Frequent complaints of banditry in areas of mixed military and commoner populations suggest that civil officials' efforts were not entirely successful.

Troops engaging in banditry were quick to exploit these administrative ambiguities between military and civil authorities. For example, in 1489, officials in Henan reported that soldiers from the Ningshan, Luzhou, Huaiqing, and Zhangde garrisons plundered widely in the area. These troops were stationed on agricultural lands at a considerable distance from their original guard unit bases. Local officials complained that they were ill supervised, and officials in the capital issued orders to tighten supervision over these units. Ultimate responsibility was given to officials from Hebei, and officers from the agricultural fields were to press charges if they discovered evidence of wrongdoing.[84]

Although the efficacy of this resolution is not reported, it clearly did not address the underlying problem: military units fell outside the jurisdiction of local civil authorities and often answered only to military superiors located in an entirely different province. As one 1473 report noted, "Insofar as military colonies and forts are far removed from the [administrative] offices of their original army camps, there is no one to oversee [them]. Even when they are within the jurisdiction of a subprefecture and county, there is still no control."[85]

This official went on to complain about the soldiers' unruliness and bullying; even when they killed livestock that strayed into the camp, local people from commoner households dared not seek their animals. While in this example the suggestion to implement a mutual responsibility organization similar to those used among commoner households was rejected as being too difficult, a similar proposal was approved for Guangping, Daming, and Shunde in 1471, and was implemented in some parts of Baoding in 1515.[86]

Even when military authorities were physically present, their relations with local civil authorities could be strained.[87] Consider, for example, the mid-fifteenth-century case of Duan Gang, a supernumerary soldier from a garrison attached to the Prince of Shen, located in Luzhou, Shanxi Province.[88] Duan himself was assigned to military agricultural lands in Weixian County, approximately 130 miles east in the neighboring Northern Metropolitan Area.[89] There, Duan joined a group of heavily armed highwaymen. The magistrate of Weixian led a band of patrolmen to apprehend Duan, who had taken refuge in the military camp. Learning that the magistrate was on his way, Duan led stolen pack animals outside the camp in an attempt to escape blame. Local civil officials nevertheless recovered a portion of the stolen goods and tried to take Duan into custody, only to encounter armed resistance.

At this point, an assistant chiliarch from the military camp arrived on the scene. Having been apprised of the situation, he feigned complete cooperation with civil authorities, turning Duan and the other bandits over to the magistrate. At the same time, however, he commanded his younger brother to gather a group of men and to seize Duan and the others as the magistrate marched them back to the county seat. Duan was successfully freed, and his bandit companions, as well as several other brigands living in nearby colonies, took the opportunity to flee the area.

The assistant chiliarch later claimed that magistrate Liu had unexpectedly arrived at the head of a contingent of more than five hundred patrolmen (*huojia*) who surrounded the camp. The assistant chiliarch maintained that he had duly placed Duan under custody and incarcerated him in the guard jail after having been informed of Duan's crimes. In this account, however, the magistrate mysteriously never forwarded orders that Duan be turned over to him. In the end, Duan was executed, the assistant chiliarch was demoted, and the Prince of Shen was criticized for his inability to control his troops.[90]

If administrative structures in the capital region powerfully shaped banditry in the area, issues of ethnicity added further complications. Mongols who had moved to China, and their descendants, valued for their martial prowess, frequently served in Ming military garrisons, usually segregated from Han troops. These Mongols were generally loyal to the dynasty and frequently exhibited great valor on the battlefield. However, some Mongols in North China took advantage of moments of dynastic crisis to engage in banditry. For instance, in the wake of the Ming army's disastrous 1449 defeat at Tumu, a small military fort just northwest of Beijing, Mongol forces under Esen plundered the suburbs of Beijing. Local bandits and Mongol troops in the service of the Ming dressed as invading Mongols and took advantage of the chaos to plunder the suburbs again in November 1449.[91]

Mongol soldiers and officers, like their Han counterparts, were part of a more systemic problem. In 1479, the powerful eunuch Wang Zhi (fl. 1476–1481) reported to the throne:[92]

[I] have recently seen that the bandits in various areas who ride horses, blockade roads, make off with merchandise, and wound people are largely Mongol army officers and Mongol supernumerary officers. After they obtain the merchandise, they secretly enter the garrison. When faced with apprehension, they gather together their cohorts and resist capture and fight back to the point that those sent to apprehend them fear their savagery. [They] dare not go forward in pursuit of this kind of person. Their barbaric nature seems to remain unaltered. [They] are not susceptible to the rewards for doing good.[93] If [we] do not make plans, [they] will grow increasingly fierce and unbridled in [their] reckless actions.[94]

Mongols used military camps as bases, pillaged in the surrounding territory, and used force to resist when confronted by authorities. The report suggests that the foreign ethnicity of Mongols concerned Ming officials, a sentiment echoed elsewhere. For instance, in 1488 the minister of war observed that Ming Mongols who engaged in brigandage in the capital region "appeared no different from Mongols of the steppe," dressed in armor and helmet, armed with bows and arrows, and mounted on horses. Without more generous rewards, the minister believed, no one would risk his life by confronting them.[95]

Other well-known bandits of foreign descent in the Northern Metropolitan Area included Xi Ying and "Song the Mongol," both active during the Chenghua reign (1465–1488).[96] An exceptional horseman and archer, Song had served in one of the imperial bodyguard units. He and a regional military commissioner turned to banditry and raided outside the walls of Beijing, eluding capture for many years. When his companion was captured, Song reportedly disguised himself by shaving his head and dressing as a Buddhist monk. Government reports maintained that Song was planning to flee to the "northern barbarians" when he was apprehended, suggesting direct links between Mongols in the service of the Ming and those north of the Great Wall.[97]

The roughly contemporaneous exploits of Xi Ying were even better known, recounted in at least two miscellaneas, the *Veritable Records* and a detailed chronicle of the famed statesman and thinker Wang Shouren (1472–1529).[98] Xi Ying, formerly a Mongol commander in the Ming army, and his compatriot, Wang Yong, a former Mongol supernumerary officer (*she*), were highly skilled in archery and possessed of unusual bravery. To avoid punishment for unspecified crimes,[99] the two had fled the capital and turned to plundering in the area around Gu'an and Bazhou, two counties south of Beijing. Incredible as it might seem, at one point the two former military men reportedly rode back into Beijing on horseback, swords drawn, in search of an enemy.[100] According to one account, the two had been clients of the powerful eunuch Wang Zhi and had turned to banditry when their patron fell from power.[101] Although they eluded government forces on several occasions, they eventually were apprehended and executed.

The ethnicity of Mongols serving in the Ming military rendered them especially dangerous to certain officials. In the eyes of some, they were dauntingly fierce, while others feared the Mongols might collude with their brethren on the steppe. Despite officials' apparent concern with ethnicity, Mongol banditry grew from the same factors that figured in brigandage by Han military personnel. Many were underemployed men who possessed some military skills, enjoyed ready access to the arms of the day, and knew how to exploit relatively light government supervision. As the minister of war observed of the growing number of Mongols in Hejian, Baoding, and Dingzhou early in 1488, "They have no other way to support themselves, so they plunder as bandits."[102]

If jurisdictional ambiguities and complicating ethnic considerations facilitated banditry, the capital drill rotation system during the middle Ming was seen by some as practically an invitation to robbery and violence. Close to 100,000 soldiers and officers from the North China provinces of Henan, Shandong, Shanxi, and parts of the Northern Metropolitan Area traveled each spring and autumn to Beijing for military training with the capital garrisons. Discipline was loose, and incidents of banditry and mayhem were common. In November 1452, not only did large numbers of soldiers desert on the way to drill in the capital, many plundered once they arrived in the vicinity of Beijing.[103] In 1470, one regional inspector described the situation in stark detail:

[Cangzhou is located at] a critical juncture of water and land routes. Travelers from the two capitals pass to and fro unceasingly. In recent years, capital rotation troops from the Regional Military Commissions of Shandong, Henan, along with [the troops] from Huai-[an] and Yang-[zhou] of the [Southern] Metropolitan Area have passed through [Cang-zhou]. Those traveling by water display arms on the boats in which they ride. [They] use this to awe [other people]. Among them, the law abiding are few and the blackguards many. Whenever they pass deserted stretches, and they encounter on the Grand Canal the boats of traveling merchants or "great households" [dahu] delivering tax grain and monies, [or even] a small vessel belonging to officials or commoners, they create an incident by running into it. Using this as a pretext, they accost them and board their vessel. [The soldiers] thereupon transport and seize their merchandise, humiliate their wives, and in extreme cases even beat people and throw them into the waters. People have died of these injuries. . . . Those troops who take the overland route [are] soldiers who have tarried too long at home and fear that they will arrive late. They gird their weapons, mount their horses, and form into groups in the guise of [a troop of soldiers]. In the deep of night, they perpetrate their misdeeds. They rob whomever they encounter. During the day, when they pass through villages, they steal domestic fowl and lead off all the livestock. They have caused hurt and suffering so great as to defy description. For pity's sake, let the [supervising] officials be charged with failure to control their subordinates. Owing to this [situation], for years now, soldiers have been able to get away with whatever they wanted, and there is nothing that anyone has been able to do about it.[104]

Later that year, it was discovered that most of the mounted bandits active in Tongzhou, Zhuozhou, and Liangxiang were actually troops training in the capital, Mongol officers, and Mongol supernumerary officers.[105] According to the same report, when challenged by local police authorities, these bands would claim that they were on their way to drill. Once the authorities had passed by, the troops would resume their predatory activities.[106] Authorities were aware of the problem. During the fall of 1504, one thousand Mongol troops from Baoding and Hejian scheduled to train in Beijing were ordered not to come, lest they create "unease among the people."[107] Although this is likely another instance of a heightened sense of danger because of the Mongols' ethnicity, much of the concern arose from ongoing institutional problems that encouraged banditry by Han soldiers, as well as by Mongols.

The soldiers' proclivity for pillaging on their way to and from training in the capital owed something to their receiving no wages while on the road. In March 1493, the Ministry of War noted that because of fiscal difficulties, the early Ming practice of providing wages to soldiers on campaign or en route to training in the capital had recently been discontinued.[108] Although the Filial Ancestor (Xiaozong, r. 1488–1505) approved the ministry's recommendation that these wages be reinstated, given the fiscal straits of the latter half of his reign, the order probably was not scrupulously observed.[109]

Examples of soldiers committing banditry in the region could be easily multiplied.[110] Perhaps a more telling sign of the chronic nature of the problem is a 1489 memorial that addressed the fate of the sons and grandsons of officers found guilty of brigandage. The sons and grandsons of officers who had already been executed for their crimes were to serve as soldiers in a border guard, while those of officers still being held in jail were to inherit the post but serve in a border guard.[111] The memorial suggests that military officers were being found guilty of brigandry so often that a more institutionalized method of replacing them within the hereditary system had become necessary.

Maintaining Order in the Empire

The Ming government drew on a wide-ranging and sophisticated body of strategies for dealing with banditry, many dating from the Song dynasty (960–1279) and earlier. During outbreaks of banditry, government authorities often attempted to strengthen control over local populations by establishing mutual responsibility organizations (like the *baojia*) and, in conjunction, intensifying household registration efforts.[112] Forts and stockades were built along important routes leading to Beijing. Imperial troops, particularly capital garrison forces and the Imperial Guard, were periodically dispatched to crush powerful bandit groups active in the Northern Metropolitan Area.[113] Private forces and community covenants were also used to meet the challenges of brigands.[114]

By Ming times, the use of mutual responsibility organizations already had a long history. As to security, they served a dual function. First, they discouraged crime within neighborhoods by making all members of the community responsible for any single member's violation of the law. This arrangement was also intended to eliminate such links between criminals and communities as safe houses and fencing operations. Second, when threatened with violence from outside the community, members were to take up arms, establish patrols, and make a concerted effort to apprehend criminals.

Although mutual responsibility systems could be highly effective in maintaining local security, their successful implementation was difficult. It was predicated on detailed and up-to-date registers, the government's willingness and ability to closely supervise local affairs, and some degree of community solidarity. By the late fifteenth century, all were problematic in the Northern Metropolitan Area.

This is not to say, however, that government officials completely abandoned attempts to organize the populace into self-regulating units. For instance, in an attempt to reduce crime in Beijing, in January 1489 the emperor approved security measures that included posting census certificates outside the gates of residences, punishing those who harbored illegal residents in the capital, and calling for community members to be on the alert for those with non-native speech or clothing.[115] Repeated calls for implementation of mutual responsibility units in Beijing and the Northern Metropolitan Area appeared in the following decades.[116] The frequent proposals to establish or more stringently implement the mutual responsibility organizations suggest that without special efforts, they tended to fall into disuse relatively quickly. They also suggest that Ming officials viewed the mutual responsibility units as a tool to be used periodically for limited lengths of time.

When mutual responsibility units proved insufficient to stem the tide of banditry, the court often dispatched government troops. Usually, a censor and a chiliarch or centurion from the Imperial Guard jointly oversaw campaigns to apprehend brigands.[117] The court also seasonally dispatched chiliarchs and centurions to supervise bandit-suppression troops stationed in and around the capital, such as Tongzhou, Zhangjiawan, and Hexiwu.[118] This periodic rotation was intended to prevent the development of patronage networks, presumably between outlaws and the men responsible for apprehending them.[119]

Another method to increase imperial security and to protect travelers against highwaymen was the system of forts and walls constructed along some of the major overland routes in North China. For instance, in a 1456 edict, the emperor ordered five forts to be established between Tongzhou, east of Beijing, and Zhigu, near Tianjin, with soldiers stationed in each to guarantee the safety of travelers.[120] Again in May 1468, because of banditry between Beijing and Zhangjiawan, an entrepôt to the southeast, the court ordered a police stand to be built every five *li,* each to be manned with ten men and equipped with arms and warning gongs.[121]

Nearly two decades later, Hanlin academician and famed statecraft writer Qiu Jun (1420–1495) proposed that because of its unique political and symbolic importance, the capital region should be protected by defenses intriguingly similar to those found along China's northern border. Qiu recommended that a series of watchtowers were to be constructed along all major routes leading to Beijing. Each of these towers was to be equipped not only with warning gongs and arms but with signal fires and white pennants. When banditry was discovered, patrols were to raise the white pennant and burn signal fires to alert nearby towers and summon reinforcements. Qiu does not seem to have been particularly sanguine about the efficacy of reforms that depended on more severe penalties for officials who failed to meet strict deadlines for apprehending bandits. Referring to his proposed watchtowers, he wrote, "If such measures are implemented, [even] without severely enforcing supervisory responsibilities, banditry is certain to stop on its own."[122]

In 1488, Zhang Ding (1431–1495), a grand coordinator of the

Northern Metropolitan Area, implemented a slightly less rigorous version of this defense system farther to the south. Complaining of "an extremely urgent" situation, in which "brigands block roads and rob people," the emperor ordered Zhang to increase security and strengthen fortifications at critical passes in the region.[123] Zhang responded by constructing a series of stockades and defensive trenches along the main highways of Baoding and Zhending. Although the project was abandoned when a high-ranking eunuch sharply criticized the project to the emperor,[124] in 1492 the prefectural magistrate of Fengyang Prefecture again called for forts along the overland route from Beijing to Tongzhou, Zhangjiawan, Liangxiang, Zhuozhou, Zhending, Baoding, Hejian, and Linqing.[125] The fact that 1492 was a year for autumnal examinations and court audiences, when thousands more officials and students would be traveling to and from the capital, accounts for some of the anxiety over banditry.[126] Stockades were also built along the major roads in the vicinity of Zhangde and Weihui in northern Henan.[127]

Greater numbers of soldiers and more extensive fortifications were common responses to rising levels of brigandage, but equally important were the politics of maintaining order in the region. Officials charged with maintaining order did not merely passively implement measures handed down by the court. As members of vast patronage networks, local officials struggled to balance the demands of patrons and clients in a way that worked to their advantage.

Although strong political support from administrative superiors was vital for a successful career, maintaining good working relations with less "reputable" members of local society was also important. Officials in mid-Ming China recruited the services of locally prominent men of force in the Northern Metropolitan Area. Drawing on a tradition dating back to at least the twelfth century, Yang Yiqing, one of the most influential officials of the early sixteenth century, proposed enlisting the services of outlaws during the 1510 Rebellion campaigns.[128] Many of the chief rebel leaders, including the Liu brothers and Tiger Yang, had previously assisted local magistrates and regional officials in putting down bandits (see chapter 5). This appears to have been standard practice among local officials; the author of a well-known seventeenth-century guide for local magistrates recommended the use of some local bandits and criminals to control the rest.[129]

Ming law prescribed strict time limits for the apprehension of criminals by law enforcement personnel. In general, police officers were allowed thirty days to capture outlaws, beginning with the local magistrate's orders for the criminals' arrest.[130] For robbery, law enforcement personnel who failed to bring in the accused within the prescribed time limits were subject to fines and beatings: twenty blows of the bamboo rod after thirty days, thirty blows after two months, and forty blows after three months.[131] The time limits and severity of punishments meted out to those who failed to meet the deadlines varied according to time, offense, and community.

During the sixteenth century, specific clauses appended to the Ming law code addressed the whistling-arrow bandits, who plundered in the capital and its environs. When whistling-arrow bandits perpetrated brigandage in broad daylight, police officers were allowed two months to apprehend the bandits. Failure to do so resulted in a demotion of two ranks and a transfer to a guard unit on the border. If whistling-arrow bandits were not involved, or if the area plundered was desolate and far removed from the capital, similar penalties would not result until ten incidents had occurred in one year.[132] Security in Beijing and its environs was tighter than in more outlying areas, and punishment for failure to maintain that security was harsher than in other areas.

Law enforcement authorities had an interest in maintaining a supply of criminals.[133] Apprehending criminals was an important source of rewards and promotions for law enforcement officials, and afforded opportunities for redemption for past offenses, such as having failed to prevent an outbreak of banditry in the first place. As one might expect, however, the apprehension of "brigands" was ripe with potential for abuse. False charges were not unknown as officials attempted to fulfill quotas or secure rewards and promotions.[134] Members of the Imperial Guard were notorious for such violations.[135] Ming law awarded at least half the assets of a convicted criminal to those who informed on him,[136] a powerful incentive to "create" outlaws. For instance, in August 1461, the emperor dispatched men from the Imperial Guard to take into custody people in and around Beijing who falsely accused others of banditry as a pretext for seizing their goods. Those found guilty of this crime were to be beaten in public as a warning to others.[137] Some apparently did not heed the warnings, for a report in March 1476 recommended punishment for those who falsely accused enemies of brigandage for merit and profit.[138]

As instances like these suggest, terms such as "bandit" were labels, the result of processes and considerations often far removed from the seizure of others' goods by force. In one sense, bureaucratic incentives for officials to apprehend bandits and the system of rewards for informants were themselves motivation to see that a sufficient number of "brigands" was maintained. The following chapters will demonstrate in more depth the ambiguity and flux surrounding the status of "bandit" in Ming China.[139]

Banditry in the capital region was a situation rich in irony. The great wealth that supported an enviable lifestyle for some capital residents also attracted a steady supply of brigands and swindlers, who sought to enrich themselves with silver, goods, and grain bound for Beijing. The capital's elite, who owed their status, wealth, and influence to the dynasty, were also tied to less-exalted elements of society through extortion, intimidation, theft, and robbery. Finally, the scores of imperial guard units stationed in and around Beijing, which were intended for the defense of the dynasty against enemies from within and without, also directly contributed to the region's chronic brigandage.

Like brigandage, the maintenance of order in the capital region tended to blur the distinctions between society and state, between outlaws and the forces devoted to their suppression. Men responsible for maintaining order worked to balance the demands of patrons and clients in ways that brought rewards and advancement. Order was preserved through complex negotiations in which all interested parties had their own separate but generally complementary goals. As local officials recruited bandits to assist in law enforcement, the boundary between licit and illicit force became less distinct. The Rebellion of 1510 fully revealed how fragile this web of relation and obligation could be—and once rent, how costly to restore.

4
The Management of Violence

Besides yin and yang, male and female, inner and outer, China and the barbarians, another binary pair frequently appeared in imperial records and private writings of the late imperial period: *wen* and *wu*. *Wen* connotes culture, letters, education, and civil order; *wu* refers to the military and the martial. As with many other pairs of complementary opposites, both aspects were essential, but one was generally ascendant. From the tenth to nineteenth centuries, *wen* and its ancillary cluster of connotative attributes generally enjoyed far greater prestige and power than did *wu* and its attributes. This relationship is encapsulated in the phrase *zhongwen qingwu*: "to hold important *wen*, to regard lightly *wu*."

Tired as this cliché might be, it nevertheless reflects certain realities in the Chinese government during the Ming dynasty (1368–1644).[1] The civil bureaucracy drew men from successful candidates in the extremely taxing civil service examinations.[2] These civil bureaucrats held positions of the greatest prestige and power, fully eclipsing those of their military counterparts in the highest echelons of the court. Although there was a military examination, it was not analogous to the civil service system. Not only did it lack the social prestige of the civil service examination, but it also afforded fewer and less-powerful positions to successful candidates, produced less-qualified men, and drew on an entirely different pool of talent. China's civil bureaucrats could in theory come from almost any sort of household, whereas military officers were overwhelmingly drawn from within a hereditary household system. The military examination merely assigned higher and lower ranks to men already registered in the hereditary system.[3] Thus, while the highly competitive and prestigious civil service examination was designed to draw out the best *wen* or literary talent in the empire, the military examination ran a distant second and was never considered a completely satisfactory method for recruiting men whose skills lay beyond the realm of letters.[4]

Although this imbalance was never fully remedied, many contemporary observers were nonetheless aware of the need somehow to regulate the martial side of society and its attendant illicit violence. After relating a famous anecdote from the Warring States period (approximately 400–221 B.C.) about petty thieves whose unusual talents saved the life of their patron, the Ming raconteur Ling Mengchu (1580–1644) noted with regret that during his day:

> Only the examination system is valued. If one is not a graduate of the examination system, then even if one were possessed of extraordinary talents, one would not be employed. Thus those with marvelous gifts and clever stratagems have no way to put them to use, and most turn to illegal schemes. If one who properly employed men of talent were to gather them up, not only might he possibly gain their aid, he would also save them from falling in with the bandits.[5]

The Ming government attempted to compensate for this shortcoming in several ways, including the recruitment of men of force into more formalized military organizations. Running throughout all such endeavors was a deep-seated belief that the state bureaucracy could successfully regulate Chinese society. The civil service examination not only supplied the Ming bureaucracy with a body of extremely literate men familiar with a wide corpus of government-approved texts, it also proffered a route to fame and riches to men who might otherwise have employed their time and energy in pursuits inimical to the stability of the dynasty. Many Ming officials also believed that it was necessary to allow men of force into the ranks of the social order to ensure dynastic stability. If they could be convinced to offer their talents to the state, officials reasoned, they would bolster imperial defenses; more important, these "unfettered heroes," as they were sometimes called, would be deterred from challenging the dynasty.

This chapter examines attempts to regulate the Ming economy of violence through recruitment into a variety of military and paramilitary organizations during the fifteenth and early sixteenth centuries.[6] Although many of the general attitudes related to the management of violence discussed below were common throughout the late imperial period, in certain ways they were specific to the social, military, economic, and intellectual conditions of the fifteenth century.

The first half of the chapter is in four sections. First, I briefly review some of the principal changes affecting the Ming military during the fifteenth century. Second, I examine the recruitment of volatile elements of the population into military units, into the forces of civil officials, and into local defenses organized by elites. Third, I discuss some of the problems inherent to this strategy, and fourth, I offer a preliminary discussion of the prevalence and regulation of arms in Ming society. I conclude with a few comments on how imperial attempts to manage the economy of violence brought the central government and its local representatives into competition with local landed elites, unallied men of force, and outlaws as all strove to win the services of daring men who excelled in martial pursuits.

Developments Affecting the Ming Military

By the early sixteenth century, many Chinese observers wistfully recalled the golden age of the early Ming as a time of order, when social hierarchies were clear and respected, when simple and pure agrarian values prevailed, and when government was firm and vigorous. The early Ming order reflected the experiences of the dynastic founder, Zhu Yuanzhang (1328–1398), known posthumously as Taizu, the Great Progenitor (r. 1368–1398).[7] Haunted by painful memories of privation and disorder during the chaotic last decades of the Yuan period (1279–1367), the Great Progenitor labored mightily to restore order in China and to establish administrative and ideological mechanisms that would ensure its durability. He envisioned an empire composed of small, self-sufficient agricultural villages reminiscent of the pastoral ideals limned in the great Taoist classic *The Power and the Way*. Those who wished to travel more than 100 *li* (approximately 30 miles) were required to detail their destination and objective to village elders. Under normal conditions, local officials, clerks, and urban elites were expressly forbidden to visit rural villages.[8]

A premium was placed on achieving an order that was largely self-replicating and that required minimal direct government intervention. Administrative communities of approximately 110 households were formed, often on the basis of pre-existing groups. Village elders, selected by villagers for their economic and moral standing, were responsible for what in other contexts would have been the provenance of government. They oversaw the collection of summer and autumn taxes to be forwarded to the county government and resolved most local conflicts through mediation and moral suasion. Village elders were also to encourage correct morals, which were understood to mean adherence to a paternalistic hierarchy, which subsumed both the family and the state. Through the monthly reading of the *Great Maxims*, sons were reminded to show respect and obedience to their parents, wives to their husbands, and everyone to the dynasty. Errant behavior was discouraged through personal admonition, public ridicule, and corporal punishment. This combined system of administrative structures and ideological guides was known as the *lijia* system.[9] Through it, the Grand Progenitor believed he could foster a society in which the status quo would be accepted as natural and beyond question. To the founder, this was the surest way to maintain order and peace in a society that he knew from personal experience to have the awful potential for naked cruelty and unremitting chaos.

The founder seems to have placed tremendous faith in the ordering power of the bureaucratic state. In an effort to stabilize society and maximize the resources available to the state, the Ming founder was deeply committed to fitting everyone in society into an appropriate administrative category, which would determine their tax and corvée obligations to the dynasty, as well as influence the laws and restrictions to which they were subject. To this end, the founder continued the Yuan system of hereditary households, which divided the population into a very large number of categories, principal among them being commoners, the military, artisans, and saltworkers.[10] As the noted Ming authority Wang Yuqian has observed, "In Ming times, the performance of labor services for the imperial court was an obligation and duty of every household in the Ming empire, and so every household was assigned to a certain category of labor service."[11] Besides these administrative and institutional efforts to order China, the Ming government also made systematic use of law codes and an extensive program of officially sponsored moral suasion in an attempt to create the proper social environment that would lead to stability and order.

Yet as the founder knew well from his own experience, threats to this precious order were never far away. He himself had been one for most of his life: a vagrant, a beggar, a member of a millenarian sect, and a rebel—all roles that involved differing levels and varieties of violence. Thus, in the "Placard of People's Instructions," the imperially compiled set of moral injunctions to be read aloud in villages throughout the empire, the founder specifically discussed how local elders were to deal with the "robbers, thieves, bandits, military deserters, escaped prisoners or trouble-makers among the common people, . . . the unregistered rowdies causing trouble and committing crimes day after day, refusing to mend their ways and dominating and coercing people," and "deserters from military or corvée services who have come back home."[12]

Of course, despite the romanticized views of later observers, the challenge of illicit violence and the threat of chaos had never really been fully vanquished. Even during the early years of the dynasty, a period often characterized as a time of rural reconstruction, largely positive government policies, agricultural recovery, and growing stability, there was no shortage of insurrections throughout the empire. At least 190 insurrections of varying scale occurred during the Hongwu reign (1368–1398) alone, while the *Veritable Records* documents more than four hundred incidents of unrest during the first sixty years of the dynasty.[13] If this is not surprising, given China's enormous size and population, it is still worth bearing in mind that illicit violence was always a matter of concern during the Ming. Over the course of the fifteenth century, the speed of social, economic, military, and intellectual change accelerated, rendering the threat of illicit violence ever more urgent for many observers.

General facets of the Ming military system have been outlined earlier, but before examining recruiting practices in the imperial military system, it is useful to bear in mind several trends and signal events of the early Ming period related to the military. The hereditary military household system undergirding the Ming armies served several functions, only one of which was to secure a stable supply of men for imperial forces. Also important were the system's social and fiscal aspects. Through the military household registration system and its periodic updates, the Ming garrison system was intended as a way to organize and control a large portion of Ming society. In some regions, military personnel composed a quarter or more of the general population. Besides overseeing millions of people, the military also controlled considerable agricultural and pasturelands, from which the military was not only to support itself but also to generate revenue for the central government. The garrison system also figured in the dynasty's penal system, as convicts received sentences of military exile both to interior and border garrisons.[14] Thus, one cannot view military institutions in isolation. Changes in the military directly influenced all of Ming society and, conversely, larger social, economic, and political developments profoundly affected the military.

Over the course of the fifteenth century, several factors eroded the integrity of this hereditary system. Despite Herculean efforts by the Ming government, the military registrars compiled to monitor performance, posts gained, and changes in the composition of the household (births, deaths, injuries, etc.) were gradually subject to the corrosive influences of corruption, inefficiency, and incompetence. A well-placed bribe or, in some cases, the threat of force, enabled many to escape the registration system and all its responsibilities. In other cases, the names of those who had died or had deserted were left on the roster; their monthly stipends, meager as they were, enriched local military officers who pocketed the money. Still other soldiers paid a monthly fee to their commanding officers in exchange for exemption from their military duties.[15]

Officials of the day were aware of these problems and proposed various solutions, ranging from stricter registration policies, harsher penalties for officers who abused their subordinates, and punishments for deserting soldiers. During the fifteenth century, government policies toward the ballooning numbers of supernumerary soldiers in the garrisons also changed noticeably. Supernumerary soldiers were those males in military households who did not serve as imperial regulars. Exempted in theory from corvée and tax responsibilities, as well as from active military service, supernumerary soldiers were to help defray expenses incurred by the imperial regular in their family, preferably through farming. Beginning no later than the first decade of the fifteenth century, however, officials began to complain that these supernumerary soldiers exploited their corvée and tax exemptions to engage in commerce and handicrafts.[16] Although others were forced to work on various public works projects related to the rebuilding of the northern capital slightly later, during the early fifteenth century,[17] many supernumerary soldiers remained under only light military and civil supervision.

During the fifteenth century, imperial authorities made repeated efforts to place these men under closer control and make more effective use of them. As imperial regulars in Jiangxi Province were saddled with growing corvéelike responsibilities (the most important being the transportation of imperial tribute grain to the capital), supernumerary soldiers increasingly served in a military capacity in order to maintain adequate manpower levels.[18] Supernumerary soldiers in the strategically critical northwestern provinces of China were drawn into active military service to bolster border defenses during the late fifteenth century.[19] Both developments demonstrate how shifting institutional imperatives changed personnel policies in the garrison system, and suggest that the tendency simply to dismiss Ming military institutions as being in terminal decay after the early fifteenth century needs reconsideration, a question that will be addressed more fully in the concluding remarks of this study.[20]

That being said, serious problems did plague the system, and the number of battle-ready troops fell steadily through the fifteenth century. By 1500, few garrisons could field more than a quarter of their prescriptive 5,600 men. For many contemporaries, there was no more telling proof of the advanced decay of the Ming military than the 1449 Tumu Incident. In October 1449, Eastern Oirat Mongols under the command of their dynamic leader, Esen, routed a large elite Ming expedition personally led by the emperor. The Mongols decimated the heart of the Ming forces, captured the emperor, and stood poised for a direct assault on the capital.[21] The last time a reigning emperor had been taken captive by foreign invaders, in the late thirteenth century, the dynasty fell, and "barbarian" Mongol forces established a new ruling house in China. Thus, while Ming forces campaigned with some success in the southern provinces of Fujian, Guangzhou, and Sichuan during these years, the Tumu Incident left Chinese officialdom vulnerable[22] and desperate for ways to strengthen the defenses of North China in particular and of China in general.

Recruiting Efforts
Military Units
The military crisis of the Tumu Incident sparked frantic efforts to defend the capital and to reorganize the capital garrisons.[23] The crisis also provided a clear and urgent incentive to intensify recruiting efforts.[24] For instance, in the immediate wake of the Tumu Incident, the Ministry of War reported in November 1449 that it had recruited more than four hundred strong and courageous men from among the ranks of imperial regulars. The best among them were to be awarded posts, silver, and military equipment. The ministry recruited an additional 130 men, who were willing to supply their own mounts and fight against the Mongols.[25] We see a similar report early in 1450 from one of the leading generals of the day, Yang Hong (1381–1451),[26] who requested that supernumerary soldiers in the garrisons of Wanquan Regional Military Commission, men who theoretically did not have any military responsibilities, be organized into a battalion and be drilled for battle.[27]

In another long memorial of early 1450, a supervising secretary in the Office of Scrutiny for War argued that in the light of the officer corps' corruption and incompetence, and the pathetic state of their soldiers, an elite unit should be organized from five thousand "soldiers who dare death." To be well armed and under the command of a courageous general, this new unit was to serve exclusively as a vanguard, for charging into battle immediately after the initial artillery barrage and engaging the Mongols in close-quarters fighting, thus robbing the Mongols of their chief advantage, mounted combat.[28]

While this official advocated reorganization of personnel within

existing military units, others called for recruiting new men from outside the military. For instance, little more than a year later, in mid-
January 1451, the minister of revenue submitted a memorial calling for
the recruitment of "loyal, righteous heroes" along the lines of such illus-
trious historical military figures as Li Guang, Ban Chao, Li Xun, and
Yue Fei, to bolster Ming defenses. Although officials were to coordinate
recruitment of these "heroes" in several areas in North China, it appears
that Jin expected "sons of officers [guanshe], men of military and commoner households, government stipend students, jailers, priests, and
others" to do the actual recruiting, promising them positions commen-
surate with the number of men they were able to assemble. These forces
were then to be given government-issued armor, weapons, and training and to be stationed in strategic sites in North China, including Linqing, Taiyuan, Zhangde, Changan, Huaian, and Daming. The best
among these recruits, he suggested, could be used to reinforce capital
defenses in case of Mongol incursions, while the rest could be used to
protect the local population in areas where they were stationed. This
measure clearly supplemented ongoing efforts at recruitment, as the
emperor ordered officials supervising the recruiting to assist grand
defenders and grand coordinators who were already in place in the
recruitment process. The emperor, however, warned against recruiting
in areas from which people's stalwarts had already been drawn, "for
fear that it may provoke revolt."[29]

Lesser regional threats on occasion prompted calls for wider recruiting efforts. In July 1505, as part of Ming efforts to bolster border
defenses against increasingly frequent Mongol incursions, plans were
again drawn up to recruit with rewards "men who were fierce, courageous, and talented in martial pursuits." These men were to be settled
around the capital, where during times of peace they were apparently
to be under military command. The policy was intended in a single
stroke to intimidate the Mongols and to eradicate any potential domestic
challengers.[30] To increase troop strength along the northern border, Liu
Jian (1433–1526), a junior grand secretary, proposed that "in addition to
those registered in hereditary military households, anyone, without
regard to whether he is a supernumerary officer or villager who is brave
and strong and can be put into battle should be recruited and selected
in many ways. They shall be provided with provisions according to
what imperial regulars receive. They should be given armor, weapons,
and mounts."[31] Thus, while the crisis of 1449 sparked a flurry of recruiting drives, such drives were by no means restricted to moments of
national crisis.

In fact, recruiting efforts continued during periods of relative peace and stability. For instance, early in 1466, a time of comparative calm, the emperor ordered the Ministry of War to post announcements in and around Beijing encouraging men of great strength, bravery, and clever stratagems to place their talents at the service of the dynasty. In this case, the court seems to have targeted men who had neither registered in Shuntian Prefecture nor had any prior military obligations to the state. Those willing to offer their talents were to be organized into a separate unit, trained, and called into action in times of crisis. These men were to be eligible for the same rewards and promotions as imperial regulars. Furthermore, anyone willing could join the capital garrisons and receive the same wages.[32]

Recruiting continued during periods of relative peace and stability, suggesting that factors beyond the simple desire to maintain adequate levels of military strength were at work. In some instances, the impetus for recruiting drives was not any obvious military need but rather what appears to have been an administrator's desire to make the numbers come out properly. Late in the summer of 1476, efforts were made to increase manpower in several garrisons in northeastern China, where in some units troop strength had dropped by more than 90 percent. Local military and civil authorities observed that men were available locally but that many of them were hiding out because of military regulations that forced them to report to garrisons in faraway southern China rather than serve in their home regions. These officials proposed that the men be allowed to surrender to local garrison authorities and be reregistered in the local garrisons, where they would take up their duties. Here the emphasis was less on the recruitment of unfettered heroes or men of superior martial skills than on an attempt to improve administrative efficiency.[33]

This was in part attributable to the administrator's love of neatness. It was also, however, inextricably tied to questions of political and moral legitimacy during the Ming. The administrative practices established by the dynastic founder during the late fourteenth century had lasting authority. During his later years, the founder had insisted that the institutions and guidelines he established were inviolate and would serve as eternal standards. Thus, depending on the orientation of an official and political demands, any variation from those practices, no matter how well they might meet contemporary social, military, or economic needs, could be portrayed as deviation from the golden age of the early dynasty and a sign of disrespect for the founder.

However justifiable as to moral and political legitimacy, restora-

tionist impulses that sought to bring things more in line with guidelines of the early Ming sometimes reflected a poor grasp on social reality.
For instance, in one memorial, the renowned scholar Qiu Jun (1420–
1495), a member of the prestigious Hanlin Academy, the bureaucratic
organization responsible for drafting imperial edicts, exclaimed, "If all
the registered men in the seventeen subprefectures and forty-eight counties of the capital region were to become soldiers, we would then have
between 400,000 and 500,000 troops." He then gushed about the military impact of these "potent troops" on the defenses of the capital.[34] In
effect, he was calling for a militarization of the entire male population
of the capital region. Given the countless incidents of banditry that
grew out of a poorly supervised military population in the capital
region,[35] it is unclear if doubling the military population would significantly have improved social control or military strength. Qiu's proposal
was not put into action.

The risk of increased banditry aside, there were other reasons why
some officials rejected the forcible registration of commoner men into
military households. When recruits were forcibly registered into military households and burdened with all the attendant responsibilities, it
made subsequent recruiting difficult. Few men wished to risk registration just for the few ounces of silver they stood to earn from serving in
what should have been a temporary militia. Criticizing such practices
in the strategically northwestern province of Shaanxi, Li Dongyang
(1447–1516), another official in the Hanlin Academy, observed:

> Recently, recruits have been forced into construction projects and reg-
> istered in garrisons—that is to say, they have become real soldiers. In
> severe cases, they have [been forced to] designate their own successors,
> [thus] making soldiering a hereditary obligation. Thus while there
> have been vigorous efforts at recruiting, no one responds. Since sol-
> diers and commoners are distinct in the first place, to register farmers
> as soldiers would not seem to be of their volition. Furthermore, when
> they are forced into bondage, it renders them equivalent to convicts.
> Who then would be willing to [respond to the recruiting]?[36]

Whether men were willing to respond to recruiting drives was of
some import, because recruiting was often used as a way to bring suspect segments of society under firmer imperial control. These efforts
could be effective only if they held some appeal for their target audience. Often, calls for more aggressive recruiting campaigns were linked

to a general undercurrent of social instability: violent crime, vagrancy, and disturbing levels of physical mobility among the populace were all problems that seem to have been most keenly felt in urban environments, like the capital. *Wuji zhi tu,* literally "unregistered ones," almost always appear in government records and official memorials as socially disruptive and prone to engage in illegal activities.[37] For instance, writing about the large number of mendicant Buddhist monks in Beijing, one bureaucrat expressed a sentiment common among many government officials.[38] He noted with acute concern the monks' lack of a fixed abode and the fact that they were not actively engaged in productive agricultural work. He described them as "dressing in the clothing of barbarians [i.e., non-Chinese garb], and harboring the thoughts of wild animals. Their treachery and duplicity, too, defy enumeration."[39] Discounting the official's hyperbole, he clearly worried about people who were not under firm state control through the registration system. Recruiting and registering groups that authorities believed posed the greatest risk to imperial order was one method of solving this problem.[40]

It is in this context that we should understand the recommendation of Liu Jian (1433–1526), a grand secretary and a leading late-fifteenth-century statesman. After noting the limited success of previous recruitment efforts, Liu observed, "Unregistered people in and around the capital are legion." He suggested that the Ministry of War "thoroughly investigate these men. [The Ministry] should find a way to track down the native place and address of all those strapping men not registered with government authorities. They should be made to perform military duties. Thus the garrisons would achieve full strength."[41] Recruiting and its attendant registration were an attempt to extend some kind of supervision and control over segments of the population perceived most likely to create trouble.

Foreign military threats also heightened domestic security concerns.[42] This is perhaps most obvious with such "outsiders" as the Mongols serving in the Ming army. In the wake of the Tumu Incident of 1449, Mongols in China were viewed with grave suspicion. Not content merely to heap calumny upon the Mongols, officials also transferred large numbers of Mongol officers and soldiers to China's deep south on military campaigns against various non-Han peoples—thus conveniently precluding the possibility of Mongol collusion with their brethren to the north of the Great Wall.[43]

Such concerns, however, were not restricted to ethnic outsiders, and all military threats, both foreign and domestic, heightened fears that

marginal or volatile elements of society would exploit periods of imperial weakness to commit nefarious acts. Thus, even those recruiting
drives that might at first blush appear to have been motivated exclusively by military considerations may also have been prompted in part
by a desire for greater domestic social control.[44] For example, shortly
after the Tumu debacle, which occurred north of Beijing, one grand
coordinator responsible for the capital region expressed his fears about
potential outbreaks of banditry in the southern capital, Nanjing. He
explicitly mentioned "the powerful and lawless among military and
commoner households," whom he believed would turn to banditry or
revolt unless they quickly received some protection from grasping, corrupt civil and military authorities.[45]

Finally, before turning to the subject of recruiting by civil officials,
there is one more category of recruits to note—private military retainers.
For many military officers, securing these military retainers was essential to developing effective fighting forces.[46] While the use of private
military retainers would reach its height only during the last decades
of the dynasty, several studies have demonstrated that the practice
originated no later than the fifteenth century.[47] To cite only a few instances, during the 1510 Rebellion, several generals made effective use
of their highly trained, well-provisioned, and deeply loyal retainers in
fighting against rebel forces. In fact, the noted man of letters and Hanlin
bachelor Lu Shen (1477–1544) commented that at the peak of the rebels'
powers, "The only thing they feared was [General] Xu Tai's retainers."[48]
The retainer forces of Shi Xi, a commander in Wuping Garrison in
modern-day northwestern Anhui Province, figured in the elimination
of one of the most important leaders of the 1510 Rebellion.

In the years after the 1510 Rebellion, reports of military retainers
sporadically appear. For instance, one Vice-Commander Yuan Jie of the
capital garrison maintained military retainers. In October 1516, in the
face of a growing Mongol threat on the northern border, he was ordered
to take his retainers, with five hundred men from Hejian Garrison and
five hundred men from the capital garrison, to take up a position in the
important entrepôt Tongzhou, just east of the capital.[49] Days after receiving his orders, Yuan was granted permission to send the capital garrison
troops home and to receive provisions for his retainers and the troops
from Hejian.[50] As is evident in the examples noted above, the chief motivation for maintaining military retainers was a desire for personally
loyal soldiers of proven ability to direct imperial campaigns. The potential to misuse such forces in the personal interests of officers, however,
posed a constant threat.

Civil Officials

Not only military officers maintained retainers; civil officers ranging in rank from local magistrates to grand coordinators also augmented their forces through recruiting able-bodied men. Grand coordinators were high-ranking civil officials who were appointed to oversee various operations, which often spanned one or more provinces. From the mid-fifteenth century onward, the majority of many grand coordinators' duties involved military operations.[51]

In 1509, for instance, the emperor ordered Grand Coordinator Ning Gao to eradicate a particularly virulent outbreak of banditry in North China and granted him permission to take with him his personal military retainers.[52] This force apparently was insufficient, and he recruited more than one thousand men from the area. Although the source of these new recruits is unclear, there are indications that they were taken from outside the hereditary military system. The 1549 edition of the *Zhending Prefectural Gazetteer* notes, "Grand Coordinator Ning Gao was determined to suppress the bandits, and he implemented unrighteous methods. He recruited brave and martial men from among the people, who were then called his assault troops [*jibing*]."[53]

Local magistrates also made use of men of force to maintain order in their jurisdictions. Much of the reason why local officials not only tolerated but often actively sought out these men of force lies with magistrates' responsibilities and the resources at their disposal to fulfill those duties.[54] Although Ming magistrates across the empire wielded considerable political power in local society, they were also under great pressure from various authorities—fellow officials, their immediate superiors, provincial officials, the central government, and local elites. Failure to successfully negotiate their varied and often contradictory demands could result in broken careers and an assortment of corporal, economic, and administrative punishments.[55] Magistrates were asked to do much locally with very little assistance from the central government: collect taxes, impose corvée labor, maintain order, encourage proper social mores, and more. In these circumstances, the key to good government and a successful tenure in office was effective use of local resources.

Perhaps foremost among these local resources was the yamen staff of clerks and runners, which could number in the hundreds. Most Ming magistrates depended almost exclusively on yamen personnel for the daily operation of much of county government.[56] In contrast to the magistrate, who by law was an outsider to the area, the yamen staff was familiar with local conditions and established practices. Although high-minded literati roundly criticized these clerks, many of whom were off the books, as venal, corrupt, shameless bullies, they nonetheless constituted one of the magistrate's most critical links to the local community. They served as the chief sources of information used in the periodic imperial administrative evaluations of local officials, and thus enjoyed some leverage over their superiors.[57]

Both the magistrate's salary and the overall administrative costs of county government depended on the efficacious use of local and unofficial sources of revenue. Set at low levels, Ming officials' salaries were generally insufficient to support themselves and their families or to entertain associates and visiting officials.[58] One partial solution was to permit the magistrate to pocket the monies set aside for fictitious lictors; a recent study suggests that this unofficial source was often equal to half the magistrate's official salary.[59] Underfunded county governments also commonly resorted to unofficial, and occasionally technically illegal, practices to cover the expenses of local governance.[60]

It is in this historical context that one must understand Ming magistrates' apparently frequent use of local men of force. As yamen clerks were most familiar with local administrative practices and the intricacies of political interaction, so the men of force possessed an intimate knowledge of local bandit groups, toughs, and other potential troublemakers. The yamen clerks' proclivity to abuse their power gained through association with the county government paralleled the tendency of men of force to exploit the aura of authority and legitimacy lent by government service. Additionally, most magistrates were not fully aware of either group's full range of activities. Finally, despite all these abuses, contemporaries took it for granted that local government would grind to a rapid halt without the benefit of these ambitious men.

Of course, the comparison cannot be pushed too far. In contrast to yamen clerks, whose influence dramatically diminished once they lost their government posts, men of force depended less exclusively on association with government officials. They enjoyed reputations for martial skills and the effective use of violence, which predated their association with county officials, and they retained these qualities even after they parted ways with local authorities. It goes without saying, however, that those groups who severed their links with local government faced an uncertain future. They could easily become the target of new "bandit catchers."

On some occasions, government officials incorporated bandit and rebel chiefs directly into the local security forces. For instance, in 1445, having surrendered to authorities in Yongfeng County, Jiangxi, thirty-five men under the command of rebel leader Wang Neng received lands and positions in the local constabulary. They then assisted the security forces of six surrounding counties.[61]

In 1498, Hu Shining (1469–1530) articulated the reasoning behind co-opting unfettered heroes:

> Banditry among the people is largely by unfettered heroes. Your humble minister believes that if we were to gather these men then not only would we acquire talent for generals, but also we would eliminate banditry. This is the superior policy for banditry. I would that Your Majesty order the Ministry of War to formulate plans for promulgation throughout the realm: Civil and military authorities are to carefully investigate those among military and commoner households who possess surpassing strength and extreme proficiency in martial arts. . . . Officials are not to coerce those commoners of good standing who are unwilling [to join]. When selecting those with posts, if they are of military households, they shall be appointed squad leader. Those from commoner households shall be granted such titles as head instructor, etc. They shall be given slightly better provisions. Have them accompany the troops in training. For those who are able to capture bandits and accumulate much merit, they shall be granted posts accordingly in order to recognize and reward [their efforts].[62]

Several facets of Hu's report bear mentioning. First, in Hu's eyes, these "unfettered heroes" were as likely to appear among commoners' households as military households, suggesting that they were not the exclusive product of military culture. And while the specific provisions for co-opting men of different backgrounds vary, the state's desire to win the alliance of these men remained the same. Second, as noted above, Hu maintains that the government's gain was the bandits' loss. This was true not only in the sense that every man who joined government forces reduced the bandit ranks by one. More important, Hu and other officials believed that the unfettered heroes provided the essential leadership and spark of potential rebel groups. The key for the government was the elimination of disaffected, unfettered heroes through appeasement, co-option, or execution. Bereft of galvanizing leadership, rebel forces quickly would disintegrate into nothing more than directionless mobs, or so the reasoning went.

Like the vast majority of similar proposals to identify and organize unfettered heroes, Hu assumed that these men could be brought to heel by the state. Hu's contemporary Chu Quan (1457–1513) makes this assumption explicit and offers a fascinating analogy. Chu compares "men of talent and martial prowess" to such steppe people as the Mongols. Both are possessed of great military skill but are wild and fierce. He notes that the Mongols in the service of the Ming must be put under the command of Chinese officers and campaign in Ming ranks before the state can "break their spirit [make them submit] and obtain their strength. Otherwise, it would be to no advantage." Similarly, men of talent and martial prowess were to be identified, registered, and "controlled through the ranks in order to alter their practices [customs]." He concludes, "When bravos are congregated in the capital armies, not only will [the dynasty] be able to overawe its enemies and keep in check distant foes. Those traitorous men plotting to gather mobs or attempt armed revolt will also fall into our trap. [Thus, through this measure], these problems will resolve themselves of their own accord."[63]

Chu's comments not only confirm what seems to have been a prevalent confidence in the transformative powers of the imperial state but also provide insight into contemporary conceptions of violence and culture. In regard to the Mongols, Chu repeats the well-worn observation, "They are not of our kind; their minds must be different." Far more interesting is that Chu implicitly applies this reasoning to the village bravos, who were all Han Chinese. It seems reasonable to assume that when Chu talks about "our kind," he refers either to highly educated men of substance like himself or to suitably domesticated commoners. In either case, Chu's perception of unregulated violence as distinctly foreign is striking and suggests that, at least in his mind, only those who were duly registered and under the control of the imperial government were fully Chinese.

Slightly later, in the early sixteenth century, the minister of personnel, Yang Yiqing (1454–1530), also advocated policies designed to absorb into the service of the state as much talent from society as possible. During the 1510 Rebellion, Yang hoped to rally locally prominent families, university students, and retired officials to the defense of their native regions.[64] Yang argued that with the promise of office and commendation by the throne, local elites were certain to strive to outdo one another in apprehending bandits.[65]

More directly relevant to our concerns here was Yang's proposal to use segments of local society usually more closely associated with crime and violence than with local defense. Yang quoted from the famous Song dynasty literatus Su Shi (1036–1101), who urged that "the powerful and lawless" (haohua) should be offered the possibility of an official post in return for their aid in combating bandits. Su Shi argued that recruiting men into the government through only the examination

system left the "simple and coarse, the fierce and difficult to transform" with no way to advance in government. Unallied to the dynasty,
these men and their families often turned to rebellion. Using several historical examples from earlier dynasties, Su Shi insisted that by securing
the loyalty of these men, the dynasty could increase its source of talented men and deprive bandits of leaders. Even reformed bandit leaders
could be useful to the throne.[66] Facing a considerable threat to Ming
power, Yang reiterated Su's claim: winning the loyalty of these men
deprived common bandits of a vital source of talented and ambitious
leaders.[67]

Yang also referred to another famous Song figure, Qin Guan (1049–
1100), who wrote that the most important technique for eliminating
bandits was to win the loyalty of "men of outstanding talents" (haojun).[68]
Once these men were swung to the side of the dynasty, common bandits
were easily disposed of, regardless of how many there might be.[69] Because bandits and banditry varied widely, Qin emphasized a flexible
approach to dealing with brigands, including the use of methods and
personnel outside existing government regulations. Like Su Shi, Qin also
argued that only when brigands were led by a haojun, "a man of outstanding talent," would they become dangerous to the state. Qin recommended recruiting these "men of outstanding talent" through the
civil and military examinations. Qin concluded that the state could
greatly expand the pool of talent from which it drew by including these
haojun. Even if a few of them did cause trouble, the damage would be
limited if they had been co-opted by the government.

Early in the sixteenth century, Yang took for granted a large supply
of men of force and stressed the need to recruit aggressively among
them. To this end, he recommended that grand coordinators—civil officials who supervised one or more provinces—travel throughout their
jurisdiction to summon all men possessed of great strength and courage
or who excelled in mounted archery.[70] Additionally, Yang was interested in those who had studied the use of the fist, cudgel, spear, sword,
or metal-linked whip—martial artists.[71]

Yang also sought to make use of known criminals. Thieves, pickpockets, urban toughs (lahu)—that is, members of urban gangs and
gamblers who rendered meritorious service would enjoy what
amounted to a pardon for previous crimes. They would also receive
rewards on the same basis as anyone else for apprehending bandits. By
recruiting these men, the dynasty was diminishing a source of brigand
recruits, thus sapping their morale.[72]

At the conclusion of the campaign, all these ad hoc local security forces were to be immediately disbanded and the men returned to their lands. According to Yang, men would be willing to offer their services against the bandits only when secure in the knowledge that they would not be forced into permanent obligations or registered as military households.[73] Another unstated motive for immediate disbandment was almost certainly the highly volatile nature of these forces. Organized, armed, and equipped with the prestige and influence afforded by association with local officials, men once valuable for suppressing threats to the dynasty could easily become problems themselves.[74]

Both Hu Shining and Yang Yiqing probably were influenced by the writings of Qiu Jun (1421–1495), author of the most influential work on statecraft penned during the fifteenth century.[75] Qiu had singled out the writings of Su Shi and Qin Guan as signally important to the question of banditry and had included lengthy segments of their memorials in his magnum opus, the *Daxue yanyi bu*. Qiu also strongly advocated the recruitment of bold men through two methods. The first way was the establishment of special examinations for men who were literate, familiar with history, knowledgeable about military books, and skilled in martial arts but incapable of meeting the stringent requirements of the regular civil service examination. A second avenue was to order military officers to recruit aggressively those who were expert on border conditions, adept at martial arts, or possessed of surpassing strength. Quoting another Song-dynasty thinker, Qiu argued that if these measures were implemented, "All talent in the realm would have a use [to the dynasty], and none would have thoughts of moving beyond their station."[76] Qiu Jun's essays on eradicating banditry continued to exercise a broad influence, being reprinted in most major compilations of statecraft writings of the sixteenth and early seventeenth centuries.[77]

Finally, before turning to private recruiting efforts by local elites, a word on eunuchs and their military retainers. The court regularly dispatched eunuchs on military campaigns throughout the empire. As military commanders, eunuchs needed able fighting men who would serve as their bodyguards and could be counted on to inspire others in battle. To note only a few instances, during the mid-fifteenth century, the eunuch Cao Jixiang developed a following of Mongol soldiers serving in the Ming imperial army during several campaigns in the southern provinces of Yunnan and Fujian.[78] During the early sixteenth century, the palace eunuchs Zhang Zhong and Gu Dayong were prominent military commanders in the campaign against North China rebels, while fellow eunuch Zhang Yong led the elite capital garrison forces to suppress a revolt by an imperial prince.[79] In each instance, eunuchs encountered bitter criticism for the large number of men in their entourages.[80]

Given civil officials' propensity to damn nearly every activity of eunuchs, it is not surprising that eunuchs came under sharp attack for maintaining military retainers. Everyone in eunuch entourages was dismissed as a useless camp-follower, fraudulently laying claim to military merit, rewards, and promotions. Without question, many who followed the eunuchs on the campaign trail were not above falsely claiming credit for battlefield heroics. To dismiss all such followers, however, seriously distorts both the military role of eunuchs and the prevalence of retainers.

We gain oblique recognition of the fact that at least a portion of eunuchs' entourages were capable fighting men in a report by senior statesman Liu Daxia (1437–1516), from the late fifteenth or early sixteenth century.[81] Liu fulminated against "unregistered men" who offered their services as military retainers to eunuch grand defenders and others, arguing that "upon encountering bandits, they immediately flee and [then] falsely claim credit." Although he proposed that the majority of men be returned to their original place of registration or original garrisons, those men whom he verified *were in fact knowledgeable about military affairs and adept in archery and horsemanship* will be allowed to follow [these officials]"[82] (emphasis added). Liu's remarks suggest that at least a portion of these followers were recruited for their military skills and usefulness in battle, even if many others were simply padding the rolls.

Local Elites

Most government officials assumed that local elites possessed some resources of violence. This knowledge could be a comfort during times of crisis, when local government forces proved insufficient and magistrates turned to local elites for assistance. During such times, especially the waning years of a dynasty, gentry organized local militias and fortifications, providing a measure of protection and security for at least a portion of the local community.[83] Although gentry-organized local militias (*xiangbing*) were more prevalent during the last decades of the Yuan and Ming dynasties, such forces were not unusual during the fifteenth and early sixteenth centuries.[84] For instance, during the late fifteenth century, one official in the southern coastal county of Pingyang, Zhejiang, failed to subdue with regular imperial troops a group of "miner bandits" in the area. These rogue miners reportedly had killed several yamen clerks and arrogated imperial-sounding titles. Discovering that a member of the local gentry (*shimin*) had gathered a group of "men who dared death," he paid a visit to the local notable. Moved that the magistrate would thus honor him, the gentleman agreed to lend his forces to the campaign of suppression. The outlaw miners were quickly suppressed.[85]

During the 1510 Rebellion in North China, several elite families organized local defenses. For example, in 1510, a retired official sojourning in Cangzhou played a critical role in the week-long defense of that city, and later, in 1511, a retired censor in Yuzhou reportedly was able to assemble three thousand local men for battle.[86] One "man of righteousness" from Xiayi County, in Henan Province, Wang Hai, displayed a long-standing interest in public affairs, expressed primarily through contributions of grains and silver in times of crisis. During the 1510 Rebellion, Wang contributed grain to the local government, donated funds to pay for the repair of the city walls and moats, and fed the troops of an imperial general when they passed through Xiayi. He rejected rebel demands for silver in exchange for sparing the city, and instead distributed rewards of 20 taels of silver (about twice the amount an unskilled laborer would earn in a year) to militiamen who defended Xiayi. Later, in the early 1520s, during a virulent outbreak of banditry, Wang dispatched his retainers to fight, supplying them with more than 200 taels of silver to cover their expenses. Eventually, his meritorious acts were acknowledged even by the throne; the emperor Shizong (r. 1522–1566) ordered that an account of Wang's deeds be compiled as a lasting tribute, an act of considerable imperial favor.[87]

In at least one occurrence, local elites themselves formed the core of a "dare death" squad. The eldest Lu brother of Fuyang, Henan, was granted a position in the Imperial Guard for his merit on the battlefield, and after his death, a temple was founded in his honor.[88] In these instances, the local elites responded to the request of the magistrate and willingly put their personal resources at the service of the state. For such behavior they were often recognized by the throne or given laudatory biographies in local gazetteers.

Dangers of Recruiting and Private Retainers

All the strategies outlined above, designed to regulate force in the middle Ming, posed potential dangers to the dynasty. Militias under the dominance of local elites represented a threat to the dynasty's monopoly on legitimate violence. Volatile men who were incorporated into government armies could easily disrupt discipline and order in the imperial ranks. Men of force who served as private military retainers presented financial, security, and political legitimacy problems.

If during periods of crisis the Ming government gave its blessing to the use of private military retainers, it remained cognizant of the dangers presented by military forces not fully under state control. Ming officials harbored suspicions about military retainers for fiscal reasons. In a March 1503 report to the throne, the grand coordinator of the strategically vital Liaodong area in northeast China decried the abuses associated with soldiers who became "retainers" or "housemen" of their officers.[89] The grand coordinator alleged that over time, these men, their sons, and their grandsons, numbering as many as several hundred, disappeared from the military rolls. This, in turn, meant that no one in the family paid any taxes or rendered any corvée service. The official's concern was not so much with the security threat that such forces posed to the Ming government as with the fiscal challenge they presented.[90]

In other examples, military forces under private or quasi-private control threatened the authority of local officials. In January 1517, Assistant Regional Commander Shi Xi, of northwestern Anhui, then retired, was charged with "maintaining military retainers without authority to vaunt his power and prestige."[91] This officer and his band of several hundred retainers, who had performed such admirable service on behalf of the throne during the 1510 Rebellion, were now a source of worry to local civil officials. Shi's men apparently had not disbanded at the conclusion of the campaign, nor even with the officer's retirement from active service. Instead, Shi used them to advance his local interests. Shi's men seized lands, forcibly converted people's grave lots into agricultural fields and orchards, and established illegal toll stations along well-traveled highways.[92] Although the officer and his men were a potent challenge to local civil authorities, the emperor elected not to press the issue, noting that the officer had already retired.[93] Perhaps, too, the emperor wished to keep effective military forces available for future crises. Lu Shen, who had praised the efficacy of Xu Tai's retainers during the 1510 Rebellion, simultaneously observed that they were all "fierce and brave military men; they are suited only to killing rebels." He argued strenuously against integrating them into the emperor's bodyguard in the capital.[94]

Wang Hai, the man of righteousness who contributed so greatly to local defenses during the 1510 Rebellion, also constituted a potential threat to the authority of the state with his access to men of force. At one point during the rebellion, Wang took personal offense at the behavior of a military officer hailing from a region outside Xiayi. Wang believed the officer showed more interest in collecting money, cavorting with prostitutes, and quaffing wine than in defending Xiayi. He declared that a man of such behavior was himself a bandit and ordered members of the militia to seize the officer during the night. Although the details of what transpired that evening are unclear, it is said that the officer was suitably humbled after his release the next morning and quickly left the area.[95] With his control over local men of force, Wang was useful to the local government and the state in times of crisis. In exchange for his cooperation, the state was willing to overlook Wang's minor transgressions—such as kidnapping an imperial army officer and driving him out of town.

Integrating these various kinds of violence into a bureaucratic order was always a calculated risk, and the line dividing defenders of the imperial order from its challengers often blurred with disturbing ease. Writing on developments in Jiangxi during the early sixteenth century, Lin Ruozhou observed, "One variety of fierce bare sticks initially claims to be assisting officials to kill bandits, but in the process colludes with them, storing stolen goods for a profit. Later these folks take up for a living the false accusation of commoners to extort goods from them. The only thing they fear is the return of peace."[96] With peace came the restoration of normal litigation and the possibility that the misdeeds committed during the time of crisis would be brought to light and the criminals be punished.

Lin's concerns were echoed during the mid-sixteenth century by another commentator, Chen Quanzhi, who worried about the corrupt ties binding local elites, bandits, and the men charged with apprehending bandits. According to Chen, "Robbers depend on local notables to carry out crimes, while these local elites depend on the robbers in order to increase their wealth." In the few cases where the robbers were detected, the victimized family could be bought off, while the local police would, for a bribe, set the robbers free. Chen was deeply concerned about the long-term effects of this widespread corruption. He believed that every robber freed was an encouragement for others to follow in his footsteps. He wrote, "They only see the prosperity [to be gained through] robbery and do not see its price. Why should they have any further hesitation?" Eventually, Chen worried, these robbers would grow into rebels.[97]

Managing these men of force was a delicate balance, and the price of failure could be very high (see chapter 6). The same factors that made these men attractive to military officers, civil officials, and local gentry were precisely those that made them most dangerous—skill in arms, physical bravery, a willingness to use violence, a band of followers, and ties that extended beyond the confines of local society. Allied with proper authorities, these men were a potent addition to the forces of order. When relations with these men of force broke down, however, they became a frightening avatar of social chaos. In two of the most well-known instances from the mid-Ming period, both Deng Maoqi and Tiger Yang were rebel leaders who had previously enjoyed close ties to government authority. Deng had served the chief of local security forces in Fujian before turning to rebellion in 1448, a rebellion that would require the dispatch of high-ranking civil and military officials from Beijing, as well as troops from the capital garrisons, including much-vaunted Mongol cavalry units. (See chapter 5 for a detailed examination of the career of Tiger Yang as a case study of men of force and state attempts to regulate the *wu* side of Chinese society.)[98]

Weapons

As officials grappled with the existence of violent men in society—men who were simultaneously valued and feared for their special skills and temperaments—they also faced the challenge of dealing with a society in which the possession of arms was widespread.

To my knowledge, no studies have addressed the question of the variety and prevalence of arms in Ming society, and the following treatment is intended as nothing more than a brief introduction. In general terms, while the state prohibited some kinds of arms, such as cannon and certain varieties of firearms, most officials took it for granted that most households possessed such weapons as cudgels, bows and arrows, knives, spears, and swords.

A well-known passage from the *Official History of the Ming* corroborates this assumption that arms were part of Ming society by describing nearly a dozen regions celebrated for producing militia forces. In almost every example, the forces were renowned for their skill in certain kinds of arms, ranging from short swords and bows and arrows to staffs, throwing darts, shields, and even stones.[99] Put in slightly different terms, specialization in arms constituted one facet of regional identity.

We find no blanket prohibition against the possession of arms contained in the *Great Ming Code;* the closest is perhaps "The private possession of prohibited military arms." This item reads as follows:

> Everyone who privately possesses armor for horse or men, shields, tubes of fires [a primitive gun], a catapult for throwing fire, banners and signaling devices and the like—military equipment that is forbidden to the people—will, for one such item, receive eighty strokes of the heavy bamboo. For each [additional] item, add one degree. If he manufactures the items privately, add to the punishment for pos-

sessing it privately, one degree. In each case, the punishment is limited to one hundred strokes of the heavy bamboo and exile to 300 *li*. If it is not complete [so that it cannot be used], there is no penalty. He may be ordered to deliver it to the government. Bows and arrows, lances, swords, and crossbows, as well as fishing forks and pitchforks, are not within the category of prohibited objects.[100]

Other relevant laws included prohibitions against the private sale of military equipment and war horses. It was expressly pointed out, however, that the purchase of military equipment by military personnel was not a punishable offense.[101]

Early Ming regulations called for careful management of military equipment. According to a 1392 order, military officials were to compile registers of soldiers' names and their weapons. Further, the soldier's names were to be written on their weapons. It is unclear whether the concern was primarily security or economic; if the weapon were lost, the soldier was to reimburse the government.[102] A 1439 edict ordered all garrisons throughout the empire to submit monthly reports to the central government on the weapons they had manufactured that month.[103] This suggests that on the one hand, this practice either had not been mandated previously or it had lapsed, and on the other hand that the government still desired to closely monitor arms in China.

Some attempts were made to collect weapons left on the battlefield. An edict of November 1449 issued in the wake of the Tumu Incident ordered rewards for anyone who turned over weapons from battle sites to government authorities.[104] Whether this was a standing policy, we do not know; such edicts are not recorded for the early sixteenth century, when several major rebellions affected most of China.

Given the deterioration of military personnel registrars in general and the well-known phenomenon of thousands of acres of military lands falling into private hands over the course of the fifteenth century, it seems safe to assume that significant numbers of government-issue weapons escaped state control and made their way into private homes. For instance, a March 1450 report by the Ministry of War noted that because many troops stationed along the northern border had deserted or died, it was impossible to keep track either of their weapons or their horses. The ministry suggested that civil and military authorities in these areas were to submit monthly reports on personnel and equipment so the government might be better able to monitor such affairs.[105]

Additional prohibitions forbade bearing arms in certain contexts, most notably the strict laws against arms in or around the capital,[106] especially the imperial palace. Despite the extra security measures taken in Beijing, the prohibition against bearing arms in the capital was not observed. Gangs of *lahu*, or urban gang members, brandishing knives, metal whip-chains, cudgels, swords, and various other weapons were frequently reported on the streets of Beijing during the fifteenth and sixteenth centuries. The violations certainly owe something to Beijing's enormous and very mobile population (between 800,000 and one million by 1500).

Also relevant for our purposes here is the supply-side of the question of weapon control. To supply the imperial family, imperial in-laws, and central government with goods during the early Ming, large numbers of artisans were registered into hereditary households and were required to work in government workshops for a given number of days each year. During the fifteenth century, this system grew increasingly lax, and many goods that were once produced exclusively for the imperial family or the central government became available for anyone with adequate funds. Among these were weapons. During the spring of 1477, the emperor wrote, with some agitation, "In recent years, there are military and commoner artisans in and around the capital who dare to privately make armor and such items for sale to others. These people show absolutely no fear of the law."[107] In this case, although it may have struck the emperor as willful violation of his imperial law, it is probably more accurate to say that during the middle-Ming period, weapons had become a marketable commodity like so many other goods at the time.

During the summer of 1516, a band of outlaws led by a supernumerary soldier and a military artisan plundered inside and outside the walls of Beijing. Pressured by government forces, the men apparently fled south to the Jianghuai region. After several years, they returned to Beijing, where they masqueraded as members of the Imperial Guard and forged an order from the emperor purporting to give them authority to purchase weapons in Zhejiang and to make use of the official relay system. For a time, these men successfully posed as members of one of the empire's elite military organizations and, until they were discovered in Xuzhou, purchased weapons with impunity.[108]

Violations of these anti-weapons regulations were also reported in the secondary Ming capital of Nanjing. During the spring of 1453, arrows twice were shot into the area inside the Gate of Everlasting Peace, the outermost area of the Forbidden City. The motivation for these acts is unclear, but it may have been an effort to frame an enemy. On both occasions, the arrows used were marked, in accord with military regulations, with the names of their owners (one a battalion leader, the other a commander) and thus were easily traced.[109]

The state also expressly forbade the sale of prohibited arms to foreigners, for fear they would use them against the Ming. Authorities, however, seemed to have tolerated the sale of other varieties of weapons along the border.[110] It was difficult, however, to prevent the sale of even prohibited weapons, as officials discovered early in 1453 when it came to their attention that the Mongol tribute mission held in their possession several hundred suits of armor, scimitars, bows and arrows, and small firearms, presumably acquired during their sojourn in China.[111] The arms trade was too much a part of the local economy to be easily eradicated. As the Ming government traded tea and other goods for Mongolian horses, people along the northern border traded arms for horses, as we see in the 1447 case of a soldier in Shanxi who was apprehended for trading armor, probably government-issue, for Mongolian steads.[112] One regional inspector familiar with conditions in Liaodong complained during the summer of 1493, "In recent years, imperial troops, supernumerary officers, and others frequently take halberds, bows, chainmail armor, *yaodao* [short, scimitar-like swords], and copper and iron weapons to sell to the barbarians."[113] As these transactions were especially common when visitors from foreign embassies arrived, the regional inspector proposed that the ambassadors all be thoroughly searched when they left China, and that official announcements be posted from Beijing to the Great Wall prohibiting the sale of forbidden weapons to foreigners.[114]

In Beijing, too, forbidden weapons were sold to foreigners. In 1477, an attendant at the state hostelry for foreign guests served as an intermediary between a member of the Korean embassy and a garrison soldier in the capital. In exchange for ginseng and cloth, the Korean official secured "ox horn," a critical material in constructing the highly regarded Korean composite bows.[115] When the matter was discovered, an investigation was conducted, and further efforts were made to prevent the reoccurrence of such transactions.[116]

Government authorities periodically attempted to eradicate the possession of all arms among the commoner populace. For instance, on at least two occasions during the early 1450s, the Ming government issued orders forbidding the possession of arms along the southeastern coast. In September 1451, commoner and military households alike in Guangdong, Fujian, and Zhejiang were prohibited to have "privately held weapons." The entire family of anyone who failed to turn in his weapons were to be punished by serving as soldiers, and the artisans who had manufactured the weapons, and the men who had hired them, were to be executed.[117] Less than a year later, another edict was promulgated, forbidding people along the Fujian coast from selling abroad Chinese goods, manufacturing weapons, or taking to the seas to trade with the Ryūkyū Islands. The reason given for this order was the perceived link between pirates and the rebel forces of Huang Xiaoyang.[118]

Two cases from Shandong in the early 1450s suggest that well-armed populations deeply concerned Ming officials. Although in neither case were arms forbidden, one report noted explicitly that "more than one hundred thousand had weapons," while the other described the local population's great expertise in the use of long and short cudgels. Instead of a blanket prohibition, the Ming government transferred experienced and proven officials to the areas to defuse the situation.[119]

As some officials attempted to turn "unfettered heroes" and lesser potential troublemakers to the state's advantage, others sought to capitalize on people's access to arms to strengthen local defenses. For instance, in response to the 1510 Rebellion, the minister of personnel at the time, Yang Yiqing (1454–1530), argued that local villages should be turned into armed fortresses to better resist the predations of the bandits —bandits who were very soon to declare dynastic intentions and become open rebels. He presupposed that many commoners had access to weapons and recommended that each household was to keep bow and arrow, sword, spear, whip, and cudgel at hand. Young stalwarts and hired laborers serving as corvée workers were to practice and drill with these weapons.[120]

Later in the sixteenth century, the famed official Lü Kun (1536–1618), too, wanted to take advantage of the widespread presence of arms in society to strengthen local security.[121] One facet of his renowned local security program involved militia training during the winter, after autumn crops had been harvested and before spring agricultural activities had begun. Under the instruction of professional teachers, young men were to learn the correct use of "spears, swords, bow and arrows, short cudgels, rope whips, etc." and to undergo yearly proficiency tests.[122]

Some, however, apparently questioned the appropriateness of arms in the possession of commoners. Writing in the early sixteenth century, Wang Tingxiang (1474–1544), an official and a well-known poet deeply interested in neo-Confucianism, felt compelled to argue that people did indeed need such weapons as bows, arrows, and lances to protect their homes. If deprived of these weapons, he argued, they would be defenseless in the face of attack by bandits—a Ming variation of "If guns are outlawed, only outlaws will have guns." After drawing several parallels to debates during the early Han dynasty, Wang concluded, "Thus the prohibition against the possession of bows, crossbows, and long spears benefits plundering bandits and does not benefit the good people. This is as true now as it was in the past."[123]

Thus, most Ming officials recognized the widespread circulation of such arms as bows, arrows, crossbows, knives, swords, spears, and cudgels in Chinese society, a phenomenon that predates the Ming dynasty, probably by several centuries.[124] Although authorities occasionally tried to disarm the civilian populace, with the exception of certain firearms the Ming state did not make any consistent or rigorous attempts to regulate arms. Instead, the imperial government and its officials more often strove to incorporate both men and arms into local defenses during periods of crisis.

Conclusion

The recruiting of "unfettered heroes" and other potentially volatile elements of Ming society was not a narrowly military matter but rather an important attempt to manage or regulate the Ming economy of violence. The Tumu Incident of 1449 renewed attention to military preparedness in general, including the reorganization of the capital garrisons, experiments with a military examination system, a reconstitution of the officer corps, and greatly expanded local militia forces. However, the periodic attempts to absorb segments of the population into an assortment of military capacities grew out of a wide variety of impulses, including fiscal solvency, social control, and cherished administrative ideals, as well as military considerations.

To return to the contrasting spheres of *wen* (civil) and *wu* (military), both *wen* and *wu* were critical "handles" (to borrow a Legalist term) in the search for effective social control. Most secondary scholarship to date has examined efforts by the Ming central government to shape social behavior and mores through education, ideology, religion, rites, sumptuary regulations, and law codes. Along with these more cultural facets of social control, Ming elites also maintained a keen interest in the regulation of force and the economy of violence.[125] In the minds of many officials, the identification and organization of men possessed of daring and military skills represented the first step toward the regulation and control of potentially volatile elements of the populace.

Besides shedding light on general levels of force and violence in society, examination of recruiting also bears directly on the current debate about "public" and "private" in China. As we have seen, the various forms of force often were neither purely public nor private, and the men who comprised these groups often effortlessly changed hats, from garrison soldiers to enterprising local bandits, from military retainers on the staff of provincial governors and local magistrates to rebel leaders. In many cases, the services rendered and reputation acquired in one capacity directly increased one's value in another.

As the imperial government attempted to gain the services of men of force for its armies and staffs of high-ranking civil officials, it entered into direct competition with local magistrates, privately organized militias, bandit groups, and rebels, all of whom also sought to make use of this group's particular skills. This competition drew together a wide spectrum of society, from ministers in the capital to local magistrates, from military officers to members of the local gentry, from bandit chiefs and rebel leaders to concerned social thinkers. What united them was the desire to turn daring men of martial prowess to their own ends. All assumed that such men left unallied were volatile. And they even more firmly believed that violence was a necessary resource to be husbanded and used for one's own ends. In most cases, the nature of this competition was intentionally obscured, as it would have seriously undermined the awe and legitimacy that the imperial state was taking great pains to project.[126]

In the documents that openly acknowledge social control as a primary motivation behind recruiting efforts, the imperial state used the rhetoric of "trapping" unfettered bravos. The notion that the imperial state was competing with other elements of social for the loyalty and services of these men is completely omitted. Official records and even private jottings pass over the ongoing negotiations with local men of force in nearly complete silence. County magistrates may have believed that such matters were unworthy of public note. They also almost certainly wished to preserve a measure of deniability, if their dangerous clients ran too far amok. Neither did imperial officials or local elites wish to acknowledge that men of force possessed power and resources that the government and literati needed. To admit that illicit violence figured in their own power would undermine a legitimacy and privileged social position predicated on moral rectitude, superior education, and exclusive concern for the public weal.

Finally, men of force—often ambitious and independent-minded individuals—varied significantly in talent, enterprise, and social standing. From those who owned lands, pursued commercial endeavors, and cultivated ties to local, regional, and even national elites, to small-time operators of ill-repute, each brought his own desires and aspirations to the process of negotiation. Neither imperial authorities, nor local officials, nor local elites fully controlled them; indeed, at times men of force played one group of potential sponsors against another. Because it was impossible to conceal from contemporaries the fact that local officials and landed elites were intimately tied to men of force and that on occasion "unfettered heroes" managed to outwit authorities, such vulnerability was largely eliminated from official records. Including these incidents in imperial reports would have cast doubt on the government's ability to competently manage society and would have subverted the critical didactic function of the moral-literary rhetoric of late imperial China.

Although seldom visible to the eye of the modern historian, violence and its management formed a vital feature of the Ming social landscape. Of concern to nearly all levels of society, violence connected a surprisingly large cast of social actors during late imperial China. The following chapter examines a rare case from the mid-Ming period where sufficient documentation exists to more fully untangle the complex sets of personal relationships that linked men of force to the very highest levels of late imperial society.

5
Men of Force and the Son of Heaven

Such labels as "bandit" and "man of force" were products of social negotiation in at least two senses. First, societies—or, more accurately, ruling
elites—define the formal parameters of criminal behavior, through the
creation of official law codes. Ever-shifting considerations of private
profit, personal prestige, local security, official duties, and political expe-
diency, however, deeply influenced how and when such categories were
applied, which then determined whether men like Zhang Mao, the Liu
brothers, and Tiger Yang were perceived as unfettered heroes, valued
members of the local constabulary, grasping bandits, or defiant rebels.
The same behavior—intimidation, physical violence, and even robbery
—might be ignored, tacitly condoned, or even openly encouraged. The
careers of men examined in this chapter demonstrate that such dichot-
omous pairs as public and private, national and local, and licit and
illicit were relative terms, whose boundaries were in constant flux.

Given that the basic economic, social, political, and military structures of the Northern Metropolitan Area did not change dramatically
from the late fifteenth to the early sixteenth centuries, it is not surprising that the mounted bandits described in chapter 3 did not disappear
during the sixteenth century. That the patterns of violence and criminality transformed themselves into one of the largest rebellions of the
sixteenth century, however, requires some explanation, which leads us
back to the strange gathering of bandits, eunuchs, bodyguards, and the
emperor of China in 1509.

The following two chapters explore a case study of the role of violence and men of force in the capital region during the early sixteenth
century. Chapter 5 traces the fascinating set of personal relations that
linked men like Zhang Mao, the Liu brothers, and Tiger Yang to prominent civil officials, imperial eunuchs, and even the emperor. It explores
the strategies adopted by all players to maintain useful ties without
sacrificing personal interest or autonomy. It concludes at a time when,

in large part because of political rivalry at court, patronage networks in the capital region had shifted dramatically, creating new opportunities and new dangers for the court, local officials, eunuchs, and men of force.

Chapter 6 chronicles the course of the rebellion, the rebels' chief strategies, and the imperial government's response. At the same time, it draws out what the rebellion reveals about wider questions of Ming social history: the ongoing role of force in society, the relations among men of force, officials, local elites, and communities in crisis.

Many issues introduced in chapters 2, 3, and 4—patronage networks, negotiated order, links between Beijing and the capital region, the role of eunuchs, and the influence of military garrisons in local society—converged during the course of the rebellion with unusual clarity. The rebellion provoked a sense of crisis, intense policy debates, an increased flow of government documents, and greater attention to the workings of local society. The resulting paper trail suggests that Ming China was shaped by a complex system of unlikely relations that bound court politics to local society, connected the most exalted personages to the lowest, and tied the specificity of individuals and their motivations to larger enduring social structures of the capital region. Thus, the 1510 Rebellion and its origins tell us much about how China functioned in crisis and also suggests much about how it operated during less tumultuous and less heavily documented times.

Patronage Networks: Bandits, Eunuchs, and Officials

Let us begin with Zhang Mao, a critical figure in the complex web of connections linking bandits, eunuchs, government officials, and, incredibly enough, the emperor himself. According to the *Veritable Records of the Ming Dynasty*, an imperially compiled daily chronicle of the empire:

> Zhang Mao was a great bandit of Wenan. [His] house had multistoried buildings, rows of rooms, thick walls, and deep vaults. [He] gathered together desperadoes. Liu Chen [Liu the Sixth], Liu Chong [Liu the Seventh], Qi Yanming, Li Long, Li Rui, Yang Hu [Tiger Yang], and "Battalion Commander" Zhu were all his followers. [Zhang] Mao also had connections with and passed bribes to all of the emperor's personal attendants in the Leopard Quarter. Eunuch Director Zhang the Loyal [Zhang Zhong] had the courtesy name Northern Grave Zhang. Zhang's residence was contiguous with [Zhang] Mao's. They had taken an oath as brothers. Through Zhang, [he] was able to bribe everyone, [including] Ma Yongcheng, Yu Jing, and Gu Dayong. Consequently, [he

could] enter and leave the Imperial City and had occasion to attend
the emperor in playing kickball. Relying on this, [they] stood ever less
in awe [of authority].[1]

This extraordinary passage from the official annals of the Martial Ancestor's reign highlights Zhang Mao, "a great bandit of Wenan,"
a medium-sized county approximately 75 miles south of Beijing—
although it is unclear whether Zhang Mao's house was located in the
county seat of Wenan or somewhere in the surrounding countryside.
What is clear, however, is that Zhang resided inside a formidable complex, whose lofty towers and looming walls proclaimed power and influence to commoners and officials alike. According to the imperial government's nine-tier tax category schema, 70 percent of the population in
Wenan fell into the very lowest category, with almost 95 percent in the
lowest three categories. Zhang, in contrast, was a man of wealth. He
visibly commanded the resources to protect his deep vaults, which
housed stores of grain and valuables. Whatever the sources of his wealth
and influence, Zhang Mao was far from a marginal figure in local society
—a man of substance, if not respectability.

Did the people of Wenan regard Zhang Mao as "a great bandit"?
Had Zhang been an outlaw in the eyes of local authorities, and been
formally charged with banditry, the county magistrate would have had
a responsibility to apprehend and try him. Instead, Zhang was allowed
to amass resources and to assemble around himself a considerable entourage of men of force. Local authorities also permitted him the free-
dom to erect an imposing complex—in effect, to advertise his wealth
and status in local society. This suggests that regardless of Zhang Mao
eventually being charged with banditry and arrested, his status in
Wenan until then was sufficiently ambiguous that local officials felt no
pressure to formally charge him with any crime. In a word, Zhang probably was not known exclusively, or even primarily, as "a great bandit"
in Wenan.

The next important figures to appear in the text are the "emperor's
personal attendants," among whom the most prominently mentioned
is Zhang Zhong, or "Zhang the Loyal." Literati of the Ming understood
that eunuch influence extended far beyond the walls of the Imperial
City, a fact perhaps accounting for some of the bitterness with which
literati inveighed against eunuchs. Not only were eunuchs potential
rivals at court, they also posed challenges in local society. Writing during the late sixteenth century, one literatus from Hejian Prefecture, a
prime source for imperial eunuchs, observed:

The younger brothers and nephews of eunuchs are granted posts and entrusted with [their] affairs. [They] rely on [the eunuchs'] power to do wrong, assembling scoundrels and nurturing the wicked. [Their] retainers number several hundred; [their] goods [are valued at] more than 10,000 [taels]; [their] fields go on for a thousand *qing,* and [the number of their] horses reach up to one thousand. Having this property, the eunuchs are insatiably greedy and endlessly devious. Although [their] bodies are in the palace, [their] thoughts are actually in the provinces. [Those who are] in the palace and [those who are] outside the palace act together, and this is whence disaster and rebellion will inevitably arise.[2]

While the author's rhetoric must be viewed with a measure of caution, some successful palace eunuchs did translate their considerable political influence at court into wealth and status for themselves and into salaried posts in the Imperial Guard for their male relatives. At the local level, some eunuchs held large tracts of land; others took part in the construction and refurbishing of temples and public works projects. Successful eunuchs became functioning members of the local elite, and, like others of this privileged group, sought to use their position and influence to pursue their own interests.

The case of Zhang the Loyal is illustrative. Zhang first appears in government histories as the head of the Directorate of the Imperial Horses and one of the emperor's personal attendants.[3] Like any number of eunuchs during the Ming, Zhang the Loyal played an active role in the military. During the course of his career, Zhang would fight the 1510 rebels, oversee the firearms divisions of the capital garrison forces, campaign against Mongols on the northern border, and head imperial forces dispatched to put down a short-lived rebellion by one of the imperial princes.[4]

Critical to our concerns here is the fact that the power and influence gained from his association with the Martial Ancestor at court ensured that Zhang the Loyal enjoyed considerable status in local society. In 1518, Zhang, in a highly visible display of his piety and resources, would donate a large bronze bell to Wanhui Temple, located in Xin'an township, Yongqing County, not far from Bazhou and Wenan.[5] The names of nine other men with the surname Zhang, all officers in the imperial guard and probably Zhang the Loyal's close male relatives, were inscribed on the same bell. Later, in 1520, Zhang, in another public demonstration of his faith and wealth, would refurbish the Dongyue Temple in the county seat of Bazhou, a subprefecture with administrative authority over Wenan County.[6] He would also repair the "Floating

Bridge" of Bazhou in 1519, a bridge previous repaired by local magistrates.[7] Zhang unquestionably was acting as a member of the local elite.

With his powerful imperial connections and his status as a member of the local elite in Wenan and Bazhou, Zhang the Loyal was a man to be reckoned with, and to any local man of ambition, he would have been an invaluable patron. Thus, it is perhaps not surprising that Zhang Mao, the prominent local man of force, would seek to forge stronger ties with his close neighbor, known locally as Northern Grave Zhang. Perhaps taking advantage of their shared surname, the two became sworn brothers as means of sealing their relation as patron and client. Zhang the Loyal more than fulfilled his responsibilities as a patron, introducing Zhang Mao to his fellow eunuchs, who served as personal attendants to the emperor in the Leopard Quarter. Not coincidentally, the other eunuchs in the quotation from the *Veritable Records* also hailed from neighboring counties south of the capital. Zhang Mao used these new connections to vault spectacularly into the most exclusive company in all the empire—the emperor's inner world of the Leopard Quarter.

The lord of the Leopard Quarter was Zhu Houzhao, the tenth emperor of the Ming dynasty, best known to historians either by his posthumous title, Wuzong (the Martial Ancestor), or by his reign title, Zhengde (1506–1521). The Martial Ancestor was one of the most unusual and most misunderstood emperors of the late imperial period. Perhaps the most fundamental political question of the Zhengde reign was who should rightfully define the role and function of China's Son of Heaven. Raised outside the capital, the first Ming emperors were no strangers to the battlefield and had seen much of their empire with their own eyes. Although the early emperors never possessed absolute power and were forced to compromise with the civil bureaucracy on more than one occasion, they did not hesitate to exercise their imperial prerogatives. It was their dynasty, and they would run the country as they saw fit.

Over the course of the fifteenth century, however, individual emperors became subject to an ever-growing variety of restraints: the compendium of laws established by the Ming founder, called the *Ancestral Injunctions,* the growing welter of administrative precedents of all succeeding rulers, and increasing dependence on the civil bureaucracy for policy initiatives.[8] By the early sixteenth century, if not decades earlier, the civil bureaucracy had gained a much stronger voice in determining the proper role of the emperor. In its view, the Son of Heaven should placidly reside within the Forbidden City, where he would assiduously cultivate Confucian morality. From there, his transforming influence would naturally radiate in all directions, carrying order and prosperity to the most remote corners of the empire. The Son of Heaven should actively solicit his officials' advice on all matters and humbly (even gratefully) accept their remonstrances whenever he erred. Historians lavished fulsome praise on the Filial Ancestor (r. 1488–1505) for at least appearing to meet these expectations.

The behavior of his son, the Martial Ancestor (r. 1506–1521), was quite another matter. This was an emperor who traveled the streets of Beijing incognito in search of excitement, who played shopkeeper at a mock store in the Forbidden Palace, who only rarely held regular meetings with his officials, and who refused to live in the emperor's regular quarters. He donned Mongol garb, listened to Central Asian music, and created an alter identity (Great Generalissimo Zhu—Zhu was the dynastic surname) on whom he lavished praise and rewards. He and his companions burst into the homes of wealthy families and kidnapped their daughters for ransom and for thrills. He was badly mauled while hunting a wild tiger, and eventually died from complications after a drunken boating accident.[9] Clearly, the emperor did not conform to the civil bureaucracy's ideals. The more fundamental question remains: was he simply an immature, moral reprobate, oblivious to matters of state and the welfare of the people, as most have argued, or was there some method to his apparent madness?[10]

Let us consider one example of the Martial Ancestor's seemingly lighthearted frivolity that bears directly on the opening quotation. In the fall of 1507, less than a year and a half into his reign, the emperor began construction of the two-hundred-room Leopard Quarter, located outside the Forbidden City and built at the considerable cost of more than 240,000 ounces of silver. Here, warriors of the imperial bodyguard outnumbered civil officials, heavy drinking proved more routine than ritual propriety, and hunts for wild tigers and leopards (kept in an adjoining animal park) were more frequent than court audiences.[11] Civil officials criticized the emperor for squandering limited imperial funds, evading his official responsibilities, and cavorting with sycophants and ne'er-do-wells.

The most densely argued study on the period, however, draws a different conclusion about the significance of the Leopard Quarter. Rather than a den of iniquity, the Leopard Quarter functioned as the Martial Ancestor's administrative and military headquarters. Intentionally built on the foundations of a building closely associated with one of his most martial forefathers, the third emperor Chengzu, it constituted one element of the emperor's attempt to reestablish the Son of Heaven's primacy and revive the strong martial traditions of the early dynasty at the expense of civil service's new-found dominance.[12]

The Leopard Quarter also provided a point of interface between the Son of Heaven and more humble members of local society in North China. Besides the many eunuchs around the Martial Ancestor who hailed from the counties south of the capital, musical entertainers, acrobats, and dancers were also summoned from these areas to perform for the emperor. In fact, part of the reason that Zhang the Loyal introduced Zhang Mao and his followers into the emperor's inner sanctum may have been an effort to offer the young man a new form of entertainment. The Martial Ancestor displayed an interest in dashing military men, and perhaps Zhang the Loyal thought that men of force like Zhang Mao might also prove appealing.

Before we continue with Zhang Mao's extraordinary trip to the capital, let us return to his activities in local society, which remained the center of his world and his concerns. Not only of inestimable help in extending Zhang Mao's connections in the capital, Zhang the Loyal also brought considerable resources to play locally. This became evident during the spring of 1510, when Zhang the Loyal brokered an understanding between his sworn brother, Zhang Mao, and a middle-ranking military officer, Yuan Biao, who was stationed in Hejian Prefecture to the southeast.[13] Yuan had been aggressively carrying out his charge, the eradication of bandits in his jurisdiction, and for reasons to be explained below, by this point, Zhang Mao had been declared a bandit. By late spring, Yuan had scored several successes, and Zhang Mao was sufficiently hard-pressed to seek help from his patron Zhang the Loyal.

Zhang the Loyal's solution reveals much of the workings of patronage networks south of the capital. Rather than simply order Yuan to back off, Zhang the Loyal hosted a banquet at his home in Wenan to which he invited both Yuan Biao and his sworn brother Zhang Mao. During the meal, Zhang the Loyal raised his wine cup and told Yuan Biao to address Zhang Mao by his less formal sobriquet, Zhang Yanshi. The eunuch continued, "This Yanshi is my younger brother. From now on, take good care of each other and don't get in each other's way." Turning to Zhang Mao, the eunuch again raised his cup and said to him, "Today you have formed a personal relationship with General Yuan. From now on, don't disturb the area of Hejian."[14]

Here, Zhang the Loyal takes advantage of his political power in the capital to broker a new set of personal relations in local society. Because of Zhang's influence, General Yuan is in no position to refuse the banquet invitation. At the banquet, General Yuan and Zhang Mao share food and wine, both critically important social lubricants in late imperial society. Zhang the Loyal then uses his position of power to create a new personal relationship between his sworn brother and the military officer. No longer was it a simple matter of General Yuan conscientiously prosecuting his public duty; he had been woven into a web of personal relationships. And although he did not enter into the relationship voluntarily, it is equally evident that all parties expected these private relationships to supersede imperial duty. Zhang the Loyal had forged another link in the chain of patronage relations. In fact, Ming observers noted, "The reason that Liu Chong [Liu the Sixth] and Liu Chen [Liu the Seventh] eventually turned to rebellion was that Zhang the Loyal [through his connections to Zhang Mao] gave them a free hand."[15]

Yet, Zhang the Loyal's having been compelled to intercede on behalf of his sworn brother Zhang Mao suggests these chains of personal ties were not single strands that neatly radiated out from a single powerful patron in the capital. Chance incidents and single events could reverberate through these intricate sets of relations, growing until they took on a life of their own. Tracing these ties and examining their repercussions reveals much about how social order was constructed in the Beijing and the capital region.

To explain how Zhang Mao was transformed from a local man of great substance and enviable contacts with imperial favorites into a "great bandit" of Wenan, we must return to 1508. At that time, Zhang Mao robbed a prominent official, making off with a considerable cache of silver. The official was Kang Hai (1475–1541), a famous litterateur and a member of the prestigious Hanlin Academy in Beijing, on his way home to Shaanxi Province to mourn the death of his mother.[16] What complicated matters for Zhang Mao and, later, his patron, Zhang the Loyal, was that Kang Hai was also an acquaintance of the influential eunuch Liu Jin.

At the time, Liu Jin was at the very height of his power. He, too, was a long-time personal attendant to the emperor. In fact, he had served the boy when he had still been the heir apparent, and having gained the young emperor's trust, Liu Jin had steadily expanded his power and influence. Liu Jin wielded the power to make or break bureaucratic careers; contemporary records claim that every government official who reported to the capital for regular performance evaluations paid a visit to Liu Jin and presented him with handsome gifts of silver. For a time, he was known among the populace of Beijing as "Emperor Liu," a satiric sobriquet that nonetheless reflected his puissance.[17]

According to the account in the *Veritable Records of the Martial Ancestor*, Kang quickly wrote to Liu Jin informing him of the theft and urging Liu to use his influence to ensure Zhang Mao's apprehension. Perhaps because this was not immediately possible, Liu Jin instead penalized those officials responsible for the egregious breach in security. Liu suspended the salary of the local prefect and demoted a higher-ranking official responsible for eradicating banditry in the region, Ning Gao (js. 1496). Liu was moved to fury not simply out of personal regard for his acquaintance but because Zhang Mao had struck in the Northern Metropolitan Area, in effect challenging Liu's control of the region. Kang apparently further complicated matters by misinforming the prefect, perhaps in jest, that he had been transporting the silver on behalf of Liu.[18] When the prefect learned the dangerous provenance of the silver, he took it upon himself to raise sufficient funds to replace the amount stolen.[19] To this end, he levied extra taxes on the people of Shunde Prefecture. Having collected several thousand taels of silver, presumably the amount stolen by Zhang Mao, the prefect turned the money over to Kang Hai, who relayed the information to Liu. With this, the matter was considered settled.[20]

The incident lays bare a fascinating nexus of personal relations, illustrating that at least two important patronage networks were operating in the capital region. The editors of the *Veritable Records of the Martial Ancestor* repeatedly reported that Ning Gao was under the patronage of Liu Jin.[21] But when Ning Gao failed to ensure the safety of Liu's friends and personal wealth, he was demoted, a message intended to improve his performance. The political fortunes of Kang Hai were also closely tied to Liu Jin (however unjustly); when Liu fell from power, Kang was dismissed from office.[22]

It is unclear whether relieving Kang Hai of Liu Jin's silver was Zhang Mao's first criminal endeavor. We lack convincing documentation for any such previous activities, but given the dynamics of relations between men of force and their patrons, it is highly plausible that Zhang Mao's substantial compound and Zhang the Loyal's willingness to become his sworn brother may be attributed at least in part to illegally gained wealth.[23] More certain is that although such activities previously had not earned Zhang Mao the label "great bandit"—that is, an outlaw in the eyes of officialdom, subject to arrest and prosecution —his clash with Liu Jin did.

For while the Shunde prefect's extra levies had temporarily placated Liu Jin, the matter was not settled for long. Eager to redeem himself in the eyes of "Emperor Liu," Ning Gao turned his attention to the problem of Zhang Mao. To better understand Ning Gao's circumstances and the rather formidable skills he brought to bear, it is necessary to return briefly to the summer of 1509. Late in July 1509, the emperor specially appointed four censors to suppress banditry in eastern China, two of whom were stationed in the Northern Metropolitan Area.[24] One censor was ordered to patrol the prefectures of Shuntian and Baoding, just south of the capital, while the second, Ning Gao, was made responsible for the prefectures of Guangping and Zhending, farther to the south and southeast.

All four censors received special permission to take their personal military retainers with them during their tour of duty. These forces were maintained privately by civil officials and, more commonly, military officers. Drawn at this time primarily from among the ranks of military households, the military retainers were chosen for their bravery and fighting prowess and enjoyed treatment markedly superior to that of common soldiers. The forces of Ning Gao numbered at least 1,700 men.[25] Many of these men seemed equally at ease serving as military retainers or as brigands. In fact, as government officials noted, they were often drawn from the same pool of men.

Although few of the antibanditry measures adopted in the early sixteenth century were new, the case of Ning Gao provides us with a rare level of detail. Ning owed much of his success to the effective use of terror, social organization, and public spectacle. For example, a gruesome parade took shape each time Ning's men returned to the prefectural seat from their patrols in the surrounding countryside. The military parade's cacophony of shrill flutes and resounding gongs announced the arrival of Ning's men to residents throughout the city. As Ning's patrols marched down the streets, they displayed the fruits of their labor: men seized on charges of banditry and, spiked atop long wooden poles, the heads of those already slain.[26] It is alleged that Ning personally butchered those bandits his men captured, slicing open their stomachs and severing their hands and feet.[27] These body parts were suspended from the four gates of the city, a grisly warning to all. Several accounts claim that on capturing a particularly well-known outlaw, Ning Gao cut out his heart and ate it.[28]

Although one might be tempted to dismiss this as pure hyperbole, or to conclude that Ning was a maniacal fiend, it is equally likely that Ning was making deliberate use of terror to instill fear and obedience into the subject population. Whether Ning actually consumed the heart of his foe is open to question. That such a rumor circulated, though, indicates Ning had succeeded in establishing a fearsome reputation. In the critical eyes of some, overawing the bandits was Ning's chief strategy.[29]

Ning's second line of attack involved organizing the local population into mutual responsibility units, a time-tested response to social unrest.[30] Through Ning's skillful use of this system of social and administrative organization, "There was no place for traitorous people to hide [bandits], and there were more bandits daily."[31] This was a decidedly mixed blessing. On the one hand, government control over the local population was tightened. At the same time, however, it appears that many men who might have been "pacified" were instead driven to outright brigandage. In the short run, more bandit heads meant more promotions for Ning Gao and his men.

To return to Ning Gao's plans to apprehend Zhang Mao, Ning needed the support of at least a portion of local officialdom if he hoped to succeed. Perhaps under pressure from Ning Gao, shortly after Zhang the Loyal had hosted the reconciliatory banquet for Zhang Mao and General Yuan, an assistant magistrate in the region reached a daring decision. His motivations are unclear, but they must have been compelling. Displaying enormous physical courage and considerable ingenuity, he put away his flowing silk robes, sash, and distinctive official's cap—all the sartorial signs that marked him as a servant of the throne and a member of China's elite—to take up a *pipa*, a four-stringed musical instrument, and enter the ranks of one of society's least prestigious professions, that of a wandering musician. The assistant magistrate transformed himself neither to avoid Ning's wrath nor to flee his responsibilities but to infiltrate Zhang Mao's stronghold. His purpose was to learn the layout of the complex in preparation for a daring armed raid conceived by Ning. The concert concluded and Zhang's men no wiser, the assistant magistrate left the complex and reported to Ning Gao. One can only speculate what drove an assistant magistrate to risk death with a personal foray into Zhang's complex, but it may well have been his belief that the local yamen runners and constables were too chummy with Zhang Mao and therefore could not be trusted to carry out the assignment without revealing their purpose.

In part because of the assistant magistrate's efforts, Ning Gao's surprise attack was a complete success. During the hand-to-hand combat, Zhang Mao, the great bandit of Wenan, was wounded in the leg and captured. His punishment began immediately. He was transported to Beijing, a two-day journey from Wenan along the well-maintained imperial postal highway, in a prisoner's cart, a vehicle that intentionally left the prisoner in full view of curious and jeering bystanders. Once he arrived in the capital, he was to be presented as a prisoner to the throne in a formal ceremony often conducted before the Meridian Gate, the enormous southern gate to the Forbidden City.[32] Barring some unexpected reprieve, Zhang's sentence would be death by beheading, with the body left to rot on the execution grounds and the decapitated head to be displayed publicly as a warning to others.

Was Zhang Mao's sudden fall caused exclusively by inadvertently crossing Liu Jin and his interests south of the capital by stealing Kang's silver? When one considers that Ning Gao earlier had been demoted for Zhang Mao's theft of silver from Kang Hai, and that Ning probably was still under considerable pressure to redeem himself in the eyes of his patron Liu Jin, his raid is understandable. However, Liu's stance on banditry may have been related to a broader set of more stringent policies designed to reassert imperial authority at the expense of slowly encroaching local interests. For instance, Liu Jin continued to press officials to eliminate banditry in the capital region. In May 1510, Liu learned that because of the lackadaisical efforts of two officers from the Anterior Daning Garrison, bandits continued to plunder in the region. Liu Jin had the two men arrested and incarcerated in the Ministry of Justice jail. One of them grew so terrified at what awaited him that he hanged himself in his cell. The second officer was exiled to a border garrison in Liaodong Province, at the northeastern edge of the empire.[33] Like the other unpopular and socially disruptive reforms that Liu Jin attempted to push through, the crackdown on banditry south of the capital seems to have caused more trouble than Liu had anticipated.[34]

Zhang Mao's sudden reversal also reflects the relative power of his sworn brother, Zhang the Loyal, and Liu Jin, who was displeased with the theft of his silver. While at this point Liu seems to have had the upper hand, Zhang the Loyal did not immediately abandon Zhang Mao and his followers.

Hearing of Zhang Mao's arrest, the lieutenants who had eluded capture rushed to the capital. Skilled horsemen traveling with the urgent speed that impending doom lends, they arrived in Beijing before Zhang Mao and his slow-moving prisoner's cart. They immediately sought out Zhang Mao's patron, the imperial eunuch Zhang the Loyal. Zhang the Loyal and another eunuch who had grown rich off the gifts of Zhang Mao and his group agreed to plead their case before the emperor. The men were soon informed that a gift of 20,000 taels of silver was necessary before Zhang Mao or they could be pardoned.[35] Several accounts claim that a client of the eunuch Liu Jin also took advantage of their desperate straits to demand 10,000 taels.[36] At the turn of the sixteenth century, a respectable country estate could be purchased for 1,000 taels of silver, and 2,000 taels was a colossal sum even for a treasured antique piece of calligraphy during the late Ming, when inflation had driven prices up.[37]

Whether these astronomical prices were determined through consultation with the emperor or were simply the product of the eunuchs' own entrepreneurial initiative is unclear. Even allowing for some exaggeration in the sum demanded, the price of an imperial pardon must have staggered Zhang Mao's followers. Their liquid assets woefully inadequate to meet the eunuchs' conditions, two of the more senior lieutenants, Liu the Sixth and Liu the Seventh, sent word to Tiger Yang, another important member of Zhang Mao's band, to raise the money as quickly as possible. Their choice was to plunder south of the capital. During the course of his fund raising, Tiger Yang reportedly set a government office aflame. Receiving this news, the Liu brothers apparently despaired of restoring patronage ties with Zhang the Loyal and gaining the promised imperial pardon. They and their followers instead scattered, each returning to his home region. It is said that "the bandit forces subsequently increased daily." Although extant records are silent on the matter, it seems safe to assume that on his arrival in Beijing, Zhang Mao "lost his head" over the failure of his lieutenants and the collapse of his assiduously cultivated ties to imperial power.

At this point, our narrative returns to developments outside the capital, where events unfolded to yield a rarely detailed perspective on the relations between officials and men of force during the Ming dynasty. With the demise of their leader and facing what surely seemed to be imminent imperial prosecution, Zhang Mao's men might have withdrawn quietly into the countryside until their notoriety (and criminality) faded. At the very least, avoiding the attention of local officials would seem to have been a prudent course of action.

Instead, the Liu brothers and others attempted to foster relations with new patrons capable of providing at least a measure of the protection and social status that Zhang the Loyal had offered Zhang Mao. Their desires were by no means unrequited. The magistrate of Zhuozhou, a thriving county located on a major commercial artery southwest of the capital, soon recruited the Liu brothers to apprehend other bandits.[38] "Very daring and peerless with bow and arrow," the Liu brothers soon overawed other local men of force. Here we see that reputation for skill in arms, no matter how fine its balance between legal or illegal, was a valuable asset. Thus, rather than cast away their hard-earned reputation as effective men of force, cease their activities, and go into hiding, the Liu brothers and others chose to exploit their name and to maintain their presence in the region. In this capacity of bandit catchers, the brothers rendered meritorious service and were routinely dispatched in times of crisis. Perhaps reflecting the growing reputation of the Liu brothers, a censor touring the region, an official of great rank and prestige, also employed Liu the Sixth and Liu the Seventh.

While their service to local government may have reflected a change of heart and a rejection of criminal behavior, what seems more likely is that the Liu Brothers' new employment did not preclude their previous illegal but lucrative activities. Indeed, official affiliation often only enhanced opportunities for illegitimate profit. We gain some oblique confirmation of their sideline activities from the circumstances surrounding their decision to part company with the touring censor who sought to make use of the brothers' services. The Liu brothers reportedly fled when they learned that someone had counseled the censor to "apprehend and do away with the root of disaster"—that is, themselves.[39] The Liu brothers apparently posed greater danger than they promised advantage, presumably either for their unlawful activities or for their association with a confirmed "bandit," Zhang Mao.

As the Liu brothers tried to adapt to the loss of Zhang Mao and to reestablish useful connections with new patrons in regional society, at court Liu Jin remained steadfast in his efforts to eradicate banditry in the capital region. Ning Gao continued to figure prominently in his plans. The chronology is unclear, but at some point during the spring of 1510, after Zhang Mao's fall and the Liu Brother's attempts to forge new links with local officials, Ning Gao received orders to focus his efforts on the Liu brothers. He first circulated "Wanted" posters of the Liu brothers. He then struck at their point of greatest vulnerability— their families. Although the Liu brothers remained at large and mobile, Ning destroyed their homes, imprisoned their wives and daughters, and desecrated their family graves. The Liu brothers, outraged and frustrated, resorted to undisguised brigandage in the area.[40]

What of the other men Zhang Mao had gathered beneath his roof? The case of Tiger Yang, one of the most prominent leaders of the 1510 Rebellion, in many ways parallels that of the Liu brothers. A native of Jiaohe, Hejian Prefecture, Tiger Yang, like the Liu brothers, was known for his matchless skill in archery and horsemanship. Although we do not have an exact chronology, imperial records indicate that at one point in his career, Yang served as a military retainer for Ning Gao. Tiger Yang's connections to the officials charged with eradicating banditry in the region do not end here. He seems also to have entered into a mutually beneficial relationship with a high official charged with eradicating brigandage around Tianjin, a major city just over 60 miles south-east of Beijing. Contemporary rumor held that Tiger Yang paid off the high official in exchange for a free hand in the area south of the capital. The official then invested Yang's payoffs into cultivating relationships with influential imperial eunuchs surrounding the emperor in Beijing.[41] This connection between Tiger Yang and the high official responsible for eradicating unrest south of Tianjin seems to have come to light only during the 1510 Rebellion. Possibly the relationship was formed earlier, perhaps as part of Yang's efforts to reestablish a tenable position in the region after Zhang Mao's fall.

Zhang Mao, the Liu brothers, and Tiger Yang were neither single men nor marginal social actors. Zhang enjoyed powerful social connections and an impressive residential complex, while the Liu brothers were married and had children. In fact, by 1510 if not earlier, at least one of the Liu brothers had a grandson old enough to travel with the rebel forces. Nor was Tiger Yang a single young man, as we discover from passing mention to his grandson made in later documents related to the 1510 Rebellion. Finally, the fact that the Lius' forefathers were buried in a grave complex substantial enough to be targeted for violation suggests some measure of social and economic standing in the local community. We may conclude, then, that although men like Zhang Mao, the Liu brothers, and Tiger Yang were known as men of force and violence, they were not marginal products of a bachelor subculture. Their backgrounds strongly indicate that illicit force was an integrated element of local society in the capital region.

How tightly men of force were woven into the social fabric of the capital region became apparent in the wake of Ning Gao's fall from power, in the autumn of 1510. Ning's downfall seems to have sprung directly from the misfortunes of his chief political backer, Liu Jin, who slipped from power late in September. After Ning Gao was subsequently cashiered, his former military retainers were left without employment. Rather than seek service with another imperial official, many of these former bandit catchers chose, instead, to join the forces of Liu the Sixth and Liu the Seventh, who, without official patronage, had now embarked on what appeared to be a more openly rebellious course.[42] From ashes to ashes, from dust to dust.

In the meantime, the Liu brothers negotiated a settlement with government authorities. The fall of Ning Gao and his patron Liu Jin temporarily discredited a vigorous policy of extirpation, and the court adopted a more conciliatory posture toward the Liu brothers. Many messages almost certainly passed privately between the Liu brothers

and high officials in Beijing, but the first firm evidence of efforts to negotiate a peaceful settlement was an imperial pardon offered by the court
in return for the Liu brothers' surrender. The offer was not unusual:
pardons were frequently used as bargaining chips in negotiations with
domestic troublemakers of various kinds.

Long accustomed to the process of negotiating relationships, and
still eager for some kind of relationship with officialdom, the Liu
brothers willingly entered into the give-and-take of hammering out an
understanding with the court. They provisionally accepted the government's offer, and tested the court's trustworthiness by sending their own
sister to see how she would be treated.[43] Local officials must have dealt
with her in good faith, because shortly thereafter, the Liu brothers led
thirty-four others in surrendering to the subprefectural magistrate of
Bazhou. The magistrate submitted a report, which was forwarded to
the Ministry of War for comment. Late in November 1510, the emperor
pardoned the brigands and once again ordered them to atone for their
offenses by apprehending other bandits.[44]

Lest the results seem overly predictable, all accounts agree that
"shortly thereafter," the Liu brothers and their band once again turned
to rebellion—a rebellion that would eventually grow to encompass
nearly half of Ming China.[45] There was never any guarantee that new,
mutually satisfactory relations could be formed or that negotiations
would bear fruit. For the Liu brothers and their followers, there is no
definitive answer to speculation about why they rebelled; indeed, one
would be hard pressed to identify a single defining moment that
marked the transition from men of force to imperial rebels. From what
we have seen in the preceding paragraphs, the Liu brothers and others
had broken imperial law on several occasions, sometimes in spectac-
ular fashion. Yet, an equal number of times, a new *modus vivendi* had
been achieved with government officials, whereby the talents of the men
of force were placed at the disposal of the imperial state, and the men
of force were granted protection and autonomy to continue their "sideline" activities.

A final pair of encounters between the Liu brothers and the officials
sent to apprehend them illuminates this subtle drift toward rebellion.
The first begins with a middle-ranking military officer making his way
from Beijing to Bazhou and Wenan to apprehend the Liu brothers, presumably after they had "rebelled" again—that is, resumed their normal
activities. In mid-January 1511, the officer and his force of four hundred troops from the empire's elite capital garrisons stopped to rest in
a temple in Yongqing District, some 15 to 30 miles north of Bazhou and

Wenan.[46] Liu the Sixth received information about the troops' presence from local informants, and to forestall any untoward developments, he ordered an underling to wrap 1,000 taels of silver in a money bag and take it to the officer. The officer took their silver, turned around, and led his troops back to the capital, where presumably he informed his superiors that he had been unable to locate the wily Liu brothers.

The second encounter was in March 1511, but under conditions markedly different from those of the first meeting in January. By March, imperial troops had clashed with highly mobile bandit groups in several areas of North China. Brigands had attacked imperial warehouses and prisons, and had abducted officials. Crossing provincial, prefectural, and county borders, the brigands' movements played havoc with jurisdictional lines of responsibility and defense.

Part of the confusion arose from the absence of any single, unified bandit army; instead, several smaller, independent groups operated throughout the region. The Liu brothers, Tiger Yang, and their followers were not yet the dominant leaders they would later become. In fact, only in early April 1511, at least one month after reports of widespread bandit raids had been submitted in several areas of North China, did the *Veritable Records of the Martial Ancestor* mention that "the Bazhou bandits Liu Chen [Liu the Seventh], Liu the Sixth, Qi Yanming, Gu Zimei, and others maraud through Shandong."[47] This is the first and only reference to Gu Zimei in the government records, perhaps a reflection of uncertain government intelligence and fluid bandit leadership. (The story of the imperial government's response to this growing unrest in North China will be told more fully in chapter 6.)

For our purposes here, it is enough to note that both the court and local governments had begun to commit small but growing levels of troops and money to restore local order. By mid-March, the court had dispatched a thousand men from the capital garrisons; another thousand were soon to follow. Soldiers from local garrisons in Shandong and the Northern Metropolitan Area, including Mongols in Hejian and Dingzhou, had also begun to mobilize for combat. Funds from the central government had begun to flow into Shandong to defray military costs and rewards granted for meritorious service, and the court ordered local governments to collect extra levies to cover the additional expenses of supplying troops and offering relief aid to peasants who might otherwise consider supporting the bandit groups.

Thus, intensifying unrest in North China and corresponding government concern provide the backdrop to the second mid-March encounter between the Liu brothers and the military officer who had accepted their gift during their first brush. The Liu brothers and approximately thirty of their band were lying low in Wenan, presumably taking advantage of their strong local connections to hide from imperial forces, when the officer was once again ordered to capture the outlaws.[48] This time, however, instead of leaving after collecting his payoff, he cornered the Liu brothers on the second floor of a commoner's house. For some reason, the officer did not exploit the situation to immediately press the attack but was content, it is said, merely to talk with the brothers.[49]

Separated from their band and pinned down by imperial troops, the brothers bleakly contemplated suicide, a fate seemingly preferable to the drawn-out humiliation and painful execution of Zhang Mao, their former leader. One suspects that the sudden change in fortune deeply struck the Liu brothers. Less than a year earlier, Zhang Mao had ventured into one of the most exclusive areas in the world, the Leopard Quarter, where he had watched the Son of Heaven, palace eunuchs, and members of the Imperial Guard play kickball. Zhang Mao enjoyed status, wealth, and enviable ties with a powerful patron, Zhang the Loyal, who effectively shielded the band from local authorities. Now, as the remains of Zhang Mao's rotting corpse lay intermingled with others who had met their end on the execution grounds on the capital's western side, they crouched fearfully in a nondescript house far from the glories of metropolitan Beijing.

The noisy arrival of a half dozen or so members of their band jolted them from their reverie.[50] One of the rescuers challenged the military officer, yelling, "You got a bag with one thousand taels of our silver —what are you doing returning to take us in?" He and his companions then assailed the officer and his troops with their halberds. The officer withdrew under their attack; seven of his men succumbed to the blows of the banditti. Emboldened by the arrival of help, the brothers took up their bows and showered arrows on the troops, killing several men.[51] Although no doubt grateful for the reprieve, the Liu brothers may have sensed that armed clashes with imperial troops would feature prominently in the rest of their days.

By that point, however, too much had changed for the Liu brothers and their followers to successfully resume their past roles. The speed with which the Lius fled when they heard that the censor had been advised to eliminate them illustrates their awareness of how precarious their position had grown. Their experience with the military officer at Wenan surely drove home this message. In their first encounter, he obligingly accepted their bribe in exchange for free rein in the area.

In their second encounter, however, the officer pressed the situation far closer to the brink; the Liu brothers were on the point of suicide when help finally arrived. Without a powerful patron to act as mediator, the bandits were forced to deal directly with the men charged with apprehending them. Such negotiations were always risky. As pressure mounted from the central government for the heads of the bandits, the likelihood of direct confrontations escalated.

Historiographical Questions

In the interest of clarity, the reconstruction of events presented thus far has for the most part steered clear of historiographical questions. Yet, the nature of the documents on which my reconstruction is based and the complex political agendas behind those documents must be addressed. The most striking question is why were details about the connections among local men of force (and future rebel leaders), highly placed imperial eunuchs, and the emperor himself included in the single most important imperial annal of the dynasty? The *Veritable Records of the Ming Dynasty* were often profoundly shaped by the political agendas of the scholar-officials who were ordered to compile them, a fact that contemporary observers and modern scholars have documented in convincing detail.[52]

More specifically, why did the editors choose to include all the Martial Ancestor's blemishes? During his lifetime, the emperor clashed repeatedly with many of his civil officials, who strenuously objected to his policies, his lifestyle, and his vision of the emperor's proper role. Although officials ultimately failed to prevail against the emperor during his reign, civil officials were only too willing to richly reward him posthumously. Let future emperors and officials see him for what he was! A drunk, a lecher, an escapist, a foolish and irresponsible young man dangerously susceptible to the deleterious influence of corrupting eunuchs and unlettered, uncouth military bravos. Outright fabrication was avoided whenever possible, but the records presented the emperor in the worst possible light, usually through slight embellishments, judicious omissions, and the occasional devastating editorial comment.

Read carefully, these sources are a boon to the modern historian. In their efforts to portray the emperor in an unfavorable light, the editors of the *Veritable Records of the Martial Ancestor* included unusually detailed information related to the Martial Ancestor's personal life. The critical issue is how to sift through a biased record compiled by enormously literate and highly trained bureaucrats who exercised an almost complete monopoly over the production of creditable history.

This process of evaluating the documentary record is always problematic, and even the most basic assumptions of this study are open to question. In the interest of objectivity, I explore the possibility that I, like most modern historians, have been duped by the editors of the *Veritable Records of the Martial Ancestor*. The following paragraphs will analyze briefly the iconography introduced at the outset of the chapter, which detailed the nexus of unexpected personal connections among bandits, eunuchs, and the Son of Heaven.

Linking the emperor of China with rebel leaders through the efforts of his palace eunuchs was an extraordinarily compelling image. According to Confucian orthodoxy dominant at the time, rebels were not merely reprehensible violators of imperial law and political order, they were degenerates, flouting moral standards and the social order of the realm. They displayed disregard for the very social hierarchies that made civilization possible by rising up against their elders, government officials, and the authority of the dynasty. Their delinquent behavior could induce others to emulate their example, further undermining proper social relations.

Consider the effect, then, of introducing these agents of disorder into the company of the one man who was most responsible for maintaining harmony and order—in the realm and in the cosmos. Many believed that the Son of Heaven was pivotal in the order of the cosmos. His behavior directly influenced not only the tone of government but also Heaven and Earth, the moon and the stars.

Consider, too, the site of the meeting. These men of force, avatars of chaos, were introduced into the center of imperial space and power. A frequently invoked image during the Martial Ancestor's reign was the ancient sage King Wu (r. 1027–1025 B.C.), founder of the Zhou dynasty. According to canonical texts, he "had only to let his robes fall down, fold his hands, and the empire was orderly ruled."[53] Emperors were repeatedly enjoined to remain within the walls of the imperial palace and assiduously cultivate their morality and virtue. The emperor's private quarters should have been the central point from which the emperor's all-powerful and transformative moral force radiated outward, ordering and harmonizing all beings and all events everywhere in the realm.

Instead, however, agents of disorder corrupted the great harmonizer. Thus, rather than emanating moral order, he radiated discord. The result was social unrest and rebellion. Chaos at the center meant chaos throughout the empire.

And who, according to the *Veritable Records*, had brought the empire to such a pass? The answer was the eunuchs. Abusing their positions of trust and intimacy with the emperor, the eunuchs accepted bribes from men like Zhang Mao to introduce the forces of chaos. Here, the implicit contrast is with the enormous educational, moral, and political benefits that proper companionship, that of Confucian tutors and senior statesmen, could and should have bestowed on the young ruler.

The iconography is perfect and thus immediately suspect. Zhang Mao's startling cameo in the Leopard Quarter is seamlessly woven into a powerful political and moral critique of the Martial Ancestor, the Leopard Quarter, and his deplorable personal servants, the eunuchs. The image contains a series of implicit contrasts between deeply held moral-political ideals and the Martial Ancestor's aberrant behavior. Best of all, no explicit criticism was necessary. A skillfully wrought picture is worth a thousand words of moral outrage.

Was this nothing more than a carefully polished literary-historical gem intended as a political and moral cautionary tale? Did Zhang Mao, the great bandit of Wenan, actually watch as the most powerful man in China played kickball? These are daunting questions for which no conclusive answer is possible. I believe that the meeting did take place and that the connections described in the chapter are historically accurate. I made this assessment based on what we know about the eccentricities of the Martial Ancestor, the individual eunuchs involved, and the function of the Leopard Quarter on the one hand, and the more general, long-term role of men of force in the capital region and the dynamics of patron-client relations as documented in chapters 2 through 4 on the other. The reader will make his or her own judgment.

Before we turn to the rebellion itself, a summary of certain general facets of the management of force, the structure of politics in the capital region, and the negotiated nature of order in the area will be useful. From the documents produced by the 1510 Rebellion and government efforts to explain its origins, it is clear that many officials in the Northern Metropolitan Area, ranging from local magistrates to special-duty censors, made fairly regular use of men of force in their attempts to maintain acceptable levels of order in their jurisdictions. The fact that even the minister of personnel, Yang Yiqing, actively promoted the co-opting of criminals and unfettered heroes suggests that most officials believed they could safely use these men of force to their own ends and that this recruitment of marginal elements of society had become a semi-institutionalized response to moments of crisis.

Ties between Beijing's elite and men of force from nearby counties suggest, however, that connections between China's elites and its subalterns were perhaps not so much a temporary marriage of convenience during periods of crisis as an ongoing feature of regional society. The example of the palace eunuch Zhang Zhong and his ties to local bandits illustrates these patronage networks shaping political developments in the capital region. As argued above, political rivalry and shifts in the balance of power at the court in Beijing could have immediate consequences for the surrounding region. Furthermore, this understanding of the nature of politics was evident to men of the time. Indeed, this view was a central assumption of patronage networks: after all, if the influence of one's capital patron extended no farther than the city walls of Beijing, the investment in cultivating such connections probably would not have been made in the first place. Returns in local society were the ultimate standard for many.

Finally, as noted in chapter 1, any number of excellent studies have shown how local order was not only a product of imperial dictates and institutions but also often a process of informal negotiation. This negotiated order is obvious in the compromises wrung from Yuan Biao, the official responsible for eradicating banditry in Hejian, and from the bandit Zhang Mao by the palace eunuch. The negotiations allegedly continued up to the Son of Heaven himself, as he was offered a sizable "gift" to pardon Zhang Mao and his subordinates. If this variety of bargaining was highly unusual and specific to the Martial Ancestor and his court, Yang Yiqing's proposals about the finessing of local order through the temporary recruitment of criminals and martial artists, the controlled militarization of local communities, and the courting of unfettered heroes suggest that other elements of negotiated order were more broadly and deeply rooted in the institutional memory of the imperial government than might appear at first glance.

To conclude, the particulars of the incidents related above confirm the findings of other studies about compromised imperial power but expand our understanding of the process by including negotiations that focus not on elites, whose power was based on land, education, and official titles, but on elements of society whose power was grounded in the use and threat of force and in attenuated forms of imperial favor. The next chapter demonstrates how court rivalries influenced the imperial campaigns against the rebels and how negotiation at the local level remained an ongoing feature of the management of force during periods of intense social unrest.

6
From Banditry to Rebellion and Back Again

Flamed by the winds of latent discontent, widespread drought, military incompetence, and government hesitancy, the small sporadic sparks of armed conflict grew into a mighty conflagration, spreading from Beijing in the north to the Yangzi River in the south, from the Pacific Ocean in the east to the Taihang Mountains in the west.[1] In the process, the 1510 Rebellion deeply affected the lives of tens of thousands of people, tested the resources and ability of the court, and influenced perceptions of Chinese strength throughout East Asia. What had begun as a relatively common event—rivalry among palace eunuchs and dislocation in patronage networks—ended as a national rebellion, requiring more than two years, hundreds of thousands of ounces of silver, and thousands of lives to quell. Yet for all the high drama and furious turmoil, violence's role in the social order of the capital region emerged surprisingly little changed in the wake of the rebellion. Banditry, administrative interstices, and ties among men of force, local elites, and government officials all survived the hazards of the battlefield.

This chapter is divided into three parts. The first traces the intermittent but high-stakes negotiations between the Liu brothers, Tiger Yang, and their followers on the one hand, and the imperial court and high officials on the other. The second chronicles the violence of the 1510 Rebellion as it grew both in intensity and scope. The final section revisits the question of violence and banditry in the counties south of Beijing in the wake of the suppression of the 1510 Rebellion. Rather than attempt a comprehensive account of the rebellion, the following narrative hews to the main themes developed in chapters 2 through 5. National issues and the evolving military response of the imperial government to the rebellion are briefly noted, but emphasis is placed on how the rebels absorbed local outlaw groups, how local communities dealt with violent crisis, and how the imperial government balanced military and diplomatic efforts to end the rebellion.

We have examined the consequences of the Liu brothers' somewhat adventitious involvement in the complex interactions of court and local power from the events of 1508 to the explosion of 1509–1510. That quickly became a massive armed insurrection, the largest domestic military challenge to Ming authority in the sixteenth century. Having explored the initiating elements, we must now follow the spreading rebellion across several provinces, and its violent suppression two years later.

Violence and Suasion

During the spring of 1511, bandit activity gradually spread from Shandong to the Northern and Southern Metropolitan Areas, to northeastern Henan, and to northern Huguang. By mid-April, the minister of personnel at the time, Yang Yiqing (1454–1530), had submitted to the throne a lengthy policy paper on banditry in North China. One of the foremost officials of the early sixteenth century, Yang had passed the highest level of civil service examination at the exceptionally young age of eighteen, had developed expertise in frontier affairs during his many years in China's northwest, and had helped orchestrate the eunuch Liu Jin's fall from power. He was one of the most powerful men at court, and the emperor held him in great esteem.[2] His detailed report sheds light on contemporary problems as seen by a very capable senior official.

When confronted with bandit attacks, most local officials chose between two strategies, Yang wrote. The first was passive defense—that is, closing the gates of the city and defending from the walls or filling in the city gates with pounded earth. The second was appeasement. Local officials often prepared feasts, welcomed the bandits, and offered gifts in hopes they and their city would be spared.[3] Yang held that this second strategy was disastrous. Not only did the bandits grow more confident and daring as local representatives of the central government begged for mercy, but inhabitants of the city began to doubt the ability of the government to cope with crisis.[4]

Yang stressed the need to improve the economic conditions of people in areas ravaged by bandit raiding through the elimination of official malfeasance, the granting of tax amnesties, and the distribution of relief to needy households.[5] If the people directly benefited from these reforms and were able to make ends meet, Yang insisted, they would be content with their fields and unlikely to follow the bandits.[6] Yang did not, however, assume that economic relief alone would quell the spreading unrest.

Yang suggested a wide variety of measures to strengthen local defenses. Grand coordinators were to repair city walls, dredge moats, prepare weapons, post sentries, and stockpile grain.[7] The services of local elites were to be enlisted: the promise of office and official recognition was to be dangled before the families of retired officials, imperial university students, and the wealthy as an encouragement to participate in local defense.[8] Yang's proposals to use martial artists, unfettered heroes, and convicted criminals to stiffen local village defenses, were put forward at this time. The village itself was to become an armed fort, with the construction of a wooden stockade at the entrance, the erection of watchtowers with a gong and drum, and the posting of watchmen. In sparsely populated areas, three and four communities were to band together into one unit, with a single person responsible for making sure the various communities in the unit would come to aid each other.[9]

The thoroughness of Yang Yiqing's proposal and his apparent conviction that the Ming government should muster every possible resource to suppress the rebels testify to his belief that the bandits represented an urgent problem in the empire. The brigands not only raped, pillaged, and burned; more important, in Yang's eyes, they assaulted and set aflame government offices.[10] They looted government granaries, freed prisoners from government prisons, and occupied cities for weeks at a time. The rebels issued orders, thus arrogating to themselves the authority of local government. It was because the brigands openly challenged the authority of the throne that Yang described them as an "affliction of the root and of the heart."[11]

Based on Yang Yiqing's suggestions, the Martial Ancestor appointed a military officer and a civil official, the Earl of Huai'an, Zhang Wei (d. 1535), and censor-in-chief of the left, Ma Zhongxi (1446–1512), to oversee the campaign against the rebels.[12] Ma Zhongxi was a senior official experienced both in military administration and the cut and thrust of political intrigue. Zhang Wei had inherited his position as a military officer and had served competently in several previous positions. The court put at their disposal two thousand "crack" imperial troops from the capital garrisons and granted the two men seemingly extensive powers, including authority over all provincial officials in Henan, Shandong, and the Northern Metropolitan Area and permission to execute on the spot any imperial troops who disobeyed commands in battle. More prosaically, Zhang was provided with one hundred firearms, fifty silver medals to serve as rewards, fifty tallies, and one hundred bolts of colored satin.[13] These were the military, administrative, and motivational tools with which Zhang was to destroy the brigands.

As Ma Zhongxi and Zhang Wei hurriedly prepared to leave Beijing, bandit attacks continued throughout much of Shandong and parts
of Henan. Some nineteen subprefectural and district seats in western
Shandong suffered attacks in April and May.[14] In at least three instances, local officials abandoned their posts and fled the city.[15]

Perhaps the most striking incident in Shandong during this two-
month period was an April raid on Queli, the ancestral home of Confucius, the location of the considerable estates of his descendants,
the Kong family, and the site of frequent state-sponsored ritual obser-
vances.[16] Before attacking Queli, a band of more than a thousand riders
had sacked the county seat of Quxian,[17] torching more than three hundred government, temple, and commoner buildings. After this spree of
violent mayhem, the highwaymen left for the Kong estates, where they
spent the night. Here, the brigands fed their mounts, threw several
Confucian texts into a pond, destroyed the sacrificial vessels, and
burned the gate of a lecture hall.[18] The bandits killed a licentiate who
attempted to upbraid them for their violent behavior. Three other licentiates, who had been taken captive, attempted to lecture the interlopers
on Confucian principles of righteousness. Either the topic or the delivery
was not to the liking of the outlaws; they dispatched on the spot their
three would-be moral guides. The brigands also killed a score of women,
including nine Kong wives and one of their teenage daughters. In contrast, the male Kongs fled, perhaps in an effort to fulfill their Confucian
responsibility to live and produce heirs who would carry on the family
name. The Martial Ancestor later recalled his shock at learning that the
bandits dared attack even the home of the Great Sage.[19]

The bandits soon left Queli, and late in April 1511, forces under
Liu the Sixth assaulted Tancheng, Yanzhou Prefecture, a relatively small
city located along two major routes leading to the wealthy south.[20]
While the bandits attacked scores of county seats across North China,
the events at Tancheng reveal in detail the dynamics of how local
defense actually worked—the personal negotiations, the temptations,
and the risks.

In this case, the district magistrate entrusted the defense of the
community to the relatively lowly district jailer, Kang Youhui.[21] Kang
rallied locals, assembled several hundred braves, and oversaw the construction of a defensive earthen wall, topped with doors as crenellations.
After completing these preparations, Kang selected several dozen capable men to hide in ambush outside the earthen fortifications. When
the bandits drew near, the men emerged from their hiding spots, beheading dozens of the outlaws. Kang, however, cautioned the newly

confident inhabitants of Tancheng, "The bandits are enraged and are sure to arrive in great strength. We are in a dangerous predicament."[22]

Kang's preparations continued, as he enlarged the walls, dredged low-lying lands, and put the city's weapons into order. Kang himself donned armor and helmet as he supervised the defense preparations night and day. He posted scouts at great distances. Inside the fortifications, Kang maintained strict control, meting out rewards and punishments without fail. According to one observer, Kang "faintly resembled a great general."

The bandits did indeed arrive in great strength, and some residents of Tancheng wished to jump the fortifications and flee. Hefting his battle-axe, Kang announced severely, "Whosoever dares mention flight dies by this axe."[23] While Kang used his axe to good effect against the inhabitants of Tancheng, it was cannon fire from the city walls that proved most effective against the bandits.[24] Although the brigand forces traveled on horses and were highly mobile, they had brought siegecraft and attempted to use a mobile shield (huoche) against the city walls.[25] The defenders of Tancheng, however, managed to burn it before it could be used to inflict significant damage.

Pushed back after their first assault, the bandits tried another tack. From a distance, they attempted to negotiate a deal with Kang. Standing on a bridge over the moat surrounding the city, one of the outlaw leaders cried, "Your post is base, and you will not be rewarded even if you do render meritorious service. Why bring such hardship upon yourself? Open the gates and give us a free hand. It is worth one thousand taels to you." For Kang, whose official annual salary was a few dozen ounces of silver, this was an enormous sum. Nonetheless, he heaped abuse on his tempter and ordered several dozen of his men to leap on their mounts and attack him. In his efforts to avoid them, the bandit leader jumped from the bridge into the moat and scrambled out of harm's way. The weapons and impedimenta of the dead and captive bandits were distributed among the braves defending the city. The brigands mounted seven attacks on Tancheng, but Kang and the rest of the defenders stood firm. Imperial forces eventually came to the aid of Tancheng, reportedly taking more than 150 bandit heads.

The bandit's words proved prophetic. While the magistrate, Tang Long, was promoted two ranks and hailed as a model for other local officials, the meritorious service of the lowly Kang went unreported to the throne, despite protests by local government students. When he died in office, the following year (1512), a local shrine in his honor was erected north of the district seat. Despite fame exceptional for a minor functionary, in death as in life Kang's official rank determined his position—his shrine was placed behind one built for Tang and another previous magistrate.[26]

The account of the defense of Tancheng may glorify the role of Kang Youhui, but it also reveals that local defenses were often uncertain and sometimes led by unlikely figures. In this case, responsibility for local defense fell to a relatively lowly official. Originally a clerk,[27] Kang Youhui was a district jailer *(dianshi)*, an unranked subofficial who acted as the district magistrate's police agent. Defense measures were makeshift. The account does not mention regular organized local security forces, and emphasizes that the earthen fortifications were made by scooping up dirt one handful at a time.

Perhaps most revealing was the bandits' offer of 1,000 taels of silver in exchange for a free hand in the area. Many officials did in fact accept such offers. It is perhaps precisely the frequency with which officials colluded with bandits that made Kang's refusal noteworthy. Officials and bandits alike must have been aware of the relative risks and advantages involved. An official could resolutely defend his city out of duty or in the hope of later glory and reward. He could also quietly pocket the silver and walk away. Either way, he faced risks. A failed defense often ended in death for local officials at the attackers' hands. The incident at Tancheng shows that a successful defense did not ensure reward. For those who took the bandit silver, there was no guarantee that the bandits would deal in good faith. Further, the Ming court did not look kindly on officials who abandoned their posts.

Such were the conditions in North China when Ma Zhongxi finally left the capital in mid-May 1511.[28] With only one thousand troops from the capital garrison under his direct command, Ma decided against a sustained military campaign, and instead distributed to local yamen offices announcements encouraging the bandits to surrender. These announcements were to be reprinted and posted in each region. Ma also dispatched a district jailer and an honorary official to Bazhou, the reputed home of the Liu brothers, in an effort to persuade the bandits' leaders to abandon their errant ways. Ma's success in negotiating a conclusion to the growing violence would prove to be mixed.

Government records often suggest that all the brigands in North China moved in one or two large groups, sometimes called the Henan bandits, under the putative leadership of Tiger Yang, and the Shandong bandits, under the Liu brothers. This narrative strategy, however, was in large part a desperate effort by imperial authorities to render coherent the widespread and fluid outlaw bands, which varied in strength, cohesion, and longevity. Throughout late spring and early summer, the "Shandong bandits" and the "Henan bandits" ranged through the Northern Metropolitan Area, northern Huguang Province, eastern Shanxi Province, and northern Henan.[29] By early August, two large groups under Tiger Yang and Liu the Sixth assembled for a brief but significant meeting in Wenan.[30]

The meeting irrevocably changed the life of a licentiate named Zhao Sui. During the previous Hongzhi reign (1488–1505), Zhao had been a government student at the imperially authorized county academy.[31] Later falling ill, he returned home and subsequently remained there to attend his parents.[32] While the exact nature of the Zhao family's social status is unclear, there are good reasons for believing that it numbered among Wenan's local elite. During the first half of the dynasty, Wenan boasted few advanced-degree holders; Zhao's status as a licentiate probably meant more in Wenan than in other regions. Another man sur-named Zhao with what appears to be a related personal name (quite possibly a relative) had become a tribute student in 1506. Finally, the Zhao household included several score of people.[33] Therefore, we can assume the Zhao family was counted among the region's social, cul-tural, and economic elites.

Zhao Sui enjoyed the reputation of a man of strength and bravery, fond of the Chinese "knight errant" tradition (renxia) and possessed of great ambitions.[34] His nickname, "Madman Zhao," perhaps reflects this unbridled character.

Rumors flew as the bandit forces prepared to mount an attack on the county seat of Wenan. Some said they numbered as many as ten thousand strong. Whatever the number, Madman Zhao hurriedly orga-nized his family's escape from the city. Once outside the city gates, Zhao and more than seventy members of his family, including his wife, sons, brothers, and uncle, hid among the reeds in a nearby river. How-ever, men under the command of Liu the Seventh discovered the Zhao family and forced them ashore.[35] When the brigands attempted to rape his wife, Zhao slashed out furiously, injuring two bandits, but Liu's men quickly subdued him.

At this point, Liu the Seventh favored slaying the former govern-ment student, but Tiger Yang intervened and persuaded Zhao to join the band. According to government records, in exchange, Tiger Yang allowed Zhao's family members to return home safely. Using his family's considerable local influence, he and his brothers quickly gathered five hundred additional men, who joined the outlaw forces at Hejian to the south on August 8, 1511.[36]

Zhao's motivation for recruiting these men is puzzling. Even if he was afraid that his family would be vulnerable to future attacks if he did not convincingly demonstrate his support for the outlaws, why did he feel the need to recruit so many men? Would not his personal participation suffice to secure his family's safety? Perhaps joining the outlaws appealed to Zhao's "knight errant" sensibilities—whatever its risks, such a life offered the exhilarating potential for sudden power and excitement to a man who considered himself a hero but led a decidedly unglamorous life. Whatever Zhao's motivations for joining the marauding band, in time his name would become synonymous with what grew to be China's largest rebellion of the sixteenth century.

Several months after Zhao had become a rebel leader, he composed a short poem, which reveals his mixed bravado and remorse and may shed light on his decision to join the outlaws.

> Man who has erred, belly full of worry,
> Chivalry in his bosom, great talent revealed.
> His heart full of blood and tears which splash upon his carved saddle;
> How many times has his spirit returned home in his dreams.
> Father and mother implicated, imprisoned in dour *Diaotai.*
> Overcoming and deceiving opposing generals like a tiger snags a lamb;
> Moving without restraint in all directions, who dares apprehend?
> Would that my lord's benevolence be deep like the sea,
> and free me to return home, all things made whole.[37]

If imperially compiled sources are to be believed, Zhao was not alone in his visions of grandeur. The Liu brothers, Tiger Yang, and other bandit leaders apparently also began to formulate highly ambitious plans. At a banquet, the various brigand chiefs congregated to discuss their future over food and wine.[38]

> It's going to be tough for us to succeed in establishing a new dynasty [if we continue like this]. It would be better to start from this district and then move throughout the empire. [We should] gather together several tens of thousands of men in the name of "establishing a kingdom [and] upholding the worthy." [We] must be brutal before people will surrender. If there are those who don't obey, [we] will destroy subprefectures upon encountering subprefectures and obliterate counties upon encountering counties. First [we] will have to take Hebei and Henan and later go to Nanjing, [since] there is an empty seat [i.e., a throne].[39] At that time, [we] will order you made ministers and enfeoffed as nobles. [Your] whole family will be rich and powerful. Won't that be great![40]

On a political level, this declaration of dynastic intentions may be seen as a watershed, the point from which the Liu brothers, Tiger Yang, and their followers should be viewed as rebels rather than brigands. Government sources, however, do not reflect this change; they still referred to the Lius, Tiger Yang, and their bands as *"dao,"* *"zei,"* and *"kou,"* all terms that could mean either bandit or rebel. The Liu brothers and Tiger Yang did not alter their plundering ways immediately; they subsequently launched successful attacks on the county seats of Wenan and two other counties to the south. Indeed, it is dangerous to make too much of the meeting. Although the Liu brothers, Tiger Yang, and their confreres may have consciously articulated their political aims and united, however tenuously, the various bands with promises of wealth and status, the Liu brothers and Tiger Yang had not chosen a path that would end either in total victory or utter defeat. As the narrative below makes clear, at the same time that the court and local officials responded with military force to this challenge to imperial authority, they did not rule out pardon and negotiation as a way to end the rebellion.

In mid-August 1511, Tiger Yang and the Liu brothers gathered once more in Wenan.[41] Defense forces from the capital and neighboring Tongzhou and Zhuozhou were put on alert. Imperial troops rushed to Bazhou, Wenan, and Dacheng and were commanded not to return to the capital until the insurgents were destroyed. Crack troops were selected from among the training camps in the capital in preparation for deployment.

If these defenses were not enough, on August 18, 1511, the minister of war, He Jian, made an extraordinary suggestion—deploy troops stationed along China's northern border against the rebels.[42] Powerful military figures were viewed with a mix of dread and admiration during the Ming. Military revolts by border troops in northeast China during the mid-eighth century had devastated the great Tang dynasty (618–907), and even the highly cultured Song dynasty (960–1279) had been founded by a usurping general. Thus, Ming central authorities valued border troops for their superior fighting prowess and their contributions to national defense, but remained cautious about allowing them near the capital in Beijing.

The complete failure of capital garrison forces to suppress the rebels was painfully obvious to most observers. Further, the minister of war reasoned, no immediate crisis threatened the northern frontier. He proposed that two officers each lead one thousand men from Juyong Pass to Zhuozhou.[43] Five thousand one hundred men from Zijing Pass were sent to Baoding.[44] Each of the soldiers received 2 taels of silver, and local officials were to provide fodder and grain.

As officials in Beijing finalized plans to employ thousands of battle-tested soldiers from the northern border, Ma Zhongxi and Zhang Wei continued their intermittent negotiations with the rebel leaders. On August 5, Ma had sent a messenger to the rebel camp to induce the outlaws to surrender.[45] According to government sources, the insurgents had agreed to accept the offer of pacification. Instead, they attacked three county seats in western Hejian Prefecture before becoming bogged down there by heavy rains, flooding, and impassable mud. Learning that imperial troops had blocked their exit in all directions, the insurrectionist leaders once again expressed their willingness to surrender.

Mindful of their troops' repeated failures against the mounted forces under the Liu brothers and Tiger Yang, Ma Zhongxi and Zhang Wei quickly relayed news of the rebels' professed change of heart to the throne. They also withdrew troops stationed in the area and prohibited imperial forces from attacking rebels. This pacification also proved short-lived. Before long, two counties just south of the capital suffered attacks. Once again, the rebels camped in the administrative offices of the county seat of Wenan for several days.

After this long string of rebel attacks through Hejian Prefecture and northern Shandong, Ma finally received a piece of unexpected good news. Liu the Sixth notified Ma Zhongxi through intermediaries that he wished to meet at a spot just north of Ma's headquarters at Dezhou, a strategic city located along the Grand Canal straddling the border of Shandong and the Northern Metropolitan Area. Ma again quickly accepted the invitation. One source indicates that Ma traveled with a large entourage of officials from Dezhou, befitting an official of his standing. An alternate version, which had Ma riding into the rebel camp without armor or accompaniment, seems to have been more popular among many Chinese historians, past and present.[46]

The rebel leaders are said to have been "both amazed and pleased" to see Ma, and they "circled around [him] to make obeisance, offered wine, and bowed their heads to the ground."[47] As they drank their wine, Ma attempted to persuade the leaders to surrender. While his older brother was apparently moved by Ma's words, Liu the Seventh abruptly interrupted the official. "No more of this talk! We already know that the court will not pardon the likes of us."[48] When Ma Zhongxi protested that this was not so, Liu the Seventh dramatically produced an imperial edict from within his sleeve, presumably proving that there was to be no pardon. With that, Liu the Seventh stormed out.[49]

A rare and previously unused source provides the most detailed and telling account of the failed negotiations. During the summer of 1512, a high-ranking official traveled down the Grand Canal from Beijing to Yangzhou on official business. Throughout his journey, this official met with local civil and military authorities, learning much of the details of the campaign against the Liu Rebels. In his travelogue, he reported that the Liu brothers and approximately forty of their followers all knelt in supplication beside an imperial relay station outside Dezhou to welcome Ma. When Ma arrived, they all kowtowed and begged for mercy. Ma agreed to petition the court on their behalf if they reformed their ways.

In their report to the throne, Ma Zhongxi and Zhang Wei wrote, "[Liu] Chong [i.e., Liu the Sixth] and others had previously violated the law. They were forced by hunger and cold into banditry. Although this cannot be forgiven, their original intention was no more than [the wish] to avoid death."[50]

The Ministry of War recommended that because the rebels had indeed shed their armor and reported to Ma's headquarters, they should be allowed to surrender. If their intentions were not sincere, wrote the Ministry of War, they should be destroyed.

The rebel leaders then began their negotiations in earnest: "We two-thousand-odd men are willing to be stationed in nearby garrisons and to kill rebels on behalf of the court."[51] Ma ordered that two rebels should serve as representatives of the entire group and work out the details of the settlement with local officials. The officials, though, balked at the rebels' request to serve as members of an imperial prince's personal garrison in Yanzhou Prefecture. They reasoned that because all lands and all troops in the realm belonged to the throne, what need was there to specify particular places and particular garrisons? Perhaps as a way to cool rising tempers and facilitate smoother negotiations, officials then provided a meal to the rebels. The skittish rebels, however, were thrown into a turmoil and fled when a postal rider arrived at the station; as they later explained, they feared ambush by treacherous officials.[52] Although they returned shortly later to renew negotiations with Ma and his subordinates, the rebels ultimately gave up. During their final encounter with Ma, Liu the Seventh said, "Your honor has agreed; the court has agreed; but there is someone who is trying to kill us." Ma tepidly responded, "That is beyond me: What can I do? What can I do?"[53] The rebels left in an uproar.

Details of the various accounts may differ, but they all point to the same conclusion. The Liu brothers and their followers wished to re-

negotiate their way into a secure and profitable patron-client relationship that would allow them to make good use of their proven military
skills. With insufficient pull at court, Ma simply lacked the power to
ensure real protection to the Liu brothers both at the local level and in
Beijing. For a fleeting moment, Ma and his repeated attempts at moral
suasion appeared to have successfully navigated the treacherous seas
of satisfying the demands both of the imperial court and local society.
Ultimately, however, his hopes were dashed on the pitiless shoals of
political reality and court divisiveness.

Liu the Seventh's pointed refusal to surrender must have been a
heavy blow to Ma Zhongxi. Despite a promotion early in the campaign,
he had recently come under increasing criticism and pressure to end
the rebellion in North China.[54] Late in August, before the ill-fated meeting with the Liu brothers, several censors had submitted memorials to
the throne impeaching Ma Zhongxi, Zhang Wei, and the grand coordinators responsible for territories where the insurrectionists were rampant. They complained that Ma and others were wasting military provisions in their campaign without any tangible results. They further
argued that because of the repeated defeats inflicted on the imperial
forces under Ma and Zhang Wei, the "military prestige [of the dynasty]
deteriorates daily."[55]

The Martial Ancestor replaced Ma and Zhang with other officials.
He recalled Ma Zhongxi and Zhang Wei to the capital, where they were
taken into custody and interrogated at the Ministry of Justice.[56] Although Zhang Wei eventually would receive an imperial pardon and
resume his military career, Ma did not live to long enough for a pardon.
Weak with illness and lack of food, he died on the dank floor of an
imperial prison in Beijing.

Ma's successor was the assistant minister of war, Lu Wan (1458–
1526). Lu was known as a pragmatic man, who understood the importance of good relations with his superiors.[57] The example of Ma's downfall surely illustrated the need for strong supporters at court. Lu was
now to serve concurrently as military superintendent and to oversee
the newly transferred border troops from Xuanfu and Yansui, as well
as the imperial soldiers of the capital garrisons.[58]

Spreading Rebellion

If the Martial Ancestor and his court believed that dismissing the discredited Ma Zhongxi and deploying thousands of combat-hardened
troops from the northern border would quickly end the rebellion, they
were mistaken. In fact, during the months that followed, the rebels

reached the acme of their power. During the fall of 1511, their raids expanded far beyond the Northern Metropolitan Area and Shandong into Henan Province, with its fluid population and often mountainous terrain. The rebels increasingly adopted the rhetoric and administrative forms of an imperial government. The response of local communities to these new developments reveals much about the nature of county government, its relation to local society, and the negotiated nature of local order. Despite the rebels' surge, the imperial Ming government was not cowed. In the face of imminent attack, the court carried out important solemn state rituals beyond Beijing's protective walls and formulated the beginnings of an effective response to the dynastic challengers.

The newly transferred border troops soon proved their mettle. After rebel forces attacked three county seats less than 50 miles south of Beijing and stood poised for an assault on yet another prosperous township nearby,[59] border forces sprang into action. In September 1511, they skirmished with rebel forces at least seven times in the counties south of the capital. Although Madman Zhao badly defeated the imperial troops in one encounter, reportedly killing more than three thousand troops and briefly taking captive a Ming commander, the border troops reported victories in most encounters.[60] Madman Zhao and Tiger Yang capitalized on one of their few victories in southern Hebei to put distance between the border troops and themselves by fleeing to Shandong Province.

They took temporary refuge on Mount Meng, more than 1,000 m. high and located on the southern edge of the Shandong massif. From there they once again defeated a contingent of imperial troops and seized an unspecified number of firearms, more than one hundred suits of armor, and one set of dragon robes.[61]

This was a remarkable haul. While a wide variety of firearms and cannon were in use during the Ming, with such names as "crouching tiger," "long-range awe-inspiring," and "swift thunder," their production and distribution were jealously guarded by the state.[62] More common weapons for imperial forces, and probably for many bandits as well, were bows and arrows, knives, cudgels, and a slightly curved scimitar-like sword called the *yaodao*.[63] Government forces almost certainly enjoyed a distinct advantage over the rebels in logistics, supplies, and firearms, but each seizure of firearms (and many more were to follow), eroded their technological edge.

The significance of the dragon robes can be grasped only if one remembers that during much of the late imperial period, clothes were the most immediate and visible markers of official status and position in China. "Mandarin Patches" specific to each of the imperial bureaucracy's eighteen ranks were an attempt to control status and power. Those outside the Ming bureaucracy were also subject to sumptuary regulations, which the central government issued with great regularity, if limited effectiveness.[64] In a real sense, clothes made the man.

Although conferring no immediate military advantage to the rebels, dragon robes radiated power, prestige, and authority, being imperially produced ceremonial clothing bestowed by the emperor as rewards for meritorious service.[65] Although some complained that the Martial Ancestor was too liberal in dispensing the dragon robes, still only the highest levels of the Ming elite could boast of possessing them. The rebel Tiger Yang immediately donned this symbol of imperial favor, displaying it for all to see as he traveled along the road.

All in all, the core members of Tiger Yang's forces must have cut quite a figure to the people of North China. They rode horses, wore imperial Ming armor, and carried firearms; their leader dressed in robes that exuded imperial prestige. That they repeatedly trounced local militia and routed imperial troops could only have made them even more awesome, both in the eyes of villagers and county magistrates.

(Yang made another acquisition at this time, Miss Cui. Cui had been seized in raiding, and willing or not, became Yang's companion. After Yang's death, Cui became known as Widow Yang and led forces formerly under Tiger Yang.)[66]

By late September, the rebels had amassed a considerable string of victories in northwest Shandong.[67] While worrisome to the court, the rebels' growing strength proved highly appealing to other members of Ming society. During the fall of 1511, large numbers of local bandits from Henan and Shandong joined the forces of Tiger Yang and Madman Zhao.[68] A single group of three thousand mounted brigands from Henan is said to have allied with Zhao. Links between the local brigands and the rebel forces were apparently formalized through pacts (huoyue), which are repeatedly mentioned in the confessions of Madman Zhao and Zhang Wei.[69]

While the exact nature of the pacts is unclear, the practice of establishing more formal and binding links among individuals and groups who were not related by blood, marriage, or adoption was a well-established feature of late imperial China. In most cases, such voluntary associations were innocuous, even socially respectable. Associations devoted to agricultural production, religious practices, and raising funds for funerals, marriages, and other major expenses were common.[70]

Sometimes, however, these bonds were formed for purposes that the state found less acceptable—such as banditry, rebellion, and, later during the Qing period, secret societies.[71]

Alliances between individual locally established outlaw groups and the rebel forces continued throughout the course of the rebellion, but for the most part, these ties were of limited duration. The appearance of the rebels dramatically affected local patterns of interaction among imperial authorities, local elites, and bandits. As rebel forces vividly demonstrated the limits of officials' ability to enforce local order through repeated victories over imperial troops and magistrate-led defenses, local bandit groups probably saw an opportunity to strengthen their position locally through alliances to the rebels. Rebel groups may have also pressed these bandit groups to join them. Given the rebels' proven puissance, smaller local outlaw groups were probably not in a position to decline. In fact, one official proposed to the court that it should take advantage of the tendency of rebel forces to absorb local groups by having volunteers pose as local bandits who wished to join the rebels. Once in place, they were to spy for the government and, if the opportunity presented itself, assassinate rebel leaders during the chaos of battle.[72]

The rebels' military victories did not lead to permanent political control over the territories through which they passed. Rebel forces commonly raided in the same area several times. The result was a state of flux, where government authority was shown to be insufficient to maintain local order, yet where rebel forces were unable to establish any lasting alternative. In this highly fluid context, magistrates, local elites, bandits, and the general population interacted with rebel forces.

The uncertainty of the situation was often heightened by the lack of credible and timely information about the location, size, and intentions of rebel forces and imperial troops. Rebel forces often controlled imperial highways and made traffic uncertain along the Grand Canal, thus disrupting two of the empire's most important routes of information. Although we lack detailed information about the degree to which the flow of information was disrupted during the 1510 Rebellion, events of the fall of the Ming dynasty are suggestive. One modern scholar has argued that credible news of the last emperor's suicide on Coal Hill in Beijing did not reach the Jiangnan region for nearly one month; it apparently did not arrive in Fuzhou, far to the south, for more than two months.[73]

In November, the insurrectionists dramatically demonstrated the government's inability to protect even the Grand Canal, the critical lifeline that supplied Beijing with grain, tax silver, and myriad other goods from the affluent southeastern coastal region. During an abortive attack on the thriving commercial city of Jining, rebels burned more than 1,200 of the approximately 11,600 boats that constituted the government's entire grain fleet plying the Grand Canal.[74] In the wake of the rebel attack, officials and civilians along the Grand Canal fled for safety. Fearing for their lives, soldiers assigned as transport workers there neglected work, and the canal itself reportedly fell into even greater disrepair.[75] On this and other occasions, the rebels not only destroyed boats along the canal, they also seized large numbers of them, greatly handicapping the ability of imperial troops to move back and forth across the canal.[76]

The court attempted to restore order in North China through improving the dismal performance of the capital garrisons, which had been repeatedly defeated in battles with rebel forces. By late October 1511, in response to requests by the influential eunuch Zhang Yong and the threat of the rebels, the Martial Ancestor ordered the eunuch Zhang to select more than 123,000 troops from among the capital garrison for use in the campaign, nearly trebling the number of troops originally requested, an indication of the emperor's personal interest in the campaign and his conviction that greater military resources were needed.[77]

In the end, however, it was neither the highly touted border troops nor the prestigious capital garrisons that claimed the first great success against the rebels. It was, instead, the much maligned local troops of a garrison in the Southern Metropolitan Area. The troops of Commander Shi Jian of Wuping Guard were an unlikely group to accomplish such great deeds. As fall changed to winter in 1511, rebel forces had overrun the defenses of several county seats in the Southern Metropolitan Area, taking captive at least one magistrate, freely crossing the Grand Canal, killing more than three hundred garrison troops in one battle, and seizing their commander. Shi Jian had skirmished only inconclusively with small raiding parties several times and had been unable to prevent rebel attacks in neighboring Henan Province just across the border to the west.[78]

At the county seat of Bozhou, close by Wuping Guard and located on a major overland route to Nanjing, Shi Jian's father, a retired commander, tried his hand against Tiger Yang and Madman Zhao, with even more disheartening results. Besides imperial regulars, Shi Jian's father commanded more than three hundred warrior monks, quite likely from the famed Shaolin Temple. The use of monks skilled in martial arts and battle was a well-established practice by this time, and they would again be pressed into service a few decades later against pirates marauding along China's southeastern coast.[79] The monks under Shi Jian's father suffered heavy casualties; more than one-quarter of them died in the fighting.

Shi Jian's forces, which included military retainers, fared better, engaging the rebels in combat approximately 10 miles north of Bozhou. There he reportedly took thirty rebel heads and captured Tiger Yang's grandson, Yang Jing.[80] The rebels retreated and encamped about 10 miles east of the Bozhou city walls. According to initial reports, Shi Jian and a subordinate, a centurion, sank one of the rebels' boats as they attempted to cross a river. The surviving rebels suffered further losses in a defeat by a combined force of imperial troops and local militia, before escaping into southeastern Henan Province and neighboring Fengyang Prefecture.[81] A follow-up report by inspecting censors revealed not only that the centurion's men had attacked without knowing the identity of the men in the boat but that when Shi Jian had belatedly arrived, he had taken credit for killing the rebels and had cowed the centurion into silence. Preliminary investigations into the accuracy of Shi's report were delayed when Shi's father bribed officials. In the end, the court awarded 1,000 taels of silver to the centurion, and Shi Jian was taken into custody for questioning.[82]

The significance of this series of small skirmishes and the destruction of a single boat hinges on the identity of one of the boat's passengers. On November 13, 1511, four well-dressed corpses were fished from the river.[83] Sounds of lament and accusation went up in the rebel camp: "Shi's men killed our Great Prince Yang." Paper money was burned for the Great Prince's spirit at the site where he drowned, and his followers prayed that his spirit might safely return home.[84]

Tiger Yang's grandson, captured before this, was forced by government authorities to identify the four corpses. Cradling one body in his arms, the tearful grandson said simply, "Great Prince." The corpse of Tiger Yang wore a four-cornered helmet, a style of military headgear reserved for officers of the Ming army.[85] His armor stood out for its splendor.[86] A drawing was made of the corpse and shown to a captured rebel; he also began to sob and cry the name Great Prince Yang. Only then did imperial forces believe that Tiger Yang was dead.

To modern readers, the imperial government's apparent lack of reliable information about the appearance and whereabouts of the rebel leaders is striking, but this was the norm in most premodern societies.[87] With Tiger Yang and later Liu the Seventh, imperial forces could do no better than identify especially richly dressed rebel corpses as possible candidates for rebel leaders. What is perhaps more noteworthy was the government's later ability to locate Madman Zhao after he disappeared into the countryside of southern China, well over 600 miles from the capital.

As is apparent from his followers' grief, Tiger Yang was a leader of considerable charisma. His sudden demise left his group without strong leadership or direction. Hoping to prevent the disintegration of Yang's forces, Madman Zhao and others pushed another of the rebel leaders, Liu the Third, to the head of the insurgents.[88] Having solved the problem of leadership at least temporarily, Liu the Third and Madman Zhao led their men approximately 50 miles southeast to Taihe County, where they handed government forces a major defeat. Liu's men killed more than 1,500 imperial troops and local security forces and seized two thousand pieces of armor, spears, and swords, as well as seventy pieces of artillery.[89] The transfer of leadership from Tiger Yang to Liu the Third apparently was successful; Liu's momentum only increased with his arrival in Henan.

In contrast, the court in Beijing struggled with natural disasters, the threat of rebel attack, and a creeping dread. On December 1, 1511, an earthquake struck Beijing, affecting a dozen counties around the capital. Bazhou, a county seat just north of the Liu brothers' hometown, was hardest hit, with nineteen tremors during the first three days of December. Local residents were deeply unnerved.[90] As was customary in instances of natural disaster, civil and military officials were ordered to reflect on their transgressions, and sacrifices were made at the Altars of Heaven and Earth, the Ancestral Temple, and the Altar of State.[91]

Reports that rebel forces under the Liu brothers had attacked Bazhou, little more than 40 miles south of the capital, and were active in the vicinity of Beijing in mid-December tightened panic's grip on the capital. On the first day of the twelfth lunar month (December 20, 1511), according to long-established custom, the emperor was to inspect animals to be used in the emperor's annual sacrifices at the Altar of Heaven, just south of Beijing. There was widespread and well-founded fear that the rebels might attack the vulnerable imperial procession while it was outside the capital's towering walls. Yet the sacrifices to Heaven and Earth were among the most important events of the Ming ritual calendar, an occasion when the Son of Heaven reported on the state of the realm and prayed for good weather and bountiful crops in the coming year.

Minister of War He Jian learned of the bandits' presence in Bazhou just before retiring for the evening.[92] Having no clerks at hand, the minister himself penned a note and ordered a servant to slip it into a special slot in the Gate of Everlasting Peace, through which such urgent messages could be transmitted. Once the gates to the imperial palace were closed for the night, not even the highest ministers were allowed in. The report was passed on to the eunuchs who handled incoming memorials, and the Martial Ancestor was notified at once.

All government offices in the capital were put on alert. Because the great gates of Beijing could not be opened, the emperor's orders to his field commanders were lowered from the city wall on a rope to a waiting messenger below, who delivered the message to prepare men and mounts. Troops took up positions to the south, west, and east to prevent any sudden attacks by the rebels.

The Forbidden City buzzed with activity throughout the night, and by 4:00 A.M., the various preparations for the Martial Ancestor's excursion to the Altar of Heaven were largely complete. Shortly later, the emperor ordered the Directorate of Ceremonial to summon the minister of war and Grand Secretariat Yang Tinghe to Zuoshun Gate to discuss the scheduled procession to the southern suburbs. The grand secretariat observed that the inspection of the sacrificial animals was vital. Not to go would make the emperor appear cowardly, something the dynasty could ill afford in the midst of a major rebellion. Security should be strengthened, but the Martial Ancestor should travel to the southern suburb as planned.

One of the emperor's closest eunuch attendants, the influential Zhang Yong, agreed strongly and volunteered to march in the emperor's procession.[93] On December 20, 1511, the emperor set forth from the Forbidden City at mid-morning and returned at dusk.[94] The rebels made no move against the imperial procession, perhaps having been informed that their plans had been discovered. The inspection complete and imperial authority asserted, the people were reassured.

By early January 1512, the immediate threat against Beijing had apparently passed, as the rebels attacked a string of county seats to the south in Zhending and Baoding Prefectures.[95] Lu Wan's forces followed the rebels south, and by mid-January, he had reached as far south as Henan Province.[96] Lu Wan reported that imperial troops were victorious in every encounter with the rebels, and the Martial Ancestor once again granted Lu an imperial edict encouraging him to render further meritorious service. Less than a fortnight later, however, the emperor would have cause to wonder if his praise of Lu Wan had been premature.

During 1512, the rebellion's center shifted decisively south of the Yellow River. Aside from a few minor yet highly embarrassing attacks in the vicinity of the capital, most battles were fought in central and southern

Henan, northern Huguang, sections of Jiangxi, and the Southern Metropolitan Area. This meant that the "Hebei bandits" were now operating almost exclusively in areas differing from their home regions in important ways—topographic, linguistic, agricultural, cultural, and political. The contrasting fortunes of Madman Zhao and the Liu brothers are in some measure a reflection of how they chose to bridge those gaps. Despite being active in an area of China under fairly light government control, Madman Zhao's imperial rhetoric and administrative measures failed to garner consistent local support. On the other hand, the Liu brothers' predatory raids attracted local bandits and pirates in areas close to the empire's economic and cultural center, Jiangnan. If the strategies and characteristics of the two rebel groups differed, their leaders' ultimate fate was the same—defeat, humiliation, and death. Constant military pressure by imperial armies hastened the internal disintegration of Madman Zhao's forces, while a punishing typhoon and a bloody mop-up operation by Ming armies ended the Liu brothers' predations.

Returning to developments in Henan, local officials reported during December 1511 that Liu the Third, the rebel leader who had risen to great prominence since Tiger Yang's death, had led raids on several county seats in Kaifeng Prefecture. More significant than the ease with which Liu the Third sacked administrative cities and defeated imperial forces were his increasingly bold political claims. Local officials wrote that Liu the Third planned to attack the great walled city of Kaifeng, an important administrative and economic city in North China.[97] Liu had already arrogated the title Supreme Commander Marshal. He issued placards and announcements, in the manner of the official Ming bureaucracy, forbidding teachers and students—potential participants in imperial politics and important cultural symbols for any contender seeking legitimacy—to flee the city. Further, Liu forbade his men to kill commoners indiscriminately, another attempt to stress the righteousness of his cause.[98]

In fact, the ambitions of Liu the Third and Madman Zhao were even greater than these reports would suggest; while encamped in the administrative offices of Luyi County, in northeast Henan, Liu the Third and his band began to look like earnest contenders for the throne. The retired magistrate of Xincai, two licentiates, and an elder prepared horses, four sets of wine cups and stands of chased gold, ten wine goblets and stands of silver, and two rolls of silk damask.[99] They presented these gifts to Liu the Third, along with an entreaty that he spare the lives of the people in the district. Liu accepted the gifts and allowed them to live.

It was also at Luyi that Chen Han, a man who claimed to have been a secretary in the Ministry of War, expressed his willingness to become an adopted son of Liu the Third.[100] Chen Han was made a member of the band and quickly proved his worth in the reorganization of Liu the Third's forces. Chen Han darkly warned that the band's lack of military organization would surely lead to chaos, and he insisted on the necessity of organizing the rebels into ranks and bestowing titles on the various leaders.

The new titles were based roughly on existing Ming administrative practices and were entered in formal registers. Liu the Third was named "Grand Marshal Who Receives Heaven's Mandate to Suppress Enemies."[101] Madman Zhao changed his personal name from Sui to Huaizhong, the new name meaning "embracing loyalty." Zhao took the title vice-marshal. Chen Han was appointed Counselor on Critical Military Affairs of the Empire. Other leading bandits were also given grand titles, and their duties were clearly delineated.

Chen Han and another of Liu's adopted sons oversaw the "Eastern and Western Depots." The original Eastern and Western Depots were key imperial intelligence centers located in Beijing and dominated by eunuchs who were widely feared for their terror and brutality.[102] Reorganization was not limited to the bestowal of impressive titles; at least on paper, the confederacy of bands was divided into twenty-eight brigades *(ying)*, each with the name of a corresponding heavenly constellation. Each was to be commanded by a regional military commissioner, again borrowing from the organization of the Ming military.[103]

Twenty-four multicolored damask banners and a pair of pennants embroidered in gold thread proudly flew in the rebel camp. On the gold pennants, the rebels boldly announced their intentions: "The three thousand valiants drive directly into the land of [ancient] You and Yan [Beijing]. The emperor takes his throne, the primordial heavens reopen."[104]

The rebels also posted public notices, usually issued by the imperial court or local officials, to announce policies or orders. The rebels' notices read:

Grand Marshal Liu Who Campaigns by Heaven's Order and Vice-Marshal Zhao order that officials on the road ahead are to prepare fodder, arrows, and needed utensils. [They are to] repair bridges and roads. Those who welcome [us] will not be harmed in the slightest. [For] those who resist, not a blade of grass will be spared. Those who disobey or delay will be punished according to military law [i.e., executed on the spot]. None shall disobey.[105]

One may wonder what the officials, local elites, local garrison troops, and myriad other commoners of the region made of the rebels' mix of grandiose rhetoric and detailed administrative instructions. Despite the dynasty's official position, realists at the imperial court in Beijing did not presume the unquestioning loyalty of each rural community or county seat. In fact, some were pessimistic; one important record claimed that at this point, "all yamen offices welcomed the rebels."

Each encounter between rebel forces and local society was subject to multileveled negotiation—between the rebels and the county government, between county officials and local residents, and between local residents and the rebels. Equally important were the discussions that transpired within and across each of these various subgroups. The details of these negotiations are now lost, but it is clear that there was considerable variation in the strategies adopted by the rebels and by any given county, and further that these negotiations were often marked by acute tensions and conflicting viewpoints.

In December 1511, when the rebels attacked Shangcai in central Henan, they encountered fierce resistance.[106] The new local magistrate, Huo En (1470–1512, js. 1502), had recruited troops, made defense plans, offered prayers to the gods, and vowed to the people of the city that he would die before abandoning Shangcai.[107] Huo is said to have personally led the defenses and threatened to kill on the spot anyone who tried to flee. Nonetheless, the city fell on December 13, 1511.[108]

The rebels seized Huo and attempted to enlist him in their cause. Huo's response (as recorded by a later biographer) is as follows:

> I am a servant of the court with the status of a metropolitan degree holder. How dare you cur and swine humiliate [me]. You are bandits and nothing more. Who would grant you the title of prince? I regret [only] that I am unable to mince your flesh into thousands of [little] bits [and pieces]. Would anyone be willing to call you [a prince]?[109]

With that, Huo sat down cross-legged and continued to hurl abuse at the rebels. Amazingly, the rebels did not immediately dispatch Huo. Rather, his captors the next day again attempted to persuade him to join their band. In the end, however, Huo's vitriol proved too much for the rebels. They bound Huo and killed him outside the southern gate of Shangcai. They quartered his body and hung pieces of his corpse by the four gates of the city as a gory warning to others. Huo's wife committed suicide after seeing her husband fall into rebel hands. The throne granted both of them posthumous titles.[110]

The magistrate of neighboring Xiping also opted for resistance and completed extensive defensive preparations. When the city fell, he was taken captive, suspended from a flagpole, and shot with arrows until he expired.[111] At least six other county seats in southern Henan and northern Huguang suffered from rebel attacks in late 1511.[112]

Officials who opted to resist the rebels without strong local support did so at their own risk. When a reported thirty thousand rebels attacked Yuzhou (modern-day Fangcheng) in mid-January 1512, Vice-Magistrate Yu Cai (js. 1508) stolidly rejected promptings from residents to bribe the bandits and instead personally led the defense of the eastern gate.[113] A three-thousand–man militia privately organized by a retired official who had settled locally bolstered Yuzhou's defenses.

Shortly after the fighting began, however, panicky residents, including the magistrate and several local military commanders, opened the city's western gate to flee. The rebel forces quickly breached the city's defenses. Vice-Magistrate Yu died from a head wound while fighting in the city streets.[114] In the course of the attack, the city's newly refurbished administrative buildings were reduced to rubble, and the city walls were severely damaged.[115]

Other local officials in Henan chose a more accommodating stance, often bribing the rebels to spare their cities. In Shangshui, Kaifeng Prefecture, the magistrate led Confucian teachers and students in welcoming the rebel forces, while Madman Zhao and his men occupied the branch office of the surveillance commissioner for several days.[116] During a rebel attack on another county seat in Kaifeng Prefecture, residents presented 2,000 taels of silver and twenty horses to the rebel leader Liu Hui, who then spared the city.

While only scarce details surround these "gifts," Liu Hui probably chose to interpret them not as simple bribes but as acknowledging his authority. It was this reason, rather than the material value of the goods, that persuaded Liu to spare the city. By not sacking cities that acknowledged his authority, Liu the Third provided local officials and residents with an alternative to defending to the death.[117]

In this way, during their travels through Henan, the rebel forces expanded their numbers by absorbing all manner of people, from such opportunists as the organizer Chen Han, mentioned above, to local bandits to ordinary men and women who were forced to care for horses, carry luggage, and perform other menial but vital tasks.

During the fifteenth and sixteenth centuries, mountainous southern Henan offered fertile soil for insurrection. It was known for its large, mobile, and obstreperous miner population. Outside imperial control, organized into tight work teams, supporting small nuclear families, and tied to commercial interests (often backed by local elites), the miners were known as fierce fighters. They sometimes became involved with heterodox sects, such as the one that erupted briefly in the mid-sixteenth century. Part of the fluidity was because of southern Henan's proximity to one of the Ming dynasty's largest administrative black holes—the area where the provinces of Henan, Huguang, and Sichuan meet. In 1506, one official estimated that nearly three-quarter million "floating people" had settled there.[118]

Despite the rebels' evident dynastic intentions, repeated attacks on administrative cities, and gruesome murders of several magistrates, the Martial Ancestor once again offered them a chance to surrender. Sometime in mid- to late January 1512, Madman Zhao received two imperial edicts while encamped in the county administrative offices of Baofeng, at the foot of the mountains in the western half of Henan. Madman Zhao responded:

> When, year after year, a clique of traitors has been in [power at] court, trifling with the imperial throne, and disrupting all within the seas, executing ministers who remonstrate and driving out senior officials, in none of those instances were they not betraying the dynasty. I humbly petition that your august majesty purify your spirit, make your own determination from within [the palace], and display in warning the heads of the traitorous in order to placate [the anger] of all under heaven. [Then] behead your minister [i.e., Zhao Sui] to placate [the anger] of the traitorous.[119]

Madman Zhao was attempting to elicit literati support for his position by identifying the corrupt eunuchs as the true villains in this drama. Several years before this, a censor had written a similarly phrased memorial remonstrating with the Martial Ancestor. The emperor had not been amused. The censor became something of a political martyr after dying from savage and repeated imperial beatings.[120] While Madman Zhao may have had a ready answer for the throne, more than one hundred of his followers were less certain; they took the imperial pardon to heart and fled.[121]

It is difficult to speak about the precise scale of the rebel force under Liu the Third and Madman Zhao. According to the figures contained in the *Houjian lu,* there were more than 130,000 cavalry, divided into twenty-eight garrisons or camps. The names of these 130,000 followers were kept in six books of registration, which were distributed to each leader for roll-call.[122] Zhao would later throw away these registers during his flight from pursuing imperial troops in Huguang, possibly to eliminate documentary evidence of his rebellious activities and to avoid implicating his followers.

Back in the capital, the ministers of war and revenue had met in January 1512 with other high-ranking officials to discuss counter-measures to the Liu brothers, Madman Zhao, and Liu the Third. They proposed that units from the capital garrisons be strictly separated from the border troops deployed in the area, because when the two were mixed, only blunders and the avoidance of responsibility resulted. Capital garrison troops were to defend fixed strategic points in North China, while the more competent border troops were to be divided along various routes and were ordered to actively pursue the rebel forces. Discipline was to be tightened. Anyone below the rank of regional military commissioner who failed to carry out his duties was to be beheaded in front of the troops as a warning to others.

To put these plans into action, the court again increased troop levels. Capital garrison troops and border units recently garrisoned near the capital traveled to Henan as reinforcements, while seven thousand more troops from the northern border transferred to Shandong and Henan.[123] A week later, on January 12, 1512, 50,000 taels of imperial silver from Shandong and Henan were used to secure military provisions for the border troops.[124] If troops in the various defense commands proved to be insufficient, supernumerary officers and local militia were to be recruited. Besides the border troops, the Martial Emperor dispatched five thousand aboriginal troops from the southern province of Huguang to fight in Henan in early February.[125] Frequently used by the Ming imperial government, especially in southern campaigns, aboriginal troops were renowned for their ferocity but also were much criticized for their poor discipline and their proclivity for plundering.

During February and March 1512, rebel forces overcame the defenses of a dozen localities in an area sometimes called Huaibei (north of the Huai River)—that is, southern Shandong, northern Jiangsu, and parts of Anhui, a region traditionally noted for its violent, explosive tenor. During the twelfth and thirteenth centuries, Huaibei had been the northern border of the Southern Song (1127–1279), and the site of periodic clashes with the Mongols. It was also the cradle of the Red Turban armies and the Ming dynasty. Later, during the mid-nineteenth century, this region was home to fierce Nian rebels and their series of walled communities, which evaded state control for a decade and a half.[126]

The 1510 rebels, too, successfully recruited men in the region, as they repeatedly tested the defenses of the strategic Grand Canal city of Pizhou during these months. Liu the Sixth, Liu the Seventh, and Qi Yanming directed the majority of the assaults, yet other such lesser-known leaders as Jia Mian'er (who was more frequently associated with Liu the Third and Madman Zhao) and, significantly, such strictly local figures as "Elder Mao" also appear in accounts of the attacks. In still other cases, various Ming records do not identify individual leaders, noting merely that "the rebels" assaulted such-and-such a place. While this lack of detail makes definitive judgments difficult, it seems that as in other areas, the various rebel groups did not move as a single force and readily absorbed local men, at least temporarily.

The testimony of one defector from the rebel forces reveals much about relations between the traveling rebel forces and local society. With the retreat of the rebel forces from Pizhou in mid-March 1512, the defector advanced to the city walls, where he discarded his armor and began his tale.

> I was originally from Bazhou and served as a valiant [*yongshi*] in the Right Tengxiang Guard.[127] My older brother [Liu] Zong and I were taken captive. Neither of us was willing to be used by the rebels. We were beaten. There was also one Han Kesheng. [He] often claimed to be a son in an official's family but was forced to serve the rebel dogs. Thus, he and . . . others together took a vow to kill Liu the Sixth, Liu the Seventh, and Qi Yanming and surrender [to imperial forces]. Recently, the remaining members of the Tiger Yang band of Henan sent a letter, [writing that] they wished to join forces with Liu the Sixth and Liu the Seventh. [They] wished to jointly attack Nanjing.[128]

After receiving this information, Liu had secretly sent word of this news to government authorities through several intermediaries, including a licentiate.[129]

The defector's story is significant because it corroborates other reports that the rebel bands included imperial troops. Some had been taken captive, as Liu here claims, while others joined voluntarily. Several of these men were members of the twenty-two imperial-guard units of the Ming.[130] In fact, one source claims that the Liu brothers themselves were soldiers from the Jinwu Right Guard of the imperial guard, while another noted that a soldier of Yanshan Left Guard, another of the imperial guards, supplied the rebel forces with arms and information.[131]

The defection also sheds light on relations between the rebels and the local population. The seeming ease with which this defector and his companions met with residents in the areas through which the rebel forces moved illustrates that the line between collaboration and resistance was not always distinct. The defector placed his life in the hands of several men outside the rebel band during the course of his negotiations. These men in turn do not seemed to have suffered for their associations with him.

The resolute determination of some local officials not to join the rebels is celebrated in government memorial accounts. In most cases, however, imperial records are curiously silent regarding who the rebels attempted to recruit. Was Madman Zhao really the only licentiate in China to join the rebel forces of the Liu brothers and Tiger Yang? Or, as seems more likely, were there others who persuaded the rebels of their loyalty at the time, only to deny cooperation after the rebels moved on?

After the failed assault on Pizhou, rebel attacks continued in the Huaibei area, where in March they burned several government offices along the Grand Canal.[132]

Late in January and early in February, the Martial Ancestor had offered a general pardon to those who had joined the rebels, reiterating promises of a three-year tax break for all areas affected by the fighting, and warning his officials against ignoring these orders. At the same time, the emperor increased pressure against the rebel leaders. Rewards for the heads of the rebel leaders were increased to 10,000 taels of silver and a hereditary post as full chiliarch. The commanding general of any soldier able to bring in one of the rebel leaders was also to receive 10,000 taels of silver (well over four hundred times the annual salary of a skilled craftsman and more than 160 times the official salary of a county magistrate at the time). A title of nobility was to be offered to anyone who could exterminate a group of bandits.[133]

Dire straits forced the court to reinstate officials who got things done but had lost their positions because of various abuses. Early in February, the court had ordered Ning Gao (who effectively used terror and public spectacle) and another censor to take up their former positions despite their acknowledged transgressions in the past. The Ministries of War and Revenue wrote, "Inasmuch as the rebels are at present on a rampage, [we must] use people under duress; not [even] the likes of [Ning] Gao can be discarded."[134] By late February, Ning was appointed grand coordinator of Baoding and placed in charge of the defense of the strategic Zijing Pass, an important approach to the capital from Shanxi. He was ordered to recruit stalwarts for the campaign against the rebels.[135]

None of these measures immediately stopped Madman Zhao and

Liu the Third, who in March and early April 1512 attacked more than two dozen prefectural, subprefectural, and district cities in southeastern Henan, northeastern Huguang, and the southwestern Southern Metropolitan Area, a traditional no-go area where imperial control was lax.[136] The raiding prompted at least two imperial princes who held lands in the area to directly petition the Martial Ancestor for aid.[137]

However, nearly constant skirmishes with imperial regulars, aboriginal troops, and local militia, several disastrous river crossings, and a failed attempt to seize a county seat sapped rebel strength.[138] By April, Zhao's forces seemed to have lost the initiative. For the next month, border troops, imperial regulars, aboriginal irregulars, and local militias hounded the rebels as they moved from place to place in southeastern Henan, northeastern Huguang, and the southwestern section of the Southern Metropolitan Area.

Madman Zhao and Liu the Third assembled their last large force early in May 1512, when they reportedly led ten thousand men into battle against imperial troops.[139] Before June was over, the key leaders had died in battle, surrendered, fallen captive, or committed suicide. Border forces and capital garrison troops under the supervision of General Qiu Yue finally crushed the remaining "Henan rebels" in a series of battles in northern Huguang, eastern Henan, and the Southern Metropolitan Area.[140]

Madman Zhao temporarily evaded Ming authorities. Only during the interrogation of one of his captured lieutenants did officials learn of Zhao's last known whereabouts. Zhao had proceeded in mid-June to the foot of the hills northeast of Yingshan County, in Huguang Province, only miles from the Henan border, where the sight of the assembled imperial armies from two provinces convinced him to go into hiding. A Buddhist monk, Zhen'an, shaved Zhao's head and then gave him his official certification as a clergy member. At that point, Zhao told his followers to flee for their lives. Accompanied only by Zhen'an and a second monk, Madman Zhao faded from view. He was reportedly heading for Jiangnan, where he planned to join rebel forces and once again try to win the throne.[141]

Armed with this information, the Ming government began a massive manhunt for Zhao. Troops and security forces from local counties and garrisons in southern Henan and northern Huguang searched for him, and provincial authorities in Huguang also ordered local officials to step up efforts to locate and apprehend Zhao. Beijing issued warrants for his arrest to each of the subprefectures and counties of the Metropolitan Areas, Henan, and Huguang.

The manhunt quickly bore fruit. On June 30, the Zhao brothers (same surname but no relation) of Wuchang Garrison bumped into a man of "unusual appearance" in Huanggang, the prefectural seat of Huangzhou. The brothers thought he resembled the warrant displayed in the provincial capital. Later, at a local police station, they saw government troops guarding a young boy, a relative of the rebels. The brothers asked the boy and his guards about the man they had encountered on the road. Their suspicions confirmed, they engaged one of the many security personnel dispatched from surrounding counties to track down Madman Zhao. With the security officer's assistance, they traced Zhao and one of the monks to a restaurant in Jiangxia. One of the brothers alerted local authorities while the other two went to capture Madman Zhao. Soon the local security forces arrived to assist with Zhao's arrest. Local authorities confiscated the monk's certificate and slightly more than 112 taels in "travel money" (actually a small fortune at the time) found on Zhao's person. Thus ended the imperial aspirations of Madman Zhao.

If Madman Zhao's forces were disintegrating by late May 1512, the Liu brothers and Qi Yanming remained a dangerous and ever-changing threat. They had traveled south to Huguang, where, in the words of one contemporary, they "abandoned their horses and took up boats"; they also gathered hundreds of new followers.[142] Peng Ze and Qiu Yue, the top civil and military officials who had helped end rebellion in Henan, now added their strength to the campaign against the Liu brothers and Qi Yanming. All but the highest-ranked provincial authorities were subject to the authority of the two, which included the power to execute anyone who disobeyed orders, as an example to others. Several border generals pursued the rebels, while additional border troops bolstered defenses in the Southern Metropolitan Area.

Despite the rebels' audacity, they were out of their element on water. Tiger Yang had been killed by imperial regulars while fording a river in November 1511, and during the spring of 1512, hundreds, if not thousands, of rebels had died while attempting to cross various rivers in southern Henan. On June 12, 1512, Liu the Sixth became the next rebel leader to meet a watery death. After a raid on the important commercial center of Hankou, the rebels were pursued by a group of Han and aboriginal troops along the Yangzi River.[143] A sudden gust of wind snapped the mast of Liu's boat, knocking him overboard into the river, where he drowned. His son and several others also perished in the incident.[144]

Liu the Seventh and Qi Yanming continued down the Yangzi River

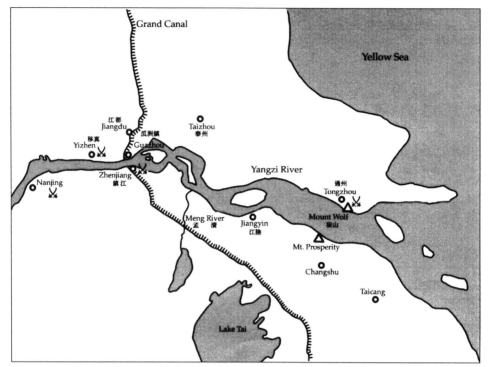

Liu the Seventh along the Yangzi River

in thirteen large boats, attracting pirates and raiding from Huangzhou to Yizhen (see map).[145] Throughout the entirety of the Ming dynasty, large groups of well-armed salt smugglers and pirates took advantage of the innumerable inlets and coves along the Yangzi River, its hundreds of tributaries, and those of Dongting and Poyang Lakes to prey on the enormous wealth of the region.[146] Some groups specialized in the highly lucrative smuggling of salt and tea, while others were more predatory, attacking the hundreds, perhaps thousands, of merchant and official grain boats that daily plied the southern waterways. Still others either trafficked in slavery, seizing children and women for sale to brothels and inns in such prosperous southern cities as Suzhou, or engaged in extortion, "requesting" contributions of grain from affluent families in the area.[147]

This criminal waterworld existed largely beyond the control of the imperial government. Its highly mobile denizens were able to avoid the imperial registration system, and the constables and patrolmen charged with enforcing Ming law and maintaining order found it easier and more profitable to turn a blind eye to certain activities or even to lend their aid in such endeavors. When government officials made more rigorous efforts to crack down on piracy and smuggling, they were met with open and armed resistance. Outlaws routinely traveled in groups of from several score to several hundred men, who navigated the waterways in fast, highly maneuverable boats.[148]

Officials in the region greeted the arrival of the northern rebel forces with considerable fear. Surprised defenders of the thriving commercial town of Guazhou looked on as Liu and Qi burned imperial war boats and seized a cache of weapons late in June 1512.[149] The rebels swept aside imperial troops from Zhenjiang on the opposite bank in one of the few instances where government troops along the river offered any resistance at all.[150] In the wake of these defeats, the Martial Ancestor transferred the forces of Peng Ze and General Qiu Yue to east of Nanjing, while the troops of Lu Wan encamped in the affluent prefectures of Suzhou, Changzhou, and Zhenjiang.[151]

Perhaps the greater fear, however, was that the scores of independent pirate groups might coalesce around the northern rebels and unite into a powerful confederation. Xia Liangsheng (1480–1538) dismissed as premature predictions of the rebels' imminent defeat. He noted, "Ruffians have long taken root among the lakes and rivers, each establishing his own band. . . . The names of the rebels are well known among the [pirate groups]. I fear that they may all respond to the [rebels'] call and pledge their allegiance." United in a common enterprise, the rebels and pirates would cooperate "like the right and left hands."[152] In fact, Xia noted with grave concern that rebel groups in Henan, Jiangxi, and Hubei might take advantage of the extensive waterways in southern China to form a unified force potent enough to frighten people even safely ensconced within the mighty city walls of Nanjing, the Ming's secondary capital.[153]

While nothing so dire occurred, from Zhenjiang, Liu the Seventh and his band sailed downstream to Mount Wolf, a little more then 6 miles south of Tongzhou on the northern bank of the Yangzi. At approximately 300 feet above sea level, Mount Wolf is actually a large and very steep hill commanding a strategic view of the surrounding area.[154] The rebels rested there for a fortnight, unaware that their next visit to Mount Wolf a few weeks later would end in a rest of a more permanent nature.

Although some officials reported that Liu the Seventh was uneasy on the water and planned to seize horses and return to the north in mid-July, the rebels moved practically unopposed along the Yangzi, carrying out day raids on many of the rich urban settlements, including Tongzhou, Taizhou, and the suburbs of Nanjing.[155] When one remembers that nearly forty imperial garrisons were stationed in Nanjing during the early sixteenth century, the rebel attacks are even more shocking.[156] That such complete tyros in river fighting could plunder largely unopposed along China's most important commercial waterway is striking, but open defiance of imperial authority in the area was not unprecedented. At the height of pirate raids during the mid-sixteenth century, as few as two or three dozen men were able to paralyze local defenses along the southeastern coast.

After several failed attempts to engage the rebels in combat, imperial regulars and border troops took up positions at Jiangyin and Zhenjiang to deny the rebels egress from the mouth of the Yangzi River. Meanwhile, six to seven hundred rebels in more than thirty boats under the command of Liu the Seventh and Qi Yanming made their way downstream on a notorious pirate haunt, the Meng River. The Meng is a tributary of the Yangzi 20 miles west of Jiangyin, where as recently as May 1505 pirates had seized nearly 150,000 pounds of rice from imperial tribute boats. The rebels also attacked cargo ships on the southern bank and assaulted at least one county seat.[157]

On August 28, local defenses prevented the rebel forces from coming ashore at prosperous Tongzhou.[158] That night a devastating typhoon assailed the rebels' fleet with a ferocity unseen in the area for decades.[159] A third of all the dwellings in Tongzhou suffered from flood damage; more than three thousand men and women died.[160] Unprotected in their ships, the majority of the rebel force boats either sank or scattered; one account claims that only eight boats survived intact.[161]

While the rebels struggled to regroup a short distance to the southeast, at Mount Wolf, imperial forces prepared for what would prove to be the coup de grâce. During the night of August 31, with the aid of local officials, the border generals and other commanders came ashore at the base of Mount Wolf and formed ranks for battle.[162] In the ensuing fighting, the rebels withdrew to a position at the top of the hill.[163] From there, the rebels rained stones and arrows down on the advancing imperial troops, who sustained heavy losses. Government troops mounted an assault from two directions; one border general attacked from the northern face of the hill, while another worked his way up the southern side.[164] Their troops crawled up the hill with culverins in their hands, while on their backs were shields so studded with rebel arrows that they resembled "the spines of a hedgehog."[165]

As imperial troops finally reached the summit, many of the rebels fell from the heights while attempting to escape. Several score of Liu the Seventh's closest followers streamed down Mount Wolf in an attempt to escape in small boats that had been prepared for just such an occasion.[166] Volleys of imperial arrows from the bank mowed down the fleeing rebels, and among the corpses found in the river waters was one dressed in fine clothes and armor. One of Liu the Seventh's women, a Miss Ding, identified the body as that of the rebel leader. At least one sixteenth-century historian suggested that Miss Ding was browbeaten into falsely identifying the body as Liu the Seventh so the battle might be declared a success and the campaign brought to a conclusion.[167] If Liu the Seventh did drown in the Yangzi, he would have been the third major rebel leader to meet a watery death.

Those rebels who managed to survive both the pounding typhoon and the devastating attack at Wolf Mountain scattered. Some drifted to nearby ports, where they were captured by government troops. Others, seriously wounded and without hope, committed suicide. Finally, some rebels attempted to return to the north. At least one group of men seized a fishing boat, sailed down the Yangzi, and then headed northward to Jiaozhou, Shandong, where they came ashore. Others traveled overland to Henan, Shandong, and the Northern Metropolitan Area. Sporadic raiding by remnants of the rebel forces was reported in several areas.[168]

The Victors and the Vanquished

As might be expected, Ming literati quickly heralded the imperial victory in poems,[169] and on October 6, 1512, slightly more than one month after the final battle at Mount Wolf, the Martial Ancestor publicly praised the efforts of his various eunuch, civil, and military officials for their meritorious service and announced their rewards.[170] The court widely distributed awards and honors, both to ranking officials and officers and to the soldiers who had fought in the campaigns. Despite criticism by civil officials, the emperor also granted generous rewards and promotions to palace eunuchs who had fought on the campaign. The Martial Ancestor wrote, "The fierce rebels were at the gate, and a string of campaigns against them brought no victory. I specially dispatched these two eunuch ministers after earlier officials had failed. Their meritorious service in quelling the rebels cannot be forgotten."[171]

And the fate of those with the temerity to challenge the August Ming dynasty? On October 11, 1512, the emperor ordered that the corpses of Liu the Seventh and Qi Yanming be dismembered; their heads were to be displayed in Bazhou, their hometown, as a warning to others. Jia Mian'er, Chen Han, Madman Zhao, and his brothers were all put into fetters and transported to Beijing.[172] According to the report in the *Houjian lu*, forty-one men and at least ten women were inter-rogated. After investigation, the Ministry of Justice determined that twenty-three men were guilty of rebellion. Based on the *Ming Code*, the ministry recommended that the sentence of "death by slicing" be car-ried out at once.[173] Widow Yang and Yang Congming, Liu the Sixth's daughter-in-law, were to be given as slaves to the households of meri-torious ministers.[174] Seven women, including Miss Ding, were released because they were judged to have been seized against their will.[175]

In its concluding remarks, the Ministry of Justice wrote:

> The rebel bandits Zhao Sui [i.e., Madman Zhao] and thirty-five others, relying on their blind intransigence, rebelled against the way of Heaven, deeply violated the injunction against plotting to kill one's lord, and together conspired to rebel. Zhao and the deceased Liu the Sixth were the first to call for rebellion. Zhao Fan, Pang Wenxuan, and others assisted in creating havoc. The larger [among them] arrogated the title "prince," [while] the lesser [among them] were falsely ap-pointed as officials. They gathered together more than 100,000 rebels, sacked scores and scores of cities, burned down houses and ware-houses, plundered all the valuables, and set free the criminals in the jails. Nothing was left in their wake. [The rebels] killed and seized officials, clerks, soldiers, and commoners beyond count. The filth of their depravity was extreme, and the viciousness of their butchery was beyond measure. [They] rocked the capital and interrupted grain shipments. [Their] poison spread throughout six provinces, lasting for more than two years. Their overflowing crimes enraged gods and men alike.[176]

On November 7, 1512, Madman Zhao and thirty-five others were "dismembered in the marketplace"—that is, their excruciating torture and deaths were offered up as a public spectacle to the residents of the capital.[177] Illustrations of the rebels' interrogation, confession, and exe-cution were distributed throughout the empire as a warning to others.[178]

The Martial Ancestor marked the end of the long rebellion in his inimitable fashion; over the objections of his ministers, the emperor reportedly had the skins of six rebel leaders stitched into his horse saddle. The saddle must have given him a macabre satisfaction; it is said that the Martial Ancestor made frequent use of it during his many riding excursions beyond the walls of the capital.[179]

Status quo ante

Most traditional narratives of the 1510 Rebellion provide a clear and glorious conclusion to the campaign. All rebel leaders were killed in battle, were captured and later executed, or were driven to commit suicide. These narratives, however, pass lightly over the consequences of the rebellion for the capital region. The 1510 Rebellion marked an intense period of unrest, but it did not fundamentally change the patterns of violence and social organization mapped in the early chapters of this study. Although the court did bolster Beijing security forces and respond to incidents of banditry in the capital region with greater alacrity than had characterized prerebellion years, no clarion call was sounded for extensive military, social, or political reforms to eliminate the underlying conditions that had contributed to the 1510 Rebellion.

Appearances can be deceiving. In 1508, 820 soldiers patrolled inside and outside the walls of Beijing. The number quickly rose. It increased to more than 1,900 in 1515, to 4,000 just before Shizong's ascension to the throne in 1522, and to 5,000 just afterward. By 1542, there were 10,018 troops in the Bandit Apprehension Garrison.[180] In three and a half decades, Beijing's security forces had increased more than twelvefold. The marked expansion of law enforcement personnel could be read as an indication of a steady breakdown of order in Beijing and its environs, and growing government incompetence, as many scholars have characterized the situation from the mid-Ming onward. Yet rather than an inexorable escalation of unrest, armed violence in the region came in waves.

Central and local governments responded as best they could to changing circumstances, establishing, bolstering, and abolishing security apparatus. For instance, consider the post of the regional commander of Hejian, a prefectural seat south of Beijing.[181] Instituted during the 1510 Rebellion, it was abolished late in 1514 (although the officer who had held the position remained in Hejian for two more years), reestablished in 1517 because of anticipated unrest in the wake of severe flooding, and once again abolished in 1521.[182] Several military defense circuits similarly established during the rebellion were deemed unnecessary by early 1516.[183] These changes suggest that the court recognized the unrest was neither constant nor always escalating. These posts required resources in men, silver, and material. To return to the initial example of the rapid expansion of Beijing's security forces in the first half of the sixteenth century—in 1551, they were halved as their numbers were reduced to five thousand.[184]

The years after the 1510 Rebellion were not kind to the Northern Metropolitan Area. Many localities suffered from severe drought and famine.[185] "Torrential downpours . . . that had not been seen for several decades" inundated Beijing, Shuntian, Hejian, Zhending, and Baoding in August 1517.[186] Grand Secretary Liang Chu (js. 1478) worried that "when the people are desperate, they are sure to turn to banditry" and proposed stockpiling grain and fodder against the eventuality of another rebellion like that of the Liu brothers.[187] The court appointed a high-ranking military officer as regional commander in Hejian late in August and placed at his disposal two thousand crack Han and Mongol troops from Hejian and Baoding.[188] In the following weeks, the court approved a series of measures designed to decrease the area's fiscal burdens.[189]

Political concerns were never far removed from discussions of social unrest. Some officials at court blamed the natural disasters and imminent social turmoil on what they considered the Martial Ancestor's outlandish behavior. The emperor had left Beijing in disguise early in September 1518, traveling to the northern border town of Xuanfu and taking up residence in a new palace there.[190] Late in November, several officials complained that the emperor had been away in Xuanfu for more than seventy days, and brigands had risen up in his absence.[191]

The following January, Grand Secretary Yang Tinghe elaborated on this theme. He noted that in several areas south of the capital, bands of forty to more than one hundred men—equipped with armor and weapons, mounted on horses, and moving in military formation with banners—plundered, took prisoners, injured imperial officials, and committed arson. The roads were impassable. Perhaps in an effort to draw officialdom's attention to the problem, even Dongzhi Gate (where supplies from the terminus of the Grand Canal at Tongzhou entered Beijing) and Dashiyong Ward (outside the main southern gate of the Inner City and the site of a large concentration of government offices) had been put on alert against possible daytime outlaw raids. Yang observed that without explicit instructions from the Martial Ancestor, further defense preparations would be difficult. He also noted that while banditry was engendered by "hunger and the cold," the brigands grew so brazen only because the Son of Heaven was not in Beijing. Yang warned of the possibility of an insurrection even more threatening than that of the Liu brothers. He begged the emperor to return to the capital at once.[192]

Although it is clear that Yang and other officials used the appearance of the brigands to rhetorically bolster their position in relation to the emperor, the situation was in fact reaching alarming proportions.[193] Because of flooding and crop failure in the Northern Metropolitan Area and Shandong, refugees streamed into the capital in search of food. Many perished on the road before reaching Beijing. Those who did reach the capital grew desperate when they discovered that the price of grain had soared beyond their means. Early in February 1518, the Martial Ancestor approved plans to bury the dead and distribute one peck (*dou*) of grain to each of the refugees. They were ordered to return home and to wait for this aid.[194] That same day, the emperor also dispatched a high-ranking official to oversee relief efforts in the Northern Metropolitan Area and disbursed more relief funds. He further ordered that the collection of taxes and material be temporarily suspended and that local officials supply cattle and seed to the farmers in need.[195]

Perhaps as a result of the 1510 Rebellion, officials were acutely aware of the need for a balanced response to brigandage. The minister of war observed that because outlaws in Gu'an had been pursued "overly aggressively," they had taken refuge in Beijing, where they were hiding among the capital's large and only partially registered population. Implicitly criticizing an excessively narrow and harsh approach, the Ministry urged that grain prices be lowered, that tax collection be temporarily suspended, and that harsh punishments be announced for anyone who harbored criminals.[196] The emperor ordered weapons, grain, and matériel to be supplied to troops in the area from the palace treasuries, drawing on stocks originally intended for Henan and Dezhou. Attempting to prevent the spread of banditry to neighboring provinces, he also instructed the grand coordinators, officials of the military defense circuits, and commandants of Shandong and Henan to guard against brigandage.[197]

Most policies relating to violence and social order in the capital region did not change after 1512. Civil officials remained firmly convinced, probably correctly, that loosely supervised military populations were hotbeds of brigandage. In October 1515, a censor touring Baoding reported the familiar view that because military camps were interspersed among civilian populations in parts of Daming Prefecture, banditry was common. The censor's solution, too, was standard; he proposed establishing "camp elders" for each camp and selecting a "headman" (*zongjia*) from every ten households, whom local civil authorities were to supervise.[198]

As might be expected, the Ming court did show keener interest in the brigandage of the capital region after the 1510 Rebellion. When banditry was reported east of Beijing in Bashang, Yutian, during the summer of 1515, the government responded decisively. Reward schedules were quickly posted. A highly decorated military officer who had campaigned against the Liu brothers, Xu Tai, was appointed to oversee elite troops from the new military headquarters located in the Imperial City who were to suppress the outlaws.[199] Later, in February 1517, a high-ranking palace eunuch was put in charge of apprehending the Bashang brigands.[200] The alacrity of the court's response and its willingness to use high-ranking officials indicate that the security of Beijing and its immediate environs assumed greater importance to the Martial Ancestor and his ministers in the years after the rebellion.

One of the most experienced and effective men at court in the years after the 1510 Rebellion was Wang Qiong (1459–1532), who in his capacity as minister of war submitted a revealing memorial, "A Proposal on Managing Local Bandits in Order to Pacify the Capital Region." The report showed that some officials believed the underlying problem of brigandage in the region stemmed from poor administrative organization. Wang quoted a report from the grand coordinator of Shuntian: " 'Bandits occupy all the hamlets and villages to the east of the Hun River [on my circuit of inspection] for 600 li, making a great number of them into [robbers'] dens.' "[201] The grand coordinator maintained that "because Han and Mongols lived mixed [among each other] and military colonies [as numerous and densely packed together] as the scales of a fish, bandits arise with ease and are pacified [only] with difficulty." The grand coordinator suggested that a yamen be established in the area, that top-quality troops from Tongzhou and Zhuozhou (to the east and southwest of the capital, respectively) be sent to lie in ambush for the bandits, that constables be dispatched, and that a single civil official be set up in a yamen to oversee defense operations.[202]

Wang Qiong agreed that the "military lands of more than seventy capital garrisons scattered throughout the areas of Wuqing and Dongan" created the problem. Even when the county magistrate was present, the "supernumerary troops of the military lands are not subject to his jurisdiction and are thus difficult to control." Wang worried that dispatching troops from other guards would cause further unrest and that appointing a civil official to oversee the military units would violate standard administrative practice.

Wang instead proposed that a certain assistant prefect in charge of apprehending bandits be sent to cooperate with an assistant commander of the Left Guard of Yanshan. This particular assistant commander had achieved considerable success in the related activities of suppressing banditry and securing local support. Their offices were to be located in one of the military forts, and they would inspect all the military lands and scattered communities. On the basis of this investigation, they were to organize patrols (*huofu*) to maintain mutual surveillance. Supernumerary troops were to be selected as bandit catchers. Wang believed it was critical that nothing be implemented unless it "accorded well with the wishes of the people and fit circumstances."[203]

The investigation of households, the organization of patrols drawn from residents, and the expansion of administrative structures were all standard bureaucratic responses to security problems. What merits particular attention here is the minister of war's reluctance to implement formal institutional change and his expansion of the powers of an individual assistant commander. Wang's attention to securing local support underscores the importance of personal governance. Local order could be maintained only through negotiation and compromise. Wang's proposal is a concrete example of the constant mediation needed to harmonize the dictates of the court with local interests ("the wishes of the people").

This chapter concludes with a brief look at violence and social order in one county, Bazhou, the epicenter of the 1510 Rebellion. Responding to widespread brigandage south of the capital during the summer of 1521,[204] the court reestablished, upgraded, and gave wider responsibilities to the military defense circuit of Bazhou. The Bazhou defense circuit had been established in 1511 to coordinate military activities in the area. An assistant commissioner who maintained offices in Bazhou oversaw security for the subprefecture of Bazhou and six surrounding counties. The defense circuit had been abolished after the end of the rebellion. The man now appointed to head the circuit, Zhang Siqi, was given the rank of vice-commissioner and had shown himself to be competent in military matters through his defense of Bozhou, in the Southern Metropolitan Area, during the 1510 Rebellion. The circuit was expanded to include the region from Hexiwu to Zijing Pass.[205] Late in July 1521, Gui Yong, the officer from capital garrisons responsible for maintaining security in and around Beijing, led imperial troops against bandits from east of the capital who were raiding in Bazhou and Yongqing. The authorities in Zhuozhou, Hejian, Bazhou, and Tianjin were ordered to be on guard against any sudden attempts by the brigands to flee.[206] After this initial flurry of activity, brigandage slipped to a lower priority for the court, although reports of Gui Yong's activities appeared periodically through the rest of 1522.[207]

The causes of this latest surge in banditry in such areas as Wuqing and Bazhou shared much in common with previous episodes. In 1521, one official observed that "undesirables" tended to congregate in Cui-huangkou, Wuqing, as it bordered on several counties. When farmland there was appropriated for use as "imperial pasturage," these undesir-ables lost their means of support and turned to banditry. It was said that "desperadoes" *(wangming)* seized the opportunity to rise up and plunder. This description would indicate that besides farmers who were pressed into brigandage, there existed a group of men outside the law who were always ready to take advantage of social unrest.[208]

Other signs indicate that men of force remained prominent in the counties south of the capital. The biography of a head of the Bazhou defense circuit noted in passing that "after the Zhengde reign (1506–1521), bandits gradually congregated in Bazhou." The account then identified several familiar problems: the large number of estates belong-ing to eunuchs and imperial relatives, shortages of land, and limited reserves of grain.[209] According to the biographer, "imperious families" seized lands and violated the law, yet officials dared not apprehend them. "Truculent people" plundered, while patrols were unable to take them into custody. In addition, we have already noted the problems generated by conflicting spheres of influence and the fact that jurisdic-tional ambiguity was routinely cited as a factor in banditry.[210]

After arriving in Bazhou, this particular head of the Bazhou defense circuit aggressively bolstered imperial authority by repairing city walls and building forts.[211] Perhaps most important, however, he recruited a one-thousand–man force in the area. He armed and trained this force, and provided generous rations to maintain a high level of combat readi-ness.[212] This approach apparently was successful: in February 1524, the official received a reward of 10 taels of silver and a set of silk garments from the throne.[213] It seems likely that this militia served the dual pur-pose of strengthening local security forces while at the same time pro-viding an alternative to banditry for men of force. Here we see clear parallels with the plans proposed by Yang Yiqing during the 1510 Rebellion, a strategy that stretched back at least to Su Shi and Qin Guan of the Song dynasty.

Bazhou continued to be known as an area "difficult to govern," where the "people are poor and customs are base," as a later head of the defense circuit observed in the mid-sixteenth century.[214] Writing in the late 1520s, Gui E (d. 1531), a leading court minister of the day, had observed that the area "east of Dongan, Bazhou, and Wuqing is desolate and sparsely populated. Thieves and robbers take refuge there. It is very much an affliction of the heart."[215]

An anecdote from a well-known miscellany of the early seventeenth century, *Wanli yehuo bian,* suggests that Bazhou and Wenan retained a measure of notoriety for their bandits late into the sixteenth century. A comely thirty-year-old woman nicknamed the Tigress had been plundering in the region for several years and had developed a reputation for her proficiency with the long spear, reputedly killing several men in combat. Fearing that her actions would eventually attract the attention of the authorities, the Tigress' lover left her and fled to Beijing. Infuriated, she selected some of her most capable lieutenants and rode to the capital in search of him. When alarmed authorities in Beijing dispatched troops to apprehend her, the Tigress and her companions fled to the suburbs of Beijing. She was later captured and executed in Beijing.[216] If this anecdote is to be believed, bandits continued to be a presence in Bazhou in the late 1500s, and on occasion they openly flouted imperial authority by venturing into the capital. Only when their activities directly impinged on the security of Beijing, however, did they draw the ire of the court.

Banditry also continued to be a serious problem in many of the other areas "pacified" in 1512. In Henan, Shanxi, and especially Shandong, bands of armed, mounted outlaws appeared with regularity during the last years of the Martial Ancestor's reign and continued into the following reign of Shizong. Throughout the late 1510s and early 1520s, bandit activity was most intense in southwestern Shandong, although the single largest group originated in Yanshenzhen, an important commercial town in central Shandong famous for its mining and porcelain production. Like the rebels of 1510–1512, these mounted, mobile outlaws often traveled in groups of several hundred and defeated imperial troops in battle.[217] Although these Shandong brigands shared similarities with the forces of the Liu brothers and Tiger Yang, there is no firm evidence of direct links between the two groups.

Some men who fought with the "Hebei bandits," recruited in Shandong, returned there, however, in 1512. Existing bandit groups had been incorporated into the ranks of the Hebei bandits during the course of the rebellion. They often had retained their own internal identity, pledging their allegiance as a group to various rebel leaders and reassessing their loyalties as circumstances dictated. When the rebellion was crushed, in 1512, it is reasonable to speculate that many of these groups, or at least individuals, returned to their native lands to take up where they had left off. This was the case of Wu Tingzhang of Jingle, Shanxi, who joined Tiger Yang's forces when they raided in the area. Wu returned home when Yang was defeated and in 1517 led a group of more than eighty men in raids in central Shanxi before being apprehended and executed.[218]

Thus, in terms of banditry and the economy of violence in North China, continuity outweighed change in the years after the 1510 Rebellion. Brigandage remained a prominent problem even after the Liu brothers, Tiger Yang, and Madman Zhao were destroyed. Government officials continued to report on men of force in counties south of the capital. Because the activities of these men did not develop into a direct threat to the dynasty, information related to their backgrounds and activities is less detailed than what is available for the Liu brothers and Tiger Yang. Local officials, however, apparently believed that many of the administrative problems that fostered brigand activity during the late fifteenth century were no less germane in the decade after the conclusion of the 1510 Rebellion. Military households were ill supervised, and troops lived interspersed among commoners, giving rise to opportunities for violence and plunder. Given that men of violence did not disappear in 1512, and that patterns of social organization in the capital did not change significantly after the 1510 Rebellion, it seems likely that patronage networks continued to link men of force to local elites and officials through much of the Ming period.

7
Conclusion
Implications for the Study of Late Imperial China

Inseparably tied to the area's demography, military institutions, economic structures, ethnic composition, and political dynamics, illicit violence constituted an integral element of the capital region's social order during the middle Ming period. Given that violent crimes like banditry and highway robbery posed perennial problems in the heart of the Ming empire even during a time of relative peace and prosperity, violence and crime probably loomed more prevalent in late imperial China than many of us may have assumed. This realization has several consequences for our understanding of the period in general.

Before considering the implications of this study for late imperial China, let us first briefly review its principal findings. Banditry constituted a recurrent problem in and around the capital of Ming China, Beijing. Gangs of armed riders, often dressed in government-issue armor and bearing imperial weapons, roamed the suburbs of Beijing and its satellite cities, compromising security and severing vital transportation links in the region. The highwaymen preyed on the ceaseless flow of merchants and government functionaries who delivered goods, grain, and taxes to the capital. The flagrant violation of imperial authority in the very shadows of the capital deeply disturbed officials, who ruminated about how much worse the problem was in areas of the empire far from heavily garrisoned Beijing, and it aggravated emperors, who railed against the inefficiency (and worse) of their officials.

Banditry in the capital region originated in the area's demographics, political dynamics, military institutions, and economic structures. The great wealth that supported an enviable lifestyle for some capital residents also attracted a steady supply of brigands and swindlers, who sought to enrich themselves with the silver, goods, and grain bound for Beijing. The capital's elite, who owed their status, wealth, and influence to the dynasty, were also tied to less-exalted elements of society through a variety of illicit activities. The relatively dense state presence in the capital region, with its overlapping layers of jurisdiction and influence, created administrative interstices in which men of force found ample room to exercise their particular talents. The scores of imperial garrisons stationed in and around Beijing, intended for the dynasty's defense against enemies both from within and without, also figured prominently in the region's chronic problems with brigandage, as underemployed and lightly supervised soldiers took up highway banditry, extortion, and violent service on behalf of capital elites.

This study has attempted to illuminate a fluid world, where shadowy patronage networks, violence (actual and threatened), and crime were an accepted part of life, figuring in the political, social, and economic strategies of a wide variety of actors. Violence drew together men —and, one suspects, women—from all levels of society. The curious meeting in the spring of 1509 brought together palace eunuchs, local men of force, and the Son of Heaven, who played kickball with members of the imperial bodyguard. While the Martial Ancestor was an unusual emperor, and his brief encounter with men of force was extraordinary, this study has demonstrated that alliances between national and local elites with men of force were in fact far more common than a cursory reading of contemporary documents might suggest.

This study's methodology, assumptions, and conclusions sharply contrast with the most influential work on collective violence during the Ming, James Tong's *Disorder under Heaven*. The core of Tong's book is based on statistical analysis of prefectural gazetteers—that is, histories compiled at an intermediate level of government, more local than the provinces but above the county level. The quality and quantity of gazetteers varied widely during the Ming according to time and place, although in general, far more gazetteers were available for the southern regions of China and in the latter half of the dynasty. Although often rich sources of local information, gazetteers were compiled to satisfy agendas that seldom included detailed discussions of local unrest.[1] Further, they often failed to adequately reflect larger institutional contexts within which individual local incidents occurred.

This study has drawn extensively from prefectural and county gazetteers, but as noted at the outset, I have found the *Veritable Records* and the *Classified Compendium* to be far richer resources, not only in the number of incidents mentioned but also in detail and in contextualization. These two centrally compiled sources often contained detailed information on local events when corresponding local histories were completely silent. Other sources, such as narratives, confessions, and various private writings by literati, also often provide invaluable information. To put the matter simply, Tong's sources are insufficient to support the sort of highly systematic social science analysis that he wishes to conduct.

Perhaps more important, however, are the questions and assumptions that Tong brings to his analysis of violence. Drawing on rational choice theory, Tong argued that banditry was more prevalent in areas far distant from the center of imperial power and from more local nodes of that power, such as garrison units and seats of local administration. His position is reasonable—men are more likely to consider the use of illegal means to attain their goals when the risk of punishment is low. As I have demonstrated above, however, risk of punishment does not necessarily increase with proximity to imperial power and its representatives. The prevalence of banditry, the prominence of men of force, and the problems of eradicating violence were often a direct result of imperial power and wealth in the capital.

Tong offers a panoramic view of nearly the whole empire through the entire 276-year dynasty, while this study has confined itself to a single geographic area and a discrete period of time. Despite the limitations of a local studies approach, it is still critical to consider violence in its local context because without such studies, the broad panoramic view can be deeply misleading. My argument here is not that there was more banditry in North China than in the south, but for the need to penetrate below the surface and to move beyond a black-and-white rendering of late imperial Chinese society. The sorts of problems revealed in this study of the capital region have parallels in other areas of the empire where mixed military-commoner or Han–non-Han populations were to be found.

Moving beyond the question of determining relative levels of violence, let us consider some of the broader implications of this study's findings. In his important study *Praying for Power: Buddhism and the Formation of Gentry Society in Late-Ming China*, Timothy Brook mounted a powerful critique of Western preoccupation with the multileveled dominance of the traditional bureaucracy on Chinese society, or, as Brook put it, seeing China as a state rather than a society. Based on his examination of gentry patronage of Buddhist temples, he concluded that during the late sixteenth and early seventeenth centuries, "The state and society began to stand apart," and he cautioned against an exclusive focus on "what elites were doing in cooperation with the state."[2] Brook and other scholars, inspired in part by the work of Habermas, have sought evidence of a "public sphere" and "civil society" in late imperial China.

With the capital region, however, it is impossible to understand local society without extensive reference to the state's presence.[3] The large number of imperial military garrisons, the high concentration of imperial estates, the remnants of the horse administration, the vast ranks of elites connected to the throne, and the presence of Mongol communities all bespoke the power of the Ming state. More important than birth, simple economic strength, education, or land, imperial power in all its articulated forms became the most highly sought commodity in the region. Ill-educated eunuchs from desperately poor families hobnobbed with leading literary lights of the day. Proud, pampered scions of the merit nobility swaggered through Beijing, publicly humiliating military officers without fear of recrimination. In one extreme example, local men of force looked on as the Son of Heaven played kickball in his private quarters.

Yet perhaps because the state's influence was so omnipresent in the area, its internal tensions and limitations emerge with special clarity. While the emperor, imperial family, imperial in-laws, eunuchs, civil officials, and military authorities were all constituent elements of the greater whole, termed "the state," the interests of each group frequently clashed. Thus, strong aggregate state presence did not mean complete state control; it contained within itself the seeds of its own subversion. The capital region case serves as a dual reminder. On the one hand, it reconfirms common wisdom: in at least some parts of the Ming empire, the state was a crucial element of local society. At the same time, however, it concretely illustrates the dangers of assuming a monolithic and united "state."

This study has argued for a more inclusive understanding of the exercise of power at the local level. Many considerations of local society–central government or state-society relations have focused on the gentry. This approach has been both natural and fruitful. In general, local gentry possessed wealth, education, political connections, and a near monopoly over writing local records. Gentry-focused studies are among the most sophisticated in the field, and they have immeasurably enriched our understanding of Ming social history. More recently, however, many have looked beyond the gentry and expanded our understanding of elite to mean "any individuals or families that exercised dominance within a local arena."[4] Usually, this has meant a focus on nondegree gentry, merchants, military leaders, and village brokers.

Based on conditions in the capital region during the mid-Ming, this study argues for an even more expansive scope of social inquiry to include such apparently marginal groups as eunuchs and men of force.

Exploiting their imperial connections and the use of violence, respectively, these groups often played critical roles in local society. Men of force were situated in complex and ongoing processes of negotiation in which they, local elites, civil and military officials, and central authorities all strove to advance their interests without riving the linking networks of favor and obligations. Often, historiographical biases obscured these negotiations through renderings of local society where all but the gentry are relegated to secondary importance, virtually eliminated from the modern historian's view. Literary constructions conspired with political, cultural, and economic concerns to produce historical records that highlight the centrality of Ming literati at the expense of potential rivals.

Finally, this study has argued that illicit force was as much a part of local order as it was a threat to that order. Coercion, assault, and banditry were all well-established facets of life in the capital region. During relatively stable periods, local officials and ambitious bandit chiefs often competed for men of force from a common pool. This competition only intensified during times of crisis, such as the 1510 Rebellion. Drawing on centuries-old tradition, the well-respected statesman Yang Yiqing explicitly recommended the recruitment of strong young farmers, martial artists, and even known criminals as a way simultaneously to bolster the ranks of imperial forces and to deprive rebels of new recruits. All officials assumed the presence of swords, bows and arrows, cudgels, and knives in commoner households. The more pressing concern was how to incorporate those weapons and their wielders into local defense efforts.

Although violence and the threat of violence were part of life in late imperial China, this study has attempted to show that specific patterns of violence must be sought in the particulars of local society. As variation in lineage structure, the composition of local elites, and religious practices have simultaneously heightened our appreciation of regional variation and deepened our understanding of late imperial China as a whole, so have variation and commonalities of illicit force provided another revealing historical perspective from which to view Chinese society.

A preliminary comparison of the violence explored in this study with the piracy along China's southeastern coast during the mid-sixteenth century illuminates both their points of commonality and the distinctive regional features of violence. Obvious points of similarity include the close links between elites and the subaltern, the subversion of imperial authority, the question of ethnicity and "the other," and the use and threat of violence to achieve ends. "Pirates in gowns and gaps" —gentry-officials and gentry-scholars who composed the local elite— invested deeply in smuggling and, often, piracy. When a high-ranking official dispatched from Beijing mounted a vigorous campaign against the smugglers and pirates, elite backers came to their aid, obstructing the campaign, undermining the official's credibility, and eventually forcing a significant liberalization of the prohibitions against foreign maritime trade. The parallel with capital elites who offered their patronage in exchange for a percentage of stolen goods or for the services of men of force is clear. In both cases, the central government failed to impose its will on local society. Finally, although the vast majority of pirates along the coast were Han Chinese, Japanese and European adventurers were also involved. In fact, Chinese records often rather indiscriminately refer to the pirates as "Japanese pirates" (or more literally "dwarf bandits," *wokou*). Here again, one might draw a parallel between the foreign component of piracy and the Mongols in the capital region who participated in banditry.[5]

The differences, however, remain important. These include geography, the character of the local economy, the nature of local elites, the composition of the outlaws, and the relative urgency assigned to each. Maritime activities profoundly influenced much of the economy in China's southeastern coastal region, and by the mid-sixteenth century, if not earlier, international trade played a crucial part in local society.[6] Whereas many of bandits in the capital region preyed on the resources flowing to and from Beijing, "pirates" along the coast were as often involved in international trade as in raiding coastal regions. Many of these affluent, highly commercialized areas made extensive use of silver. Drawing on the wealth to be made through international trade and other forms of investment, local elites successfully passed the imperial examination system, secured official positions in the national bureaucracy, and developed extremely powerful political connections.

Although elites of both regions ultimately depended on their links to the state for their power,[7] local elites in the capital region often based their position on much more direct ties to the imperial throne, whether by marriage or by personal patronage. Eunuchs, imperial in-laws, the merit nobility, and military officers were able to shield their clients from imperial justice precisely because of their personal connections. Additionally, the composition of the bandit and pirates gangs differed. Many of the highwaymen in the capital region based themselves in imperial military garrisons, whereas the pirates were drawn from coastal fishermen, merchants, and adventurers, none of whom enjoyed any special ties to Ming bureaucratic structures. Relatedly, while in both groups there was a foreign component, the Japanese and Europeans were generally considered outright outlaws, while most of the Mongols who turned to banditry were members of the Ming military, often enjoying special tax and corvée exemptions because of imperial orders. Finally, precisely because security issues involved international aspects of piracy and the more overt political challenges posed by the elites of the southeastern coastal regions, piracy became a fiercely debated policy issue in a way that the problem of banditry in the capital region never did. Even after the destructive 1510 Rebellion highlighted the problems of the capital region, no attempt was made to reorganize the garrison system, the ambiguities of civil versus military jurisdiction, or the dangerous patronage networks that linked capital elites to local men of force.

Thus, while the very preliminary comparison sketched above shows significant parallels between patterns of violence and crime in the capital region and along the southeastern coastal region, their differences remain just as important and suggest that the study of economies of violence provides a useful addition to our understanding of regional history in China.[8] Studies from other periods of Chinese history and early modern Europe suggest the value of further investigations into other facets of violence in late imperial China, such as sanctioned violence and the state, the role of violence in popular religion, regional notions of honor, revenge, and justifiable violence, and literati perceptions of the origins, regulation, and significance of violence.

If the preceding discussion has suggested the utility of further research into regional variations of violence, it is also important to consider the broader question of *wen* and *wu* in late imperial China. In the years after the 1510 Rebellion, one of the military officers prominent in suppressing the revolt, General Qiu Yue, established a residence in the suburbs of Beijing. One day during the New Year celebrations, while most of the household was away in the capital visiting family and friends, "Several dozen men armed with swords took advantage of their absence to climb the walls of the compound and enter the Qiu residence. At this time, only his son and one or two retainers attended Qiu Yue. Qiu emerged from his room, slowly drew his bow, and fired, lightly grazing the top of one man's head. He cocked another whistling arrow, and before he let go, the bandits all fled." The tale ended with the miscreants concluding that attacking the Qiu residence had indeed been a grave error.[9]

This vignette, related by the leading litterateur of his day and one of the most powerful officials at the Martial Ancestor's court, Yang Tinghe, is revealing in two ways. Most obviously, it suggests the on-going problem of armed robbery just outside the capital, a phenomenon fully corroborated by this study. More significant is Yang's intriguing attitude toward violence and physical conflict. Yang personified the ideal of *wen*, the acquisition of power through the civil service, litera-ture, and high culture. Yang placed high in the civil service examina-tions and for most of the Zhengde period served in the Inner Secreta-riat, an elite branch of government known for its literary excellence and thorough knowledge of historical precedents. Through these various accomplishments, he often had the ear of the Martial Ancestor and his successor, the Jiajing emperor. Despite these impressive *wen* credentials, Yang manifested a keen, if somewhat backhanded, interest in the ex-ploits of Qiu Yue, a social inferior much less cultured or polished than himself.

It is a commonplace assumption that the military and the martial were somehow marginal concerns during the Ming. While at least one scholar has drawn attention to the critical importance and prestige of military men and concerns in the early years of the Ming, too often the emergence of a more civil ethos within the Ming bureaucracy during the early fifteenth century has been a convenient excuse to gloss over the role of military matters as affairs of state.[10] Although the Martial An-cestor possessed an unusually intense and personal enthusiasm for military affairs,[11] in an institutional sense, the logistics, funding, and staffing for border defense and domestic campaigns of suppression, as well as the management of the mammoth hereditary military house-hold system, were perennial questions at Ming courts throughout the dynasty. As the details of the 1510 Rebellion reveal, civil officials, military officers, and palace eunuchs of the highest ranks were all inti-mately involved in the military, while military institutions and per-sonnel were important elements of Ming China, closely tied to eco-nomics, crime, land tenure, social dynamics, and the exercise of political power.[12]

Despite their importance, we know far too little about the actual functioning of Ming armies: how decisions were made, how troops were housed, trained, supplied, and transported, how generals were selected, how battles were fought, and what weapons were used. Given the enormous scale of men (and their families), land, grain, and silver involved, we need more studies that chart the institutional his-tory of the Ming military and that fully reflect the enormous regional variations occurring throughout the empire.[13] To dismissively date the beginning of the terminal decline of the Ming military to only a few decades after the founding of the dynasty seems of dubious accuracy or utility.[14]

Shifting our attention from the arena of official government policy and institutions to the murkier realm of what might be called "cultural inclination," we see again that the military and the martial held keen interest for many elements of Ming society. This facet of Ming culture often goes unremarked, perhaps because it does not seem to fit neatly with one of the most common generalizations in all Chinese history, one related to the great constellations of changes called the "Tang-Song Transition." A critical element of the transition from the Tang dynasty (618–907) to the Song dynasty (960–1279) was the fall of the aristocratic military elite of great families of the early Tang and the emergence of scholar-officials, who claimed legitimacy through mastery of a classic canon, literacy expertise, and government service.[15] One eminent modern historian of the Song period argued that this shift in cultural values was clearly reflected in the relative frequency of polo matches at the imperial court. His reasoning was elegantly simple. Polo was closely linked with war and was often considered a form of military training. It required formidable equestrian skills, a keen competitive drive, and a proper sense of etiquette and grace. Thus, during times when military values were ascendant (as they were during much of the Tang), polo was a central activity among elites, and when those values lapsed (as they did during most of the Song), the prominence of polo faded.[16]

This shift in attitudes, though, must not be overstated.[17] Most elite families did wish to see their sons pass the prestigious civil service examination; they also invested considerably more resources in their education than in military training. However, it is abundantly clear that many young elite males were fascinated by martial arts, assiduously practicing swordplay and enthusiastically discussing military strategy and famous battles. To cite only two examples of late Ming figures better known today for their literary skill, political involvement, and philosophical musings than for martial prowess, both Fang Yizhi and Chen Zilong (1608–1647) were deeply interested in martial arts as young men.[18] Part of their enthusiasm may have been because of the sense of crisis among some elites during the early seventeenth century.[19] Yet the many examples of elite men in this study who had longstanding interests in martial arts and strategy even during periods of relative prosperity suggest it was a much more prevalent element of elite culture. The continuing popularity of expensive editions of such heroic (or antiheroic, as Andrew Plaks has argued) action novels as *The*

Water Margins and *Romance of the Three Kingdoms* serves as yet another indication that some Ming literati never outgrew their youthful interest in violence, mayhem, and extraordinary martial skills.[20]

Interest in the military and the martial was by no means restricted to elite families. Non-elite interest in theater, professional storytelling, religious ceremonies, and popular legend that prominently, if not exclusively, featured martial exploits or themes was keen and sustained.[21] As this study shows, varying degrees of competency in martial arts were common among many elements of Ming society. Although the quality and duration of military training for members of the Ming armies varied widely, most had at least some exposure to armed and unarmed martial arts.[22] This knowledge was by no means a monopoly of Ming military personnel. Besides the hosts of men who fled the military and used their martial skills and daring to make a living (legal or otherwise) in other fields, others never had any association with the military but nonetheless were well versed in the pugilistic arts. This economy of violence linked renegade military personnel, bandit chiefs, county magistrates, and local elites into a constantly shifting set of tension-filled relations. As the study of illicit force reveals an important if often neglected side of Ming social history, the examination of *wu* promises to illumine a rich vein of Ming cultural history.

One final area that will handsomely repay closer scrutiny is crime. The varied and rich studies on European crime during these centuries have yielded important insights into popular culture and religion, social relations, gender, and contemporary understandings and exercise of power.[23] Analyses of crime in China during the Qing period have begun to shed light on family dynamics, the role of law in imperial China and how people endeavored to turn it to their advantage, and the conception of vengeance and justice, as well as contemporary definitions of female chastity.[24] While the Ming period lacks the mountainous archival resources available to scholars of the Qing dynasty, the preliminary researches of Chinese and Japanese scholars into subjects like prostitution, beggars, con artists, hired thugs, and economic felonies show that the study of crime does pay.

Further attention to violence and crime, to the military and the martial, is likely to reveal a China far removed from idealized images of order, control, and triumphant civil virtue. This should be viewed neither as academic China-bashing nor as arcane pedantry. Rather, such explorations into vital facets of Ming life will lead to a more nuanced, more realistic, and, ultimately, more human understanding of Chinese society and social interaction during the late imperial period.

Notes

Works frequently cited in the Notes have been identified by the following abbreviations:

DSJ   Zhu Guozhen, *Huang Ming dashiji*. In his *Huang Ming shigai,* 1632. Reprinted in *Yuan Ming shiliao congbian,* 1st series. Taibei: Wenhai chubanshe, 1984.

HJL   Xie Fen, *Houjian lu.* Early sixteenth century. In Xie Guozhen, ed., *Mingshi ziliao congkan,* 1st series, pp. 4–160. Jiangsu renmin chubanshe, 1981.

JSBM   Gu Yingtai, *Mingshi jishi benmo.* 1658; reprint, Taibei: Sanlian shuju, 1985.

JSWB   Chen Zilong, ed., *Huang Ming jingshi wenbian.* Pinglu tang, 1638; reprint, Taibei: Guolian chuban youxian gongsi, 1964.

MS   Zhang Tongyu et al., *Mingshi.* 1736; reprint, Beijing: Zhonghua shuju, 1974.

SZSL   *Shizong shilu* in *Ming shilu.* 1418 to mid-seventeenth century. Facsimile reproduction of *Guoli Beiping tushuguan cang hongge chaoben.* 133 vols. Taibei: Zhongyang yanjiuyuan lishi yuyan yanjiusuo, 1961–1966.

TFSLZ Dai Jin, *Huang Ming tiaofa shilei zuan.* Ca. 1531; reprint, Tokyo: Koten kenkyūkai, 1966.

TZSL   *Taizu shilu,* in *Ming shilu.* 1418 to mid-seventeenth century. Facsimile reproduction of *Guoli Beiping tushuguan cang hongge chaoben.* 133 vols. Taibei: Zhongyang yanjiuyuan lishi yuyan yanjiusuo, 1961–1966.

WZSL   *Wuzong shilu,* in *Ming shilu.* 1418 to mid-seventeenth century. Facsimile reproduction of *Guoli Beiping tushuguan cang hongge chaoben.* 133 vols. Taibei: Zhongyang yanjiuyuan lishi yuyan yanjiusuo, 1961–1966.

XNSL   *Xianzong shilu,* in *Ming shilu.* 1418 to mid-seventeenth century. Facsimile reproduction of *Guoli Beiping tushuguan cang hongge chaoben.* 133 vols. Taibei: Zhongyang yanjiuyuan lishi yuyan yanjiusuo, 1961–1966.

XOSL   *Xiaozong shilu,* in *Ming shilu.* 1418 to mid-seventeenth century. Facsimile reproduction of *Guoli Beiping tushuguan cang hongge chaoben.* 133 vols. Taibei: Zhongyang yanjiuyuan lishi yuyan yanjiusuo, 1961–1966.

YZSL   *Yingzong shilu*, in *Ming shilu*. 1418 to mid-seventeenth century. Facsimile reproduction of *Guoli Beiping tushuguan cang hongge chaoben*.
133 vols. Taibei: Zhongyang yanjiuyuan lishi yuyan yanjiusuo, 1961–
1966.

The *SZSL, TZSL, WZSL, YZSL, XNSL,* and *XOSL* are the dynastic annals of
individual reign periods. The records of all the reign periods together form the
Ming shilu—the *Ming Veritable Records.*

Chapter I   Introduction: The Economy of Violence
    1. This definition of economy is based on the *Oxford English Dictionary*
(1971 edition). In his examination of Haute Auvergne between 1587 and 1664,
Malcolm Greenshields has described the economy of violence as "an endless
round of provocations and retaliations, or affronts and private, violent justice.
This 'economy' could be a matter of individual quarrels or of massive, collective uprisings." See Greenshields, *An Economy of Violence in Early Modern France*
(University Park: Pennsylvania State University Press, 1994), pp. 1–2. As the
following discussion makes clear, my notion of economy of violence is not
restricted to provocation, retaliation, and the mediation of the two.
    2. See Frederick Brandauer, "Violence and Buddhist Idealism in the *Xiyou*
Novels," in Jonathan Lipman and Steven Harrell, eds., *Violence in China: Essays
in Culture and Counterculture* (Albany: State University of New York Press, 1990),
pp. 115–143. For thoughtful consideration of the significance of violence in the
most important vernacular novels of the sixteenth century, see Andrew Plaks,
The Four Masterworks of the Ming Novel (Princeton: Princeton University Press,
1987).
    3. For a preliminary discussion based on contemporary Taiwan, see Avron
Boretz, "Martial Arts and Magic Swords: Identity, Myth, and Violence in
Chinese Popular Religion," *Journal of Popular Culture* 29.1 (1995): 93–104. See
also Richard Shek, "Sectarian Eschatology and Violence," in Lipman and Harrell, *Violence in China*, pp. 87–109. For a more detailed consideration based on
sixteenth century France, see Natalie Davies, "Rites of Violence" in her *Society
and Culture in Early Modern France* (Stanford: Stanford University Press, 1975),
152–187.
    4. See Ann Waltner, "Breaking the Law: Family Violence, Gender, and Hier-
archy in the Legal Code of the Ming Dynasty," *Ming Studies* 36 (1996): 29–43.
    5. While Eric Hobsbawm's work on banditry and the concept of social
banditry often forms a point of departure for recent work on the subject, I have
found his approach and conclusions to be of limited use in understanding
Ming China. See Hobsbawm, *Primitive Rebels: Studies in Archaic Forms of Social
Movement in the Nineteenth and Twentieth Centuries* (Manchester: Manchester
University Press, 1959); *Bandits* (New York: Delacorte, 1969); introduction to
*Bande Armate, Banditi, Banditismo: E repressione de giustizia negli stati europei de
antico regime* (Rome: Jouvence, 1986). Anton Blok was the first in a long line to
challenge the concept of social banditry. See Blok, *The Mafia of a Sicilian Village:
1860–1960* (London: Blackwell and Mott Limited, 1974); "The peasant and the
brigand: Social banditry reconsidered," *Comparative Studies in Society and History* 19 (1972): 494–503.

6. In contrast to the relative neglect of violence in Western scholarship, for decades, the ideological imperatives of the People's Republic of China enjoined countless scholars to scour historical records for examples of social unrest; massive compilations on "peasant wars" appeared for many dynasties. Valiant peasants struggled to cast off the shackles of feudal oppression, while urban workers protested the abuses of venal landlords and corrupt officials. Throughout the 1950s, 1960s, and 1970s, scholars from the People's Republic of China (and often Japan) interpreted unrest of any kind as evidence of ongoing class struggle. These heavy-handed attempts to describe unrest and violence in a politically correct Marxist framework discredited the entire enterprise in the eyes of most scholars in the United States; and for many, instances of violence remained the exception that proved the rule of an otherwise ordered and pacific populace firmly governed by enlightened civil authorities.

For discussions of scholarly treatments of peasant rebellions in the People's Republic of China, see James Harrison, *The Communists and Chinese Peasant Rebellion: A Study in the Rewriting of Chinese History* (New York: Atheneum, 1969); Liu Kwang-ching, "World View and Peasant Rebellion: Reflections on Post–Mao Historiography," *Journal of Asian Studies* 40.2 (1981): 295–326. For an overview of some of the debates surrounding "peasant wars" in the People's Republic of China, see Chen Wutong, "Nongmin zhanzheng yanjiu de zhongzhong zhenglun," in *Jianguo yilai shixue wenti taolun juyao* (Jinan: Qi Lu shushe, 1983), pp. 210–285. For a recent review of Chinese and Japanese scholarship on Chinese peasant rebellions, see Kobayashi Kazumi, "Chūgoku nōminsensōshiron no saikentō," in Mori Masao et al., eds., *MinShin jidaishi no kihonmondai* (Tokyo: Kyūko shoin, 1997), pp. 341–375.

This is not to claim a complete absence of such English-language studies in the West. See Tsing Yuan, "Urban Riots and Disturbances," in Jonathan Spence and John Wills, eds., *From Ming to Ch'ing: Conquest, Region, and Continuity in Seventeenth Century China* (New Haven: Yale University Press, 1979), pp. 277–320; Richard Von Glahn, "Municipal Reform and Urban Social Conflict in Late Ming Jiangnan," *Journal of Asian Studies* 50.2 (May 1991): 280–307. For an English translation of a study by an important Japanese scholar, see Tanaka Masatoshi, "Popular Uprisings, Rent Resistance, and Bondservant Rebellions in the Late Ming," in Linda Grove and Christian Daniels, eds., *State and Society in China: Japanese Perspectives on Ming-Qing Social and Economic History* (Tokyo: University of Tokyo Press, 1984). More recently, Michael Lewis has translated into English Fuma Susumu's "Late Ming Urban Reform and the Popular Uprising in Hangzhou," in Linda Cooke Johnson, ed., *Cities of Jiangnan in Late Imperial China* (Albany: State University of New York, 1993), pp. 47–79.

7. For a discussion of the founder's effort to legitimate his new order, see Edward Farmer, *Zhu Yuanzhang and Early Ming Legislation: The Reordering of Chinese Society following the Era of Mongol Rule* (Leiden: E. J. Brill, 1995), and "Social Regulations of the First Ming Emperor: Orthodoxy as a Function of Authority," in Liu Kwang-ching, ed., *Orthodoxy in Late Imperial China* (Berkeley: University of California Press, 1990), pp. 103–125. For an analysis of the Ming dynasty's attempts to regulate religious deities, see Romeyn Taylor, "Official and Popular Religion and the Political Organization of Chinese Society in the Ming," in Liu Kwang-ching, *Orthodoxy in Late Imperial China*, pp. 126–157; Hama-

shima Atsutoshi, "The City-God Temples (Ch'eng-huang miao) of Chiangnan during the Ming and Ch'ing Dynasties," *Memoirs of the Research Department of the Toyo Bunko* 50 (1992): 1–28. For another recent articulation of the importance of culture in the maintenance of social order, see R. Bin Wong, Theodore Huters, and Pauline Yu, "Introduction: Shifting Paradigms of Political and Social Order," in R. Bin Wong, Theodore Huters, and Pauline Yu, eds., *Culture and State in Chinese History: Conventions, Accommodations, and Critiques* (Stanford: Stanford University Press, 1997), pp. 1–26.

8. For a thoughtful analysis of characterizations of "the gentry" during the late Ming period, see Martin Heijdra, "The Socio-Economic Development of Rural China during the Ming," in Denis Twitchett and Frederick Mote, eds., *The Cambridge History of China*, vols. 7 and 8 (pts. 1 and 2), *The Ming Dynasty, 1368–1644* (Cambridge: Cambridge University Press, 1998), 8:552–564; Wolfgang Franke, "Historical Writing during the Ming," in Twitchett and Mote, *The Cambridge History of China*, 8:726–782.

9. For an overview of a wide variety of activities that often entailed violence, see Frederick Wakeman, "Rebellion and Revolution: The Study of Popular Movements in Chinese History," *Journal of Asian Studies* 36.2 (1977): 201–237.

10. The sole English-language monograph devoted to rebellion during the Ming remains James Parson, *The Peasant Rebellions of the Late Ming Dynasty* (Tucson: University of Arizona Press, 1970). Chinese and Japanese scholars have shown much greater interest in rebellion during the Ming and have produced a voluminous literature. Major works on the late Ming rebellions include Li Wenzhi's classic *Wan Ming minbian* (Shanghai: Zhonghua shuju, 1948); Gu Cheng, *Mingmo nongmin zhanzhengshi* (Beijing: Zhongguo shehui kexue chubanshe, 1984); Yuan Liangyi, *Mingmo nongmin zhanzheng* (Beijing: Zhonghua shuju, 1987); Satō Fumitoshi, *Minmatsu nōmin hanran no kenkyū* (Tokyo: Kenbun shuppan, 1985).

11. Merrilyn Fitzpatrick, "Local Administration in Northern Chekiang and the Response to the Pirate Invasions of 1553–1556" (Ph.D. diss., Australian National University, 1976); Roland Higgins, "Piracy and Coastal Defense in the Ming Period, Governmental Responses to Coastal Disturbances, 1523–1549 (Ph.D. diss., University of Minnesota, 1981) and "Pirates in Gowns and Caps: Gentry Law-Breaking in the Mid-Ming," *Ming Studies* 10 (1980): 30–37; Charles Hucker, "Hu Tsung-hsien's Campaign against Hsu Hai, 1556," in Frank Kierman and John Fairbank, eds., *Chinese Ways in Warfare* (Cambridge: Harvard University Press, 1974), pp. 273–307; Kwan-wai So, *Japanese Piracy in Ming China during the Sixteenth Century* (Ann Arbor: Michigan State University Press, 1975). See also James Geiss, "The Chia-ching Reign, 1522–1566," in Twitchett and Mote, *The Cambridge History of China*, 7:490–505; Thomas Nimick, "Ch'i Chi-kuang and I-wu County," *Ming Studies* 34 (July 1995): 17–29; John Wills, "Maritime China from Wang Chih to Shih Lang: Themes in Peripheral History," in Spence and Wills, *From Ming to Ch'ing: Conquest, Region, and Continuity in Seventeenth Century China*, pp. 201–238.

12. Frederick Mote, "The Rise of the Ming Dynasty, 1330–1367," in Twitchett and Mote, *The Cambridge History of China*, 7:11. Mote's comments were made apropos conditions during the late Yuan and early Ming but have broader relevance.

13. James Tong, *Disorder under Heaven: Collective Violence in the Ming Dynasty* (Stanford: Stanford University Press, 1991).

14. Tong observed that collective violence was "rampant in peripheral and mountainous regions, during the reigns of wanton and decrepit emperors, and in periods when government troops were preoccupied with defending the empire against foreign invasions" (Tong, *Disorder under Heaven*, p. 7).

15. For a review of these groups during the Ming and Qing periods, see O Kŭm-sŏng (Oh, Keum-song), "Myŏng-Ch'ŏng sidae ŭi muroe: Yŏn'gu ŭi hyŏnhwang gwa gwache," *Tongyang sahak yŏn'gu* 50:4 (1995): 60–77.

16. Miyazaki Ichisada, "Mindai So-Sho chihō no shidaifu to minshū," *Shirin* 37.3 (1953): 1–33; Kawakatsu Mamoru, "Minmatsu Shinsho ni okeru dakō to hōkō—kyū Chūgoku shakai ni okeru burai no shoshiryō," *Shien* 119 (1982): 65–92 and "Kōnan shichin no seisan, ryūtsū, shōhi no rekishiteki ichi—shukōgyō seisan to burai, kontu, kyakufu," *Kyūshū daigaku Tōyōshi ronshū* 26 (1998): 1–28; Ueda Shin, "Minmatsu Shinsho: Kōnan no toshi no burai o meguru shakai kankei, dakō to kyakufu," *Shigaku zasshi* 90.12 (1981): 1619–1653.

17. A rapidly growing literature on all these activities has emerged to meet consumer demand in the People's Republic of China. For a highly entertaining romp through the ages, see Wanyan Shaoyuan, *Liumang de bianqian* (Shanghai: Shanghai guji chubanshe, 1993). For more scholarly discussions, see Wang Chunyu, "Mingdai liumang ji liuming yishi," *Shehuixue yanjiu* 2 (1991): 122–126, and Chen Baoliang, "Mingdai wulai jieceng de shehui huodong ji qi yingxiang," *Qi Lu xuekan* 2 (1992): 91–97. The use of corpses to accuse others of murder in the hope of extracting hush money is the subject of two essays by Miki Satoshi, "Keishō zuraikō-toku ni ihitsu (ifuku) to no kanren ni tsuite," *Shihō* 27 (1993): 1–18, and "Shigai no kyōkatsu-Chūgoku kinsei no zurai," in Dōrōbo kenkyūkai, ed., *Nusumi no bunkashi* (Tokyo: Seikyūsha, 1996), pp. 65–92. For an example of the use of a corpse as a tool of blackmail, see Feng Menglong, "A Squabble over a Single Copper Cash Leads to Strange Calamities," translated from the Chinese by Anne McLaren in her *Chinese Femme Fatale: Stories from the Ming Period* (Sydney: Wild Peony, 1994).

Pettifoggers are another important facet of this world that bears on the question of how the subaltern interacted with the imperial state. See Kawakatsu Mamoru, "Minmatsu Shinsho no shōshi ni tsuite-kyū Chūgoku shakai ni okeru burai chishikijin no ichikeitai," *Kyūshū daigaku Tōyōshi ronshū* 9 (1981): 111–129; Fuma Susumu, "Min-Shin jidai no shōshi to soshō seido," in Kaoru Mamoru, ed., *Chūgoku kinsei no hōsei to shakai* (Kyōto: Kyōto daigaku jinbun kagaku kenkyūjo, 1994), pp. 437–483, and "Shōshi hibon, *Shō Sō Ihistu,*" *Shirin* 77.2 (1994): 1–33, and "Shōshi hibon no sekai," in Ono Kazuko, ed., *Minmatsu Shinsho no shakai to bunka* (Kyōto: Kyōto daigaku jinbun kagaku kenkyūjo, 1996), pp. 189–238.

18. For a review of the traditional complaints against the pettifoggers, see Kawakatsu Mamoru, "Minmatsu Shinsho no shōshi ni tsuite" and Fuma Susumu, "Min-Shin jidai no shōshi to soshō seido."

19. This paragraph draws heavily on Fuma Susumu's important article "Min-Shin jidai no shōshi to soshō seido." See also Fuma's "Shōshi hibon *Shō Sō Ihistu*" and "Shōshi hibon no sekai." In addition to excerpts from romantic novels, jokes, riddles, drinking games, agricultural advice, and sundry other

items, popular encyclopedias from the late imperial period also commonly included sections from collections of court cases and so-called pettifoggers' manuals. See Ogawa Yōichi, *Nichiyō ruisho ni yoru Min-Shin shōsetsu no kenkyū* (Tokyo: Kenbun shuppan, 1995), pp. 54–58.

20. Fuma Susumu, "Min-Shin jidai no shōshi to soshō seido," pp. 441–443.

21. Harry Lamley, "Lineage Feuding in Southern Fujian and Eastern Guangdong under Qing Rule," in Lipman and Harrell, *Violence in China: Essays in Culture and Counterculture*, pp. 27–64, "Hsieh-tou: The Pathology of Violence in Southeastern China," *Ch'ing-shih Wen-t'i* 3.7 (1977): 1–39, and "Lineage and Surname Feuds in Southern Fukien and Eastern Kwangtung under the Ch'ing," in Liu, *Orthodoxy in Late Imperial China*, pp. 255–278; David Ownby, "The 'Ethnic Feud' in Qing Taiwan: What Is this Violence Business Anyway? An Interpretation of the 1782 Zhang-Quan Xiedou," *Late Imperial China* 11.1 (1990): 75–98, and *Brotherhoods and Secret Societies in Early and Mid-Qing China: The Formation of a Tradition* (Stanford: Stanford University Press, 1996). See also Johanna Menzel Meskill, *A Chinese Pioneer Family: The Lins of Wu-feng, Taiwan, 1729–1895* (Princeton: Princeton University Press, 1979).

Although violence was not her principal concern, Susan Naquin has examined how two large sectarian rebellions grew out of local society in North China during the late eighteenth and early nineteenth centuries. See Naquin, *Millenarian Rebellion in China: The Eight Trigrams Uprising of 1813* (New Haven: Yale University Press, 1976), and *Shantung Rebellion: The Wang Lun Uprising of 1774* (New Haven: Yale University Press, 1981). The vast pirate confederation that took shape off South China's coast during the late eighteenth and early nineteenth centuries is the focus of Dian Murray's fascinating study *Pirates of the South China Coast, 1790–1810* (Stanford: Stanford University Press, 1987).

22. See also Adrian Davis, "Homicide in the Home: Marital Strife and Familial Conflict in Eighteenth-Century China," (Ph.D. diss., Harvard University, 1995).

23. Thomas Buoye, "Economic Change and Rural Violence: Homicides Related to Disputes over Property Rights in Guangdong during the Eighteenth Century," *Peasant Studies* 17.4 (1990): 233–259, and "From Patrimony to Commodity: Changing Concepts of Land and Social Conflict in Guangdong Province during the Qianlong Reign (1736–1795)," *Late Imperial China* 14.2 (1993): 33–59.

24. Robert Antony, "Peasants, Heroes, and Brigands," *Modern China* 15.2 (April 1989): 123–148, "The Problem of Banditry and Bandit Suppression in Kwantung South China, 1780–1840," *Criminal Justice History: An International Annual* 11 (1990): 31–53, and "Scourges of the People: Perceptions of Robbery, Snatching, and Theft in the Mid-Qing Period," *Late Imperial China* 16.2 (December 1995): 98–132.

25. Some have warned against such characterizations. For instance, Philippa Maddern maintains that actual levels of violence in fifteenth-century England were much less than previous studies have argued. Maddern, *Violence and Social Order, East Anglia, 1422–1442* (Oxford: Clarendon Press, 1992), pp. 4–9, 226. Others, such as Claude Gauvard, draw attention to the fact that "fear of crime permeated French society in the late Middle Ages" and to the "percep-

tion that heinous crimes were on the increase." See Claude Gauvard, "Fear of Crime in Late Medieval France," in Barbara Hanawalt and David Wallace, eds., *Medieval Crime and Social Control* (Minneapolis: University of Minnesota Press, 1999), p. 1.

26. J. R. Hale, *Renaissance Europe: Individual and Society, 1480–1520* (Berkeley: University of California Press, 1971), pp. 27, 28. In a slightly later essay, Hale seems to downplay the role of violence in Renaissance Europe. See J. R. Hale, "Violence in the Late Middle Ages: A Background," in Lauro Martines, ed., *Violence and Civil Disorder in Italian Cities, 1200–1500* (Berkeley: University of California Press, 1972), p. 19.

27. Fernand Braudel, *The Mediterranean and the Mediterranean World in the Age of Philip II*, translated from the French by Siân Reynolds (New York: Harper and Row, 1973), p. 738.

28. Ibid., p. 745.

29. Ibid., p. 751.

30. Jacob Burckhardt, *The Civilization of the Renaissance in Italy* (New York: First Modern Library, 1954), p. 334. He further observed, "Premeditated crimes, committed professionally and for hire by third parties, occurred in Italy with great and appalling frequency" (p. 335).

31. For a discussion of the growing number of men under arms during the sixteenth and seventeenth centuries, see Frank Tallett, *War and Society in Early-Modern Europe, 1495–1715* (London: Routledge, 1992), pp. 4–20.

32. Charles Tilly, "War Making and State Making as Organized Crime," in Peter Evans, Dietrich Russchemeyer and Theda Skocpol, eds., *Bringing the State Back In* (Cambridge: Cambridge University Press, 1985), pp. 169–191; Pieter Spierenburg, *The Broken Spell: A Cultural and Anthropological History of Preindustrial Europe* (New Brunswick: Rutgers University Press, 1991), pp. 195, 221.

33. Lawrence Stone, "Interpersonal Violence in English Society, 1300–1980," *Past and Present* 101 (1983): 22–33.

34. J. A. Sharpe, "The History of Violence in England: Some Observations," *Past and Present* 108 (1985): 206–215. For further comments on the importance of violence in the historiography of early modern England, see Maddern, *Violence and Social Order: East Anglia 1422–1442*, pp. 1–26.

For further evidence of interest in violence and crime in late medieval and early modern European history, see John Bellamy, *Crime and Public Order in England in the Later Middle Ages* (London: Routledge and Kegan Paul, 1972); Guido Ruggiero, *Violence in Early Renaissance Venice* (New Brunswick: Rutgers University Press, 1980); Eric Johnson and Eric Monkknonen, eds., *The Civilization of Crime: Violence in Town and Country since the Middle Ages* (Urbana: University of Illinois Press, 1996); Edward Muir and Guido Ruggiero, eds., *History from Crime: Selections from Quaderni Storici* (Baltimore: Johns Hopkins University Press, 1994); Trevor Dean and K. J. P. Lowe, eds., *Crime, Society, and the Law in Renaissance Italy* (Cambridge: Cambridge University Press, 1994).

35. Karen Barkey, *Bandits and Bureaucrats: The Ottoman Route to State Centralization* (Ithaca: Cornell University Press, 1994).

36. George Sansom, *A History of Japan, 1334–1615* (Tokyo: Tuttle Books, 1990), pp. 217–406; John Whitney Hall, Nagahara Keiji, and Kozo Yamamura, eds., *Japan before Tokugawa: Political Consolidation and Economic Growth, 1500 to*

1650 (Princeton: Princeton University Press, 1981); Mary Elizabeth Berry, *Hideyoshi* (Cambridge: Harvard University Press, 1982). For a wide-ranging consideration of how violence influenced fifteenth- and sixteenth-century Kyoto, see Mary Elizabeth Berry, *Culture of Civil War in Kyoto* (Berkeley: University of California Press, 1994).

37. R. Bin Wong, *China Transformed: Historical Change and the Limits of European Experience* (Ithaca: Cornell University Press, 1997), pp. 92, 99.

38. For a synopsis of Sino-Portuguese relations in the early sixteenth century, see John Wills, "Relations with Maritime Europeans, 1514–1662," in Twitchett and Mote, *The Cambridge History of China,* 8:335–345. The letters are translated in Donald Ferguson, "Letters from Portuguese Captives in Canton, written in 1534 and 1536. With an introduction on Portuguese intercourse with China in the first half of the sixteenth century" (hereafter Ferguson letters), *Indian Antiquary* 30 (1901, 1902).

39. Ferguson letters, p. 59.

40. Ibid., p. 61.

41. Ibid., p. 20.

42. Ibid., p. 26.

43. Ibid., p. 30.

44. Ibid., pp. 56, 62.

45. Ibid., p. 22.

46. Ibid., p. 26.

47. Ibid., p. 56. In a far less bellicose account of China from the mid-sixteenth century, the Portuguese Galeote Pereira suggested, "And albeit the cities are so large as I say, yet the people are so weak (although innumerable) that with very little, one could in this country in a very short time do a great deal of Service to God and to our lord the king," presumably by conquest and conversion. See C. R. Boxer, ed. *South China in the Sixteenth Century* (Nendeln: Kraus Reprint Limited, 1967), p. 28.

48. Matteo Ricci and Nicola Trigault, *China in the Sixteenth Century: The Journals of Matthew Ricci, 1583–1610,* translated from the Latin by Louis Gallagher (New York: Random House, 1953), p. 59.

49. Ibid.

50. Braudel, *The Mediterranean,* p. 742.

51. Ibid., p. 752.

52. Jonathan Spence, *The Memory Palace of Matteo Ricci* (New York: Penguin Books, 1984), p. 27.

53. Cosme de Torres noted, "As a pastime they practice with their weapons, at which they are extremely adept. . . . They are very brave and put much faith in their weapons; boys over the age of thirteen carry a sword and dagger, and never take them off. . . . They are the best archers I have seen in this world." St. Francis Xavier wrote, "They greatly prize and value their arms, and prefer to have good weapons, decorated with gold and silver, more than anything else in the world. They carry a sword and dagger both inside and outside the house and lay them at their pillows when they sleep. Never in my life have I met people who rely so much on their arms. They are excellent archers." Rodrigo de Vivero y Velaso observed, "The Japanese are much braver and more warlike

than the people of China, Korea, Ternate and all the other nations around the Philippines." See Michael Cooper, ed., *They Came to Japan: An Anthology of European Reports on Japan, 1543–1640* (Berkeley: University of California Press, 1965), pp. 40–42.

54. For European views of China during these centuries, see Jonathan Spence, *The Chan's Great Continent: China in Western Minds* (New York: W. W. Norton, 1998), pp. 19–100; Raymond Dawson, *The Chinese Chameleon: An Analysis of European Perceptions of Chinese Civilization* (London: Oxford University Press, 1967), pp. 9–89; Colin Mackerras, *Western Images of China* (Hong Kong: Oxford University Press, 1989), pp. 15–42.

55. Gottfried Wilhem Leibniz, ed. and trans., with introduction, notes, and commentaries by Daniel J. Cook and Henry Rosemont, Jr., *Writings on China* (Chicago: Open Court, 1994), pp. 46–47. Cited in Spence, *The Chan's Great Continent*, pp. 84–85.

56. Montesquieu, *The Spirit of Laws*, ed., and Anne Cohler, Basia Miller, and Harold Stone, trans. (Cambridge: Cambridge University Press, 1994), p. 128. Cited in Spence, *The Chan's Great Continent*, p. 93.

57. On the enduring nature of images formed of China during the early modern period, see Zhang Longxi, *Mighty Opposites: From Dichotomies to Differences in the Comparative Study of China* (Stanford: Stanford University Press, 1998), pp. 19–54.

58. Heijdra, "Socio-Economic Development of Rural China during the Ming," p. 438.

59. Edward Peters, *Europe and the Middle Ages* (Englewood Cliffs, N.J.: Prentice-Hall, 1989), p. 142. I should like to thank my former colleague David Routt for bringing this source to my attention.

60. Halil Inalcik, "Introduction: Empire and Population," in Halil Inalcik with Donald Quataert, eds., *An Economic and Social History of the Ottoman Empire, 1300–1914* (Cambridge: Cambridge University Press, 1994), p. 29.

61. The other Ming capital was at Nanking. See Edward Farmer, *Early Ming Government, The Evolution of Dual Capitals* (Cambridge: Harvard University, 1976). For the development of Beijing, see James Geiss, "Peking under the Ming (1368–1644)," (Ph.D. diss., Princeton University, 1979).

62. Based on annual tonnages of tribute grain delivered to Beijing, Joanne Wakeland estimates the population of the capital as "between 800,000 and 1 million people" (p. 92). For her calculations, see "Metropolitan Administration in Ming China: Sixteenth Century Beijing" (Ph.D. diss., University of Michigan, 1982), pp. 83–92. Han Dacheng also estimates the population of Beijing to have been approximately one million by the sixteenth century; see *Mingdai chengshi yanjiu* (Beijing: Zhongguo renmin daxue chubanshe, 1991), pp. 59–60, and "Mingdai Beijing jingji shulüe," *Beijing shehui kexue* 4 (1991): 93. On the hazards of calculating Ming Beijing population figures, see Aramiya Manabu, "Mindai no shuto Pekin no toshi jinkō ni tsuite," *Yamagata daigaku shigaku ronshū* 11 (February 1991): 23–46.

63. Han Dacheng, *Mingdai chengshi yanjiu*, pp. 49, 67, 73, 74, 88, 92–103.

64. The estimate for Venice comes from Carlo Cipolla, *Before the Industrial Revolution: European Society and Economy, 1000–1700* (New York: W. W. Norton,

1980), p. 303. I should like to thank my former colleague David Routt for bringing this source to my attention. The figures for Constantinople are from Inalcik,
"Introduction: Empire and Population," p. 18.

65. On economic conditions in Eurasia during the fifteenth and sixteenth
centuries, see William Atwell, "Yūrashia no 'Daikinginkō,'" *Kokusai kōryū* 62
(1993): 54–60. For a broad overview of the Ming economy with an emphasis on
its international dimensions, see William Atwell, "Ming China and the 'Emerging World Economy,' 1470–1650," in Twitchett and Mote, *The Cambridge History
of China*, 8:376–416.

66. Andre Gunder Frank, *ReOrient: Global Economy in the Asian Age* (Berkeley: University of California Press, 1998), p. 117. Timothy Brook has also
argued that "China, not Europe, was the center of the world in Ming times."
Brook, *The Confusions of Pleasure: Commerce and Culture in Ming China* (Berkeley:
University of California Press, 1998), p. xvi.

67. Wang Ao, *Zhenze changyu* (early sixteenth century; reprinted in *Jilu
huibian*, ed. Shen Jiefu, 1617; reprint, Taibei: Taiwan shangwu chubanshe, 1969),
2.30a. This figure is also cited in John Dardess, *A Ming Society: T'ai-ho County,
Kiangsi, in the Fourteenth to Seventeenth Centuries* (Berkeley: University of California Press, 1996), p. 141. Dardess writes that subbureaucracy was approximately three times the size of the official bureaucracy, which seems very low.
Nimick has noted that by late Ming times, larger counties reportedly had as
many as 1,000 staff members, while smaller ones employed between 400 and
500 men. See Thomas Nimick, "The County, the Magistrate, and the Yamen in
Late Ming China" (Ph.D. diss., Princeton University, 1993), p. 34.

68. For the unofficial administrative units below the county level, see
Timothy Brook, "The Spatial Structure of Ming Local Administration," *Late
Imperial China* 6.1 (June 1985): 1–55.

69. The quote is from the English translation of Mendoza's *Historia de las
cosas mas notables, ritos y costumbres del gran Reyno de la China*, as cited in Donald
Lach, *Asia in the Making of Europe* (Chicago: University of Chicago Press, 1965),
1:764. Lach provides an enlightening survey of European reporting and impres-
sions of China during the sixteenth century (pp. 730–821).

70. One wonders if Barkey and others somewhat understate the amount
of negotiation that occurred in Europe. Barkey, *Bandits and Bureaucrats*, pp. 1–
17. Donald Smail has drawn attention to the unplanned and highly negotiated
nature of the transition from resolution of conflict through personal vengeance
to court-centered justice in late medieval France. See Smail, "Common Violence:
Vengeance and Inquisition in Fourteenth Century Marseille," *Past and Present*
151 (May 1996): 28–59.

71. Uwe Danker has argued that the Holy Roman Empire had a strong
interest in exaggerating the threat of bandits as a way to extend the power of
the state and as a way to emphasize the state's role as the legitimate defender
of a divinely sanctioned social order. See Danker, "Bandits and the State: Robbers and the Authorities in the Holy Roman Empire in the Late Seventeenth
and Early Eighteenth Centuries," in Richard Evans, ed., *The German Underworld: Deviants and Outcasts in German History* (London: Routledge, 1988), pp.
75–107. Nathan Brown has stressed the utility of inflating the threat of bandits
as a way to extend state control over society. See Brown, "Brigands and State

Building: The Invention of Banditry in Modern Egypt," *Comparative Studies in Society and History* 32.2 (April 1990): 258–281.

72. Parallel efforts may be seen in the state's efforts to incorporate local religious practices into officially approved traditions. See Terry Kleeman, "Licentious Cults and Bloody Victuals: Sacrifice, Reciprocity, and Violence in Traditional China," *Asia Major* (third series) 8.1 (1994): 206.

73. For an analysis that addresses violence in terms of Buddhist idealism, see Brandauer, "Violence and Buddhist Idealism in the *Xiyou* Novels." For an allegorical interpretation of the novel that stresses neo-Confucian concern with cultivation of the mind, see Andrew Plaks, *The Four Masterworks of the Ming Novel* (Princeton: Princeton University Press, 1987), pp. 183–276.

74. Conducted in the immediate wake of the founding of the People's Republic of China, the earliest studies of the rebellion were heavily influenced by ideological and political concerns that stressed the importance of peasant resistance against feudal regimes and role of such struggles as the primary driving force in Chinese history. The two most important essays of this period include Zhao Lisheng, "Mingdai Zhengdejian jici nongmin qiyi de jingguo he tedian," *Wenshizhe* 12 (1954), reprinted in Zhao Lisheng and Gao Zhaoyi, eds., *Zhongguo nongmin zhanzhengshi lunwenji* (Shanghai: Xinzhishi chubanshe, 1955), pp. 134–153; Li Guangbi, "Ming zhongye Liu Liu Liu Qi da nongmin qiyi," *Lishi jiaoxue* 4 (1951): 21–25. Later published in a slightly expanded version in Li Guangbi, et al., *Zhongguo nongmin qiyi lunji* (Beijing: Sanlian shudian, 1958), pp. 267–287.

Scholarship related to the rebellion entered a second stage during the 1970s. The Japanese scholar Nishimura Genshō made important contributions to our understanding of the rebellion in two ways. First, he vastly expanded the documentary base by making systematic use of more private jottings and imperially compiled records. Second, he offered an alternate theoretical explanation for the rebellion. Nishimura characterized the rebel leaders as *wulai*, or local toughs. Although I agree with Nishimura on many counts, his analysis of these local toughs is often panhistorical and gives insufficient attention to the importance of regional and historical variations. See Nishimura Genshō, "Ryū Roku Ryū Shichi no ran ni tsuite," *Tōyōshi kenkyū* 32.4 (1974): 44–86. Also very useful is Nishimura's annotated translation of a seventeenth-century narrative of the rebellion; see "Ryū Roku Ryū Shichi no ran," in Mori Masao and Tanigawa Michio, eds., *Chūgoku minshū hanranshi* (Tokyo: Heibonsha, 1979), 2:409–468.

People's Republic of China (PRC) scholar Chen Gaohua made similar, though independent, contributions to the scholarship on the rebellion. Chen also characterized the leadership of the rebellion less as peasants than local bandits. Perhaps even more important, Chen made available in an appendix the full text of a previously unknown manuscript that included reports made by imperial authorities based on the interrogations of two important figures in the rebellion. I make extensive use of this manuscript, which was later published in a series of important but rare Ming period primary documents. See Chen Gaohua, "Mingdai zhongye Liu Liu, Yang Hu qiyi de ji ge wenti," *Zhongguo nongmin zhanzhengshi luncong* (Shanxi: Renmin chubanshe, series no. 1, 1978), pp. 305–350. The manuscript noted above is Xie Fen, *Hou jian lu* (early sixteenth century), which was reprinted in Xie Guozhen, ed., *Mingshi ziliao congkan*

(1st series, Jiangsu renmin chubanshe, 1981), pp. 4–160. For the historical value of the *Hou jian lu,* see Wu Xinli, "Xie Fen de Hou jian lu ji qi shiliao jiazhi," *Zhongguoshi yanjiu* 1 (1980): 151–159.

A number of shorter essays have focused on a particular element of the rebellion, generally single battles, newly excavated stone inscriptions, or minor questions of dating. These articles will be mentioned when relevant in the body of the narrative.

75. Chen Baoliang's discussion of scores of related terms extends for forty pages. Chen Baoliang, *Zhongguo liumangshi* (Beijing: Zhongguo shehui kexue, 1993), pp. 1–40. For a discussion of the term *"liumang,"* with an emphasis on its use during the modern period, see Sakai Tadao, "Chūgokushijō no bō to ryūbō," in Noguchi Tetsurō, ed., *Chūgokushi ni okeru ran no kōzu* (Tokyo: Yūzankaku, 1986), pp. 11–34.

76. *Mencius,* Penguin Classics edition, 1970, p. 103.

77. See Chu Hung-lam, "Huang Zuo's Meeting with Wang Yangming and the Debate over the Unity of Knowledge and Action," *Ming Studies* 35 (August 1995): 60 n. 31.

78. For examples of the founder's use of the term *"haojie,"* see *Taizu shilu* (hereafter *TZSL*), in *Ming shilu* (1418 to mid-seventeenth century; facsimile reproduction of *Guoli Beiping tushuguan cang hongge chaoben,* 133 vols.; Taibei: Zhongyang yanjiuyuan lishi yuyan yanjiusuo, 1961–1966), 31.2a, 35.5a.

79. Zhao Yi, *Nian ershi zhaji.* Prefaces 1795 and 1800. Cited in Chen Baoliang, *Zhongguo liumangshi,* p. 38.

80. Sima Qian et al., *Shiji* (Beijing: Zhonghua shuju, 1959), chap. 124. I might also mention chapter 86 of Sima Qian, entitled "Assassins," which deals with men of varying social backgrounds who sacrificed everything in their efforts to fulfill what they understood as their duty.

This ambiguity finds a parallel in medieval European notions of chivalric violence, which as Maddern has noted, "simultaneously sustained the perfect knight and gave rise to the banditry and oppression of errant mercenaries" (Maddern, *Violence and Social Order, East Anglia, 1422–1442,* p. 13).

81. For discussions of the compilation, limitations, and biases of the *Ming Veritable Records,* see Wu Han, "Ji Ming shilu," *Zhongyang yanjiuyuan lishi yuyan yanjiusuo jikan* 18 (1948): 385–447 (in *Dushi zhaji,* 1956; reprint, Beijing: Shenghuo dushu xinzhi sanlian shudian, 1960); Mano Senryū, "Mindai rekichō jitsuroku no seiritsu," in Tamura Jitsuzō, ed., *Mindai Man-Mōshi kenkyū* (Kyōto: Kyōto daigaku bungakubu, 1963), pp. 1–72; Wolfgang Franke, "The Veritable Records of the Ming Dynasty (1368–1644)," in Edwin Pulleyblank and William Beasley, eds., *Historians of China and Japan* (London: Oxford University Press, 1961), pp. 60–77.

82. The dating of the compilation is problematic, but Franke estimates it to have been between 1531 and 1533. See Franke, *Introduction to the Sources of Ming History* (Kuala Lumpur: University of Malaya Press, 1969), p. 187. For a discussion of the work's preface and the problems surrounding its dating and authorship, see Niida Noboru, "Kyūshōhon Kō Min jōhō jiruisan shiken," *Tōyō gakuen* 27.4 (1940): 602–620; Huang Zhangjian, *Mingdai lüli huibian* (Taibei: Zhongyang yanjiuyuan lishi yuyan yanjiusuo zhuankan, no. 75, 1979), pp. 3–5. For a brief bibliographic note, see Nagasawa Kikuya, "Kō Min jōhō jirui o

miru," *Shoshigaku* 15.2 (1941): 27–32. On its value as a historical document, see Wang Yuquan, "Huang Ming tiaofa shilei zuan duhou," *Mingdai yanjiu luncong* 1 (1982): 1–28, and Li Jianziong, "Yibu you jiazhi dan chongman le yiwen de Mingdai guji," *Lishi jiaoxue wenti* 1 (1987): 55–57, 63.

83. Silas Wu, "The Transmission of Ming Memorials and the Evolution of the Transmission Network, 1368–1627," *T'oung-pao* 54 (1968): 275–287; Yin Yun-gong, *Zhongguo Mingdai xinwen chuanboshi* (Chongqing: Chongqing chuban-she, 1990), pp. 23–36. For a more detailed discussion of two chief varieties of memorials, see Sakurai Toshirō, "Mindai daisōhon seido no seiritsu to sono henyō," *Tōyōshi kenkyū* 51.2 (1992): 175–203.

84. The best discussion of this question remains Wu Han, "Ji Ming shilu."

85. *Wuzong shilu* (hereafter *WZSL*), in *Ming shilu* (1418 to mid-seventeenth century; facsimile reproduction of *Guoli Beiping tushuguan cang hongge chaoben*, 133 vols.; Taibei: Zhongyang yanjiuyuan lishi yuyan yanjiusuo, 1961–1966), 30.2b–3a.

86. The imperial state held no monopoly over this lofty rhetoric. As James Cahill has convincingly demonstrated, a considerable gap existed between the idealized rhetoric of painters and connoisseurs, who professed utter disdain for any and all commercial considerations and the extensive influence of money and negotiation in the commission, execution, and marketing of paint-ing in late imperial China. See James Cahill, *The Painter's Practice: How Artists Lived and Worked in Traditional China* (New York: Columbia University Press, 1994). For a discussion of the dangers of misleading official rhetoric in India, see Ranajit Guha, "The Prose of Counter-Insurgency," in Ranajit Guha and Gayatari Chakravotry, eds., *Selected Subaltern Studies* (Oxford: Oxford Univer-sity Press, 1988), pp. 45–86.

Chapter 2   The Capital Region

1. Edward Farmer, *Early Ming Government: The Evolution of Dual Capitals* (Cambridge: East Asian Research Center, Harvard University, 1976).

2. For an excellent account of the transformation, see James Geiss, "Peking under the Ming (1368–1644)" (Ph.D. diss., Princeton University, 1979).

3. See Philip Huang, *The Peasant Economy and Social Change in North China* (Stanford: Stanford University Press, 1985), pp. 53–66; Ramon Myers, *The Chi-nese Peasant Economy: Agricultural Development in Hopei and Shantung, 1890–1949* (Cambridge: Harvard University Press, 1970), pp. 8–12. For a description of the area with more emphasis on Shandong, see also Joseph Esherick, *Origins of the Boxer Uprising* (Berkeley: University of California Press, 1987), pp. 1–17; Martin Heijdra, "The Socio-Economic Development of Rural China during the Ming," in Denis Twitchett and Frederick Mote, eds., *The Cambridge History of China*, vols. 7 and 8 (pts. 1 and 2), *The Ming Dynasty, 1368–1644* (Cambridge: Cam-bridge University Press, 1998), 8:291–294. Most recently, Kenneth Pomeranz has discussed the ecological degradation of this region during the nineteenth and early twentieth centuries. See Pomeranz, *Making of a Hinterland: State, Society, and Economy in Inland North China, 1853–1937* (Berkeley: University of Cali-fornia Press, 1993).

4. See "Yi ling Wu jun de zheng bei ji," *Wenan xianzhi* (1922), 9.3a, 3:885; *Wenan xianzhi* (1703), 3.17a. On the role of deforestation in flooding, see Zhang

Gang, "Mingdai Beizhili diqu de nongye jingji," *Hebei xuekan* 1 (1989): 65–70, esp. p. 69.

Approximately 60 percent of Bazhou's annual rainfall of 543 mm. (about 22 inches) falls in July and August. Rainfall patterns are largely the same in Wenan, with 577 mm. (about 23 inches) of annual rainfall (Hebeisheng cehuiju, ed., *Hebeisheng fenxian dituce* [Beijing: Zhongguo ditu chubanshe, 1992], pp. 23–24). See also Francesca Bray and Joseph Needham, *Science and Civilisation in China*, vol. 6, *Biology and Biological Technology*, pt. 2, *Agriculture* (Cambridge: Cambridge University Press, 1984), p. 14.

5. The elevation of Wenan is between 2 meters in the southwest to 7.5 meters in the northeast, while Bazhou ranges between 12 and 15 meters above sea level (*Hebei sheng fenxian dituce*, pp. 23–24). For a general description of North China, see Needham and Bray, *Science and Civilisation in China*, pp. 14–15. Elizabeth Perry describes the overlapping Huaibei region in her *Rebels and Revolutionaries in North China, 1845–1945* (Stanford: Stanford University Press, 1987), pp. 18–25.

6. Ji Kejia, "Yi hou Zhenggong jianzheng bei ji," 1629 *Wenan xianzhi*, 7.66a–b.

7. Song authorities also noted that many bandit bases were located in swampy or mountainous areas, as well as places near jurisdictional borders. See Brian McKnight, *Law and Order in Sung China* (Cambridge: Cambridge University Press, 1992), pp. 109–111.

8. *Wenan xianzhi* (1629), 4.58a–b; 1548 *Bazhou zhi* 5.6a, Jiajing ed. of *Zhuozhou zhi* 3.4a. While rice is mentioned in both the *Bazhou zhi* and the *Zhuozhou zhi*, it would not be more widely cultivated in the capital region until late in the sixteenth century. See Han Dacheng, *Mingdai chengshi yanjiu* (Beijing: Zhongguo renmin daxue chubanshe, 1991), pp. 22–24; Cong Hanxiang, "14 shiji houqi zhi 16 shijimo Huabei pingyuan nongcun jingji fazhan de kaocha," *Zhongguo jingjishi yanjiu* 3 (1986): 18–20. Also, Zhang Gang, "Mingdai Beizhili diqu de nongye jingji," pp. 65–70.

9. *Wenan xianzhi* (1629), 4.58a–b; 1548 *Bazhou zhi* 5.9b; JJ *Zhuozhou zhi* 3.4a–b. Also, Zhang Gang, "Mingdai Beizhili diqu de nongye jingji," pp. 67–68; Cong Hanxiang, "Shisi shiji houqi zhi shiliu shiji mo Huabei pingyuan nongcun fazhan de kaocha," *Zhongguo jingjishi yanjiu* 3 (1986): 21–22.

10. While salt merchants would reach the apogee of wealth only later in the Ming, even by 1540 they were prominent in the region (1540 *Hejian fuzhi* 10.3b). See Zhang Zengyuan, "Tianjin yanshang yiqie," *Tianjinshi yanjiu* 2 (1986): 12–19; Lin Chunye and Zhang Zengyuan, "Ming-Qing caoyun he yanye yu Tianjin chengshi de fazhan," *Tianjinshi yanjiu* 2 (1987): 13–24. A Salt Distribution Commissioner was based in Cangzhou.

11. Kataoka Shibako, "Minmatsu Shinsho no Kahoku ni okeru nōka keiei," *Shakai keizai shigaku* 25.2–3 (June 1959): 77–100; Adachi Keiji, "Shindai Kahoku no nōgyō keiei to shakai kōzō," *Shirin* 64.4 (July 1981): 66–93; Philip Huang, *The Peasant Economy and Social Change in North China*, pp. 85–105.

12. For an overview of North China's economy with an emphasis on the late Ming, see Xu Hong, "Mingdai houqi huabei shangpin jingji de fazhan yu shehui fengqi de bianqian," *Dierci Zhongguo jindai jingjishi huiyi* (Taibei: Institute of Economics, Academica Sinica, 1989), 1:107–173. In a 1960 article, Yamane

Yukio argued that periodic markets first reemerged in North China (he examined Shandong in most detail) during the Zhengde period and again with greater strength in the Wanli period. See Yamane, "Min-Shin jidai Kahoku ni okeru teikishi," *Tōkyō joshi daigaku shiron* 8 (1960): 495 (reprinted in Yamane Yukio, *Min-Shin kahoku teikishi no kenkyū* [Tokyo: Kyūko shoen, 1995]). This article was translated as "Periodic Markets in North China during the Ming and Ch'ing Periods," *Occasional Papers of Research Publications and Translations* 23 (1967): 109–142. He later revised his evaluation, saying that they reemerged during the later half of the fifteenth century (1465–1521) and gained strength during the Jiajing period (1522–1566). See "Min-Shinsho no Kahoku no shishū to shinshi to gōmin," in *Nakayama Hachirō kyōju shōju kinen Min Shinshi ronsō* (Tokyo: Ryōgen shoten, 1977), pp. 305–330. Reprinted in *Min-Shin Kahoku teikishi no kenkyū*. Two more of Yamane's articles bear directly on the markets of North China: "Min-Shin jidai Kahoku shishū no gakō," in *Hoshi hakushi taikan kinen Chūgokushi ronshū* (Yamagata: Hoshi Ayao sensei taikan kinen jigyōkai, 1978), pp. 227–248. Reprinted in his *Min-Shin kahoku teikishi no kenkyū*; Yamane Yukio, "Kahoku no byōkai: Santōshō o chūshin ni shite," *Tōkyō joshi daigaku shiron* 17 (1967): 1–22. Reprinted in his *Min-Shin kahoku teikishi no kenkyū*. See also Han Dacheng's *Mingdai chengshi yanjiu* for two appendices on *zhenshi* in the Ming (pp. 666–703).

For an overview of cities on the Grand Canal during the Ming and Qing, see Yang Zhengtai, "Ming Qing shiqi Changjiang yi beiyunhe chengzhen de tedian yu bianqian," *Lishi dili yanjiu* 1 (1986): 104–129.

13. *Wenan xianzhi* (1629), 2.18a–b.

14. *Bazhou zhi* (1548), 1.17b; JJ *Zhuozhou zhi* 2.6a–b. There were four periodic markets in Fangshan (*Zhouzhou zhi* 2.8a–b). In Bazhou, eight of the thirteen markets were outside the city walls, while in Zhuozhou and Fangshan, the numbers were five and three, respectively.

15. *Hejian fuzhi* (1540), 10.3b. For instance, iron agricultural implements were transported by carts from Linqing to Potou.

16. Ishihara Jun, "Kahokushō ni okeru Min-Shin-Minkoku jidai no teiki-ichi-funpu, kaisō oyobi chūshin shūraku no kankei ni tsuite," *Chirigaku hyōron* 46.4 (1973): 245–263. For charts of numbers, distribution of markets, and relation to population density, see pp. 247–251. While this is the most sophisticated work covering the Ming period for Hebei, Ishihara takes population figures contained in local gazetteers at face value. His estimates for population density and their relation to periodic markets must therefore be viewed with caution.

17. Cong Hanxiang, "Shisi shiji houqi zhi shiliu shiji mo Huabei pingyuan nongcun fazhan de kaocha," pp. 21–22; Adachi, "Shindai kahoku no nōgyō keiei to shakai kōzō, p. 66. On the economic status of Henan and Shandong during the Ming, see Fu Yiling, "Mingdai jingjishi shang de Shandong he Henan," *Shehui kexue zhanxian* 3 (1983): 119–127.

18. The classic work on the economic life of Beijing is Xu Daling's "Mingdai Beijing de jingji shenghuo," *Beijing daxue xuebao* 42 (1959): 185–207. See also James Geiss, "Peking under the Ming," (Ph.D. diss., Princeton University, 1979), and Han Dacheng, "Mingdai Beijing jingji shulüe," *Beijing shehui kexue* 4 (1991): 93–105.

19. Wang Ling, *Beijing yu zhouwei chengshi guanxishi* (Beijing: Beijing Yan-

shan chubanshe, 1988), pp. 81–105; Guo Yunjing, "Ming-Qing shiqi Tianjin yuye," *Tianjinshi yanjiu* 1 (1987): 1–5. Wang Ling's work represents an important attempt to explain the complex connections between Beijing and the other cities of Hebei.

20. Wang Ling, *Beijing yu zhouwei chengshi guanxishi*, p. 81.

21. Ibid., p. 128.

22. Ray Huang, "The Grand Canal during the Ming Dynasty, 1368–1644," (Ph.D. diss., University of Michigan, 1964), p. 66.

23. See Xu, "Mingdai Beijing de jingji shenghuo," esp. n. 6, for description of goods in Beijing. See also Geiss, "Peking under the Ming (1368–1644)," for mercantile activities in Beijing.

24. One reflection of this is that imperial relatives and favorites attempted to use their political influence in these places for economic gain. See Han Dacheng, *Mingdai shehui jingji chutan*, pp. 356–394. On thriving commerce in Liangxiang and close ties to the capital, see Yuan Zhongdao, "Chi ci Wanshou Chanyuan bei ji" (composed 1617), in *Liangxiang xianzhi* (1924), 8.41b–42a, and Liu Wenchen, "Chong xiu Liangxiang xianshu bei" (composed 1506), 8.39b.

25. William Skinner, "Regional Urbanization in Nineteenth Century China," and "Cities and the Hierarchy of Local Systems," in Skinner, ed., *The City in Late Imperial China* (Stanford: Stanford University Press, 1977), pp. 211–236 and pp. 281–301.

26. The best discussion of the internal migration policies during the early Ming is Xu Hong (Hung Hsu), "Ming Hongwu nianjian de renkou yixi," in Zhongyang yanjiuyuan sanmin zhuyi yanjiusuo, ed., *Dierjie lishi yu Zhongguo shehui bianqian yantaohui* (Taibei: Zhongyang yanjiuyuan sanmin zhuyi yanjiuyuan, 1982), pp. 252–293. A later, shorter article in English by Xu summarizes the important points of his 1982 essay and expands the discussion to the Yongle reign. See "The Internal Migration Policy during the Early Ming Period," *Taiwan daxue Wen shi zhe xuebao* 36 (December 1989): 51–76. See also Cao Shuji, "Hongwu shiqi Hebei diqu de renkou qianyi," *Zhongguo nongshi* 14.3 (1995): 12–27; "Yongle nianjian Hebei diqu de renkou qianyi," *Zhongguo nongshi* 15.3 (1996): 33–53, 61; Zhang Gang, "Guanyu Mingchu Hebei yimin de kaocha," *Hebei xuekan* 4 (1983): 144–148; Tian Weiping and Liang Yong, "Mingdai Hebei yimin wenti chuyi," *Hebei shiyuan xuebao* 2 (1988): 58–64. For the garrisons relocated into the area, see Wei Lianke, "Mingchu Hebei yimin shiliao jibu," *Hebei xuekan* 5 (1989): 75–77. For more on the origins and numbers of those relocated to Hebei during the early Ming, see Ishida Hiroshi, "Kaihōzen no Kahoku nōson no ichi seikaku-toku ni sonraku to byō to no kanren ni oite," (1); *Kansei daigaku keizai ronshū*, 32.2–3 (1984). Reprinted in Ishida, *Chūgoku nōson shakai keizai kōzō no kenkyū* (Kyoto: Kōyō shobo, 1986), pp. 141–305, esp. 144–153.

27. See Wang Yuquan, *Mingdai de juntun* (Beijing: Zhonghua shuju, 1965); Foon Ming Liew, "Tuntian Farming of the Ming Dynasty" (Ph.D. diss., University of Hamburg, 1984).

28. Lu Liang, "Mingchu yimin dui Hebei juluo diming de yingxiang," *Diming zhishi* 1 (1988): 28–30; Yin Junke, "Mingdai Beijing jiaoqu cunluo de fazhan," *Lishi dili* 3 (1983): 121–130. See also Cao Shumei, "Tangshan Mingdai yimin dimingqun," *Diming zhishi* 5 (1991): 20.

29. Mengcun Huizu zizhixian gaikuang, ed., *Mengcun Huizu zizhixian gai-*

kuang (Shijiazhuang: Hebei Renmin chubanshe, 1983), p. 8; Li Heping, "Hebei de Huihui minzu," *Ningxia shehui kexue* 1 (1986): 35.

30. Mengcun, *Mengcun Huizu zizhixian gaikuang*, p. 9; Yang Shaoyou and Mo Junqin, *Mingdai minzushi* (Chengdu: Sichuan minzu chubanshe, 1996), pp. 186–187.

31. Mu Dequan, "Mingdai Huizu de fenbu," *Ningxia daxue xuebao* 3 (1987): 87.

32. For the history of Bajiquan, see Wu Lianzhi, *Goshi kaimon hachikyūken* (Tokyo: Beisubourumagajinsha, 1991), pp. 5–15.

33. Henry Serruys, "Landgrants to the Mongols in China: 1400–1460," *Monumenta Serica* 25 (1966): 394. In addition to Serruys' meticulous work, a few Chinese scholars have touched on the question of the Mongols in Ming China. See Xu Hong, "Ming Hongwu nianjian de renkou qianxi," pp. 238–239; Wu Yunting, "Tumu zhi bian qianhou de Menggu jiangren," *Hebei xuekan* 3 (1989): 106–111; He Guanbiao, *Yuan Ming jian Zhongguo jingnei Mengguren zhi nongye gaikuang* (Hong Kong: Xuejin chubanshe, 1977); Yang Shaoyou and Mo Junqin, *Mingdai minzushi*, pp. 117–121; Di Fusheng, "Shilun Mingchao chuqi juzhu zai neidi de Mengguren," *Minzu yanjiu* 3 (1996): 70–77.

34. Henry Serruys, "The Mongols in China: 1400–1450," *Monumenta Serica* 27 (1968): 234, 256–265, and "Foreigners in the Metropolitan Police during the Fifteenth Century," *Oriens Extremus* 8.1 (1961): 59–83.

35. Henry Serruys, "Remains of Mongol Customs in China during the Early Ming Period," *Monumenta Serica* 16 (1957): 137–190 (reprinted in *The Mongols and Ming China: Customs and History*, ed. Françoise Aubin, Variorum Reprints, 1987, London); "Landgrants to the Mongols in China: 1400–1450," pp. 395–396, 404; "The Mongols in China: 1400–1450," pp. 285, 304–305. While Serruys' work extends through only the fifteenth century, my readings indicate that these communities retained much of their Mongol culture and customs well into the sixteenth century.

36. Serruys, "The Mongols in China: 1400–1450," pp. 241–244, 305, and "Foreigners in the Metropolitan Police during the Fifteenth Century," p. 83. See also David Robinson, "Politics, Force, and Ethnicity in Ming China: Mongols and the Abortive Coup of 1461," *Harvard Journal of Asiatic Studies* 59.1 (June 1999): 79–123.

37. Shen Dingping, "Mingdai qianqi jieji douzheng shulun," *Mingshi yanjiu luncong* 3 (1985): 214–238. Shen's arguments about the latter stages of feudalism and class conflict are less interesting than the sense of movement in much of China during the fifteenth century conveyed in this article.

38. For a discussion of the problems involved with population estimates for the Ming, see Heijdra, "Socio-Economic Development of Rural China during the Ming," pp. 428–433.

39. Wanli *Da Ming huidian, juan* 19, 1:341–349, used in Liang Fangzhong, *Zhongguo lidai hukou, tiandi, tianfu tongji* (Shanghai: Shanghai renmin chubanshe, 1980), pp. 203. See also Gao Shulin, "Hebei gudai renkou fazhan gaishu," *Hebei xuekan* 3 (1985): 68–72, esp. pp. 71–72. Gao's analysis is based almost exclusively on official government figures found in the standard histories. Ray Huang has noted that sixteenth-century population reports were even less reliable than official land reports and that underreporting was universal (*Taxation*

and Governmental Finance in Sixteenth Century China [Cambridge: Cambridge University Press, 1974], p. 61).

40. *Shuntian fuzhi* (1593), 3.1b–9a.

41. *Bazhou zhi* (1548), 5.1a. This is markedly lower than the figure of 65,356 given in the 1593 *Shuntian Prefectural Gazetteer*, 3.1b–9a. While the [Wanli period] *Shuntian fuzhi* (1593) also gives the official figure of 3720, the editors write that the actual number was 3,072 (3.1b–9a).

42. *Bazhou zhi* (1548), 5.1b.

43. Ibid., 4.2a–3a.

44. *Hejian fuzhi* (1540), 8.2a.

45. Some observers commented on Bazhou's wealth. For instance, a 1486 essay commemorating the repair of Bazhou's city walls noted, "In terms of the steadfastness of its city walls, the density of markets, prosperity of people's material goods, Bazhou is superior to other [neighboring?] counties" (Liu Ji, "Liu hou xiuzao ji," *Bazhou zhi* [1548], 8.13b). In the same piece, however, the authors note that because of its proximity to the capital, Bazhou was burdened with supplying Beijing with various goods and services.

46. Heijdra, "The Socio-Economic Development of Rural China during the Ming," pp. 484–485.

47. Heijdra suggests that degree holders in the early to mid-Ming were small in number and limited in influence (pp. 329–332). The Korean scholar O Kŭm-sŏng has observed that "if a lineage were able to secure even the status of a licentiate generation after generation, as a privileged group, they would be able to lord it over commoners in the village" (*Mindai shakai keizaishi kenkyū* [Tokyo: Kyūko shoin, 1990], p. 53).

48. *Wenan xianzhi* (1922), 4.26a–29a (4:355–361), 4.43b–44a (pp. 390–391), 4.45b–46b (pp. 394–396).

49. Ibid., 4.7a–9b, 1:317–322. O Kŭm-sŏng has estimated that between four and five thousand provincial scholars were in China as a whole during the early sixteenth century (*Mindai shakai keizaishi kenkyū*, p. 59).

50. *Wenan xianzhi* (1922), 4.1b, 1:306.

51. This estimate is derived by counting all who received degrees between 1450 and 1510.

52. Judging from their considerable burial complexes listed in the 1629 *Wenan xianzhi*, as well as the frequency with which they appear in other sections of the gazetteer, the Ji, Wang, Hao, Jiang, and Zhao lineages appear to have been the dominant families by the late Ming (2.20a–21a). On the significance of burial practices in Hebei, see Myron Cohen, "Lineage Organization in North China," *Journal of Asian Studies* 44.3 (August 1990): 509–534.

53. Li Shi, "Xiu cheng ji," *Wenan xianzhi* (1922), 9.7a, 3:893.

54. See David Robinson, "Notes on Hebei Eunuchs during the Mid-Ming," *Ming Studies* 34 (July 1995): 1–16. For an anecdotal introduction to eunuchs in Chinese history, see Mitamura Taisuke, *Chinese Eunuchs: The Structure of Intimate Politics* (Tokyo: Charles E. Tuttle Company, 1970, 2d printing 1992), a translation of *Kangan: Sokkin seiji no kōzō* (Tokyo: Chūō kōronsha, 1963). For the most comprehensive treatment available in English of eunuchs during the Ming, see Henry Shih-shan Tsai, *The Eunuchs of the Ming Dynasty* (Albany: State University of New York Press, 1996).

55. Huang Zhangjian, "Lun *Huang Ming zuxun lu* suoji Mingchu huan-guan zhidu," *Zhongyang yanjiuyuan lishi yuyan yanjiusuo jikan* 32 (1961): 77–97.

56. Robert Crawford, "Eunuch Power in the Ming Dynasty," *T'oung-pao* 49.3 (1961): 115–148; Noda Tōru, "Minchō kangan no seijiteki chii ni tsuite," *Kyūshū daigaku Tōyōshi kenkyū ronshū* 21 (1993): 47–64. For eunuchs' role as pro-vincial "Grand Defenders," see Fang Zhiyuan, "Mingdai de zhenshou zhong-guan zhidu," *Wenshi* 49 (1994): 131–145; Noda Tōru, "Mindai gaikangan no ichi keitai ni tsuite-chinshu kangan o megutte," *Kyūshū daigaku Tōyōshi kenkyū ronshū* 24 (1996): 34–44. For their supervisory role over the "Four Guards" and the "Valiants Garrison," see Fang Zhiyuan, "Mingdai de siwei, yongshi ying," *Dierjie Ming Qingshi guoji xueshu taolunhui lunwenji* (Tianjin: Tianjin renmin chubanshe, 1993), pp. 489–499.

57. The numbers involved could be large. For instance, Wang Hong (js. 1503) wrote that more than 3,500 castrated men of commoner and military households from Shuntian Prefecture petitioned the throne for positions dur-ing the Zhengde reign (cited in Shimizu Taiji, "Jikyū kangan no kenkyū," *Shi-gaku zasshi* 43.1 [1931]: 120). For the fate of those men who did not gain a post, see below.

Gu Dayong, Ma Yongcheng, and Zhang Zhong, all well-known eunuchs, were said to have been from Bazhou or Wenan (*Jishi jiwen, juan* 4, p. 93). For a more detailed description of Zhang Zhong and his role as a local mediator in Bazhou, see below. Zhang Yong was a native of Xincheng, Baoding (Zhang Tingyu et al., eds., *Mingshi* [hereafter *MS*] [1736; reprint, Beijing: Zhonghua shuju, 1974], 26.304.7792). The prefectures south of Beijing continued to pro-duce influential eunuchs through the rest of the dynasty. For instance, Feng Bao, Zhang Jing, Chen Ju, Wang An, Wei Zhongxian, Wang Tiqian, and Li Yongzhen were all from the prefectures of Baoding, Zhending, and Hejian. See *MS* 26.304.7800–7825.

58. See Ma Deqing and Zhou Chunhui, "Qinggong taijian huiyilu," *Wan Qing gongting shenghuo jianwen*, pp. 173–177.

59. For example, sixty-two palace eunuchs are mentioned in twelve of fifty inscriptions from the Ming listed in the 1779 edition of *Yongqing xianzhi* (reprint, Taibei: Xuesheng shuju, 1968), 2:1009–1056. Temple inscriptions are a critical source for understanding the role of eunuchs in local society. Most gazetteer editors in the Northern Metropolitan Area were far less meticulous than Zhang Xuecheng, however, and consequently, much valuable information has been lost. The collection of stele rubbings held by the Beijing Library illus-trates the kinds of information that may be gleaned from this source. Most of the stele rubbings in this collection, though, are either from Beijing and its immediate environs or other provinces. Funerary inscriptions of eunuchs are periodically unearthed, though only a portion of these texts are actually pub-lished (generally for lack of interest and funds). When I visited Hebei in July 1993, members of the Yongqing Gazetteer Office informed me that several of the stelae listed in Zhang's *Yongqing xianzhi* were destroyed during the Cul-tural Revolution. The whereabouts of an even greater number are not known. Some, like the Xinglong Temple Stele at Fenwangzhuang, have been recovered, though in several pieces. The temple itself was torn down in 1947. The stele was blasted in 1957, and the bottom half of the stele was used for construction

materials. The top half did not resurface until July of 1993, when members of the gazetteer office went down to the country in response to my inquiries about stelae.

60. For example, Ni Yue (1444–1501), a minister of rites during the Hong-zhi reign, composed a eulogy for the eunuch Niu Yu, a native of Zhuozhou. Niu's elegantly constructed tomb was discovered in 1976 and is now under the care of the Hebei Cultural Artifacts Office. See Baoding diqu bowuguan, "Ming liangjing sili taijian Niu Yu mu fajue jianbao," *Wenwu* 2 (1983): 76–80. The text of the eulogy is appended. It is worth noting that the eulogy for Niu is not included in Ni's collected works *Qingxi mangao* (1514 preface; reprinted in Ding Bing, Wulin wangzhe yizhu houbian, 1894–1900).

61. *WZSL* 30.3a–b.

62. Tan Qian, *Guoque* (Beijing: Zhonghua shuju, 1988), *juan* 49, p. 3045. Shen Defu wrote that "only one out of ten" gained posts (*Wanli yehuobian, juan* 6, p. 179).

63. His phrase is ambiguous, perhaps intentionally so. The term *"fuyao"* may be a reference to genitals, rather than money belt.

64. Shen Defu, *Wanli ye huo bian* (Beijing: Zhonghua shuju, 1980), *juan* 6, p. 178.

65. Shimizu, "Jikyū kangan no kenkyū," p. 120.

66. *Shizong shilu* (hereafter *SZSL*), in *Ming shilu* (1418 to mid-seventeenth century; facsimile reproduction of *Guoli Beiping tushuguan cang hongge chaoben,* 133 vols.; Taibei: Zhongyang yanjiuyuan lishi yuyan yanjiusuo, 1961–1966), 24.4a.

67. For more details, see Qiu Zhonglin, "Mingdai zigong qiuyong xian-xiang zailun," *Danjiang shixue* 6 (1994): 125–146.

68. While these estates were spread throughout the region, they were most heavily concentrated in the prefectures of Shuntian, Hejian, and Baoding.

69. *Xiaozong shilu* [hereafter *XOSL*], in *Ming shilu* (1418 to mid-seventeenth century; facsimile reproduction of *Guoli Beiping tushuguan cang hongge chaoben,* 133 vols.; Taibei: Zhongyang yanjiuyuan lishi yuyan yanjiusuo, 1961–1966), 28.13a; Lin Jun, "Chuan feng chi yu chakan jinei tiandi shu," in Chen Zilong, ed., *Huang Ming jingshi wenbian* (hereafter *JSWB*) (Pinglu tang, 1638; reprint, Taibei: Guolian chuban youxian gongsi, 1964), 88.9a.

70. For a discussion of these estates, see Zheng Kecheng, *Mingdai zheng-zheng tanyuan* (Tianjin: Tianjin guji chubanshe, 1988), pp. 114–121.

71. Chang Sha added 2,328,200 acres (166,300 *qing*) in other estate lands to the 37,595 figure and divided by 6,895,966 acres (492,569 *qing*), the total acreage of the Northern Metropolitan Region, to arrive at his estimate of more than 40 percent ("Mingdai Jingji 'zhuangtian' xiaoyi," *Zhongguoshi yanjiu* 3 [1985]: 108). Dividing 37,595 by 269,707, the amount of taxable land in the eight prefectures of the Northern Metropolitan Area according to the Wanli edition of the *Da Ming huidian,* Zheng Kecheng arrived at his estimation of 1/7 (*Mingdai zheng-zheng tanyuan,* p. 131). James Geiss divided the 37,595 by the amount of taxable land given in the Zhengde edition of the *Da Ming huidian* for his estimate of 1/6 ("Peking under the Ming," p. 101). All figures must be approached cautiously. None of the above authors address the question of the reliability of either the estate land surveys or the nettlesome problem of the tax land surveys. See Ray

Huang for tables in which he estimates acreage and annual income from these lands (*Taxation in Sixteenth Century China*, pp. 325–326).

72. *XOSL* 28.13a–b; Qin Jin, "Lun huangzhuang shu" (early Jiajing period), *JSWB*, 174.3a–4a.

73. See Zheng Kecheng, *Mingdai zhengzheng tanyuan*, pp. 143–145, 170–174. Wang Yuquan has argued that in many cases tenants on these estates paid more than twice this amount ("Mingdai xungui dizhu de dianhu," *Laiwuji* [Beijing: Zhonghua shuju, 1983], pp. 268–269). Ray Huang instead believes that rents from the estate properties were very similar to land taxes. He notes an example from Xianghe county nearby Beijing where the rent rate was 0.03 taels/mu versus an estimated 0.027 tax rate (*Taxation in Sixteenth Century China*, p. 107). Princely estates shared the controversy over control of revenue. For a detailed discussion of this question and of tenant rent rates, see Wang Yuquan, "Mingdai de wangfu zhuangtian," *Laiwu ji*, pp. 166–193.

74. Ray Huang, "Ming Fiscal Administration," in Twitchett and Mote, *The Cambridge History of China*, 8:134.

75. Ray Huang has argued, in contrast, that in most cases magistrates collected the revenue and remitted it to the estate holder (*Taxation in Sixteenth Century China*, p. 107). Estate holders did not present a united front against the civil bureaucracy. The desire to control greater tracts of land and increased revenue pitted all those with access to the throne in an internecine struggle for influence. For the fortunes of the Zhang family, one of the most notorious imperial in-laws during the late fifteenth and early sixteenth centuries, see Satō Fumitoshi, "Mindai chūqi no gaiseki, Chōshi kyōdai," *Tōyōshi kenkyū* 49.3 (December 1990): 63–86.

In at least some cases, those who sold their lands to princely estates and became their tenants were still forced to pay taxes to the local government and render corvée labor (Wang, "Mingdai de wangfu zhuangtian," p. 207).

76. Eunuchs also oversaw the management of estates belonging to imperial princes. They were accompanied by servants and several dozen low-ranking military officers drawn from the prince's military guard. Like the other varieties of estates, the direct managers of these lands were often called "zhuangtou" (ibid., pp. 166–168).

77. One 1466 report wrote of "desperadoes led by [estate] servants who ride horses and mules, carrying bow and arrows, swords, and military equipment" (Dai Jin, *Huang Ming tiaofa shilei zuan* [hereafter TFSLZ] [ca. 1531; reprint, Tokyo: Koten kenkyūkai, 1966], *juan* 13, 1:314, quoted in Zheng Kecheng, *Mingdai zhengzheng tanyuan*, pp. 149–153).

78. Lin Jun, "Chuanfeng chiyu chakan jinei tiandi shu," in *JSWB* 88.9a–10a; *XOSL* 28.13a–b. Also Wang, "Mingdai de wangfu zhuangtian," pp. 191–192 and "Mingchao xungui baoheng zhi yiban," pp. 326–341. A 1479 report charged that "servants and estate managers assembled desperadoes, bullied officials, and bitterly harmed soldiers and commoners" (*TFSLZ, juan* 13, 1:316, quoted in Zheng Kecheng, *Mingdai zhengzheng tanyuan*, p. 151).

79. Lin Jun, "Chuanfeng chiyu chakan jinei tiandi shu," in *JSWB* 88.3b. Wang Yuquan has noted that not only local magistrates but also grand coordinators and regional inspectors were known to have adopted a laissez-faire attitude toward the matters of princely estates ("Mingdai de wangfu zhuangtian,"

p. 165, also pp. 217–218). Consequently, some tenants on these properties acted with a degree of immunity from local officials ("Mingdai xungui dizhu de dianhu," pp. 259–262).

80. Henri Serruys, *Sino-Mongol Relations during the Ming*, vol. 3, *Trade Relations; The Horse Fairs, 1400–1600*. In *Mélanges chinois et bouddhiques*, vol. 14, 1966–1967 (Bruxelles: l'Institut belge des hautes études chinoises, 1967).

81. Nan Bingwen estimates that more than 41,000 households in Shuntian Prefecture were charged with caring for these "entrusted mounts" during the fifteenth century. There were an additional 6,400 in Baoding Prefecture and 3,700 in Hejian Prefecture. By the late sixteenth century, these numbers had dropped by more than half. See Nan Bingwen, "Mingdai liangji, Lu, Yu de minyang guanma zhidu," in *Ming-Qingshi guoji xueshu taolunhui lunwenji* (Tianjin: Tianjin renmin chubanshe, 1982), pp. 484–487. The description of the entrusted mounts is by Peng Ze, "Ti fu jiupian bubi yi qi yu mazheng shi," *Mingchen jingji lu, juan* 36. Cited in Li Jixian, "Mingdai mahu shulun," *Mingshi yanjiu* 3 (1993): 17.

82. For examples, see Li Jixian, "Mingdai mahu shulun," pp. 19–20. Li explicitly links the burdens of horse administration to the 1510 Rebellion, noting "this area provided an optimal breeding ground for peasant rebellion; that the peasant rebellion armies led by Liu the Sixth, Liu the Seventh, and Tiger Yang erupted in this region was only to be expected (p. 20)." Li offers no convincing evidence for this statement. The authoritative work on the Ming horse administration is Tani Mitsutaka's *Mindai basei no kenkyū* (Kyoto: Tōyōshi kenkyūkai, 1972). For a short introduction in English to the horse administration system, see Tani Mitsutaka, "A Study on Horse Administration in the Ming Period," *Acta Asiatica* 38 (1980): 73–97.

83. See Frederick Mote, "The Ch'eng-hua and Hung-chih Reigns, 1465–1505" (in Twitchett and Mote, *The Cambridge History of China*, 7:370–376), for an excellent sketch of the structure and problems of the Ming military in the latter half of the fifteenth century. His description is no less germane for most of the sixteenth century.

84. For an account of social organization based on hereditary households divided by occupation under the Yuan, see Meng Siming, *Yuandai shehui jieji zhidu* (Beijing: Hafo Yanjing xueshe, 1937; facsimile reproduction, Hong Kong: Longmen shudian). On Yuan military households, see Chen Gaohua, "Yuandai de junhu," *Yuanshi yanjiu lungao* (Beijing: Zhonghua shuju, 1991), pp. 127–155. On the Yuan origins of the military organization of the Ming, see Romeyn Taylor, "Yuan Origins of the Wei-so System," in Charles Hucker, ed., *Chinese Government in Ming Times: Seven Studies* (New York: Columbia University Press, 1969), pp. 23–40. For general overviews of the Ming military, see Wu Han, "Mingdai de junbing," *Zhongguo shehui jingjishi jikan* 2.2 (1937): 147–200 (reprinted in his *Dushi zhaji* [Beijing: Sanlian shudian, 1956]); Xie Yucai, "Mingdai weisuo zhidu xingshuai kao," *Shuowen yuekan* 2 (1940): 9–12 (reprinted in Bao Zunpeng, ed., *Mingdai zhengzhi* [Taibei: Xuesheng shuju, 1968], pp. 155–247); Wang Yuquan, "Mingdai de junhu," *Lishi yanjiu* 8 (1959): 21–34 (reprinted in his *Laiwu ji* [Beijing: Zhonghua shuju, 1983], pp. 342–361). See also Yun Chŏng-bun, "Myŏngdae kunhoche wa uisoche e taehayŏ," *Tongbang hakchi* 43 (1984): 305–329. For a more recent overview of the entire Ming military, see Shen Dingping, "Ming-

chao junzhi," in Liu Zhan, ed., *Zhongguo gudai junzhishi* (Junshi kexue chuban-she, 1992), pp. 407–461. For a concise overview of the Ming military in English, see Liew, "Tuntian Farming of the Ming Dynasty," pp. 61–73. See also Liew's very important two-volume translation and detailed commentary, *The Treatises on Military Affairs of the Ming Dynastic History (1368–1644)* (Hamburg: Gesellschaft Für natur- Und Völkerkunde Ostasiens, 1998).

85. While the favored principle of succession was from father to eldest son of the principal wife, a wide variety of substitutes within the military household was permitted according to circumstances. For a detailed explanation of the process of inheriting officer's posts, see Yu Zhijia, *Mingdai junhu shixi zhidu* (Taibei: Xuesheng shuju, 1987), pp. 142–155, and also Kawagoe Yasuhiro, "Mindai eisho no shajin ni tsuite," *Chūō daigaku bungakubu kiyō* 31 (March 1987): 77–107.

86. Wang Yuquan, "Mingdai de junhu," pp. 356–357.

87. Ray Huang has described the scale of the one-hundred-year deterioration from 1450 as "unprecedented in Chinese history" (*Taxation in Sixteenth Century China*, p. 67).

88. For a detailed discussion of the military registers and the abuses that occurred during the "clarification of military registers" (*qing jun*), when military and civil authorities sought replacements for soldiers who had died, retired, or deserted, see Yu, *Mindai junhu shixi zhidu*, pp. 50–108. For a shorter overview, see Cao Guoqing, "Lun Mingdai de qingjun," *Dierjie Ming Qingshi guoji xueshu taolunhui lunwenji* (Tianjin: Tianjin renmin chubanshe, 1993), pp. 503–509. For a brief note in English on the Ming military registers (*weixuanbu*, actually more like personnel files used for performance evaluation and promotion), see Wade Wilkinson, "Newly Discovered Ming Military Registers," *Ming Studies* 3 (1976): 36–45.

For more thorough discussions, see Yu Zhijia, "Mingdai wuzhi xuanbu yu weisuo wuguanzhi de yanjiu-ji zhongyanyuan shiyu suo cang Mingdai wuzhi xuanbu canben jian ping Kawagoe Yasuhiro de xuanbu yanjiu," *Zhongyang yanjiuyuan lishi yuyan yanjiusuo jikan* 69.1 (1998): 45–74, and Yu Zhijia, "Mingdang de liyong he Mingdai weisuo zhidu yanjiu," *Dalu zazhi* 99.5 (1999): 201–218.

89. Yu Zhijia, *Mingdai junhu shixi zhidu*, pp. 64, 155 n. 1, pp. 177–178; Ma Zishu, "Mingdai jundui shuairuo de neizai yinsu," *Gugong bowuyuan yuankan* 2 (1987): 11–17.

90. See Liang Yong, "Qianlun Mingdai Hebei de weisuo he juntun," *Hebei shifan daxue xuebao* 2 (1987): 81. Liang Yong estimates that military forces constituted 60 percent of the Northern Metropolitan Area population, which is highly questionable. Based on information in the *Military Treatise* of the *MS*, Liang writes that if we assume there were 5,500 men in each of the 80 garrisons, plus transfers from other areas, one would reach a figure higher than 500,000. There is, of course, no way to know how many men were actually in each of the garrisons. For his estimate of the population of the Northern Metropolitan Area, Liang uses a 1403 figure of 189,000 households and then multiplies this by what he reckons was the average household size at the time, 5. His calculations can be taken only as an upper ceiling.

91. *MS* 8.90.2197–2222.

92. Ma Zishu, "Mingdai jundui shuailuo de neizai yinsu," *Gugong bowu-yuan yuankan* 2 (1987): 11–12. According to Chen Hongmo and Wang Ao, there were 896,000 troops in the Ming army during the Zhengde reign (*Jishi jiwen* [early sixteenth century; reprint, Beijing: Zhonghua shuju, 1985], *juan* 5, p. 107; *Zhenze chang yu* [early sixteenth century; reprint, Taibei: Taiwan shangwu yin-shuguan, 1969], 2.30a).

93. On the formation of the capital garrisons in the early fifteenth century, see Aoyama Jirō, "Mindai ni okeru keiei no keisei ni tsuite," *Tōhōgaku* 42 (1971): 64–81. Later reprinted in the author's *Mindai keieishi kenkyū* (Sapporo: Kyobunsha, 1996). For the capital garrisons during the mid-Ming, see Oku-yama Norio, "Mindai chūki no keiei ni kansuru ichi kōsatsu," *Mindaishi kenkyū* 8 (1980): 1–19. The battle effectiveness of the capital garrisons suffered irrepa-rable damage with the Tumu Incident of 1449. See Frederick Mote, "The T'u-mu Incident of 1449," in Frank Kierman and John Fairbank, eds., *Chinese Ways of Warfare* (Cambridge: Harvard University Press, 1974), pp. 243–272. While reforms designed to restore the prowess of the capital garrisons began shortly after the 1449 debacle and continued for more than a century, results were mixed. For accounts of these reforms and the garrisons' decline, see Luo Lixin, "Mingdai jingying zhi xingcheng yu shuaibai," *Mingshi yanjiu zhuankan* 6 (1983): 1–36; Huang Miantang, "Lun Mingdai de jingying," *Shixue jikan* 3 (1992): 28–35.

94. Wu Han, "Mingdai de junbing," p. 165.

95. Ray Huang writes that military colonies in the interior often operated at 10 percent of prescribed strength by the early sixteenth century (*Taxation in Sixteenth Century China*, p. 68).

96. *Hejian fuzhi* (1540), 11.6b–7b.

97. Ibid., 11.7a. The phenomenon was not restricted to the Northern Metropolitan Area. For the large number of supernumerary troops in Jiangxi, see Yu Zhijia, "Mingdai Jiangxi bingzhi de yanbian," *Zhongyang yanjiuyuan lishi yuyan yanjiusuo jikan* 66.4 (1995): 1018, chart 3.

98. Yu Zhijia, "Mingdai Jiangxi weisuo junyi de yanbian," *Zhongyang yan-jiuyuan shiyusuo yanjiusuo jikan* 68.1 (1997): 1–51; Sŏ In-bŏm, "Minchūki no hokuhen bōei-ei to gunko-zaiei no yotei o chūshin toshite," *Shūkan Tōyōgaku* 78 (1997): 81–103.

99. See Kawagoe Yasuhiro, "Mindai hangun banjōkō," *Chūō daigaku bun-gakubu kiyō* 22 (1977): 133–162.

100. Ibid., p. 138. The second figure is derived from materials on pp. 139–140 and includes men only from Henan, Shandong, and the Metropolitan Areas, the largest contributors to the rotational forces.

101. Yu Zhijia, "Shilun zupu zhong suojian de Mingdai junhu," *Zhong-yang yanjiuyuan lishi yuyan yanjiusuo jikan* 57.4 (1986): 637–642. Yu observes that the regulation requiring soldiers to take their wives dates from 1436. Based on genealogical materials, Yu notes that before this, men often took their wives along. However, there were numerous cases of men not leaving their wives at home both before and following the promulgation of the 1436 regulation.

102. Housing was often insufficient at garrisons. Qiu Jun (1420–1495) com-plained that because the soldiers stationed in Beijing lived scattered through-out the capital's mazelike streets and several miles outside the walls, assem-

bling them quickly in a crisis would be impossible. Cited in Yu Zhijia, *Mingdai junhu shixi zhidu*, p. 118, n. 52.

103. This view is most succinctly expressed in Wang Yuquan, "Mingdai de junhu."

104. Matteo Ricci and Nicola Trigault, *China in the Sixteenth Century: The Journals of Matthew Ricci, 1583–1610* (New York: Random House, 1953), p. 91.

105. Wang Yuquan, "Mingdai de junhu," p. 355. Cavalry troops could be responsible for supplying their own mounts, while soldiers assigned to work in postal relay stations were required to provide their own saddles, bedding, and miscellaneous objects for the station.

106. Chen Wenshi, "Mingdai weisuo de jun," *Zhongyang yanjiuyuan lishi yuyan yanjiuyuan jikan* 48.2 (1977): 177–203, p. 189. His figures are from the *MS*, *juan* 82. These are the prescriptive figures for soldiers with families. Those without families received half this amount; those whose sentences had been reduced from execution to service as soldiers also received less rice and salt. See also Kawagoe Yasuhiro, "Dai Min kaiten ni mieru Mindai eijokan no getsuryōgaku o megutte," *Kyūko* 15 (1989): 37–42. Kawagoe notes that the revenue source for officers' salaries changed significantly during the Ming period.

107. For cases of officers abusing subordinate soldiers, see Wu Han, "Mingdai de junbing," p. 169; Chen Wenshi, "Mingdai weisuo de jun," pp. 188–189; Wang Yuquan, "Mingdai de junhu," p. 355; Yu Zhijia, *Mingdai junhu shixi zhidu*, p. 155. On some of the economic difficulties facing the soldiers of Hejian Prefecture, see *Hejian fuzhi* (1540), 11.8b.

108. See *TFSLZ, juan* 3, 1:56, 57, 62. See also Wu Han, "Mingdai de junbing," p. 169; Xie Yucai, "Mingdai weisuo zhidu xingshuai kao," pp. 216–217; Chen Wenshi, "Mingdai weisuo de jun," p. 194. Ray Huang has described the Beijing garrisons as a "huge labor gang" (*Taxation in Sixteenth-Century China*, pp. 58, 68).

109. See also Wang Yuquan, "Mingdai de junhu," p. 357; Li Longqian, "Mingdai junhu zhidu qianlun," *Beijing shiyuan xuebao* 1 (1982): 48–50.

110. Although Yu Zhijia also noted the misery of hereditary military households in her *Mingdai junhu shixi zhidu*, in subsequent articles, she examined marriage patterns, success in the examination system, and official appointments, demonstrating that the fortunes of military households varied considerably. See "Mindai gunko no shakaiteki chii ni tsuite: Gunko no kon-in o megutte," *Mindaishi kenkyū* 18 (1990): 7–32; "Mindai gunko no shakaiteki chii ni tsuite: Kakyo to ninkan ni oite," *Tōyō gakuhō* 71.3–4 (1990): 91–131.

111. Yu Zhijia, "Shilun zupu zhong suojian de Mingdai junhu"; Li Longqian, "Mingdai junhu zhidu qianlun."

112. *TFSLZ, juan* 3, 1:68–69.

113. Gu Cheng, "Tan Mingdai de weiji," *Beijing shifan daxue xuebao* 5 (1989): 61. An updated and expanded version of this article is available in translation by Aramiya Manabu, "Mindai no eiseki ni tsuite—jinbutsu likai no tameni," *Tōhoku daigaku Tōyōshi ronshū* 7 (1998): 239–265.

114. Revenue produced by females of these households awaits further research. Registration as a military household brought certain tax and corvée exemptions. Some long-term residents of Beijing sought to avoid these obligations by falsely claiming to be military households (*Wanli Da Ming huidian*

[Collected statutes of the Ming dynasty], Shen Shixing et al., eds. [1587; reprint, Taibei: Dongnan shubaoshe, 1964], 19.29a, 1:355).

115. *TFSLZ, juan* 34, 2:35–36.

116. Zhu Guozhen, *Yongchuang xiaopin, juan* 32 (reprint, Beijing: Zhonghua shuju, 1959), pp. 771–772. The soldiers are said to have presented at least one to eunuchs within the imperial palace, calling it "The Miraculous Method of Transmigration." The eunuchs handsomely rewarded them.

117. See Ma Chujian, "Mingdai de jiading," *Mingshi yanjiu zhuankan* 8 (December 1985): 191–252; Suzuki Tadashi, "Mindai kahei kō," *Shikan* 22–23 (1940): 1–26; "Mindai katei kō," *Shikan* 37 (1952): 23–40; Xiao Xu, "Mingdai jiangshuai jiading de xingshuai jiqi yingxiang," *Nankai shixue* 1 (1984): 102–122; Zhao Zhongnan, "Lun Mingdai junduizhong jiading de tedian yu diwei," *Shehui kexue zhanxian* 3 (1988): 144–149; and Zhao Zhongnan, "Lun Mingdai junshi jiading zhidu xingcheng de shehui jingji tiaojian jiqi fazhan," *Shehui kexue jikan* 2 (1991): 86–90.

118. Zheng Kecheng, *Mingdai zhengzheng tanyuan*, pp. 149–150.

119. Other efforts at maintaining local order involved organizing residents into *lijia, baojia,* and community compacts *(xiangyue)*. On the *baojia* during the first half of the Ming, see Sakai Tadao, "Mindai zenchūki no hōkasei ni tsuite," in Shimizu hakushi tsuitō kinen henshū iinkai, ed., *Shimizu hakushi tsuitō kinen: Mindaishi ronsō* (Tokyo: Daian, 1962), pp. 577–610. On the community compacts as attempts to restore social order during the mid-Ming, see Chu Hung-lam (Zhu Honglin), "Mingdai zhongqi fangshe zhian chongjian lixiang zhi zhanxian," *Chungguk hakpo* 32 (1992): 87–100. It is worth noting that the large-scale community pact of the Qiu Clan of Xiongshan, Shanxi, was established in 1511, during the rebellion (Zhu Honglin, "Mingdai zhongqi fangshe zhian chongjian lixiang zhi zhanxian," p. 91, also n. 50).

120. On the limited role of regular *weisuo* units during the antipiracy campaigns of the mid-sixteenth century, see Ray Huang, *Taxation in Sixteenth-Century China*, p. 292).

121. On the evolution of Ming militias, see Liang Fangzhong, "Mingdai de minbing," *Zhongguo shehui jingjishi jikan* 5.2 (1937): 200–234, in Wu Zhihe, ed., *Mingshi yanjiu luncong* (Tabei: Dali chubanshe, 1982), 1:243–276. Saeki Tomi discusses the incorporation of the "people's stalwarts" into the corvée service system from the mid-sixteenth century "Min Shin jidai no minsō ni tsuite," *Tōyōshi kenkyū* 15.4:33–64. As Mote and others have noted, the people's stalwarts for a while overshadowed regular guard troops in military significance. In time, however, the people's stalwarts lost their effectiveness and were partially supplanted by hired soldiers. See Wu Han, "Mingdai de junbing," pp. 147–149, 182–190; Li Du, "Mingdai mubing zhidu jianlun," *Wen shi zhe* 2 (1986): 62–68; Sŏ In-bŏm, "Tomoku no hen to kinōhei—giyū to minsō chūshin toshite," *Tōyō gakuhō* 82.1 (2000): 1–28. The use of garrison forces, militia troops, and hired soldiers overlapped considerably during the fifteenth, sixteenth, and early seventeenth centuries. As Liang Fangzhong notes, the central government, during periods of crisis, often incorporated local militias into national armies ("Mingdai de minbing," p. 244).

122. Saeki Tomi argues that the commutation into silver of the militia corvée service had begun by at least the Hongzhi period (1488–1505) and had

become widespread by the Jiajing period (1522–1566) ("Min Shin jidai no minsō ni tsuite," pp. 48, 53–62).

123. This follows secondary scholarship, which argues that the terms *"kuaishou," "jibing," "dashou," "makuaishou,"* and others were varieties of local militias *(minbing)*. See Liang Fangzhong, "Mingdai de minbing," p. 258; Sakai Tadao, "Mindai zenchūki no hōkasei ni tsuite," pp. 577–610, esp. p. 601; Saeki Tomi, "Min Shin jidai no minsō ni tsuite," pp. 33–64, esp. p. 41; Yamane Yukio, *Mindai yōeki seido no tenkai* (Tokyo: Tōkyō joshi daigaku gakkai, 1966), p. 156. This description finds corroboration in the following Ming sources: *Zhangde fuzhi* (1552), 8.42a; *Dongchang fuzhi* (1600), 13.6a; *WZSL* 61.8a–b.

124. Those based at yamen offices included: *kuaishou, bingkuai, makuaishou,* and *minkuai.* Those who served in the local constabularies *(xunjiansi)* were commonly called *"gongbing."* For a more detailed description of these posts in the Ming, see Miao Quanji, *Mingdai xuli* (Taibei: Jiaxin shuini gongsi wenhua jijinhui, 1969), pp. 74–80. Miao notes that by the late fifteenth century, *gongbing* often functioned as nothing more than yamen runners (p. 76). According to Miao, the general trend was true for people's stalwarts and *kuaishou* as well, though they retained more of their security functions (p. 77). Following Lu Kun (1536–1618), Miao writes that while *kuaishou* and *minzhuang* were both varieties of local militias, in cases of especially difficult brigands, *kuaishou* were those selected from among the people's stalwarts as especially nimble (p. 78). For the role of *kuaishou* during the Qing, see Ch'u T'ung-tsu, *Local Government in China during the Ch'ing* (Cambridge: Harvard University Press, 1962), pp. 57–70, 237, n. 39. Ch'u describes them as yamen runners, as does Thomas Nimick, *The County, the Magistrate, and the Yamen in Late Ming China* (Ph.D. diss., Princeton University, 1993), p. 80.

125. *MS*, 6.75.1852. See also Charles Hucker, *Dictionary of Official Titles in Imperial China* (Stanford: Stanford University Press, 1985), p. 254.

Lu Kun observed, "Those who apprehend bandits are the *kuai[shou]* and people's stalwarts. Those who commit banditry are also the *kuai[shou]* and people's stalwarts" (*Shizheng lu* 7.33, quoted in Miao, *Mingdai xuli,* p. 79). Chen Longzheng (js. 1634) similarly wrote, "Bandit catchers nurture bandits and also commit brigandage" (*Jiting waishu* 4.44, quoted in Miao, *Mingdai xuli,* p. 79).

126. *Bazhou zhi* (1548), 4.7b.

127. Sporadic and rather fruitless debate exists over exactly which year saw the establishment of the people's stalwarts. For more on the stalwarts, see Liang Fangzhong, "Mingdai de Minbing," pp. 257–268; Saeki Tomi, "Min Shin jidai no minso ni tsuite"; Sŏ In-bŏm, "Mindai chūki no Sensei no tohei ni tsuite, *Shūkan Tōyōgaku* 74 (1995): 60–79. For a brief note in English, see Frederick Mote, "The Ch'eng-hua and Hung-chih Reigns, 1465–1505," in Twitchett and Mote, *The Cambridge History of China*, 7:374–375.

128. *Hejian fuzhi* (1540), 11.10a–b; *Bazhou zhi* (1548), 4.7b.

129. This was the case in Hejian at the time the 1540 gazetteer was compiled. The editor, Fan Shen, comments that the militia *(minbing)* were all opportunists useless in battle. The greater fault, however, lay with officials who collected silver and hired replacements with the idea of making a profit (*Hejian fuzhi* [1540], 11.11a). See also *Da Ming huidian* for complaints about the quality of the hired replacements (137.20.14b, 4:1919). In some areas, the hired replace-

ments were called *"jibing"* (*Huang Ming shifa lu* 44.19a; *MS*, 7.91.2250). For more on methods of conscription, silver payments, and hired replacements, see Liang Fangzhong, "Mingdai de minbing," pp. 259–264, and Saeki Tomi, "Min Shin jidai no minsō ni tsuite," pp. 42–63.

130. There were often various other forces such as the "great men" *(dahan)* of Bazhou. The "great men" were those of great height and strong limb. The great men were originally organized in a "past year" because of Mongol incursions, probably a reference to the events of 1449 (*Bazhou zhi* [1548], 4.7b).

Assistant prefects were commonly charged with bandit apprehension. According to the Wanli edition of the *Da Ming huidian*, assistant prefects and assistant magistrates responsible for arresting brigands were added to local governments in the Hongzhi period (136.19a, 1a, 4:1924). One of these officials is listed for each of the districts of Hejian Prefecture, and in most cases they were called "bandit apprehension officials" *(xunbu guan)* (*Hejian fuzhi* [1540], 11.10a–b). However, the number of these positions fluctuated. For instance, on March 13, 1507, and again on April 17, 1507, the court reduced the number of bandit-apprehension officials (*WZSL* 22.12a–b, 24.1b).

131. See chapter 4.

132. Chen Baoliang, "Mingdai de minbing yu xiangbing," *Zhongguoshi yanjiu* 1 (1994): 85–87, and "Mingdai xiangcun de fangyu tizhi," *Qi Lu xuekan* 6 (1993): 104–105.

133. On local elites' role in local defense during the late Yuan, see Yamane Yukio, "Genmatsu no ran to Minchō shihai no kakuritsu," *Higashi Ajia sekai no tenkai 2*, Iwanami kōzō ed., *Sekai rekishi 12, chūsei 6* (Tokyo: Iwanami shoten, 1979), pp. 17–56. On their role in the rebellions of the late Ming, see Li Wenzhi, "Mingmo de zhaibao yu yijun," *Wenshi zazhi* 3:7–8 (1944), in Wu Zhihe, ed., *Mingshi yanjiu luncong*, 2:262–274; Yamane Yukio, "Minmatsu nōmin hanran to shishisō no taiō," in Nakajima Satoshi sensei koki jigyōkai, ed., *Nakajima Satoshi sensei koki kinen ronshū* (Tokyo: Kyuko shoin, 1981), 2:359–377; Taniguchi Kikuo, "Minmatsu gohei gihei ni tsuite-Minmatsu seikyaku hitokusari" (Kōbe daigaku bungakubu), *Kenkyū* 43 (1969): 99–122; Wang Xiande, "Minmatsu dōranki ni okeru kyōson bōei," *Mindaishi kenkyū* 2 (1975): 25–49, and *Mingmo xiangcun ziwei zhi yanjiu* (Gaoxiong: Fuwen tushu chubanshe, 1992), pp. 155–156, 166–173, 251–268.

134. For anecdotes from the early sixteenth century related to women from Bazhou and a village just outside Beijing serving in the imperial harem (however briefly), see Zhu Guozhen, *Yongzhuang xiaopin, juan* 32, p. 768; Li Xun, *Zhengde huangdi dazhuan* (Shenyang: Liaoning jiaoyu chubanshe, 1993), pp. 22–32.

Chapter 3   Banditry during the Mid-Ming Period

1. *TFSLZ, juan* 33, 2:20–21.

2. James Tong, *Disorder under Heaven: Collective Violence in the Ming Dynasty* (Stanford: Stanford University Press, 1991), pp. 50, 52, 63, table 3.12.

3. Ibid., p. 58, table 3.7.

4. For a recent overview of rational choice models, see Tong, *Disorder under Heaven*, pp. 76–95. The idea that peripheral areas far removed from the central government were particularly subject to brigandage is extremely prevalent in the literature. See Eric Hobsbawm, *Bandits* (New York: Delacorte, 1969), pp. 16–17. In the China field, it is present in the work of Tong (noted above)

and Elizabeth Perry, *Rebellion and Revolution in North China, 1845–1945* (Stanford: Stanford University Press, 1980). This assumption is implicit in Joseph Esherick's argument that the lack of a dominant gentry in western Shandong (i.e., one committed to Confucian ideology and the support of the state) contributed to (and was at the same time a product of) widespread banditry from at least the late Ming; see his *Origins of the Boxer Uprising* (Berkeley: University of California Press, 1987), chapter 2.

5. Qiu Jun, "Edao zhi ji shang," *Daxue yanyi bu* (1487; reprint, 1632; Rare Book Collection, Harvard-Yenching Library, Harvard University), 136.5a.

6. *TFSLZ, juan* 45, 2:298.

7. Ibid., p. 294.

8. *SZSL* 62.6b–7a.

9. For detailed definitions of *"dao"* and *"zei,"* see *Hanyu dacidian* (Shanghai: Shanghai cishu chubanshe, 1986–1994), 7:1431–1432, 10:183.

Both terms could mean either bandit or rebel, depending on the context. As Frederick Mote, noted historian of the Ming, has observed, "The distinction between banditry and rebellion in the Chinese taxonomy of social disorders is somewhat like that between mice and rats in traditional Chinese zoological taxonomy—they are the same species, but the latter have grown larger than the former. The critical difference administrators had to discern was that while banditry constituted a hazard to local order and safety, rebellion challenged the state and might threaten it" ("The Ch'eng-hua and Hung-chih Reigns, 1465–1505," in Twitchett and Mote, *The Cambridge History of China*, 7:376–377). For an insightful discussion of a similar range of meaning and usage of the term *"latro,"* or *"bandit,"* see Brent Shaw, "Bandits in the Roman Empire," *Past and Present* 105 (November 1984): 3–52.

10. For the relevant sections of the Ming Code, see Huang Zhangjian, ed., *Mingdai lüli huibian* (Taibei: Zhongyang yanjiuyuan lishi yuyan yanjiusuo zhuankan, no. 75, 1979), pp. 755–760. Statutes enacted during the late fifteenth and early sixteenth centuries dictated that after execution, the decapitated head of the offender was to be displayed in the area where he had committed banditry, as a lesson to others.

For a brief discussion of terminology related to banditry and robbery during the Song, see Brian McKnight, *Law and Order in Sung China* (Cambridge: Cambridge University Press, 1992), pp. 89–94.

11. For the best discussion of Beijing's security forces during the Ming, see Qiu Zhonglin, "Mingdai Beijing dushi shenghuo yu zhi-an de zhuanbian," *Jiuzhou xuekan* 5.2 (October 1992): 90–95. See also Shi Yuan, "Mingdai de hongpu," *Zhonghe yuekan* 2.3 (1941): 125–127.

12. Joanne Wakeland, "Metropolitan Administration in Ming China: Sixteenth Century Peking" (Ph.D. diss., University of Michigan, 1982), pp. 250–260.

13. *TFSLZ, juan* 45, 2:308 (a report from January 10, 1473).

14. A 1515 report estimated that 384,745 military personnel in the capital drew salaries. Subsequent investigation revealed that far fewer were actually available for combat (*WZSL* 126.6b–7a).

A 1507 report noted that the autumn salary of the capital's 23,908 officers amounted to 394,713 piculs of rice (converted to nearly 100,000 taels of silver). See *WZSL* 32.4b.

15. *XOSL* 22.6b–7a.

16. *TFSLZ, juan* 34, 2:34.

17. Ibid., *juan* 45, 2:293 (February 2, 1468, and May 11, 1468), p. 296 (March 8, 1476); *Xianzong shilu* (hereafter *XNSL*), in *Ming shilu* (1418 to mid-seventeenth century; facsimile reproduction of *Guoli Beiping tushuguan cang hongge chaoben*, 133 vols.; Taibei: Zhongyang yanjiuyuan lishi yuyan yanjiusuo, 1961–1966), 55.2a–3a, 209.3b–4a, 263.7b–8a; *Da Ming huidian* 136.2b.

18. *Hanyu dacidian*, 3:413. *La* here seems to mean "harsh," as in the compound *"lazui"* (*Jin ping Mei cidian* [Beijing: Beijing shuju, 1991], p. 305). Other related terms include *"lahuo,"* or "ruffian" *(wulai)* and *"lazi"* (also defined as ruffian). See *Ming Qing xiaoshuo cidian* (Shijiazhuang: Huashan wenyi chubanshe, 1992), p. 462. For examples of gangs of young men in other urban centers during the Ming, see Han Dacheng, *Mingdai chengshi yanjiu* (Beijing: Zhongguo renmin daxue chubanshe, 1991), pp. 431–445. For a discussion of urban crime during the Song, see McKnight, *Law and Order*, pp. 285–320.

19. Chen Baoliang, *Zhongguo liumangshi* (Beijing: Zhongguo shehui kexue, 1993), pp. 158–159.

20. *TFSLZ, juan* 34, 2:43.

21. Ibid., p. 44.

22. Chen Baoliang, "Mingdai de mimi shehui yu Tiandihui de yuanyuan," *Shixue jikan* 1 (1994): 7.

23. For more details on the gambling dens of the Ming, see Han Dacheng, *Mingdai chengshi yanjiu*, pp. 348–351.

24. *XNSL* 209.3b–4a.

25. Luo Qi, "Song Jinyi Zhang Hou chuluo xu," *Luo kuifeng ji*, in *JSWB* 125.5a.

26. *TFSLZ, juan* 34, 2:47–49; *XNSL* 263.7b–8a; Yu Jideng, *Diangu jiwen* in Wang Hao, ed., *Jifu congshu* (Singzhou: Wanshi kanben, 1879–1892), 15.15b. For more on "dominating" markets, see Huang Zhangjian, *Mingdai lüli huibian*, 2:579–582; George Staunton, *Ta Tsing Leu Lee; Being the Fundamental Laws . . . of the Penal Code of China* (London: Cadell and Davies, 1810; reprint, Taibei: Chengwen chubanshe, 1966), pp. 164–165. For more on prostitution in Ming cities, see Han Dacheng, *Mingdai chengshi yanjiu*, pp. 359–366.

27. For details on prostitution in Beijing during the Ming, see Qiu Zhonglin, "Mingdai Beijing dushi shenghuo," pp. 63–69. The cosmetics tax is noted in Albert Chan, "Peking at the Time of the Wan-li Emperor," in *Proceedings of the Second Biennial Conference, International Association of Historians of Asia* (Taibei, 1962), 2:141.

28. Han Dacheng, *Mingdai chengshi yanjiu*, p. 363.

29. *XNSL* 55.2a–3a; Chen Baoliang, *Zhongguo liumangshi*, p. 158.

30. *TFSLZ, juan* 33, 2:47.

31. Ibid., p. 43.

32. For instance, a March 16, 1468, entry of the *XNSL* notes that thirteen retainers of Marquis Xining had been arrested on charges of assault and plundering in and around Beijing in broad daylight. They were found guilty and received punishments ranging from beatings with the rod to death (*XNSL* 53.9a).

Of course, this practice was not restricted to Beijing. For examples from other urban areas in Ming times, see Han Dacheng, *Mingdai chengshi yanjiu*, pp. 358–359.

33. *Huang Ming Changshu wenxian zhi, juan* 6, cited in Han Dacheng, *Mingdai chengshi yanjiu,* p. 358.

34. *XOSL* 212.4a.

35. Ibid., 212.18a–18b.

36. *TFSLZ, juan* 34, 2:62–63. That little more than half a tael was divided among such a large number of men raises questions about the amount of money reported in the case and the motives of the men for agreeing to collect the debt.

Another case involving the Xu household illustrates women's importance in negotiations. To avoid rendering corvée services, the Li brothers, proprietors of a palanquin shop, a mill, and a tavern, decided to "commend" themselves to the Xu household. Through the introduction of a nun they knew, the wife of the elder Li brother presented the wife of a son of the Duke of Dingguo (née Yuan) with a bolt of green silk and eight platters of pastries. Having been accepted as retainers, Li is said to have had his wife request a *hongmu pai,* a pass, from Yuan in order to avoid corvée service. Yuan initially demurred, but on the occasion of her second son's birthday, Li's wife produced a sheep, two platters of pork and mutton, two platters of noodles, and two bottles of wine. With this, Yuan gave a pass to Li's wife, who turned it over to Li. Li promptly had a copy made. He gave the original pass to his brother for use in their palanquin shop, while he put up the second one outside his shop. See *TFSLZ, juan* 34, 2:63–64.

37. It is also possible that the duke's son had much greater knowledge of Huang's activities and benefited handsomely. It was not unusual that influential individuals were able to convince authorities that they were unaware of their minions' activities, thereby significantly reducing their own responsibilities. In this case, however, the incidents appear so petty and the sums of money involved so meager, it is likely Huang and his associates were acting on their own.

38. *XOSL* 212.18a.

39. *Yingzong shilu* (hereafter *YZSL*), in *Ming shilu* (1418 to mid-seventeenth century; facsimile reproduction of *Guoli Beiping tushuguan cang hongge chaoben,* 133 vols.; Taibei: Zhongyang yanjiuyuan lishi yuyan yanjiusuo, 1961–1966), 197.2b, 223.a, 232.7a, 259.2a, 272.3a, 297.4a.

40. *TFSLZ, juan* 33, 2:20. Cf. *juan* 45, 2:293.

41. *XNSL* 55.2b–3a.

42. *Hanyu dacidian,* 12:663. See also Huang Zhangjian, *Mingdai lüli huibian,* pp. 756–757. Herbert Giles translates the term *"xiangma"* as "mounted highwaymen" (*A Chinese-English Dictionary,* 2d ed. [Shanghai: Kelly and Walsh, 1912], p. 531).

43. *TFSLZ, juan* 45, 2:299. A March 1476 report mentions banditry in Beijing (*XNSL* 150.7a).

44. Wanli *Da Ming huidian* 129.15b. In 1492, a year for autumnal examinations in the capital, worried officials reported banditry around the capital and in the Northern Metropolitan Area (*XOSL* 67.1a–1b; Wanli *Da Ming huidian* 136.8a).

45. *TFSLZ, juan* 45, 2:308 (January 10, 1473, report).

46. Ibid., p. 310.

47. *SZSL* (December 5, 1521), 8.4a, 8.15b. For details of the 1510 Rebellion, see chapters 5 and 6; for more on the 1518 insurrection, see chapter 6.

48. *SZSL* 16.5b–6a, 23.2b, 31.3a–3b, 88.1a. Although beyond the scope of the present study, there were also many celebrated tax silver heists outside Beijing's walls during the early seventeenth century. See Yang Guoxiang et al., *Mingshilu leizuan: Beijing shiliaojuan* (Wuhan: Wuhan chubanshe, 1992), pp. 462–465.

49. *Tongzhou zhilüe* (1549), *juan* 2.

50. For Tongzhou's strategic location, see *TFSLZ*, *juan* 34, 2:43. For the commercial activities of imperial in-laws, eunuchs, and other favorites of the emperor in Tongzhou and other important economic centers in and around Beijing, see Han Dacheng, *Mingdai shehui jingji chutan* (Beijing: Zhongguo renmin chubanshe, 1986), pp. 356–394.

51. From the emperor Yingzong's orders to the new Grand Defender on July 13, 1458. The edict is preserved in the 1553 *Liuhe xianzhi*, 6.3a–4a.

52. Ni Yue, "Da Ming gu Ronglu dafu houjun dudufu du du tongzhi Chen Gong muzhiming," *Qingxi mangao* (reprint, Taibei: Taiwan shangwu yinshuguan, 1983), 22.14b–15a; *XNSL* 30.8b.

53. *XNSL* 29.1a. For another report of mounted bandits in Tongzhou (who are said to have been mostly imperial soldiers), see *TFSLZ*, *juan* 45, 2:295.

54. *XNSL* 187.2a.

55. *Tongzhou zhilüe* (1549), 8.2b–3b. There was a branch office for the Imperial Guard located in Tongzhou. Banditry was reported to be widespread during the early 1520s (*WZSL* 105.6b, 120.3a).

56. Resources allocated to Chinese police forces may seem limited by contemporary standards, but when compared to, say, those of Western Europe during similar time periods, they were considerable. For instance, in late sixteenth-century Haute Auvergne, fewer than two dozen men were responsible for a "rugged area of almost 200,000 square kilometers and a population that probably varied between 150,000 and 200,000." See Malcolm Greenshields, *An Economy of Violence in Early Modern France: Crime and Justice in the Haute Auvergne, 1587–1664* (University Park: Pennsylvania State University Press, 1994), p. 49.

57. *Tongzhou zhilüe* (1549), 8.3b–4b.

58. Ibid.

59. *XOSL* 63.10a–10b.

60. *TFSLZ*, *juan* 45, 2:295; Wanli *Da Ming huidian* 136.2a–2b.

61. Ling Mengchu, "Liu Dongshan kuaji Shunchengmen, Shiba xiong zongqi cun jiusi," *Pai-an jingqi* (Late Ming; reprint, Hong Kong: Youlian chubanshe, 1966), *juan* 2, p. 64. Translated in Yang Xianyi and Gladys Yang, *The Courtesan's Jewel Box: Chinese Stories of the Tenth to Seventeenth Centuries* (Beijing: Foreign Language Press, 1981), p. 438.

For security measures between Beijing and Liangxiang during the early seventeenth century, see Guangxu *Shuntian fuzhi* (1884–1886), 7:2323.

62. Shen, *Wanli yehuobian, juan* 24, p. 618.

63. Jiang Yikui, *Chang'an kehua, juan* 6, p. 120. As a sign of Zhangjiawan's prosperity, Jiang noted the sounds of "strings [of musical instruments] and song"; that is, houses of prostitution.

64. Ibid., p. 124; "The Two Brothers," in *The Courtesan's Jewel Box,* p. 117.

65. *TFSLZ, juan* 45, 2:303; *juan* 29, 1:711–712; *juan* 35, 2:60; *juan* 45, 2:311.

66. Ibid., *juan* 29, 1:711–712; *juan* 35, 2:60; *juan* 45, 2:303, 311.

67. Ibid., *juan* 3, 1:69–70; *juan* 45, 2:311.

68. Ibid., *juan* 45, 2:311, from a March 5, 1476, report.

69. Ibid., *juan* 35, 2:723–724.

70. Ibid.

71. Qiu Jun, "Edao zhi ji shang," *Daxue yanyi bu,* 136.4b–5a.

72. *WZSL* 165.4b.

73. *Guangping fuzhi* (1549), 11.11b. The military colonists were from Shen-yang Garrison. This region had experienced bad harvests at the time, which had resulted in land flight. This almost certainly exacerbated whatever existing tensions might have existed between the military colonists and the other local residents.

74. Ibid., 4.12b–13a. The editors of the 1607 *Baoding fuzhi* wrote with similar despair of the descendants of households relocated from Shanxi to Mancheng during the Yongle period. They maintained that the relocated households had originally been criminals and were called "the recalcitrant people." This example suggests that the reputation for unruliness attached to the military camps and colonists may be because they were not "natives." Tensions do seem to have existed between the "newcomers" and the natives. This is another facet of social history in the Northern Metropolitan Area that deserves further investigation.

75. *Baoding fuzhi* (1607), 16.11a–11b, p. 398. The editors' descriptions of soldiers and colonists stationed in other counties are equally unflattering.

76. *Guangping fuzhi* (1549), 16.7b.

77. Qiu Jun, *Qiu Wenzhuang gong ji* 5.8a–8b, reprinted in *JSWB* 75.8a–8b.

78. Jiajing *Tongzhou zhi, juan* 8. For accusations that commanding officers in Daming, Shunde, and Guangping sold abandoned military lands and harbored people fleeing the household registration system, see *XNSL* 86.6a. Problems of housing shortages for troops in Beijing had arisen as early as 1437 (*YZSL* 28.2b–3a).

79. *TFSLZ, juan* 34, 2:59. The grand coordinator of Baoding made similar complaints about military units and banditry in 1515 (*WZSL* 129.5b). For problems of mixed populations and collusion among corrupt clerks and errant military personnel in Changyuan during the early fifteenth century, see Xu You-zhen, "Xiao Jiezhi muzhiming," *Wugong ji,* 4.101, reprinted in Wenyuan ge ed. of *Siku quanshu,* 1245:184.

80. Chen Hongmo, *Jishi jiwen* (reprint, Beijing: Zhonghua shuju, 1985), *juan* 4, p. 93. Gu Yingtai found Chen's comment striking enough to include it verbatim in his narrative of the "Hebei bandits" (*Mingshi jishi benmo* [hereafter *JSBM*]; 1658; reprint, Taibei: Sanlian shuju, 1985, *juan* 45, p. 463).

The grand coordinator of Shandong, Yuan Jie also noted the potential danger of mixed military and commoner populations in Dezhou. See *XNSL* 51.8a. On this question in Daming and Zhending prefectures, see *XOSL* 68.6b. Similar complaints were made in 1480 about the mixed populations of Tong-zhou (*TFSLZ, juan* 34, 2:43).

81. *TFSLZ, juan* 34, 2:59. Those who fenced the goods were called "re-ceivers" *(jieshou)* or "short-footed buyers" *(shoumai duanjiao)* (*TFSLZ, juan* 34, 2:58–59).

82. *XNSL* 71.6b.

83. According to the *Great Ming Commandment,* even travel passes were to be issued separately. Military personnel were to request permits from garrison commanders, while civilians were to request them from subprefectural or county authorities. See Great Ming Commandment, IV.72. Translated in Edward Farmer, *Zhu Yuanzhang and Early Ming Legislation: The Reordering of Chinese Society following the Era of Mongol Rule* (Leiden: E. J. Brill, 1995).

84. *XOSL* 25.5a–5b.

85. *TFSLZ, juan* 33, 2:24.

86. Ibid., *juan* 33, p. 25; *XNSL* (January 9, 1471), 86.6a–6b. It was suggested that the inhabitants of military camps be forced to live together, that registers be posted beside the gates of households, and that the inhabitants be organized into units of ten households. In cases of banditry or conflicts with commoner households, patrols drawn from the mutual responsibility units *(huojia)* were to apprehend the offending parties. In August 1515, the grand coordinator of Baoding recommended that a "colony elder" *(tunlao)* be selected from every military colony and that households be organized into units of ten, from which a "headman" *(zongjia)* would be picked. The grand coordinator felt that bandits were frequently harbored in the camps and believed that mutual security units would eliminate the problem. See *WZSL* 129.5b.

87. It is hardly surprising that local civil officials harbored suspicions of their military colleagues, a sentiment we see reflected in a warning in a magistrate's handbook from the sixteenth century: "Whenever one encounters military officers, one should treat them with courtesy. On no account [however] should one make a practice of drinking with them for fear that with their unruly dispositions, they may inflict injury [on one]. Avoid [drinking with them]. Avoid [it]!" See Jiang Tingbi, *Guozi xiansheng Pushan Jiang Gong zhengxun* (1560), 1.30b; reprinted in *Guanzhenshu jicheng* (Hefei: Huangshan shushe, 1997), p. 16.

88. *TFSLZ, juan* 2, 1.38–40.

89. For more on Shanxi garrison lands located in the Northern Metropolitan Area, see Wang Yuquan, *Mingdai de juntun* (Beijing: Zhonghua shuju, 1965), p. 193, n. 4. It was not unusual for the jurisdiction of a regional military commission not to coincide with that of the Provincial Administration Commission. See Xie Yukai, "Mingdai weisuo zhidu xingshuai kao," *Shuowen yuekan* 2 (1940): 188–191; Tan Qixiang, "Shi Mingdai dusi weisuo zhidu," *Yugong banyue kan* 3.10 (1935): 459–464.

90. *TFSLZ, juan* 2, 1:38–40.

91. *YZSL* 184.17b, 184.19b, 184.20b.

92. For a biographical note on Wang Zhi, see Carrington Goodrich and Chaoying Fang, eds., *Dictionary of Ming Biography, 1368–1644* (New York and London: Columbia University Press, 1976), pp. 1357–1358.

93. The characters in the text are *"li shi,"* but I suspect this is a scribe's error. I have followed Professor Frederick Mote's suggested reading in the translation.

94. *TFSLZ, juan* 45, 2:624. Although the specific regions are not mentioned in Wang Zhi's memorial as recorded in the *TFSLZ,* an abbreviated version preserved in a March 13, 1479, entry from the *XNSL* indicates that the bandits in question were of the capital region (187.4a).

95. *TFSLZ* 45:298. Also in 1488, the new grand coordinator of the Northern Metropolitan Area was told to keep an eye on the Ming Mongols, who might otherwise turn to banditry. See *XOSL* 10.7a.

96. Song was actually of Jurchen descent.

97. *XNSL* 151.5a–5b.

98. See Zhu, *Yongzhuang xiaopin* (1621) (reprint, Beijing: Zhonghua shuju, 1959), *juan* 32, pp. 757–758; Huang Wei, *Pengchuang leiji* (1526), in *Hanfenlou biji*, ed. Sun Yuxiu; reprint, Taibei: Taibei shangwu yinshuguan, 1967, *juan* 5, p. 47b. Wang Shouren heard tales of Xi and Wang during his sojourn in Beijing in 1486 when he was fourteen. See *Wang Yangming quanji* (Shanghai: Shanghai guji chubanshe, 1992), p. 1222.

99. Xi Ying, Song Quan, and Wang Yong were probably all members of an abortive 1461 coup d'état. See David Robinson, "Politics, Force, and Ethnicity in Ming China: Mongols and the Abortive Coup of 1461," *Harvard Journal of Asiatic Studies* 59.1 (June 1999).

100. *XNSL* 265.7a.

101. Huang Wei, *Pengchuang leiji*, 5.47b. There is a striking similarity between Xi and Wang turning to banditry after the decline of their political patron and the conditions that led the leaders of the 1510 Rebellion to defy the dynasty after the fall of their patron Liu Jin. See chapter 5.

102. *TFSLZ*, *juan* 45, 2:298.

103. *YZSL* 222.4a, 222.1b.

104. *TFSLZ*, *juan* 34, 2:39. For an example of similar complaints in the 1420s, see Yu Jideng, *Diangu jiwen*, in *Jifu congshu*, no. 14, *Baibu congshu jicheng*, no. 94, 8.1b.

Writing in the 1530s, the noted Italian statesman Guicciardini wrote of the "licentiousness of soldiers no less destructive to friends than foes" (quoted in J. R. Hale, *War and Society in Renaissance Europe: 1450–1620* [New York: St. Martin's Press, 1985], p. 179. See also pp. 180–200).

105. *TFSLZ*, *juan* 45, 2:295.

106. Ibid., p. 296.

107. *XOSL* 215.6a; *Guo que*, p. 2820. It was further noted that because the Mongols on the northern border were not a pressing threat at the time, sending the Mongols from Baoding and Hejian to train in the capital would be a waste of money.

108. *XOSL* 72.4a–4b.

109. For the fiscal difficulties of Xiaozong's reign, see Li Shaoqiang, "Shilun Ming Xiaozong de fushui zhengce," *Beifang luncong* 5 (1992): 62–66; Zheng Kecheng, *Mingdai zhengzheng tanyuan* (Tianjin: Tianjin guji chubanshe, 1988), pp. 287–297.

110. For example, see Zhu Ji's 1468 report on banditry, in which he notes that many were from military units (*XNSL* 55.2b–3a; *TFSLZ*, *juan* 33, 2:20–21). Also *XNSL* 53.9a, 71.6b; *TFSLZ*, *juan* 35, 2:723–724 (a 1490 case); and *XOSL* 211.10b–11a.

The problem of imperial soldiers engaging in banditry was by no means restricted to the Ming. For a brief discussion of soldiers, especially deserting soldiers, who took up brigandage during the Song, see McKnight, *Law and Order*, pp. 70–73.

111. This memorial by the famed statesman Ma Wensheng is recorded in *XOSL* 28.12a.

112. On mutual responsibility systems, the *baojia,* and urban security during the Song, see McKnight, *Law and Order,* pp. 121–129, 137–145, 289–320. For more on the *baojia* system in the Ming, see Sakai Tadao, "Mindai zenchūki no hōkasei ni tsuite," pp. 577–610; Chen Baoliang, "Mingdai de baojia yu huojia," *Mingshi yanjiu* 3 (1993), pp. 59–66, 134. On the mutual security organizations of Ming Beijing, see Wakeland, "Metropolitan Administration in Ming China," pp. 250–260. For the role of detailed census records in maintaining order in Qing Beijing, see Alison Dray-Novey, "Spatial Order and Police in Imperial Beijing," *Journal of Asian Studies* 52.4 (1993): 897–902.

113. On the use of troops in the policing of the Song capital of Kaifeng, see McKnight, *Law and Order,* pp. 296–303.

114. On the community covenants as a way to shore up local order during the mid-Ming, see Zhu Honglin, "Mingdai zhongqi fangshe zhian chongjian lixiang zhi zhanxian," *Chungguk hakpo* 32 (1992): 87–100.

115. *XOSL* 21.4a–4b. In another undated memorial, Yu Zijun suggested door-to-door inspections to rout out criminals, and the establishment of citizen patrols *(huofu)* ("Yanbu daozei shi," in Huang Xun, ed., *Huang Ming mingchen jingji lu* [1551; photographic reprint of copy held in Naikaku bunko], 40.5a).

116. For Hongzhi-period Daming, see Zhang Xuan, *Xiyuan wenjian lu, juan* 96, cited in Chen Baoliang, "Mingdai de baojia yu huofu," p. 60; for Zhengde-period Zhending and Guangping, see chapter 5; for a general call during the late-Zhengde period, see *SZSL* 6.10a–10b; for late-Zhengde-period Beijing, see *SZSL* 8.15b; for Jiajing-period Beijing, see *SZSL* 50.21a; for Shunde during the late 1530s, see *SZSL* 218.3b; Xu Guo, "Tiaoshang midao fanglue," in *JSWB,* 392.8b–10a.

117. For example, see *XNSL* 29.1a, where a regional military commissioner and a censor were appointed to oversee the area from Tongzhou to Linqing, while a highly ranked officer of the Imperial Guard and a second censor were ordered to supervise the eradication of bandits from Linqing to Yizhen. In a commemorative essay dedicated to an officer in the Imperial Guard about to commence these seasonal patrols, Luo Qi notes that the officer had gained his present post for valor in battle against Jurchen tribesmen in the northeast. "In the dead of night during the fighting at Jianzhou," the officer "had taken the head of a caitiff and presented it to headquarters [for promotion and reward]. It was as if he had been killing nothing more than a fox in the city walls or a mouse on the altar." Luo felt certain that the officer would make short work of the bandits south of the capital. See his "Song Jinyi Zhang Hou chuluo xu," *Luokuifeng ji,* in *TSWB* 125.6a.

118. *Da Ming huidian* (1587), 228.9a; *Tongzhou zhilüe* 2.8a.

119. Chen Quanzhi, *Pengchuang rilu* (1565; reprint, Shanghai: Shanghai shudian, 1985), "Huanyu," 1.22b.

120. *YZSL* 272.3a. Widespread flooding had been reported at the time in the prefectures of Shuntian, Hejian, and Baoding (*YZSL* 272.2a).

121. *XNSL* 53.8a–8b; *Da Ming huidian* (1587) 136.2a. The banditry should be understood in the context of widespread drought and massive crop failure

in Shandong, Henan, the Southern and Northern Metropolitan Areas, and Huguang (*XNSL* 53.7b).

122. Qiu Jun, "Edao zhi ji shang," *Daxue yanyi bu*, 136.4b.

123. *XOSL* 10.6b–7a.

124. Ibid., 17.8b–9a.

125. Ibid., 67.1a–1b.

126. *Da Ming huidian* (1587), 136.8a.

127. *Shuilu lucheng* 6.5a. This work was originally published by Huang Bian in 1570 under the title *Yitong lucheng tuji*. In 1617, it was republished by Shang Jun under the title *Shuilu lucheng*. See Timothy Brook, *Geographical Sources for Ming-Qing History* (Ann Arbor: University of Michigan, 1988), p. 38.

128. See chapter 4 for details.

129. Huang Liuhong, *Fuhui quanshu* (1694; reprint, Tokyo: Kyūko shoten, 1973), 17.1b–2a, p. 192.

130. Punishment could be avoided if (1) at least half of the accused were apprehended, or (2) the most wanted among the accused were captured. See Huang Zhangjian, *Mingdai lüli huibian*, 2:959; Staunton, *Ta Tsing Leu Lee*, pp. 420–421.

131. Huang Zhangjian, *Mingdai lüli huibian*, 2:969.

132. Ibid., p. 971.

133. One might also note that grain paid in fines in many areas of the capital region and the Northern Metropolitan Area was transported to strategic garrisons in North China. See *YZSL* 223.13b.

134. For instance, in 1488 the vice-director of the Ministry of Revenue recommended that except in very important cases, intendants (*guanxiao*) from the Eastern Depot should not be dispatched outside the capital. See *XOSL* 9.9a.

135. See *Mingdai tewu zhengzhi*, pp. 36–38; Xiao Lijun, "Mingdai de zhifa fanfa ji chengzhi cuoshi," *Wenshi zashi* 5 (1994): 42–43.

136. In December 1452, the court announced that the offenses of bandits who surrendered and turned their fellow criminals in to authorities would receive half the family assets of those who failed to turn themselves in (*YZSL* 223.7a).

137. *YZSL* 330.4a.

138. *XNSL* 150.2b.

139. For the variety of realities comprehended by the term "*tuan lian*," local defense during the first half of the nineteenth century, see Philip Khun, "The T'uan-lien Local Defense System at the Time of the Taiping Rebellion," *Harvard Journal of Asiatic Studies* 27 (1967): 218–255.

Chapter 4   The Management of Violence

1. Edward Dreyer has argued that during the first decades of the dynasty, the martial and the military elements of the government and society were more prominent than they would be later. See his *Early Ming China: A Political History, 1355–1435* (Stanford: Stanford University Press, 1982).

2. This is not to suggest complete satisfaction with the examination system as a way to recruit talent for the government. During the early Ming, some, like Gui Yanliang, insisted on the need to actively seek promising scholars,

regardless of their social status or occupation. See his "Shang taiping zhiyao shier tiao," *Gui Zheng zi ji,* reprinted in *JSWB,* 7.8a–8b.

For a magisterial account of the examination system during the late imperial period, see Benjamin Elman, *A Cultural History of Civil Service Examinations in Late Imperial China* (Berkeley: University of California Press, 2000).

3. The way important military posts were filled changed during the course of the dynasty. Over the fifteenth century, such posts as commissioner-in-chief, vice-commissioner-in-chief, assistant commissioner-in-chief, regional commander, and heads of capital garrisons increasingly were occupied by lower-ranking officers with field experience rather than hereditary nobles, as during the early decades of the dynasty. See Matsumoto Takaharu, "Mindai bukyo ni tsuite no ichi kōsatsu," in *Yamane Yukio kyōju taikyū kinen Mindaishi ronsō* (Tokyo: Mindaishi ronsō henshūiinkai, 1990), pp. 131–147; Okuyama Norio, "Mindai chūki no keiei ni kansuru ichi kōsatsu," *Mindaishi kenkyū* 8 (1980): 1–19. Tani Mitsutaka has argued that this trend accelerated in the wake of Altan Khan's attack on Beijing in 1550 ("Mindai no kunshin ni kansuru ichi kōsatsu," *Tōyōshi kenkyū* 29.4 [1971]: 66–113).

4. For introductory discussions of the military examinations during the Ming period, see Matsumoto, "Mindai bukyo ni tsuite no ichi kōsatsu"; Chao Zhongchen and Chen Fenglu, "Mingdai de wuju zhidu," *Mingshi yanjiu* 3 (1993): 52–58, 92. There was a clear recognition that military talent was neither hereditary nor the monopoly of the families of generals. Some early Ming observers were confident that a military examination would be sufficient to identify military talent and place it at the disposal of the state. See Xu Youzhen (js. 1433), "Tiao yi wu shi shu," *Xu wu gong wenji,* reprinted in *JSWB* 37.3a; Xie Jin, "Da Paoxi fengshi," *Xie Xueshi wenji,* reprinted in *JSWB* 11.9b.

5. Ling Mengchu, "Shentou jixing yi zhi mei: Xiadao guanxing sanmei xi," in Ling Mengchu, *Erke pai'an jingqi* (1632; reprint, 1983; Shanghai: Shanghai guji chubanshe), *juan* 39, pp. 713–714. For a short biographical note on Ling, see Carrington Goodrich and Chaoying Fang, eds., *Dictionary of Ming Biography, 1368–1644* (New York: Columbia University Press, 1976), pp. 930–931. One might note that Ling himself passed only the lowest level of the three-tiered civil service examination.

6. In a general sense, the recruitment of soldiers predates the formal establishment of the Ming dynasty, as Zhu Yuanzhang worked to increase the size of his forces. Recruiting took on new importance for social control as Zhu's principal enemies were defeated, and the empire was inundated with recently demobilized soldiers. The founder noted the problems that these soldiers might cause if they returned to their villages. See *TZSL* 72.3a.

7. The standard biography of Zhu Yuanzhang remains Wu Han's classic, *Zhu Yuanzhang zhuan* (Hong Kong: Zhuanji wenxue she, 1949).

8. This section draws heavily on Edward Farmer's recent *Zhu Yuanzhang and Early Ming Legislation: The Reordering of Chinese Society following the Era of Mongol Rule* (Leiden: E. J. Brill, 1995). See also Timothy Brook, *The Confusions of Pleasure: Commerce and Culture in Ming China* (Berkeley: University of California Press, 1998).

9. On the *lijia* system, see Tsurumi Naohiro, "Rural Control in the Ming Dynasty." Originally published as "Mindai ni okeru kyōson shihai" in *Iwanami*

kōza sekaishi, vol. 12 (Tokyo: Iwanami shoten, 1971); translated by Timothy Brook and James Cole, in Linda Groves and Christian Daniels, eds., *State and Society in China: Japanese Perspectives on Ming-Qing Social and Economic History* (Tokyo: University of Tokyo Press, 1984), pp. 245–277. On the elders system, see Chang Der-lang, "The Village Elder System of the Early Ming Dynasty," *Ming Studies* 7 (Fall 1978): 53–72. For an insightful treatment of both these systems, see Martin Heijdra, "The Socio-Economic Development of Rural China during the Ming," in Denis Twitchett and Frederick Mote, eds., *The Cambridge History of China,* vols. 7 and 8 (pts. 1 and 2), *The Ming Dynasty, 1368–1644* (Cambridge: Cambridge University Press, 1998), 8:458–475.

10. Wang Yuqian, "Some Salient Features of the Ming Labor Service System," *Ming Studies* 21 (Spring 1986): 3. For a partial list of the household categories under the Ming, see the appendix of Wang's article.

11. Ibid., p. 10.

12. Translated by Chang Der-lang, "The Village Elder System of the Early Ming Dynasty," pp. 65–66. According to one government estimate, nearly 50,000 soldiers deserted armies under the command of the founder and his commanders during the period from 1367 to 1371. See *TZSL* 59.8a.

13. Lin Jinshu, "Hongwuchao nongmin qiyi chutan," *Zhongguo nongmin zhanzhengshi luncong* 4 (1982): 430; Shen Dingping, "Mingdai qianqi jieji douzheng shulun," *Mingshi yanjiu luncong* 3 (1985): 215.

14. For the impact of these military exiles on China's northeastern region of Liaodong, see Yang Yang, Liang De, and Hong Yun, "Mingdai zheyu Liaodong liuren yanjiu," *Mingshi yanjiu* 2 (1992): 122–131.

15. The relevant scholarship is voluminous. Excellent treatments may be found in Yu Zhijia, *Mingdai junhu shixi zhidu* (Taibei: Xuesheng shuju, 1987); Wang Yuquan, "Mingdai de junhu," *Lishi yanjiu* 8 (1959): 21–34; reprinted in his *Laiwu ji* (Beijing: Zhonghua shuju, 1983), pp. 342–361; Wang Yuquan, *Mingdai de juntun* (Beijing: Zhonghua shuju, 1965).

16. Wang Shuying (d. 1402), "Zizhi ce shu," *Wang Hanlin zoushu,* reprinted in *JSWB* 12.1b, 12.3a.

17. Li Shimian (1374–1450), "Bianmin shi shu," *Li Zhongwen zoushi,* reprinted in *JSWB* 21.10a.

18. Yu Zhijia, "Mingdai Jiangxi weisuo junyi de yanbian," *Zhongyang yanjiuyuan shiyusuo yanjiusuo jikan* 68.1 (1997): 1–51.

19. Sŏ In-bŏm, "Minchūki no hokuben bōei to gunko—zaiei no yotei o chūshin toshite," *Shūkan Tōyōgaku* 78 (1997): 81–103.

20. Yu Zhijia notes that by the end of the sixteenth century, more and more functions performed by supernumerary soldiers had been commuted into silver payments ("Mingdai Jiangxi weisuo junyi de yanbian"). The question of who was hired to actually perform those functions remains unclear. For a trenchant criticism of dismissing the Ming military as being in terminal decline from the early fifteenth century, see Kawagoe Yasuhiro, "Mindai gunjishi ni kansuru kenkyūjōkyō o megutte," in Mori Masao, Noguchi Tetsurō, and Hamashima Atsutoshi, eds., *Min-Shin jidaishi no kihon mondai* (Tokyo: Kyūko shoin, 1997), pp. 268–270.

21. The standard account in English is Frederick Mote, "The T'u-mu Incident of 1449," in Frank Kierman and John Fairbank, eds., *Chinese Ways in War-*

fare (Cambridge: Harvard University Press, 1974). For Tumu's impact on Ming court politics, see Philip de Heer, *The Caretaker Emperor: Aspects of the Imperial Institution in Fifteenth-Century China As Reflected in the Political History of the Reign of Chu Ch'i-yü* (Leiden: E. J. Brill, 1985). For a biographical note on Esen, see Morris Rossabi in Carrington Goodrich and Chaoying Fang, eds., *Dictionary of Ming Biography, 1368–1644* (New York: Columbia University Press, 1976), pp. 416–422. For a revisionist interpretation of the campaign, see Kawagoe Yasuhiro, "Tomoku no hen to shinseigun," *Tōyōshi kenkyū* 52.1 (June 1993): 24–55.

22. Some officials explicitly linked the problems along the northern border with threats in the south. See the comments of Liu Bin (js. 1445), "Fuchou shu," *Liu Huangmen zoushu*, reprinted in *JSWB*, 23.6b. Sun Yuanzhen (js. 1415) called for a heightened defensive posture along the eastern coast, presumably in anticipation of attacks by Japanese pirates (Sun, "Bian wu," *Sun Sima zoushu*, reprinted in *JSWB*, 24.9b–13a). For comments on the Tumu Incident's influence on intellectual developments, see Chu Hung-lam, "Intellectual Trends in the Fifteenth Century," *Ming Studies* 27 (Spring 1989): 1–33. See de Heer, *The Caretaker Emperor*, for a detailed discussion of Beijing's defense.

23. On the reorganization of the capital garrisons in the immediate wake of the Tumu Incident, see Luo Lixin, "Mingdai jingying zhi xingcheng yu shuaibai," *Mingshi yanjiu zhuankan* 6 (1983): 12–16; Shen Dingping, "Mingchao junzhi," in Liu Zhan, ed., *Zhongguo gudai junzhishi* (Junshi kexue chubanshe, 1992), pp. 423–424.

24. For the impact of the Tumu Incident on the recruitment of "people's stalwarts" and local militias, see Sŏ, "Tomoku no hen to kinōhei," *Tōyō gakuhō* 82:1 (2000). Sŏ does not consider recruiting in the light of social control.

This is not to suggest that the recruitment of competent military talent became an important issue only after the Tumu Incident. As Matsumoto Takaharu has noted, the issue of identifying qualified military officers had been discussed at court from at least the early fifteenth century, and several proposals regarding the establishment of a military examination system were advanced ("Mindai bukyo," pp. 131–136). There were also periodic calls for men of superior strength or martial abilities to register with local civil and military authorities prior to 1449. For instance, see Chen Zhi's 1439 memorial (*YZSL* 57.7a–8a), cited in Matsumoto, p. 134. Chen's proposed recruiting drive was restricted to men within the hereditary military system.

25. *YZSL* 184.6b.

26. For biographical information on Yang Hong and his sons, see *MS* 15.173.4607–4613.

27. *YZSL* 187.11b.

28. Ibid., 186.22a–22b. The memorial was included in the *JSWB* 23.6b–12a (Liu Bin, "Fuchou shu" *Liu Huangmen zoushu*).

29. *YZSL* 189.4b–5a.

30. *WZSL* 2.15b. The plan was proposed by Chu Quan (1457–1513). The full text of his memorial can be found in Chu's collected works, entitled *Chaixu ji* (photographic facsimile, Rare Book Collection, Gest Oriental Library, Princeton University; original, Naikaku bunko), 12.10a–10b.

31. See Liu Jian, "Yulu anbian shiyi shu," *Liu wenjing gong zoushu*, reprinted in *JSWB* 52.16b. This memorial appears to date from the late fifteenth or early sixteenth century.

32. "Touchong junyi shoucao ganyou yingqiu maixianzhe diaowei chong-junli," Bingbulei, *TFSLZ* 2:436–437.

33. "Jizhou Yongpingfu Shanhai dengchu," Bingbulei, *TFSLZ* 2:432–433.

34. Qiu Jun, "Dingjun zhi yi," in *JSWB* 74.3a.

35. See chapter 3 for details.

36. Li Dongyang, "Quan Shaan bianbei," in *Li Wenzheng,* reprinted in *JSWB* 54.7b. Recruits who served in militia forces were on occasion subject to later reenlistment, not always on a voluntary basis. For instance, during the mid-fifteenth century, the prominent official Li Xian proposed to the throne that braves who had been demobilized from militias in Shanxi and Shaanxi be reassembled to bolster defenses against Mongol incursions. See Li Xian, "Bian-fang shiyi," in Li Xian, *Li Wenda wenji,* reprinted in *JSWB* 36.24a–24b.

37. This practice of recruiting "unregistered ones" has clear parallels in early-modern Europe. For instance, in 1626, the Privy Council ordered the Lords Lieutenant to press "unnecessary persons that now want employment and live lewdly or unprofitably." According to Frank Tallett, this practice had been "pre-figured in Elizabethan poor law legislation between 1585 and 1602" (*War and Society in Early-Modern Europe, 1495–1715* [London: Routledge, 1992], pp. 81–82).

38. For the ubiquity of suspicions surrounding mendicant monks during the Qing period, see Philip Kuhn, *Soulstealers* (Cambridge: Harvard University Press, 1990).

39. Lin Cong (1417–1482), "Xiude mizai ershi shi shu," *Lin zhuang min zoushu,* reprinted in *JSWB* 45.10b–12a. The quotation appears on 45.11b.

40. There were other efforts to absorb this somewhat ill-defined portion of Beijing society. For instance, Qiu Jun advocated commuting into silver pay-ments a number of corvée labor responsibilities borne by people in the coun-ties south of the capital. Government authorities were then to use the silver to hire "the loafers and the lazy in the city" as substitutes. See Qiu, "Dingjun zhi yi," in *JSWB* 74.5b.

41. Liu Jian, "Yulu anbian shiyi shu," 52.18a.

42. During an outbreak of piracy along China's southeastern coast in 1382, the emperor ordered ten thousand boat people in Guangdong to be regis-tered as imperial sailors. These households previously had no fixed residences and reportedly engaged in piracy on occasion. See *TZSL* 143.5b.

43. David Robinson, "Politics, Force, and Ethnicity in Ming China: Mongols and the Abortive Coup of 1461," *Harvard Journal of Asiatic Studies* 59.1 (June 1999): 85–96.

44. Again, similar motivations may be found in early-modern Europe. Frank Tallet writes, "The real target of impressment and militia legislation were the masterless and unemployed. . . . In enlisting such men officials hoped not merely to find recruits for the army, but also rid the body politic of undesirable elements" (*War and Society,* p. 87).

45. Zhang Chun (js. 1421), "Fuchou shu," *Zhang Zhongcheng zoushu,* re-printed in *JSWB,* 23.4a.

46. The most common terms during the middle Ming period seem to have been *"jiading," "jianer,"* and, more ambiguously, *"jiaren."* For a more compre-hensive list, see Ma Chujian, "Mingdai de jiading," *Mingshi yanjiu zhuankan* 8 (December 1985): 191–252.

47. See Ma Chujian, "Mingdai de jiading"; Suzuki Tadashi, "Mindai kahei

kō," *Shikan* 22–23 (1940): 1–26, and "Mindai katei kō," *Shikan* 37 (1952): 23–40; Xiao Xu, "Mingdai jiangshuai jiading de xingshuai ji qi yingxiang," *Nankai shixue* 1 (1984): 102–122; Zhao Zhongnan, "Lun Mingdai junduizhong jiading de tedian yu diwei," *Shehui kexue zhanxian* 3 (1988): 144–149, and "Shilun Mingdai junshi jiading zhidu xingcheng de shehui jingji tiaojian jiqi fazhan," *Shehui kexue jikan* 2 (1991): 86–90.

48. Lu Shen (1477–1544), "Nilun quhui dudu yongshi zhuang," in *Lu Wenlu gong wenji* in *JSWB, juan* 155.

49. *WZSL* 141.3a.

50. Ibid., 141.4a.

51. Okuyama Norio, "Mindai junbu seido no hensen," *Tōyōshi kenkyū* 45.2 (September 1986): 55–88.

52. It is unclear whether his troops accompanied him from a previous post or were recruited locally. For instance, Weng Wanda (1498–1552) noted that mercenaries under the grand coordinator, called "troops of the standard," were recruited from among "those between battalion leaders and farmers." He observed that among these were martial arts adepts, convicts, military officers and retainers who had been relieved of their duties, as well as non-Han peoples from north of the Great Wall ("Liangchu bingma shu," in *JSWB* 224.2a; cited in Okuyama Norio, "Mindai junbu seido no hensen," p. 75).

53. *Zhending fuzhi* (1549), 9.22b. Ning developed a reputation for brutality and an inability or unwillingness to exercise proper discipline over his men. The same passage in the gazetteer notes that Ning's men were not above killing innocent commoners and passing their heads off as those of bandits to claim rewards.

54. The recruiting of brigands and local toughs to enforce local order dates back at least to the early Han dynasty. See Sima Qian, "Harsh Officials," in *Records of the Historian*, translated by Burton Watson (New York: Columbia University Press, 1969), pp. 300–332.

55. Thomas Nimick, "The County, the Magistrate, and the Yamen in Late Ming China" (Ph.D. diss., Princeton University, 1993), pp. 148–192; Bo Hua, "Mingdai zhouxian guanli chengchu guizhi chouyi," *Mingshi yanjiu* 4 (1994): 60–67, and "Mingdai zhixian de guanxiwang," *Shixue jikan* 4 (1993): 47–55. Bo Hua seems to overstate officials' ability to escape punishment for their various administrative, economic, and moral transgressions. For local elite's attempts to discredit magistrates by leaking (and not infrequently fabricating) their misdeeds to administrative superiors, see Wada Masahiro, "Minmatsu kahō no shutsugen katei," *Tōyōshi kenkyū* 62.1–2 (1980): 71–98.

56. Nimick, "The County, the Magistrate, and the Yamen," pp. 32–34; Li Xun, "Lun Mingdai de li," *Mingshi yanjiu* 4 (1994): 51–59. On the growth of administrative retinues during the Qing period, see Miao Quanji, "Qingdai mufu zhidu zhi chengzhang yuanyin," *Si yu yan* 5.3 (September 1967): 25–33. By the late Ming period, some magistrates also traveled from post to post with their own modest administrative retinues.

57. Cha Hye-wǒn, "Minmatsu chihōkan no ninji idō to chihō yōron," *Shirin* 79.1 (January 1996): 32–60.

58. For an overview of Ming salaries, see Wang Yinghua, "Mingdai guanfengzhi qianxi," *Shixue jikan* 2 (2000): 82–89.

59. Wu Yue, "Mindai no saishingin ni tsuite: Yōeki to kanryō shūnyū no kankei," *Shirin* 78.4 (July 1995): 98–123; later reprinted in a slightly revised form in the author's *Min Shin jidai no yōeki seido to chihōgyōsei* (Ōsaka: Ōsaka keizai hōka daigaku shuppansha, 2000); Nimick, "The County, the Magistrate, and the Yamen," p. 128.

60. Nimick, "The County, the Magistrate, and the Yamen," pp. 129–131. For details of the use of corvée services to cover administrative costs, see Wu Yue, "Sōko o meguru saeki ni tsuite—Min-Shin jidai ni okeru yōeki to gyōsei no kankei" (in three parts), *Osaka keizai hōka daigaku Higashi Ajia kenkyū* 11–13 (1996): 49–56, 39–54, 63–71, and "Administrative Costs of Local Governments during the Ming-Qing Period," *Transactions of the International Conference of Eastern Studies* 41 (1996): 105–113.

61. Gu Yanwu, *Tianxia junguo libing shu* 82.20b–21a. Cited in Saeki Tomi, "Min-Shin jidai no minsō ni tsuite," *Tōyōshi kenkyū* 15.4 (1957): 51.

62. Hu Shining, "Chenyan shizheng bianbei shu," in *Hu Duanmin zouyi*, reprinted in *Siku quanshu zhenben*, series 7, 76:1.16b–17a.

63. Chu Quan, "Ti yi fang luhuan," *Chaixu wenji*, 12.10a–10b.

64. Yang Yiqing, "Chenyan chuzhi difang jinji zeiqing shu." A much-abbreviated version of Yang's memorial is recorded in the *WZSL* (73.6a–6b). A slightly abbreviated version of the memorial is contained in *Huang Ming shuchao*, a 1584 collection of memorials edited by Sun Xun (reprint, Taibei: Xuesheng shuju, 1986), 11:4688–4715. For a brief note on the content and editions of Sun's work, see Wolfgang Franke, *An Introduction to the Sources of Ming History* (Kuala Lumpur, University of Malaya Press, 1968), pp. 122–123. While the contents of the two fuller versions of Yang's memorial do not differ greatly, the imperial rescript of the Martial Ancestor is found only in *Libu xianna gao*, a collection of Yang's memorials submitted during his tenure as Minister of Personnel (microfilm, Rare Book Collection, Gest Oriental Library, Princeton University). The citations below refer to the more widely available Taibei reprint. See Sun Xun, *Huang Ming shuchao*, p. 4706.

65. Yang Yiqing, in *Huang Ming shuchao*, p. 4698.

66. Ibid. For Su Shi's memorial, "Dai Li Zong lun jingdong daozei zhuang" (A Memorial on behalf of Li Zong Discussing Banditry in Jingdong), see *Su Shi wenji* (Beijing: Zhonghua shuju, 1992), 3:1058–1060.

67. Yang Yiqing, in *Huang Ming shuchao*, p. 4698.

68. Ibid. For details of Qin's life, see Julia Ching, in *Sung Biographies*, ed. Herbert Franke (Weisbaden: Franz Steiner Verlag GMBH, 1976), 1:235–241. The passage that Yang Yiqing quoted is from the last of a series of three memorials on the question of banditry that Qin submitted to the throne (*Huaihaiji juan* 17 in the Wenyuange edition of the *Siku quanshu*, Taibei reprint, 1983, 1115:512–515). In the first memorial, Qin argued that while banditry did not represent the obvious threat that foreign enemies did, it should nevertheless be snuffed out in its early stages. The key to doing so lay in the merciless execution of the bandit leaders and the offer of pardon to those followers who surrendered to the authorities.

69. Yang Yiqing, in *Huang Ming shuchao*, 4698.

70. Ibid., 4699.

71. Ibid.

72. Ibid., 4701.

73. Ibid.

74. The mid-nineteenth-century Nien Rebellion of the Huaibei region is just one of the more well-known instances of how government-sponsored militarization could in turn feed rebellion. See Elizabeth Perry, *Rebels and Revolutionaries in North China, 1845–1945* (Stanford: Stanford University, 1980), pp. 122–123.

75. For a brief biographical note on Qiu, see Goodrich and Chaoying Fang, eds., *Dictionary of Ming Biography*, pp. 249–252. The authoritative work on Qiu's massive work, the *Daxue yanyibu*, is Chu Hung-lam's "Ch'iu Chün (1421–1495) and the *Ta-hsueh yen-i-pu*: Statecraft Thought in Fifteenth-Century China" (Ph.D. diss., Princeton University, 1983).

76. Qiu Jun, "Edao zhi ji xia," *Daxue yanyibu* (1506; 1632 ed., Rare Book Collection, Harvard-Yenching Library, Harvard University), 138.9a.

77. They appear in the following collections (for bibliographic details, see Yamane Yukio and Yu Zhijia, *Mindai keiseibun bunrui mokuroku* [Tokyo: Tōyō bunko, 1986]); Chen Zilong et al., eds., *JSWB*; *Huang Ming jingji wenlu*, ed., *Huang Ming jingji wenlu*; Chen Jiude, ed., *Huang Ming Mingchen jingjilu*; and Huang Xun, ed., *Huang Ming Mingchen jingjilu*.

78. Robinson, "Politics, Force, and Ethnicity in Ming China," pp. 99–100.

79. For further details on Zhang Zhong's military career, see David Robinson, "Banditry and Rebellion in the Capital Region during the Mid-Ming (1450–1525)" (Ph.D. diss., Princeton University, 1995), 192–195.

80. For a discussion of criticisms leveled against eunuchs for their entourages, see Noda Tōru, "Mindai gaikangan no ichi keitai ni tsuite—chinshu kangan o megutte," *Kyūshū daigaku Tōyōshi kenkyū ronshū* 24 (1996): 34–44. Noda does not consider the possibility that entourage members may have had any actual military function.

81. For a biographical note on Liu Daxia, see Goodrich and Chaoying Fang, eds., *Dictionary of Ming Biography*, pp. 958–962.

82. Liu Daxia, "Zaiyi chen sanshi shu," *Liu Zhongxuan ji*, in *JSWB* 79.9a–9b.

83. Yamane Yukio, "Genmatsu no ran to Minchō shihai no kakuritsu," in *Higashi Ajia sekai no tenkai, 2: Sekai rekishi 12, chūsei 6*, ed. Iwanami kōzō (Tokyo: Iwanami shoten, 1979), pp. 17–56; Taniguchi Kikuo, "Minmatsu kyōhei gihei ni tsuite-Minmatsu seikyoku hitokusari" (Kōbe daigaku bungakubu), *Kenkyū* 43 (1969): 99–122, and "Minmatsu Shinsho no hosai ni tsuite," [Hiratsuka] *Tōkai daigaku shigakki* 9 (1973): 1–15; Li Wenzhi, "Mingmo de zhaibao yu yijun," *Wenshi zazhi* 3.7–8 (1944), reprinted in *Mingshi yanjiu luncong*, ed. Wu Zhihe (Taibei: Dali chubanshe, 1984), 2:262–274.

84. See Chen Baoliang, "Mingdai xiangcun de fangyu tizhi," *Qi Lu xuekan* 6 (1993): 100–108, and "Mingdai de minbing yu xiangbing," *Zhongguoshi yanjiu* 1 (1994): 82–92.

85. Lu Shen, "Chengdelang gongbu zhushi Liu gong zeng anren Zhao shi hezang muzhiming," *Yanshan ji* 73.3a–3b, reprinted in Wenyuan ge edition of *Siku quanshu* 1268:467. For what appears to be a derivative version, see Zhu Guozhen, *Yongzhuang xiaopin* (1621; reprint, Beijing: Zhonghua shuju, 1959), p. 757. Lu's account holds that the local magnate was a "local close to the outlaw," while Zhu maintains that he was a member of the local gentry. As Lu's account makes clear later, cooperating with authorities had its own dangers.

Not only did the magnate relocate to the city (perhaps because of dangers in rural areas), but he fell victim to competition among local officials.

86. For the defense of Cangzhou, see Xie Fen, *Houjian lu* (hereafter *HJL*) (early sixteenth century; in Xie Guozhen, ed., *Mingshi ziliao congkan*, 1st series, pp. 4–160 [Jiangsu renmin chubanshe, 1981]), p. 20; *Cangzhou zhi* (1603), 1.9b, 2.1b; Guo Tingxun, *Benchao fensheng renwu kao* (1622; reprint, Taibei: Chengwen chubanshe, 1971), 99.15b–18a; and *WZSL* 79.1b–2a. For the defense of Yuzhou, see Robinson, "Banditry and Rebellion," p. 338.

87. Ma Li and Wei Wenying, "Qinci biaolu Wang yishi xingshiji," *Xiayi xianzhi* (1548) (reprinted in *Tianyige cang Mingdai fangzhi xuankan*. Shanghai: Shanghai guji shudian, 1982), 8.71a–74b, 7.18a–19b.

88. *Fuyang xianzhi* (1755) (reprint, Taibei: Chengwen chubanshe, 1985), 3.16a–16b, 2:641–642. Known as the General Lu Temple, the temple still stood in the mid-1750s.

89. Abuses associated with housemen and retainers appear to have been especially severe in Liaodong because of the unusual power of military commanders and officers in this strategically critical region. For a brief discussion of Liaodong elites during the late Ming, see Jiang Shoupeng, "Mingmo Liaodong shizu," *Shehui kexue zhanxian* 2 (1987): 203–209.

90. *XOSL* 196.7a.

91. *WZSL* 144.1b.

92. *Bozhou zhi* (1564); (microfilm, Rare Book Collection, Gest Oriental Library, Princeton University), 4.40a–40b.

93. *WZSL* 144.1b.

94. Lu Shen, "Nilun quhui dudu yongshi zhuang," 155.

95. Ma Li and Wei Wenying, "Qinci biaolu Wang yishi xingshiji," *Xiayi xianzhi* (1548) (reprinted in *Tianyige cang Mingdai fangzhi xuankan*. Shanghai: Shanghai guji shudian, 1982), 8.71a–74b, 7.18a–19b.

96. Lin Ruozhou, "Jie xingcheng yitu changzhi jiuan shu," reprinted in Wang Shaoquan, ed., *Huang Ming zoushu leichao* (1588; photographic reprint, Hishi copy, Rare Book Collection, Gest Oriental Library, Princeton University), 39.46a. Lin's references to Peng Ze and Chen Jin as the officials supervising the campaign in Jiangxi make clear that the memorial was written during the early sixteenth century.

97. Chen Quanzhi, "Shiji," *Pengchuang rilu* (1565; reprint, Shanghai: Shanghai shudian, 1985), 2.32a–32b, 2.34a.

98. For a brief note by Hok-lam Chan on Deng Maoqi with references to most of the relevant secondary scholarship, see Goodrich and Chaoying Fang, eds., *Dictionary of Ming Biography*, pp. 1275–1277. One might also note the example of Li Mao, a pirate who surrendered to imperial authorities and, in exchange, received a series of local security appointments. Exploiting these connections, Li turned his attention to preying on pearl cultivators along the Pearl Delta in southeast China (see Kishi Kazuyuki, "Canton chihō shakai ni okeru buraizō-Minmakki no Shuchidō o megutte," in *Gen-Min-Shin ki ni okeru kokka shihai to minshū no saikentō-shihai no Chūgokuteki tokushitsu* [Kyūshū daigaku tōyōshi kenkyūshitsu, 1983], pp. 156–166).

99. *MS* 91.2252. For a slightly fuller list, see Chen Renxi, *Huang Ming Shifalu* (1630; reprint, Taibei: Xuesheng shuju, 1965), 44.13a–13b.

100. "Sicang yingjin junqi," "Junzheng," "Binglü," no. 2, *Da Minglü*, in

Huang Zhangjian, *Mingdai lüli huibian* 2:655. The translation is by William Jones from *The Great Qing Code* (Oxford: Clarendon Press, 1994), pp. 206–207. The subsequent Qing dynasty retained this passage without alteration. Under the Tang Code, the possession of "bows, arrows, swords, shields, and short spears" had been permitted, but crossbows apparently were not. See *The T'ang Code*, vol. 2, *Specific Articles*, translated by Wallace Johnson (Princeton: Princeton University Press, 1997), pp. 284–285.

101. "Simai zhanma" and "Simai junqi," "Junzheng," "Binglü," no. 2, *Da Minglü*, in Huang Zhangjian, *Mingdai lüli huibian* 2:654–655.

102. "Junqi junzhuang," *Zhengde Da Ming huidian* 156.5a.

103. Ibid., 156.5b. The only exception was some garrisons in Huguang Province, which, because of their distance, were allowed to submit annual rather than monthly reports.

104. *YZSL* 184.20b.

105. Ibid., 189.1a–1b.

106. An imperial edict of June 1521 expressly forbade anyone but [on-duty?] garrison solders and patrols from carrying bows and arrows in the capital region (*SZSL* 2.16b).

107. "Jinyue sizao yingjin junqi huomaili," Bingbulei, in *TFSLZ* 2:442.

108. *WZSL* 138.6a–6b.

109. *YZSL* 226.12a–12b.

110. Ibid., 246.5a–5b. This is clear from the remarks of Li Bing, the military superintendent of Xuanfu, in November of 1454. "Prior to this, when Mongol tribute missions entered Chinese territory, [Chinese] people along the way were allowed to trade weapons that were not prohibited. . . . However, recently prohibitions have been tightened. There have been whole families exiled to Hainan when members of military and commoner households have privately talked with the missions or traded with them. Thus now when the embassies arrive at the border markets, people avoid them." The emperor approved Li's recommendation that the prohibition be relaxed so the Mongols would not doubt the sincerity of the Ming policies of "cherishing those from afar."

111. Ibid., 223.11b.

112. Ibid., 149.6a.

113. This translation is tentative.

114. "Jinyue Shaanxi Gansu dengchu junren guanshe ren dengbu xu jiang yingjin junqi mai yu yiren weizhe ge diao bianwei chongjun bing chacao li," Bingbulei, in *TFSLZ* 2:444.

115. Koreans were largely dependent on foreign supplies of *niujiao* to complete the composite bows, which were one of the tribute items presented annually to the Ming. See Udagawa Takehisa, *Higashi ajia heiki kōryūshi no kenkyū* (Tokyo: Yoshikawa kōbunkan, 1993), p. 3. For a cross-sectional diagram illustrating the structural components of a Qing period bow, see Joseph Needham, Robin Yates, and Krzysztof Gawlikowkowski, eds., *Science and Civilisation in China*, vol. 5, *Chemistry and Chemical Technology*, pt. 6, *Military Technology: Missiles and Sieges* (Cambridge: Cambridge University Press, 1994), pt. 6 , p. 104. China had encouraged tributary states to present horn from at least the third century A.D. See Needham, Yates, and Gawlikowkowski, *Science and Civilisation in China*, vol. 5, pt. 6, p. 110, n. "n."

116. "Mai yu yiren qijun wuliao bing yu shuohua fanren liandang fang-
jiaxiao fabianyuan chongjun ge ju qinshu ju chongfaqianli," Bingbulei, in
TFSLZ 2:442.

117. *YZSL* 207.7b–8a.

118. Ibid., 217.5b.

119. Ibid., 241.1b, 206.7b.

120. Yang Yiqing, "Chenyan chuzhi difang jinji zeiqing shu," reprinted in
Sun Xun, *Huang Ming shuchao*, p. 4705.

121. For a biography of Lü, see Joanna F. Handlin, *Action in Late Ming
Thought: The Reorientation of Lü Kun and Other Scholar-Officials* (Berkeley: University of California Press, 1983).

122. Lü Kun, "Xiangjia yue," *Shizhenglu*, vol. 5. Cited in Wang Xiande,
Mingmo xiangcun ziwei zhi yanjiu (Gaoxiong: Fuwen tushu chubanshe, 1992),
p. 128.

123. Wang Tingxiang, "Shang xunfu Chen Gong zhidaoyi," *Wang Shi jia-
cangji, juan* 26, reprinted in *Wang Tingxiang ji* (Beijing: Zhonghua shuju, 1989),
2:473.

124. Robin Yates and Edward McEwen have noted the "wide popularity"
and "the perennial ubiquity of the crossbow" in China by the Song period (see
Needham, Yates, and Gawlikokowshi, *Science and Civilisation in China*, pp. 145–
146). It seems reasonable to speculate that weapons of less advanced technology were probably even more common during the late imperial period.

125. In fact, some officials of the early Ming complained that local magistrates' commitment to these cultural "handles" was woefully insufficient. See
Ye Boju's 1376 memorial, "Wanyan shu" in *Ye Jusheng zoushu*, reprinted in
JSWB 8.10a–10b. The founder was so offended by Ye's criticisms that he had Ye
put in jail, where he died.

126. This tendency to downplay or obscure negotiations with men of
force contrasts with what Karen Barkey has found in the Ottoman Empire during the seventeenth century. There, negotiations with bandit leaders were
openly acknowledged. Indeed, Barkey argues that these negotiations constituted a central facet of state consolidation. While many aspects of negotiations
between men of force in Ming China and the Ottoman Empire were similar
(co-option, negotiation, periodic recruitment, etc.), the state's conception of
itself and the image of state-society relations seem to have been very different.
See Karen Barkey, *Bandits and Bureaucrats: The Ottoman Route to State Centralization* (Ithaca: Cornell University Press, 1994).

Chapter 5 Men of Force and the Son of Heaven

1. *WZSL* 91.7b; *MS* 26.304.7795. In his *Mingshi jishi benmo*, Gu Yingtai
writes only that Zhang Mao "observed" the emperor's play (1658; reprint,
Taibei: Sanlian shuju, 1985, p. 463).

2. Yu Jideng, *Huang Ming diangu jiwen* (1601) *juan* 14, cited in Wang Chunyu
and Du Wanyan, eds., *Mingdai huanguan yu jingji shiliao chutan* (Beijing: Zhongguo shehui kexueyuan, 1986), p. 380.

3. *MS* 26.304.7795.

4. For details, see David Robinson, "Banditry and Rebellion in the Capital
Region during the Mid-Ming (1450–1525)" (Ph.D. diss., Princeton University,

1995), pp. 192–195. For an informative essay on the links between the Directorate of the Imperial Horses, which Zhang Zhong headed, and the military, see Fang Zhiyuan, "Mingdai de Yumajian," *Zhongguoshi yanjiu* 2 (1997): 140–148. Zhang also was among several eunuchs to oversee the troops of the Eastern Imperial Office, select troops from the capital garrisons. The most detailed treatment of these troops is Aoyama Jirō, "Mindai Seitokki no keiei ni tsuite—toku ni iwayuru Tōsai kanchōgun no jittai ni tsuite," *Sundai shigaku* 98 (September 1996): 83–118.

5. *Yongqing xianzhi* (1780), 5.9b; personal communication with Han Qunbao, local historian of Yongqing (July 1993).

6. *Bazhou zhi* (1548), 2.7b. During a trip to Bazhou in July 1993, I learned that the temple had been razed to construct housing. The Dongyue Temple, known locally as the Tianqi Temple, was listed in the 1934 edition of *Baxian xinzhi* (reprint, Taibei: 1968, 2.20a, 1:109).

7. *Bazhou zhi* (1548), 1.18b.

8. This is not to say that succeeding emperors were slaves to the laws created by the founder; the large body of ad hoc legislation developed throughout the dynasty clearly demonstrates otherwise. See John Langlois, "The Code and ad hoc Legislation in Ming Law," *Asia Major* (third series) 6.2 (1993): 85–112.

9. For the best Western treatment of the reign, see Geiss, "The Cheng-te Reign, 1506–1521," in Denis Twitchett and Frederick Mote, eds., *The Ming Dynasty, 1368–1644* (pts. 1 and 2), vols. 7 and 8 of *The Cambridge History of China* (Cambridge: Cambridge University Press, 1988), pt. 1. For the most comprehensive study of the period, see Li Xun, *Zhengde huangdi dazhuan* (Shenyang: Liaoning jiaoyu chubanshe, 1993).

10. For a typically negative portrait of the Martial Ancestor in modern scholarship, see So Kwan-wai's entry in Carrington Goodrich and Chaoying Fang, eds., *Dictionary of Ming Biography, 1368–1644* (New York: Columbia University Press, 1976), pp. 307–315. For the Martial Ancestor's portrayal in vernacular literature and theater, see Chen Baocheng, "Ming Wuzong cong lishi renwu dao wenyi xingxiang," *Zhengzhou daxue xuekan* 6 (1995): 54–60.

11. See James Geiss, "The Leopard Quarter during the Cheng-te Reign," *Ming Studies* 24 (1987): 1–38.

12. Ibid., p. 1. For PRC reactions to Geiss' views, see Wei Zuhui, "Baofang yu Ming Wuzong: Jian yu Gai Jiemin, Ye Zufu xiansheng shangque," *Gugong bowuyuan yuankan* 1 (1992): 29–33; Ye Zufu, "Xiyuan baofang ye yang bao," *Gugong bowuyuan yuankan* 2 (1989): 24–25. Though often unacknowledged, Geiss' revisionist interpretation of the Martial Ancestor has prompted several mainland scholars to reconsider the reign. See Li Xun, "Ming Wuzong he ta suo daibiao de fengjian guizu jieji," in *Dierjie Ming Qingshi guoji xueshu taolunhui lunwenji* (Tianjin: Tianjin renmin chubanshe, 1993), p. 605; Li Xun, "Ming Wuzong yu zhujin," *Shixue jikan* 2 (1993): 13–17, 48; Teng Xincai, "Ming Wuzong xinlun," *Sichuan shifan daxue xuebao* 5 (1989): 85–89.

In some ways, Ray Huang's interpretation of the Martial Ancestor anticipated Geiss' work. See his *1587, Year of No Significance: The Ming Dynasty in Decline* (New Haven: Yale University Press, 1981), pp. 95–102. For an intriguing, but entirely speculative, essay arguing that the Leopard Quarter functioned as something of a mosque and served as a military and administrative center, see Ma Mingdao, *Mingchao huangjia xinyangkao chugao* (Taibei?: Zhongguo Huijiao wenhua jiaoyu jijinhui chuban, n.d.), pp. 69–76.

13. Yuan Biao received his assignment as Commandant of Hejian in August 1505. See *WZSL* 3.2b–3a.

14. Ibid., 91.7b.

15. Ibid., 197.5b. This note is also found in Xu Xueju, *Guochao dianhui* (1601; reprint, Taibei: Xuesheng shuju, 1965), 33.58a, 2:726; *Yanshantang bieji, juan* 97, 4:1847.

16. For biographical details on Kang Hai, see Tilemann Grimm, in Goodrich and Chaoying Fang, eds., *Dictionary of Ming Biography, 1368–1644*, pp. 692–694.

17. Fu Tongqin and (Zheng) Ke Cheng, "Mingdai da taijian Liu Jin," *Gugong bowuyuan yuankan* 2 (1980): 25–28, 71; Sawada Mizuho, "Taikan Ryū Kin," *Tenri daigaku gakuhō* 54 (1967): 1–31.

18. Zha Jizuo, who took great pains to refute claims that Kang had become one of Liu's followers, wrote that "it was falsely reported to the prefect" that the purloined silver belonged to Liu. The sentence's subject is unclear, but given what we know of Kang's personality, one wonders if Kang did not misinform the prefect as a way to expose the official's venality—the prefect was spurred to rigorous action because of the money's connection to Liu Jin, not simply because a robbery had occurred in his jurisdiction. See Zha, "Kang Hai," *Zui wei lu* (ca. 1670; reprint, Shanghai: *Sibu congkan*, third series, 1936), *zhuan* 14.16b.

19. One biographer, a close friend of Kang, claims the prefect was inspired to aid Kang solely by his long-standing admiration of Kang and his status as a Hanlin scholar. See Zhang Zhidao, "Hanlinyuan xiuzhuan Kang Hai xing-zhuang," reprinted in *Xianzhenglu* 21.47b.

20. *WZSL* 65.1a–1b.

21. Ibid., 52.4a, 60.4a; *Guoque, juan* 47, 3:2951.

22. *WZSL* 65.1a–1b. For the role of a rival eunuch in Liu Jin's fall, see Mano Senryū, "Kangan Ryū Kin to Chō Ei to no tairitsu," *Ritsumeikan bungaku* 418–421 (1980): 273–289.

23. As the *Official History of the Ming* notes, "[Zhang] Zhong valued the Great Bandit Zhang Mao's riches, [thus he] joined his [sworn] brother" (*MS* 26.304.7795).

24. *WZSL* 52.4a.

25. Ibid., 90.6a. It is unclear whether the other three censors had forces of similar scale.

26. Lei Li, *Guochao lieqing ji* (after 1592; reprint, Taibei: Chengwen chubanshe, 1970), 124.18b, 20:6570; Wang Shizhen, "Zuo qian duyushi Ning Gao zhuan," *Yanzhou bieji*; reprint, Jiao Hong, *Guochao xianzhenglu* (1594–1616); reprinted in no. 6 of *Zhongguo shixue congshu* (Taibei, 1965), 63.41a–41b, 4:2714. Wang's biography of Ning must be used carefully, as it contains a number of errors.

27. Wang Shizhen, "Zuo qian duyushi Ning Gao zhuan."

28. Wang Hongxu, *Mingshi gao* (1723; reprint, Taibei: Mingwen shuju, 1991), 172.7a; *Guochao lieqing ji* 124.18b.

29. Wang Hongxu, *Mingshi gao* 172.7a.

30. For a discussion of the precinct captains of Beijing and its hinterland, see Joanne Wakeland, "Metropolitan Administration in Ming China: Sixteenth Century Peking" (Ph.D. diss., University of Michigan, 1982), p. 251. For the use of mutual responsibility units in fifteenth-century Fujian, see Nishimura Gen-shō's annotated translation of *juan* 6 of *Shuanghuai suichao* in Mori Masao and Tanigawa Michio, eds., *Chūgoku minshū hanranshi* (Tokyo: Heibonsha, 1979), 2:368–408.

31. *Guochao lieqingji,* 124.18b. For details on mutual responsibility units, see the "Maintaining Order in the Empire" section in chapter 3.

32. *WZSL* 91.7b–8a.

33. Ibid., 50.1a.

34. For an excellent discussion of Liu Jin's attempted reforms and the resistance they provoked, see Liao Xinyi, "Liu Jin 'bianluan jiuzhi' kaolüe," *Mingshi yanjiu luncong* 3 (1985): 139–166.

35. *WZSL* 91.8a.

36. Zhu Guozhen, *Huang Ming dashiji* (hereafter *DSJ*), in his *Huang Ming shigai,* 1632; reprinted in *Yuan Ming shiliao congbian,* 1st series (Taibei: Wenhai chubanshe, 1984), 25.2a; *JSBM, juan* 45, p. 464.

37. See "Selected prices for works of art and antique artifacts c. 1560–1620," in Craig Clunas, *Superfluous Things: Material Culture and Social Status in Early Modern China* (Urbana: University of Illinois Press, 1991), p. 181.

38. *DSJ* 25.2a–2b; *JSBM, juan* 45, p. 464.

39. *DSJ* 25.2b; *JSBM, juan* 45, p. 464.

40. Ibid.; *WZSL* 68.7a–7b. On the desecration of the Liu brothers' family graves, see Shao Bao (1460–1527), "Bing bu shilang Li gong zhuan," *Rongchun tang houji* (Huaximin edition, Zhengde-Jiajing period; Rare Book Collection, Harvard-Yenching Library, Harvard University), 7.33a.

41. *WZSL* 91.10b–11a.

42. *DSJ* 25.2b; *JSBM, juan* 45, p. 464. One version maintains that they joined Bai Ying, the most prominent bandit in the capital region, who by this time had already moved into Shandong.

43. *DSJ* 25.2b; *JSBM, juan* 45, p. 464.

44. *WZSL* 68.7a–7b; *DSJ* 25.2b; *JSBM, juan* 45, p. 464.

45. *DSJ* 25.2b.

46. *HJL,* p. 17.

47. *WZSL* 73.2a.

48. *HJL,* pp. 17–18. For the incident in Wenan, see Robinson, "Banditry and Rebellion," pp. 203–204, n. 63.

49. *HJL,* p. 18; *WZSL* 91.8a. The *HJS* chronology is to be preferred over that of the *WZSL* here.

50. *WZSL* 91.8a.

51. Ibid.; *HJL,* p. 18.

52. See Wu Han, "Ji Ming shilu," *Zhongyang yanjiuyuan lishi yuyan yan-jiusuo jikan* 18 (1948): 385–477 (in *Dushi zhaji,* 1956; reprint, Beijing: Sanlian shu-dian, 1960); Wolfgang Franke, *An Introduction to the Sources of Ming History* (Kuala Lumpur: University of Malaya Press, 1968). Several scholars have argued that the editors of the *Veritable Records* distorted the relationship between Kang Hai and Liu Jin to portray Kang as Liu's sychophantic follower. In addition to

the biographies of Kang by Zhang Zhidao and Zha Jizuo noted above, also see Li Kaixian, "Duishan Kang xiuzhuan zhuan," *Xianju ji* (reprinted in *Li Kaixian ji*, Beijing: Xinhua shuju, 1959), pp. 593–597; Huang Yunmei, *Mingshi kaozheng* (Beijing: Zhonghua shuju, 1979–1986), 7:2239.

53. See James Legge, trans., *The Chinese Classics* (2d ed., 1893; reprint, Taibei, 1969), 3:316. Cited in Geiss, "Leopard Quarter," p. 19.

Chapter 6　From Banditry to Rebellion and Back Again

1. For a more detailed examination of the course of the rebellion and related historiographical issues, see David Robinson, "Banditry and Rebellion, in the Capital Region during the Mid-Ming (1450–1525)" (Ph.D. diss., Princeton University, 1995)," pp. 213–430.

2. Carrington Goodrich and Chaoying Fang, eds., *Dictionary of Ming Biography, 1368–1644* (New York: Columbia University Press, 1976), pp. 1516–1519.

3. Just days before Yang's report, in an unmistakable gesture of deference, a retired magistrate went out to meet the bandits when they arrived in the suburbs of Yingshan in northern Huguang (*Yingshan xianzhi* [1540], *xia*.28b, 46a).

4. Yang Yiqing, "Chenyan chuzhi difang jinji zeiqing shu," in Sun Xun, *Huang Ming shuchao* (reprint, Taibei: Xuesheng shuju, 1986), p. 4689.

5. Ibid., 4693–4694, 4701.

6. Ibid., 4694.

7. Ibid., 4714.

8. Ibid., 4706.

9. Ibid., 4705. For the Korean Ch'oe Pu's experience with local defense in Ningbo Prefecture, see John Meskill, *Ch'oe P'u's Diary: A Record of Drifting Across the Sea* (Tucson: University of Arizona Press, 1965), p. 50.

10. Yang Yiqing, "Chenyan chuzhi difang jinji zeiqing shu," pp. 4688–4689.

11. Ibid., 4691.

12. *WZSL* 73.8a. Two regional military commissioners were to serve as assistant regional commanders.

13. In the Martial Ancestor's May 7, 1511, orders to Ma Zhongxi, he instructed Ma to grant silver medals to those rendering extraordinary service in battle (*Gucheng xianzhi*, 4.8a).

14. *WZSL* 73.1b, 3a, 6b, 8b, 9b, 12b, 13a; 74.2a, 3b. In mid-May 1511, the regional inspector of Shandong reported that brigands had attacked more than twenty places in Shandong since the first lunar month of the sixth year of the reign (74.5b).

15. *WZSL* 73.6b, 8b; 74.2a. For details of the various accounts of the magistrate of Laiwu, Xiong Can, see Robinson, "Banditry and Rebellion," pp. 234–235, n. 150. For those killed in Laiwu, see *Laiwu xianzhi* (1548), 2.6a, 6.3b.

16. *WZSL* 73.9b.

17. Fei Hong, "Cheng Queli ji," *Tai bao Fei Wenxian Gong zhai gao* 8.42a–44a (reprint, Taiwan: Wenhai chubanshe, 1970, 15a:691–695). A portion of Fei's account is included in Bao Zunxin, "Ming 'Cheng Queli ji' beiwen fanying de qiyi nongmin dui kongjiao de mieqi," *Wenwu* 208.9 (1973): 2–6. The stele measures 216 cm. high (about 85 inches) and 100 cm. across (about 39 inches). On the dating of this incident, see Robinson, "Banditry and Rebellion," pp. 235–236, n. 152.

18. Fei, 8.42b, p. 692. In another stele account engraved in 1520, Xiong Xiang noted that "almost all" of the books of Kuiwen Hall were burned by the bandits in 1511. See Xiong, "Kuiwenge chongzhi shuji ji," (*Quelizhi*, Zhengde ed., 10.38a; also reprinted in *Qufu xianzhi* [1774], reprint, Taibei: 1968, 52.25a, 4:1519). A largely illegible photograph of a rubbing of the inscription may be found in Qufu shifan xueyuan lishixi, "Cong Qufu yidai de jikuai beike kan lishishang nongmin qiyizhong de fan Kong douzheng," *Wenwu* 213 (1974), p. 2. Both articles appeared in the midst of the "Criticize Confucius Campaign," and they emphasize the revolutionary aspects of the attacks on the Kong Estates. Bao in particular claims that the bandits' act of throwing the books from Kuiwen Hall into the pond constituted a conscious rejection of the feudal order anchored by Confucian orthodoxy. For a rebuttal of Bao Zunxin's claims, see Takeuchi Teruo, "Ketsuri no hibun ni tsuite," *Uno Tetsujin sensei hakuju shukuga kinen Tōyōgaku ronsō* (Tokyo, 1974), pp. 711–720.

The Ming official Wang Qiong wrote that the Sagelike Duke (the senior male descendent of Confucius) was married to the daughter of Li Dongyang, a senior court official. When the bandits raided Queli, Kong complained to Li, who thought provincial officials were at fault for allowing the attack. They were imprisoned. Wang disagreed, arguing that the bandits were too strong for provincial officials to restrain unaided. See Wang Qiong, *Shuangxi zaji* (reprinted in *Jinxian huiyan* and in *Baibu congshu jicheng* [Taibei: Yiwen yinshuguan, 1966], 16a–16b).

19. *Qufu xianzhi* (1774), 29.13a. For the construction of a wall to protect Queli, see Fei Hong, *Taibao Fei Wenxian gong zhaigao*, juan 20, p. 693. For the emperor's reaction and postrebellion placatory sacrifices, see *WZSL* 93.7b.

20. *Guoque, juan* 48, pp. 2997–2998. This account is not found in the *Veritable Records of the Martial Ancestor*.

21. Zhang Jinghua, "Kanggong ciji," *Tancheng xianzhi* (1673), 10.27a–27b.

22. *Guoque, juan* 48, pp. 2997–2998.

23. Ibid., 2998.

24. Xu Jie, "Guanglu dafu taizibao libu shangshu zeng shaobao shi Wenxiang Tanggong muzhiming," *Guochao xianzhenglu*, 205.26b, 2:1034. On Ming canon, see Joseph Needham, Robin Yates, and Krzysztof Gawlikokowshi, eds., *Science and Civilisation in China*, vol. 5, *Chemistry and Chemical Technology*, pt. 7, *Military Technology, the Gunpowder Epic* (Cambridge: Cambridge University Press, 1994), p. 333.

25. For an illustration of the mobile shield, see Needham, Yates, and Gawlikokowski, *Science and Civilisation in China*, vol. 5, pt. 7, p. 421; Cheng Dong, *Zhongguo gudai bingqi tuji* (Beijing: Jiefangjun chubanshe, 1990), p. 249.

26. *WZSL* 76.4b–5a; *MS* 24.289.7430; *Guo que*, p. 2998; *Tancheng xianzhi* (1673), 6.24b, 10.28a.

27. *Tancheng xianzhi* (1673), 6.24b.

28. *HJL*, p. 18.

29. *WZSL* 75.4b.

30. Ibid., 76.5b, 7b; *Dashji* 25.6b–7a; *Guoque*, vol. 3, *juan* 48, p. 3003. The *HJL* account indicates that Tiger Yang once again joined Liu the Sixth in raiding in Shandong (p. 19).

31. *HJL*, p. 5. Zhao was an "added government student" (*zengguang sheng-*

yuan), who, in contrast to regular government students *(shengyuan* or *linheng),* was not entitled to imperial stipends. Ho Pingti has estimated that out of a registered population of 65,000,000 in 1450, only 30,000 to 32,500 were regular government students. Ho writes that in 1428, quotas were established for added government students at the same ratio as for those of regular government students, in theory doubling the total pool. See his *Ladder of Success in Imperial China* (New York: Columbia University Press, 1962), p. 173.

32. *HJL,* p. 5.

33. Ho Ping-ti has warned against overstating the social status of licentiates during the Ming. See *The Ladder of Success in Imperial China,* pp. 28–40. On the other Zhao who became a tribute student, see *Wenan xianzhi* (1922), 4.28b, 1:360. The Zhao brothers all used the metal radical in their personal names.

34. *JSBM, juan* 45, p. 464; *DSJ* 25.3a; *MS* 15.175.4662.

35. The reed marshes afforded protection to many of Wenan's residents. A woman Dong also took refuge and like the Zhao family was discovered. A martyrs' shrine was established for Dong and other local women who resisted the rebels *(Wenan xianzhi* [1629], 6.6a). On the condition of Wenan's walls at approximately the time of the attack, see "Xiu cheng ji," *Wenan xianzhi* (1922), 9.7a.

36. The date August 8, 1511, is from *HJL,* p. 5. For further details, see Robinson, "Banditry and Rebellion," pp. 254–255, n. 192.

37. *HJL,* p. 7. A precise date is not given for this poem. Judging, however, from the sequence of events given in the *HJL,* it probably was written sometime before October 21, 1511.

38. Ibid., pp. 5–6. The precise date of the meeting is unclear. In the earliest extant primary source, the *HJL,* the gathering occurred after the addition of Zhao to the band and before the raids on Dacheng, Qingxian, and the subsequent flight into Shandong. Mid-July 1511 would seem to be a safe estimation in the light of materials available at present.

39. In 1460, Li Tianbao, a native of Macheng, Huguang, had rebelled, declared himself a descendent of Taizong of the Tang dynasty, arrogated imperial titles, and allied himself with Miao tribesmen. He had also pledged to take them to Nanjing and "mount the throne" *(YZSL* 319.6a–6b).

40. *HJL,* pp. 5–6.

41. *WZSL* 77.5b, 77.8a–8b.

42. Ibid., 77.8b. The biography of Hanlin academician Chen Ji (1465–1539) suggests that Yang Tinghe supported Chen's later proposal that border troops be used in Henan *(MS* 17.190.5032).

43. Juyong Pass is located 85 km. (about 53 miles) north of Zhuozhou.

44. Zijing Pass is located 75 km. (about 46 miles) northwest of the seat of Baoding Prefecture.

45. *HJL,* p. 20. The report on Madman Zhao notes that Ma, Censor Bian Xian, and the regional military commissioner of Dezhou were all involved in the offer of surrender. The dating of the incident is, however, unclear in this account *(HJL,* p. 7).

46. For example, see *DSJ* 25.8a.

47. Ibid.

48. *WZSL* 91.8a–8b.

49. Ibid., 91.8a. The *HJL* does not include this bit of drama. It instead merely notes that on learning that the court had once again dispatched troops against them, the rebels left in a furor (p. 20). Another oft-repeated variation is found in the sixteenth-century *Jishi jiwen* by Chen Hongmo (which in turn provides the basis for much of the famous seventeenth-century *JSBM* account). After listening to Ma's appeal, Liu the Seventh challenged him, saying, "At present, eunuchs control the affairs of the dynasty. Can Executive Censor Ma make good on his words?" He thereupon secretly dispatched someone to the capital, only to find that the court had no intention of accepting the rebels' surrender. They then transported all the booty gained through raiding in Shandong and offered it as a bribe to the "powerful and favored." When a pardon still was not forthcoming, the rebels became even bolder in their pillaging (Chen, *juan* 4, p. 95; Gu, *juan* 45, pp. 465–466).

50. *WZSL*, 78.1b–2a.

51. Lu Shen, *Huaifeng riji*, in his *Yanshan waiji* (Luji ed., Jiajing period; Rare Book Collection, Harvard-Yenching Library, Harvard University), 8.3a.

52. Ibid.

53. Ibid., 8.3b.

54. Late in June 1511, the court promoted Ma from "censor-in-chief of the right" to "censor-in-chief of the left." After the successful completion of the campaign against the rebels, Ma was to be made head of the Censorate (*WZSL* 75.5b).

55. *WZSL* 77.10a.

56. Ibid., 78.8b; *Guoque*, p. 3007. The information is in a September 19, 1511, entry relating previous events.

57. A point stressed in his biography in the *Official History of the Ming*. See *MS* 16.187.4957.

58. *WZSL* (August 24, 1511), 78.2a; *Guoque*, p. 3006.

59. Yang Tinghe, *Shicao yulu*, in *Yang wen zhong san lu* (1607; reprinted in *Wenguange skiu quanshu*; reprint, Taibei: Taiwan shangwu yinshuguan, 1983, vol. 423), 1.9a–9b; *WZSL* 78.4a, 5a; *Guoque*, p. 3007; *DSJ* 25.9a–9b; *JSBM*, p. 466; *Ming tongjian*, 2:1648. If Zhu Yunming's account is to be believed, fifty riders under Liu the Sixth had sacked Dacheng County on August 11, 1511, and gone on to raid Gu'an (Zhu Yunming, *Jianghai jianqu ji*, in *Congshu jicheng chubian* [Shanghai: Shanghai shangwu yinshuguan, 1936], p. 6).

60. *WZSL* 79.2a, 86.2a; *DSJ* 25.10b; Zhu Yunming, *Jianghai jianqu ji*, p. 7; *JSBM*, p. 466.

61. *HJL*, p. 7; *JSBM*, p. 467. The term used for the firearms is *"shenqiang."*

62. For a detailed discussion of firearms during the Ming, see Needham, Yates, and Gawlikokowski, *Science and Civilisation in China*, vol. 5, pt. 7, sec. 30. For observations on restricted access to military technology during the Ming, see ibid., pp. 310 and 341.

63. These were the standard weapons for most of the troops under the renowned Ming general Qi Jiguang (1528–1588), and both weapons appear frequently in the Ming novel *Shuihu zhuan*. See Yang Hong, *Zhongguo gubingqi luncong* (1980, rev. ed. 1985, Beijing: Wenwu chubanshe), pp. 129–130. Another question deserving further consideration is the role of martial arts teachers in local and regional society. For a preliminary discussion of this question during the Qing, see Susan Naquin, *Millenarian Rebellion in China: The Eight Trigrams Uprising of 1813* (New Haven: Yale University Press, 1976).

64. See Qiu Zhonglin, "Mingdai Beijing de shehui fengqi bianhua—lizhi yu jiazhiguan de gaibian," *Dalu zazhi* 88.3 (1994): 28–42, and "Cong jinli lüshen kan Mingdai Beijing shehui fengqi de bianqian guocheng," *Danjiang shixue* 6 (1992): 67–88.

65. If the dragon robes were a sign of rare imperial favor for most civil and military officials, they were the customary habiliment of eunuchs attending the emperor in his personal quarters from the third decade of the fifteenth century onward. The editors of the *MS* note enviously that it was rare for even civil and military officials of the first rank to be given the *mang* robes (see *MS* 6.67.1638–1647). For illustrations of several varieties of dragon robes, see Zhou Xibao, *Zhongguo gudai fushi shi* (Beijing: Zhongguo xiju chubanshe, 1984), pp. 386–388, 392, and color plates 24–25; Zhou Xun and Gao Chunming, *Zhongguo fushi wuqian nian* (Hong Kong: Shangwu yinshuguan, 1984), p. 155, illustrations 261–262. For a treatment of the dragon robes in the context of international diplomacy, see Schuyler Cammann, "Presentation of Dragon Robes by the Ming and Ch'ing Courts for Diplomatic Purposes," *Sinologica: Review of Chinese Culture and Science* 3 (1953): 193–202.

66. *HJL*, p. 7.

67. *WZSL* 79.2a–2b; *Guoque*, p. 3009: *JSBM*, p. 467.

68. *HJL*, p. 7; *JSBM*, p. 467.

69. *HJL*, p. 7.

70. David Ownby, *Brotherhoods and Secret Societies in Early and Mid-Qing China: The Formation of a Tradition* (Stanford: Stanford University Press, 1996), pp. 33–42.

71. Ibid.

72. Xia Liangsheng , "Lun yongbing shier bianyi zhuang," *Xia Dongzhou wenji*, reprinted in *JSWB* 154.2a–2b.

73. Kishimoto Mio, "Sūtei jūnananen no Kōnan shakai to Pekin jōhō," in Ono Kazuko, ed., *Minmatsu Shinsho no shakai to bunka* (Kyōto: Kyōto daigaku jinbun kagaku kenkyūjo, 1996), pp. 347–364. During the late fifteenth century, the official Han Yong (1422–1478) commented that during the chaos of Mongol raids along the northern border, postal couriers "all absconded in every direction." Consequently, intelligence about the whereabouts of Mongol raiding parties did not reach the court, and counterattacks could not be launched. See Han Yong, "Juluo xinchengji," *Han Xiangyi ji*, in *JSWB* 55.1b.

74. For details of the attack on Jining, see *Jining zhili zhouzhi* (1860), 1.7a; *Jining zhouzhi* (1673), 4.21b; *WZSL* 80.1b–2a; *DSJ* 25.10b; *Guoque*, p. 3011; *JSBM*, p. 467; Xia Xie, *Ming tong jian* (ca. 1870; reprint, Beijing: Zhonghua shuju, 1959), p. 1651. The number of official grain boats on the Grand Canal comes from Ray Huang, "The Grand Canal during the Ming Dynasty (1368–1644)" (Ph.D. diss., University of Michigan, 1964), p. 71. For more on Jining as a city, see Han Dacheng, *Mingdai chengshi yanjiu* (Beijing: Zhongguo renmin daxue chubanshe, 1991), pp. 92–94.

75. Shao Bao, *Rongchun tang xuji*, in *Wenyuange siku quanshu* (1773–1783; reprint, Taibei: Taiwan shangwu yinshuguan, 1983), 6.21a–25a, 1258:499–501.

76. Cong Lan, "Qingcha Yansui tiaoyi," in *Congsikong zouyi* 1.9b, reprinted in *JSWB* 8:17.

77. *WZSL* 80.2b–3a; *Guoque*, p. 3011; Xia Xie, *Ming tong jian*, p. 1652.

78. *HJL*, pp. 7–8; *JSBM*, p. 467; Zhang Xuan, *Xiyuan wenjian lu* (1632; reprint,

Taibei: Mingwen chubanshe, 1991), p. 5948; Zhu Yunming, *Jianghai jianqu ji*, pp. 9–10; *Xiayi xianzhi* (1548), 7.8a, 13b; 8.11b–12b.

79. Zhu Yunming, *Jianghai jianqu ji*, p. 10; *HJL*, p. 8; *Bozhou zhi* (1775), 7.42a, 2:539; Zeng Weihua and Yan Yaozhong, "Cong Mindai Shaolin si de ji fang beitamingwen kan Mingdai sengbing," *Shanghai shifan xueyuan xuebao* 2 (1984): 75–77.

80. We know very little about the personal backgrounds of the bandit leaders; even their ages are unknown. However, that Yang Hu had a grandson would seem to indicate that Yang was at least in his late forties and probably closer to his mid-fifties. The 1564 *Bozhou zhi* incorrectly notes that Yang and his "nephew" were captured and executed at this time (1.10a).

81. For details of the rebels' activities in Suzhou, see the *Suzhou fuzhi* (1537), 6.25b.

82. *WZSL* 98.3a–3b.

83. The following account is from Zhu Yunming's *Jianghai jianqu ji*, p. 11.

84. Contrast this with the claim that Tiger Yang was a native of Jiaohe. The dearth of information on the personal background of the rebel leaders does not allow a definitive answer to the question of their places of origin.

85. My thanks to Dr. James Geiss for identifying this helmet.

86. For examples of an excavated helmet and armor from the Ming period, see *Dingling*, the archeological report on the imperial mausoleum of the Wanli emperor and his two empresses (Beijing: Wenwu chubanshe, 1990, vol. 2), plates 311, 312, 316, and 317. I should like to thank James Geiss for bringing this book to my attention.

87. On the difficulties of establishing the identities of alleged criminals in the courts of the Netherlands during the seventeenth and eighteenth centuries, see Florike Egmond, *Underworlds: Organized Crime in the Netherlands, 1650–1800* (Cambridge: Polity Press, 1993), pp. 87–91.

88. *HJL*, p. 8.

89. Ibid.; *JSBM*, p. 467.

90. *WZSL* 81.3b.

91. Ibid., 81.4a–4b.

92. Chen Hongmo, *Jishi jiwen* (early sixteenth century; reprint, Beijing: Zhonghua shuju, 1985), p. 97; *JSBM*, p. 468. In most respects, the account in the *JSBM* is more detailed, but it fails to mention that the grand secretary and Zhang Zhong were also present at the emergency conference. See also *MS* 16.187.4948. An imperial host under the joint command of Gu Dayong and Mao Rui had encamped in Linqing.

93. Eunuch attendants commonly accompanied the emperor's procession to inspect the animals to be used in the sacrificial offerings. In fact, some court officials criticized the growing number of such attendants during the Martial Ancestor's reign. See Liu Jian, "Neishi suijian shu," *Liu Wenjing zoushu*, reprinted in *JSWB*, 53.5a–6b.

94. Chen Hongmo, *Jishi jiwen*, p. 97; *WZSL* 82.1a.

95. *WZSL* 82.7a, 82.9b. For one example, see *Dingzhou zhi* (1850), 11.38a, 2:1133, 1232.

96. *WZSL* 82.12a.

97. Han Dacheng, *Mingdai chengshi yanjiu*, pp. 66–72.

98. *WZSL* 82.7a–7b; *HJL,* p. 9.

99. *HJL,* p. 8. In *JSBM,* Gu Yingtai writes that Liu the Third and Zhao Sui advanced to Xincai, 150 km. (about 93 miles) to the southeast, when the retired magistrate presented the rebels with tens of thousands of taels of silver and silks (p. 468). Nishimura Genshō's synthesis of the materials is confusing. While he uses Zhang Xuan's *Xiyuan wenjian lu* (a later, slightly less detailed derivative of the *HJL* report) for the details of what was given as bribe to Liu, he follows two Qing dynasty works (*JSBM* and *Zui wei lu)* in writing that Liu the Third received the gifts in Xincai ("Ryū, Roku Ryū Nana no ran ni tsuite," *Tōyōshi kenkyū* 32.4 [1974]: 60 and "Ryū Roku Ryū Nana no ran," in Mori Masao and Tanigawa Michio, eds., *Chūgoku minshū hanranshi,* vol. 2 [Tokyo: Heigbonsha, 1979], pp. 437–438). Both the *HJL* and the derivative *Xiyuan wenjianlu* state explicitly that Zhang traveled to Luyi to present the gifts to Liu the Third. Nishimura also claims that the reorganization of Liu's band, which I describe in detail below, occurred in Xincai. He calls the rebels' slogan the "Xincai Declaration." I have followed the narrative in *HJL* in which Luyi is the last place-name given before the description of titles, banners, and the band's reorganization.

100. *HJL,* p. 8; *JSBM,* p. 468.

101. In the well–known novel *Shui hu zhuan,* the Jade Emperor of Heaven dispatched a military and civil star from the sky to serve the future Song emperor Ren Zong (1023–1063) (Shi Nai-an and Luo Guanzhong [Beijing: Renmin wenwue chubanshe, 1985], p. 2; Sidney Shapiro's translation of Shi Nai-an and Luo Guanzhong, *Outlaws of the Marsh* [Beijing: Foreign Language Press, 1980], p. 3). This may have been another rhetorical attempt to present themselves as loyal servants of the throne by allusion to a widely known story.

102. On the Eastern and Western Depots, see Ding Yi's *Mingdai tewu zhengzhi* (Beijing: Zhongwai chubanshe, 1950) and Wu Han's "Mingdai de Jinyiwei he Dong-Xi chang," in *Dengxia ji* (Beijing: Shenghuo, dushu, xinzhi sanlian shuydian, 1960; reprint; 1983), pp. 83–93.

103. Rebel forces of the late Ming also organized themselves into brigades, which were only very loosely linked. See Frederick Wakeman, *The Great Enterprise: The Manchu Reconstruction of Imperial Order in Seventeenth-Century China* (Berkeley: University of California Press, 1985), 2:788.

104. *HJL,* p. 9. Nearly every account of the rebellion repeats these lines, probably because they succinctly illustrate that this was a true rebellion and that Madman Zhao and Liu the Third had dynastic ambitions. As Nishimura Genshō has pointed out, this slogan can be traced back at least to the rebellions of the late Yuan. The founder of the Ming dynasty, Zhu Yuanzhang, used a slogan that differed only by two characters; Zhu used "the Great Song" instead of "the primordial heavens." See Nishimura's annotated translation of chapter 45 of *JSBM* in *Chūgoku minshū hanranshi* 2:438, nn. 5 through 10. Also Chen Gaohua, "Yuanmo qiyi nongmin de kouhao," *Yuanshi yanjiu lungao* (Beijing: Zhonghua shuju, 1991), pp. 257–267 (a revised version of the original "Yuanmo nongmin de sixiang wuqi," *Guangming ribao,* December 1, 1965), and his "Yuanmo nongmin qiyijun minghao xiaoding," *Nankai daxue xuebao* 2 (1970): 95–96.

105. *HJL,* p. 9.

106. Ibid., p. 10. See Ma Shizhi, "Liu Liu, Liu Qi qiyi jingong Shangcai wenti shitan," *Xuchang shizhuan xuebao* 4 (1985): 72–75, for a somewhat faulty dating of the attack on Shangcai. For details, see Robinson, "Banditry and Rebellion," pp. 331–332, n. 92.

107. Huo was born into a household of military officers of Maoshan Guard in the Northern Metropolitan Area. Although Huo passed the palace examination in 1502, his grandfather, father, and one of his sons served in Maoshan Guard as chiliarchs. His various biographers stress both his knowledge of military affairs and his decision to fight to the end.

108. The rebels occupied an old fort near the walls of Shangcai, from which they showered arrows down upon the defenders (*WZSL* 83.5a).

109. Li Xunxue, "Chi zeng Guanglusi shaoqing Huogong cibei," *Shangcai xianzhi* (1691), 14.37, 4:1296. The Qing scholar Xia Xie mistakenly attributes this dialogue to Kong Huan, the instructor in the Confucian academy of Xihua (*Ming tong jian*, p. 1657).

110. Gao Shusi, "Huo Shangcai mubiao," in *Guochao xianzhenglu* 93.45a, 6:4052.

111. *HJL*, p. 9; *WZSL* 83.5b; *JSBM*, p. 469, *DSJ* 25.12a. Zhu Guozhen incorrectly claims that the magistrate in question, Wang Zuo, was magistrate at Suiping.

112. *HJL*, p. 9; *DSJ* 25.12a; *JSBM*, p. 469; *Nanyang fuzhi* (1695), pp. 218, 1176; *Yexian zhi* (1542), 1.29a–29b; *Guangshan xianzhi* (1556), 3.2a–2b, 7.24a.

113. Liu Dong, "Shuangzhong ci ji," *Nanyang fuzhi* (1694), 6.79a, 5:2096. For details on the stele from which this information was gleaned, see Liu Yusheng, "Fanying Mingdai Liu Liu Liu Qi nongmin qiyi zhangong de 'Shuangzhong ciji' bei," *Zhongyuan wenwu* 5 (1983): 115–118; *WZSL* 84.5b.

114. Liu, "Shuangzhong ciji," 6.79b; Xia Xie, *Ming tong jian*, p. 1656. Zhuang Shijun, an imperial son-in-law from the Prince of Tang's administrative offices, provided Yu with a burial. Yu was posthumously made a vice-minister in the Court of Imperial Entertainments, and one of his sons was made a student in the National University. A shrine was ordered erected in Yuzhou, where he shared honor with Ren Xian, the retired official who organized the militia forces, in the Loyal Pair Shrine, and in Yu's native Shanyin. See *Yuzhou zhi* (1546), 2.19a; *Shanyin xianzhi* (1551), 4.14b, 15a, 8.49b–51b; *DSJ* 25.13a.

115. *Yuzhou zhi* (1546), 2.2b, 12a. The city walls were repaired in 1515.

116. *HJL*, p. 9.

117. Ibid.; *JSBM*, p. 496.

118. This description of southern Henan is drawn from Ōsawa Akihiro, "Minmatsu shūkyōteki hanran no ichi kōsatsu" (*Tōyōshi kenkyū* 44:1 [1985]: 45–76). The estimate on the floating population was by He Jian (*WZSL* 11.9a; cited in Ōsawa, p. 50).

119. *HJL*, p. 10.

120. Ibid. The censor in question was Jiang Qin. For an excerpt of the memorial, see *MS* 16.188.4982–4983; cf. *MS* pp. 1490, 4978, 4981, 7788. See also Nishimura Genshō, "Ryū Roku Ryū Nana no ran ni tsuite," p. 82, n. 129.

On the question of the king's justice, the usurpation of power by evil ministers, and the utopia of a direct relationship between a monarch and his subjects in early modern Europe, see Yves-Marie Bercé, *Revolt and Revolution in*

Early Modern Europe: An Essay on the History of Political Violence (Manchester: Manchester University Press, 1987), pp. 28–33.

121. *HJL*, p. 10; *DSJ* 25.12b. Both the *JSBM* and *DSJ* accounts note that Zhao executed a man who had seized the wife of a magistrate, an apparent attempt to enforce discipline and improve the image of the rebel forces in the eyes of local officials.

122. *HJL*, p. 10.

123. *WZSL* 82.7a–7b.

124. Ibid., 82.10a.

125. Ibid., 83.5a.

126. For details on the geography of the region and treatment of the Nian rebels, see Ssu-yü Teng, *The Nien Army and Their Guerrilla Warfare, 1851–1868* (Paris: Mouton, 1961; reprint, Westport, Conn.: Greenwood Press, 1984); Siang-tseh Chiang, *The Nien Rebellion* (Seattle: University of Washington Press, 1967); Elizabeth Perry, *Rebels and Revolutionaries in North China, 1845–1945* (Stanford: Stanford University Press, 1980).

127. See Na Zhiliang and William Kohler, *The Emperor's Procession: Two Scrolls of the Ming Dynasty* (Taibei: National Palace Museum, 1970), for numerous examples of how *yongshi* were represented in art during the reign of Shizong (1522–1566).

One of the "Four Guards" formed in 1434, Tengxiang Guard was part of the emperor's personal bodyguard (*MS* 8.9.2204). Eunuchs were responsible for the supervision of the Four Guards. For more on the Four Guards and contemporary views of them, see Okuyama Norio, "Mindai chūki no keiei ni kansuru ichi kōsatsu," *Mindaishi kenkyū* 8 (1980): 10–11.

128. Zhu Yunming, *Jianghai jianqu ji*, p. 16.

129. Ibid., pp. 16–17.

130. *MS* 8.90.2204–2255.

131. *Bazhou zhi* (1548), 9.2b; *DSJ* 25.13b.

132. Zhu Yunming, *Jianghai jianqu ji*, p. 17; *Xuzhou zhi* (1557), pp. 706–707. Rebels also raided in Henan; see *WZSL* 85.9a–9b; *Guoque*, p. 3022; and *DSJ* 25.14b.

133. *WZSL* 83.3b. Price information is from Peng Xinwei, *Zhongguo huobi shi* (1st ed., Shanghai: Chunlian chuban she, 1954; 2d ed., Shanghai: Renmin chubanshe, 1958; 3d ed., Shanghai: Renmin chubanshe, 1965), pp. 721–722. Cited in James Tong, *Disorder under Heaven: Collective Violence in the Ming Dynasty* (Stanford: Stanford University Press, 1991), p. xvi.

134. *WZSL* 83.6a. Ma Ang, another military officer previously dismissed for having bribed Liu Jin, was summoned to take up a post suppressing bandits in Fengyang weeks later (*WZSL* [February 25, 1512], 84.2b). Shi Xi, the retired regional military commissioner of Wuping Guard who shared credit for killing Tiger Yang, was appointed to serve as assistant regional commander and lead mobile troops (*you bing*) in the Southern Metropolitan Area and Henan (*WZSL* [March 3, 1512], 84.5a). Shi Xi was not given permission to retire to his original guard until January 8, 1513, months after the conclusion of the campaign against the rebels (*WZSL* 95.1a).

135. *WZSL* 84.2a.

136. *HJL*, pp. 11–12; *JSBM*, p. 470.

137. *HJL*, p. 11; *WZSL* 86.5a; *DSJ* 25.16b; Li Mengyang, "Yanling xian cheng

bei," *Tongkong ji* (reprint, Taibei: Weiwen tushu chubanshe, 1976), 40.11b–13a, 3:1138–1141. In Yanling, besides raiding the administrative offices and imperial warehouses, the rebels also pillaged the residence of Liu Jing, the former Minister of Justice, and made off with the patent confirming his office *(gaoming)*. Liu was issued another one when he reported its loss to the throne. Liu's report alerted the throne that Yanling's magistrate, Sun Zan, had presented the rebels with a gift of silver and silk, and that the assistant magistrate, Wang Yu, had lowered himself down the wall of the city by rope to escape (*WZSL* 86.5a).

From his princedom in Anlu, Huguang, a worried Prince of Xing, had requested additional imperial troops to bolster the defenses of critical points in Xiangyang and De'an on March 18, 1512 (*WZSL* 85.1b). A day later, the Prince of Zheng petitioned the throne not to transfer imperial forces away from Huaiqing to other areas in Henan (*WZSL* 85.2a).

138. *HJL*, pp. 12–13; *JSBM*, p. 470.

139. *HJL*, p. 13; *JSBM*, p. 471.

140. The following narrative is based largely on information from a July 1, 1512, entry of the *WZSL* in which no specific dates are provided. The account in *JSBM* relates a similar set of events, though in a different order. It, too, lacks dates.

141. *HJL*, pp. 14–15; *JSBM*, p. 472.

142. Zhu Yunming, *Jianghai jianqu ji*, p. 19; *WZSL* 88.10b–11a; *JSBM*, p. 472.

143. *HJL*, p. 15; *WZSL* 87.9b–10a; *JSBM*, p. 472.

144. Zhu Yunming, *Jianghai jianqu ji*, p. 20; *JSBM*, p. 472. The account in *HJL* notes merely that Liu and his son fell into the water while being pursued by imperial troops (p. 15). The account in *WZSL* claims that Liu drowned after being struck by a government arrow (87.9b–10a).

145. *WZSL* 89.3b; *JSBM*, p. 472. On piracy in this region during the Ming, see Wu Zhihe, "Mingdai de jianghu dao," *Mingshi yanjiu zhuankan* 1 (1978): 107–137. One might note that during the mid-nineteenth century, Taiping rebels also attracted the support of pirates as they made their way along the Yangzi toward Nanjing. See Albert Feuerwerker, *Rebellion in Nineteenth Century China* (Ann Arbor, Mich.: Center for Chinese Studies, 1975), p. 17.

146. For example, during the early years of the Chenghua reign (1465–1488), armed salt smugglers roamed the Yangzi between Suzhou and Jiujiang. More than one hundred men were aboard each of these large sea-faring boats, from which they plundered imperial, commoner, and commercial vessels. See *XNSL* 21.6b–7a, 44.9.

147. Wu Zhihe, "Mingdai de jianghu dao."

148. Ibid.

149. Zhu Yunming, *Jianghai jianqu ji*, p. 21.

150. *WZSL* 89.3b; *JSBM*, p. 472.

151. *WZSL* 89.3b; Zhu Yunming, *Jianghai jianqu ji*, p. 21. For more on Suzhou, see Han Dacheng, *Mingdai chengshi yanjiu*, pp. 77–86.

152. Xia Liangsheng, "Lun nizei ru jianghu zhuang," *Xia Dongzhou wenji*, reprinted in *JSWB* 154.7b–7a. Perhaps Xia had in mind earlier events in Jiangxi Province, where, during the late fifteenth century, bandits in Ganzhou had attracted followers from neighboring regions. See He Qiaoxin's comments on this snowballing effect, "Xinjian xunfuyuan ji," *Jiao Qiu wenji*, reprinted in *JSWB* 67.11a–11b.

153. Late in the fifteenth century, Minister of War Ma Wensheng had also voiced concerns about Nanjing's vulnerability to river-borne rebels. He noted the decrepitude of defenses along the Yangzi: the lack of city walls, insufficient manpower, low grain reserves, and the absence of message-relay towers and patrol boats. See Ma Wensheng, "Tiwei yinzaibian sihuan yufang yi baogu Nandu shishu," *Ma Duansu gong zoushu,* reprinted in *JSWB* 62.25a–27b. Ma's unease over Nanjing's defenses increased when news of Prince Ning's ambitions spread during the early sixteenth century. See Ma, "Wei shen shoubei yi fang buyu shishu," *Ma Duansu gong zoushu,* reprinted in *JSWB* 63.19a–20a.

154. Zhu Yunming, *Jianghai jianqu ji,* p. 21; *HJL,* p. 15. Information on Mount Wolf (Langshan) is from *Jiangsu mingchenglu,* p. 319; *Jiangsu dili,* pp. 3 and 55; Jiangsusheng difangzhi bian weiyuanhui bangongshi, ed., *Jiangsu shixian gaikuang* (Jiangsu: Jiangsu jiaoyu chubanshe, 1991), p. 548.

155. Zhu Yunming, *Jianghai jianqu ji,* p. 21; *WZSL* 89.4a.

156. *Nanji zhi* (1534), 3.21a–23a. For more on the garrisons of Nanjing, see Yu Zhijia, "Mingdai liangjing jiandu yu weisuo junhu qianxi zhi guanxi," *Zhongyang yanjiuyuan lishi yuyan yanjiusuo jikan* 64.1 (1993): 137–148.

157. Zhu Yunming, *Jianghai jianqu ji,* pp. 22–23; *WZSL* 91.7a; *Zhenjiang fuzhi* (1596), 14.48a–48b; *XOSL* 223.11b.

158. *WZSL* 91.7a.

159. Zhu Yunming, *Jianghai jianqu ji,* p. 24; *WZSL* 91.7a. In contemporary Jiangsu, the months of July, August, and September are the typhoon season. Since 1950, Jiangsu typically has experienced two or three typhoons each year (*Jiangsu dili,* p. 70).

160. *Tongzhou zhi* (1578), 2.6b.

161. Zhu Yunming, *Jianghai jianqu ji,* p. 24; *WZSL* 91.7a.

162. *WZSL* 91.7a; Chen Yao, *Daguanlou manlu* 8.28a. The one *juan Da guan lou man lu* was excerpted in the 1578 *Tongzhou zhi,* where it is identified only as *Da guan lou.* The full title, as well as several other no longer extant works, such as *Zunsheng lu* (*juan* 1), *Guiyang xingji* (*juan* 1), and *Dongyuan riji* (*juan* 20), are listed in the 1755 edition of the *Tongzhou zhi* (19.16a). The Treatise on Literary Arts in the *MS* lists Chen Yao's *Wu gang wenji* (*juan* 5) and *shiji* (*juan* 3) (*MS* 8.99.2478).

163. *WZSL* 91.7a.

164. Ibid., 91.7a–7b; *JSBM,* p. 473.

165. *WZSL* 91.7b; *JSBM,* p. 473. Only the *JSBM* account mentions the *qiangpao,* translated here as "hand culverin" in the text. See Malcolm Vale, *War and Chivalry: Warfare and Aristocratic Culture in England, France and Burgundy at the End of the Middle Ages* (Athens: University of Georgia Press, 1981), pp. 134–135, for photographs and description of use of culverin in fifteenth-century Europe. See also Needham, Yates, and Gawlikokowski, *Science and Civilisation in China,* vol. 5, pt. 7, pp. 367–376.

166. *WZSL* 91.7b; *JSBM,* pp. 473–474.

167. *Tongzhou zhi* (1578), 8.28a–28b. For more details of these issues and their historiographical implications, see Robinson, "Banditry and Rebellion," pp. 422–427.

168. *HJL,* pp. 15–16. In an October 8, 1512, entry in the *Guoque,* we learn of an attack on Cangzhou by these remnant forces (p. 3034).

169. *Tongzhou zhi* (1578), 5.11b–12a.

170. For a detailed list of rewards, see Robinson, "Banditry and Rebellion," pp. 416–418.

171. *WZSL* 97.3a–3b. The two "ministers" were Gu Dayong and Lu Yin.

172. Ibid., 92.1a.

173. *HJL*, p. 16. For the relevant text in the *Ming Code, juan* 18; Huang Zhangjian, *Mingdai lüli huibian*, 2:731.

174. *HJL*, p. 16. Yang Congming was the wife of Liu Zhonghuai, Liu the Sixth's son (p. 15). As the wife and daughter, respectively, of those who conspired to rebel, Miss Big Liu and Zhang Younu were also put to work in the household of a meritorious official as punishment. The cases of three of these women, Miss Big Liu, Miss Little Liu, and the young daughter of Yang Congming, were later put to the emperor for a final decision (*HJL*, p. 17).

175. *HJL*, p. 17.

176. Ibid.

177. *WZSL* 92.7b. See *Da Ming lü*, Huang Zhangjian, *Mingdai lüli huibian*, 2:731.

178. *HJL*, p. 17.

179. *WZSL* 92.8a; Tan Qian, *Guo que* (ca. 1653; reprint, Beijing: Zhonghua shuju, 1988), p. 3035. See also *MS* 8.94.2324.

180. Qiu Zhonglin, "Mingdai Beijing dushi shenghuo yu zhi'an de zhuanbian," *Jiuzhou xuekan* 5.2 (1992): 94–95.

181. Charles Hucker, *A Dictionary of Official Titles in Imperial China* (Stanford: Stanford University Press, 1985), p. 533.

182. *WZSL* 118.6b, 134.3a; Wang Qiong, "Wei shuihuan yichang zanshe bingbei deng guan yufang daozei shi," in Wan Biao, ed., *Huang Ming jingji wenlu* 18.16a–17a. Cf. *WZSL* 152.4a, 152.5a, 164.5b, 165.4a; *SZSL* 2.6b.

183. For instance, the military defense circuits of Daming Prefecture, Caozhou, and Wuding zhou were discontinued in January of 1516. Such areas as Xuzhou, the Southern Metropolitan Area, and Jiujiang to the south, however, maintained the positions. See *WZSL* 132.6b.

184. *SZSL* 373.4b–5a.

185. *WZSL* 114.5a, 123.7b, 136.6a, 142.8b, 144.4a, 144.4b–5a, 146.7b.

186. Ibid., 151.4b.

187. Ibid., 151.5a. See also *WZSL* 151.6b.

188. *WZSL* 152.4a; Wang Qiong, "Wei shuihuan yichang zanshe bingbei dengguan yufang daozei shi," 18.16a–17a; *WZSL* 152.4a.

189. *WZSL* 152.5a–5b, 153.3b.

190. For more of the Martial Ancestor's exploits at this time, see James Geiss, "The Cheng-te Reign, 1506–1521," in Denis Twitchett and Frederick Mote, eds., *The Cambridge History of China*, vols. 7 and 8 (pts. 1 and 2), *The Ming Dynasty, 1368–1644* (Cambridge: Cambridge University Press, 1998), 7:420–421.

191. *WZSL* 155.6a.

192. Yang Tinghe, "Lun jingji zeiqing shu," *Yang Wenzhong sanlu*, 1.11a–12a, in *Wenyuange siku quanshu*, 428:759. A slightly edited version is found in *WZSL* 157.1a–2a. The date is from the *WZSL* entry. This memorial was only one of at least half a dozen that Yang submitted in an effort to persuade the emperor to return to Beijing from Xuanfu. See *Yang Wenzhong sanlu*, 1.7a–10b, 428:756–758.

193. In Zang Feng's August 10, 1517 memorial, he had argued against fur-

ther hunting trips by the Marital Ancestor for fear that his entourage would trample what little crops had survived the flooding in Shuntian. Supervising Secretary Liu Qi presented a general critique of the Martial Ancestor in a February 4, 1518, memorial, making reference to repeated disasters and rampant banditry (*WZSL* 157.3b–4a).

194. *WZSL* 158.4b.

195. Ibid., 158.4b–5a.

196. Ibid., 158.3b.

197. Ibid., 158.4a.

198. Ibid., 129.5b.

199. Ibid., 127.1a. Bashang was originally established early in the Yongle reign as an imperial horse pasturage. Like other areas, the lands were gradually either sold off into private hands or were given to imperial relatives by the emperor. It was reported that many landowners with links to the throne were able to shift the tax burden for those lands onto local commoners. For more details, see *SZSL* 3.5b–6a. The report must be evaluated carefully, for it was written soon after the new emperor, Shizong, took the throne; many of those who had enjoyed favor under the Martial Ancestor were coming under intense attack.

200. *WZSL* 146.3a–3b. Earlier in November of 1515, the court suspended the salary of an assistant regional military commissioner for two months because he failed to eradicate brigandry in the area (*WZSL* 130.4a).

201. Wang Qiong, "Wei yichu tuzei yi jing jingdian shi," *Wang Jinxi benbing fuzou*, in *JSWB* 1.4a.

202. The court rewarded this grand coordinator, Zhang Run, with silver and a set of dragon robes for his efforts. See Nie Bao, "Zhang Gong Run muzhiming," *Guochao xianzheng lu* 27.41a; cf. *Benchao fensheng renwukao* 100.38a.

203. Wang Qiong, "Wei yichu tuzie yi jing jingxun shi," *Wang Jinxi benbing fuzou* 1.5a.

204. On Shizong's accession and the political infighting it engendered, see James Geiss, "The Chia-ching Reign, 1522–1566," in Twitchett and Mote, *The Cambridge History of China*, 7:440–450. Before this, the court had been concerned about brigandage in Tongzhou, Yongping, and Baoding (and about officials' tendency to conceal such incidents). See *WZSL* 196.5b.

205. *SZSL* 3.4a; *Bazhou zhi* (1548) 6.1a–2b; *Wanli Da Ming huidian* 128.2b, 4:1827. Prior to this, the vice-commissioner from the military defense circuit of Tianjin had overseen Bazhou. See *WZSL* (March 5, 1514), 109.5b.

206. *SZSL* 3.19a. See also *SZSL* 4.11a.

207. Gui was rewarded for his efforts on July 31, 1522 (*SZSL* 16.4a), while officials from Shuntian were recognized in October 1522 for capturing the "notorious bandit" Ma Xi (*SZSL* 18.4a). Over the objections of the Ministry of Works, Shizong approved Gui's request for clothes and shoes for men from the bandit-apprehension guard (*SZSL* 20.14a).

208. *SZSL* 6.7a–7b.

209. According to the *Bazhou Gazetteer*, the region also suffered from torrential downpours and flooding in 1523 and 1525 (*Bazhou zhi* (1548), 9.2b).

210. Kang Hai, "Sichuan anchasi anchashi Ma Jun Yinglong muzhiming," in *Guochao xianzhenglu* 98.57b.

211. Part of Ma's initiatives included the expansion and refurbishing of the offices of the military training field in Bazhou, completed in 1525 (*Bazhou zhi* (1548), 8.23b–24a).

212. Kang Hai, "Sichuan anchasi anchashi Ma Jun Yinglong muzhiming."

213. *SZSL* 35.2a. Cf. *Lintao fuzhi* (1605), 19.23a–23b; *Bazhou zhi* (1548), 6.16a–16b.

214. *Bazhou zhi* 8.32a.

215. Gui E, "Jin yuditu shu," *Gui Wenxiang ji* 4.3b in *JSWB* 182.3b. Later geographies widely copied Gui's description. See Chen Quanzhi, *Pengchuang rilu,* "Huanyu," 1.21b; Cai Runan, *Yudi lüe* (1543, manuscript; Rare Book Collection, Beijing University Library, Beijing University), 1.9a; Guo Zizhang, *Junxian shiming* (1615 preface: Hishi copy held at Kyoto Jinbunken; original, Naikaku Collection), 1.2a. Similar descriptions of the area may be found in Hu Wenhuan's *Huayi fengtu zhi* (1613, preface; Hishi copy, Kyoto Jinbunken; original, Naikaku Bunko Collection), 1.1b–4a.

216. Shen Defu, *Wanli yehuobian, juan* 28, p. 757.

217. For details of banditry in Shandong, Henan, and Shanxi in the decade following the 1510 Rebellion, see Robinson, "Banditry and Rebellion," pp. 457–469.

218. *WZSL* 155.4a–4b.

Chapter 7 Conclusion: Implications for the Study of Late Imperial China

1. For a preliminary discussion of the place of gazetteers during the late imperial period and the motivations behind their compilation, see Inoue Susumu, "Hōshi no ichi," in Mindaishi ronsō henshūiinkai, *Yamane Yukio kyōju taikyū kinen Mindaishi ronsō* (Tokyo: Mindaishi ronsō henshūiinkai, 1990), pp. 1289–1306. Inoue argues that local elites compiled gazetteers for fellow local elites in an effort to advertise their success and social standing. For a more narrow examination of the Ming period in the evolution of gazetteers as an historical genre, see Huang Yansheng, "Mingdai de difangzhi," *Shixueshi yanjiu* 4 (1989): 56–70.

2. Timothy Brook, *Praying for Power: Buddhism and the Formation of Gentry Society in Late-Ming China* (Cambridge: Council on East Asian Studies, Harvard University, 1993), pp. 21 and 26. Many of Brook's observations seem to build on the introductory comments by Joseph Esherick and Mary Rankin in their *Chinese Local Elites and Patterns of Dominance* (Berkeley, University of California Press, 1990), pp. 1–24.

3. In more recent writings, Brook has stressed the need to bring the state back in. See Timothy Brook and B. Michael Frolic, "The Ambiguous Challenge of Civil Society," in Timothy Brook and B. Michael Frolic, eds., *Civil Society in China* (Armonk, N.Y.: M. E. Sharpe, 1997), pp. 3–16; Timothy Brook, "Auto-Organization in Chinese Society," in *Civil Society in China*, pp. 19–45. R. Bin Wong has also strongly argued for the need to reconsider the role of the state in late-imperial Chinese society. See R. Bin Wong, *China Transformed: Historical Change and the Limits of European Historical Experience* (Ithaca: Cornell University Press, 1997).

4. Esherick and Rankin, *Chinese Elites and Patterns of Dominance*, p. 10.

5. Roland Higgins, "Piracy and Coastal Defense in the Ming Period: Gov-

ernmental Response to Coastal Disturbances, 1523–1549" (Ph.D. diss., University of Minnesota, 1981) and "Pirates in Gowns and Caps: Gentry Law-Breaking in the Mid-Ming," *Ming Studies* 10 (1980): 30–37; Merrilyn Fitzpatrick, "Local Administration in Northern Chekiang and the Response to the Pirate Invasions of 1553–1556" (Ph.D. diss., Australian National University, 1976); Charles Hucker, "Hu Tsung-hsien's Campaign against Hsu Hai, 1556," in Frank Kierman and John Fairbank, eds., *Chinese Ways in Warfare* (Cambridge: Harvard University Press, 1974); Kwan-wai So, *Japanese Piracy in Ming China during the Sixteenth Century* (Ann Arbor: Michigan State University Press, 1975); Geiss, "The Chia-ching Reign, 1522–1566," pp. 490–505; Thomas Nimick, "Ch'i Chi-kuang and I-wu County," *Ming Studies* 34 (July 1995): 17–29.

6. For a discussion of international trade and society in Fujian, see Chang Pin-tsun, "Chinese Maritime Trade: The Case of Sixteenth Century Fu-chien (Fukien)" (Ph.D. diss., Princeton University, 1983).

7. For a discussion of this question during the Song period, see Peter Bol, "Government, Society, and State: On the Political Visions of Ssu-ma Kuang and Wang An-shih," in Robert Hymes and Conrad Schirokauer, eds., *Ordering the World: Approaches to State and Society in Sung Dynasty China* (Berkeley: University of California Press, 1993), pp. 128–192.

8. For a consideration of links between men of force and elite families in Jiangxi Province during the middle Ming period, see Imaminato Yoshinobu, "Mindai chūki no tōzoku ni tsuite," in Noguchi Tetsurō, ed., *Chūgokushi ni okeru ran no kōzo* (Tokyo: Yūzankuku, 1986), pp. 273–307. For discussion of links between men of force and local elites in the Pearl Delta during the late Ming, see Kishi Kazuyuki, "Canton chihō shakai ni okeru buraisō-Minmakki no Shuchidō o megutte," in *Gen-Min-Shin ki ni okeru kokka shihai to minshū no saikentō-shihai no Chūgokuteki tokushitsu* (Kyūshū daigaku tōyōshi kenkyūshitsu, 1983), pp. 156–166.

9. Yang Tinghe, "Xian Ning bo jinfeng hou shi Wuxiang Qiu Yue muzhi," in Jiao Hong, *Guochao xianzheng lu* (1594–1616; reprint, Taibei: Xuesheng shuju, 1965), 10.63a.

10. Edward Dreyer, *Early Ming China: A Political History, 1355–1435* (Stanford: Stanford University Press, 1982).

11. James Geiss, "The Leopard Quarters during the Cheng-te Reign," *Ming Studies* 24 (Fall 1987): 1–38.

12. PRC scholar Gu Cheng has stressed the broad importance of the garrison system for Ming society. See his "Mingdiguo de jiangtu guanli tizhi," *Lishi yanjiu* 3 (1989), "Mingdai gengdishu xintan," *Zhongguo shehui kexue* 4 (1986), "Tan Mingdai de weiji," *Beijing shifan daxue xuebao* 5 (1989): 56–65, and "Mindai no eiseki ni tsuite—jinbutsu likai no tameni," *Tōhoku daigaku Tōyōshi ronshū* 7 (1998): 239–265. See also Aramiya Manabu's translation of and commentary on Gu's article.

13. Kawagoe Yasuhiro, Yu Zhijia, Aoyama Jirō, and Okuyama Norio are among the leading scholars in this field. For a brief review of scholarship in China on the Ming military since the 1930s, see Zhao Ming, "Mingdai bingzhi liushinian zhi huigu," *Zhongguoshi yanjiu dongtai* 8 (1993): 14–20. For a recent essay outlining some of the major institutional changes in securing manpower, logistics, and command structure, see Fan Zhongyi, "Lun Mingchao junzhi de

yanbian," *Zhongguoshi yanjiu* 2 (1998): 129–139. For a preliminary discussion of regional differences in how garrisons secured troops during the earliest years of the Ming dynasty, see Sŏ In-bŏm, "Eijyo to eijyogun—gunshi no senjūhōhō o chūshin ni," *Mindaishi kenkyū* 27 (1999): 5–19. For a sophisticated discussion of the interplay of court politics and military strategy during the Ming period, see Arthur Waldron, *The Great Wall of China: From History to Myth* (Cambridge: Cambridge University Press, 1990). For discussion of organization and leadership of Ming armies, see Fang Zhiyuan, "Mingchao jundui de bianzhi yu lingdao tizhi," *Minshi yanjiu* 3 (1993): 35–44.

14. Kawagoe Yasuhiro stresses this point in his recent overview of Japanese scholarship on the Ming military. See his "Mindai gunjishi ni kansuru kenkyūjōkyō o megutte," in Mori Masao, Nogushi Testsurō, and Hamashima Atsutoshi, eds., *Min-Shin jidaishi no kihon mondai* (Tokyo: Ryūko shoin, 1997), pp. 268–270.

15. For a concise overview of the Tang-Song Transition, see Peter Bol, *"This Culture of Ours": Intellectual Transitions in T'ang and Sung China* (Stanford: Stanford University Press, 1992), pp. 32–75.

16. James T. C. Liu, "Polo and Cultural Change: From Tang to Sung China," *Harvard Journal of Asiatic Studies* 45 (June 1985): 203–224.

17. In fact, one prominent Yuan specialist has objected to both Liu's methodology and conclusion. In a short article, Chen Gaohua demonstrated that polo playing at the court did not vanish during the Song. Instead, it continued through the Yuan period and into the early Ming. See Chen Gaohua, "Song Yuan he Mingchu de maqiu," *Lishi yanjiu* 4 (1984): 177–181. Chen was reacting against an earlier version of Liu's article published in Chinese in 1980.

18. For Fang's martial activities, see Willard Peterson, *The Bitter Gourd: Fang I-chi and the Impetus for Intellectual Change* (New Haven: Yale University Press, 1979), p. 88. For a more extended discussion of Fang's notions of "men of action," see pp. 84–100. For Chen's involvement, see William Atwell, "Ch'en Tzu-lung (1608–1647): A Scholar-Official of the Late Ming Dynasty," (Ph.D. diss., Princeton University, 1974), pp. 25, 112–114.

19. Chen Baoliang points out that the repeated military crises during the latter half of the sixteenth and the beginning half of the seventeenth century spurred many young literati into the study of martial arts and strategy. However, he also argues that the new emphasis on martial activities among young elite males should also be seen as part of the "statecraft" school and its insistence on practicality and efficacy. See Chen, "Wan Ming de shangwu jingshen," *Mingshi yanjiu* 1 (1991): 248–259.

20. For descriptions of the various editions of the novels and how their narratives were understood by some sophisticated readers, see Andrew Plaks, *The Four Masterworks of the Ming Novel* (Princeton: Princeton University Press, 1987), pp. 279–495.

21. In a different vein, Krzysztof Gawlikokowski has noted that classical theories of war were "part of popular culture." See Joseph Needham, Robin Yates, and Krzysztof Gawlikokowski, *Science and Civilisation in China*, vol. 5, *Chemistry and Chemical Technology*, pt. 6, *Military Technology: Missiles and Seiges* (Cambridge: Cambridge University Press, 1994), p. 80. After remarking on the pervasive nature of acting troupes and popular fiction highlighting martial

themes, Gawlikokowski somewhat contradictorily stressed Chinese culture's "negative attitude to war, the disdainful treatment of martial values, of military service and soldiering, and indeed, of anything related to combat" (p. 98). While the audience for *huaben* stories is debated, it seems safe to say that it was wider than the one that read the expensive deluxe editions issued during the mid to late Ming. See Y. M. Ma, "The Knight-Errants in Hua-pen Stories," *T'oung-pao* 61 (75): 266–300.

22. For some sense of the martial training that the famed Ming general Qi Jiguang (1528–1588) gave his men, see his military manual *Jixiao xinshu* (1526; reprint, Beijing: Renmin tiyu chubanshe, 1988).

23. The relevant literature is voluminous. For an introduction to the range of questions accessible through the prism of crime, see J. A. Sharpe, *Crime in Early Modern England, 1550–1750* (New York: Longman, 1984). Although based on particulars in early medieval western Europe, a recent and useful discussion of violence is Guy Halsall, "Violence and Society in the Early Medieval West: An Introductory Survey," in Guy Halsall, ed., *Violence and Society in the Early Medieval West* (Woodbridge: Boydell Press, 1998), pp. 1–45.

24. Adrian Davis, "Homicide in the Home: Marital Strife and Familial Conflict in Eighteenth-Century China" (Ph.D. diss., Harvard University, 1995); Jonathan Ocko, "Hierarchy and Harmony: Family Conflicts As Seen in Ch'ing Legal Cases," in Kwang-ching Liu, ed., *Orthodoxy in Late Imperial China* (Berkeley: University of California Press, 1990), pp. 212–230; Vivien Ng, "Ideology and Sexuality: Rape Laws in Ch'ing China," *Journal of Asian Studies* 46.1 (1987): 57–70.

Character Glossary

Anlu 安陸

bachi 把持
Bai Ying 白英
Bajiquan 八極拳
Ban Zhao 班超
Baoding 保定
baojia 保甲
Bashang 壩上
Bazhou 霸州
biaobing 標兵
buxia 布俠

Cangzhou 滄州
Cao Jixiang 曹吉祥
Caozhou 曹州
Chang'an 長安
Changyuan 長垣
Changzhou 常州
Chen Han 陳翰
Chen Ju 陳矩
Chen Kui 陳逵
Chen Quanzhi 陳全之
Cheng'an 成安
Chu Quan 儲巏
Cui Shi 崔氏
Cuihuangkou 崔黃口

Dacheng 大成
dahan 大漢
dahang 打行
dahu 大戶
Daming 大名

Damingfu 大名府
daozei 盜賊
Dashiyong 大時雍
dashou 打手
Dean 德安
Deng Maoqi 鄧茂七
dianshi 典史
Ding Shi 丁氏
Dingguo Gong 定國公
Dongyuesi 東嶽寺
Dongzhimen 東直門
Dou 斗

Erlanggang 二郎崗

Fangcheng 方城
Feng Bao 馮保
Fuqing 福清
Fuyang 阜陽
fuyao 腹腰

Ganzhou 贛州
gaoming 誥命
gongbing 弓兵
Gu Dayong 谷大用
Gu Zimei 顧子美
Gu'an 固安
guanggun 光棍
Guangping 廣平
guanshe 官舍
guanxiao 官校
Guazhouzhen 瓜洲鎮
Gui E 桂萼

241

Gui Yanliang 桂彥良

haohua junmin 豪猾軍民
haohua 豪猾
haojie 豪傑
haojun 豪俊
He Jian 何鑑
He Qiaoxin 何喬新
Hejian 河間
Hexiwu 河西務
Houjianlu 後鑒錄
Hu Shining 胡世寧
Huai'an 淮安
Huaibei 淮北
Huaiqing 懷慶
Huaizhong 懷忠
Huang Xiaoyang 黃蕭養
Huanggang 黃岡
Huangzhou 黃州
Hunhe 渾河
Huo En 霍恩
huoche 火車
huofu 伙夫
huojia 伙甲
huoyue 伙約

Jia Mian'er 賈免兒
jiading 家丁
jian'er 健兒
Jiang Qin 蔣欽
Jianghuai 江淮
Jiangxia 江下
Jiangyin 江陰
Jiaohe 交河
Jiaozhou 膠州
jiaren 家人
jibing 擊兵
jibing 機兵
jieshou 接手
jinbing 勁兵
Jingle 靜樂

Jining 濟寧
jinshi 進士
Jinwu youwei 金吾右衛
juren 舉人
Juyongguan 居庸關

Kaifengfu 開封府
Kang Youhui 康友惠
kou 寇
kuaishou 快手

lahu 喇唬
lahuo 喇伙
Langshan 狼山
laoren 老人
lazi 喇子
lazui 喇嘴
Li Dongyang 李東陽
Li Guang 李廣
Li Long 李隆
Li Rui 李銳
Li Shimian 李時勉
li 例
Liang Chu 梁儲
Liangxiang 良鄉
lijia 里甲
Lin Cong 林聰
Lin Ruzhou 林若周
Ling Mengchu 凌濛初
Linqing 臨清
lishi 利實
Liu Bin 劉斌
Liu Chong 劉寵
Liu Daxia 劉大夏
Liu Hui 劉惠
Liu Jian 劉健
liumang 流氓
Lu Shen 陸深
Lu Wan 陸完
Luzhou 潞州
Luyi 鹿邑

Ma Ang 馬昂
Ma Yongcheng 馬永成
Ma Zhongxi 馬忠錫
makuaishou 馬快手
Mancheng 滿城
Mao Rui 毛銳
Mengcun 孟村
Mengdu 孟瀆
Mengshan 蒙山
min 民
minbing 民兵
minkuai 民快
minzhuang 民壯

Ning Gao 寧杲
Ningshan 寧山
Niu Yu 牛玉
niujiao 牛角

Pang Wenxuan 龐文宣
Pingyang 平陽
Pizhou 邳州
Potouzhen 泊頭鎮

qi 氣
qiangpao 槍砲
qijiu 耆舊
Qin Guan 秦觀
Qingdu 慶都
qingjun 清軍
Qiu Jun 丘濬
Queli 闕里
Quxian 曲縣

Renqui 任丘
renxia 任俠
Rongcheng 容城

sandeng jiuze 三等九則
Shangcai 上蔡
Shangshui 商水

Shangyuanxian 上元縣
Shenyang wei 瀋陽衛
sheyu 舍餘
Shi Jian 石堅
Shi Xi 石璽
shimin 士民
Shizong 世宗
shoumai duanjiao 收買短腳
Shunde 順德
sishi 死士
Song Quan 宋全
songshi 訟師
Sun Yuanzhen 孫原真
Suzhou 蘇州

Taihangshan 太行山
Taihe 泰和
Taiyuan 太原
Taizu 太祖
Tancheng 郯城
Tang Long 唐龍
Tangxian 唐縣
Tengxiangyou wei 騰驤右衛
Tongzhou 通州
tuhao 土豪
tunlao 屯老

Wang An 王安
Wang Hai 王海
Wang Qiong 王瓊
Wang Shouren 王守仁
Wang Ying Shu 王英叔
Wang Zhi 汪直
wangming 亡命
Wanhuisi 萬彗寺
Wanquan dusi 萬全都司
Wei Zhongxian 魏忠賢
Weixian 威縣
weixuanbu 衛選簿
wen 文
Wenan 文安

Weng Wanda 翁萬達
Wu Tingzhang 武廷章
wu 武
Wuchang wei 武昌衛
Wudingzhou 武定州
wuji zhi tu 無籍之徒
wulai 無賴
Wuping wei 武平衛
Wuzong 武宗
Wuqing 武清

Xi Ying 席英
Xia Fen 謝蕡
Xia Liangsheng 夏良勝
xia 俠
xiangbing 鄉兵
xiangma 響馬
xiangmazei 響馬賊
Xiangyang 襄陽
xiangyue 鄉約
xianshou 閑手
Xiayi 夏邑
Xin'anzhen 信安鎮
Xincai 新蔡
Xincheng 新城
Xiping 西平
Xu Yongning 徐永寧
Xu Youzhen 徐有貞
xunbuguan 巡捕官
xunjiansi 巡檢司

Yan Qiming 齊彥名
Yan 燕
Yang Congming 楊聰明
Yang Hong 楊洪
Yang Hu (Tiger Yang) 楊虎
Yang Tinghe 楊廷和
Yang Yiqing 楊一清
Yanshan zuowei 燕山左衛
Yanshenzhen 顏神鎮

Yanzhou 兗州
yaodao 腰刀
Ye Boju 葉伯巨
Yingshan 應山
Yingyou 營幽
yinzibu 印子鋪
yiyong 義勇
yiyongbing 義勇兵
Yizhen 移真
Yongfeng 永豐
Yongqing 永清
yongshi 勇士
youbing 遊兵
youshou 游手
youxia 遊俠
Yu Cai 郁采
Yu Jing 于經
Yu Zijun 于子俊
Yuan Biao 袁彪
Yuan Jie 袁傑
Yue Fei 岳飛
Yutian 玉田
Yuzhou 裕州

Zhang Chun 張純
Zhang Ding 張鼎
Zhang Jing 張鯨
Zhang Run 張潤
Zhang Siqi 張思齊
Zhang Wei 張偉
Zhang Yong 張永
Zhang Zhong 張忠
Zhangde 彰德
Zhangjiawan 張家灣
Zhao Fengzi 趙瘋子
Zhao Pan 趙鐇
Zhao Sui 趙鐩
zhen 鎮
Zhen'an 真安
Zhending 真定

zhengjun 正軍
Zhenjiang 鎮江
zhongwen qingwu 重文輕武
Zhouzhou 涿州
Zhu Qianhu 朱千戶

zhuangtou 莊頭
zidibing 子弟兵
Zijing 紫荊
zongjia 總甲

References

Adachi Keiji 足立啓二. "Shindai kahoku no nōgyō keiei to shakai kōzō" 清代華北の農業経営と社會構造. *Shirin* 史林 64.4 (July 1981): 66–93.

Antony, Robert. "Peasants, Heroes, and Brigands." *Modern China* 15.2 (April 1989): 123–148.

———. "The Problem of Banditry and Bandit Suppression in Kwantung South China, 1780–1840." *Criminal Justice History: An International Annual* 11 (1990): 31–53.

———. "Scourges of the People: Perceptions of Robbery, Snatching, and Theft in the Mid-Qing Period." *Late Imperial China* 16.2 (December 1995): 98–132.

Aoyama Jirō 青山治郎. *Mindai keieishi kenkyū* 明代京営研究. Sapporo: Kyobun-sha, 1996.

———. "Mindai ni okeru keiei no keisei ni tsuite" 明代いおける京営の形成について. *Tōhōgaku* 東洋学 42 (1971): 64–81.

———. "Mindai Seitokki no keiei ni tsuite—toku ni iwayuru Tōsai kanchōgun no jittai ni tsuite" 明代正徳期の京営について―特に所謂東西官庁軍の実態について. *Sundai shigaku* 駿台史学 98 (September 1996): 83–118.

Aramiya (Satō) Manabu 新宮學. "Mindai no shuto Pekin no toshi jinkō ni tsuite" 明代の首都北京の都市人口について. *Yamagata daigaku shigaku ronshū* 山形大学史学論集 11 (February 1991): 23–46.

Atwell, William. "Ch'en Tzu-lung (1608–1647): A Scholar-Official of the Late Ming Dynasty." Ph.D. diss., Princeton University, 1974.

———. "Ming China and the 'Emerging World Economy,' 1470–1650." In Denis Twitchett and Frederick Mote, eds., *The Cambridge History of China*. Vol. 8, *The Ming Dynasty, 1368–1644*, pt. 2. Cambridge: Cambridge University Press, 1998.

———. "The T'ai-ch'ang, T'ien-ch'i, and Ch'ung-chen Reigns, 1620–1644." In Denis Twitchett and Frederick Mote, eds., *The Cambridge History of China*. Vol. 7, *The Ming Dynasty, 1368–1644*, pt. 1, 585–640. Cambridge: Cambridge University Press, 1988.

———. "Yūrashia no 'Daikinginkō'" ユーラシアの大金銀荒. *Kokusai kōryū* 国際交流 62 (1993): 54–60.

Bao Zunxin 包遵信. "Ming 'cheng Quji' beiwen fanying de nongmin qiyi dui Kongjiao de mieqi" 明《城關里記》碑文反映的農民起義對孔教的蔑棄. *Wenwu* 文物 208 (1973): 2–6.

Baoding diqu bowuguan 保定地區博物館. "Ming liangjing sili taijian Niu Yu mu fajue jianbao" 明兩京司禮太監牛玉墓發掘簡報. *Wenwu* 文物 2 (1983): 76–80.

Barfield, Thomas. *The Perilous Frontier.* Cambridge: Basil Blackwell, 1989.

Barkey, Karen. *Bandits and Bureaucrats: The Ottoman Route to State Centralization.* Ithaca: Cornell University Press, 1994.

Bellamy, John. *Crime and Public Order in England in the Later Middle Ages.* London: Routledge and Kegan Paul, 1972.

Bercé, Yves-Marie. *Revolt and Revolution in Early Modern Europe: An Essay on the History of Political Violence.* Manchester: Manchester University Press, 1987.

Berry, Mary Elizabeth. *Culture of Civil War in Kyoto.* Berkeley: University of California Press, 1994.

Billingsley, Phil. *Bandits in Republican China.* Stanford: Stanford University Press, 1988.

Blok, Anton. *The Mafia of a Sicilian Village: 1860–1960.* London: Blackwell and Mott Limited, 1974.

———. "The Peasant and the Brigand: Social Banditry Reconsidered." *Comparative Studies in Society and History* 19 (1972): 494–503.

Bo Hua 柏樺. "Mingdai zhixian de guanxiwang" 明代知縣的關係网. *Shixue jikan* 史學集刊 3 (1993): 47–55.

———. "Mingdai zhouxian guanli chengchu guizhi chouyi" 明代州縣官吏懲處規制芻議. *Mingshi yanjiu* 明史研究 4 (1994): 60–67.

Bol, Peter. "Government, Society, and State: On the Political Visions of Ssu-ma Kuang and Wang An-shih." In Robert Hymes and Conrad Schirokauer, eds., *Ordering the World: Approaches to State and Society in Sung Dynasty China.* Berkeley: University of California Press, 1993.

———. *"This Culture of Ours": Intellectual Transitions in T'ang and Sung China.* Stanford: Stanford University Press, 1992.

Boretz, Avron. "Martial Arts and Magic Swords: Identity, Myth, and Violence in Chinese Popular Religion." *Journal of Popular Culture* 29.1 (1995): 93–104.

Boxer, C. R., ed. *South China in the Sixteenth Century.* Nendeln: Kraus Reprint Limited, 1967.

Brandauer, Frederick. "Violence and Buddhist Idealism in the *Xiyou* Novels." In Lipman and Harrell, eds., *Violence in China: Essays in Culture and Counterculture.* Albany: State University of New York Press, 1990.

Braudel, Fernand. *The Mediterranean and the Mediterranean World in the Age of Philip II.* Translated from the French by Sian Reynolds. New York: Harper and Row, 1973.

Bray, Francesca, and Joseph Needham. *Science and Civilization in China.* Vol. 6, *Biology and Biological Technology*, pt. 2, *Agriculture.* Cambridge: Cambridge University Press, 1984.

Brook, Timothy. "Auto-Organization in Chinese Society." In Timothy Brook and B. Michael Frolic, eds., *Civil Society in China.* Armonk N.Y.: M. E. Sharpe, 1997.

————. *The Confusions of Pleasure: Commerce and Culture in Ming China*. Berkeley: University of California Press, 1998.

————. *Geographical Sources for Ming-Qing History*. Ann Arbor: University of Michigan, 1988.

————. *Praying for Power: Buddhism and the Formation of Gentry Society in Late-Ming China*. Cambridge: Council on East Asian Studies, Harvard University, 1993.

————. "The Spatial Structure of Ming Local Administration." *Late Imperial China* 6.1 (June 1985): 1–55.

Brook, Timothy, and B. Michael Frolic. "The Ambiguous Challenge of Civil Society." In Timothy Brook and B. Michael Frolic, eds., *Civil Society in China*. Armonk N.Y.: M. E. Sharpe, 1997.

Brown, Nathan. "Brigands and State Building: The Invention of Banditry in Modern Egypt." *Comparative Studies in Society and History* 32.2 (April 1990): 258–281.

Buoye, Thomas. "Economic Change and Rural Violence: Homicides Related to Disputes over Property Rights in Guangdong during the Eighteenth Century." *Peasant Studies* 17.4 (1990): 233–259.

————. "From Patrimony to Commodity: Changing Concepts of Land and Social Conflict in Guangdong Province during the Qianlong Reign (1736–1795)." *Late Imperial China* 14.2 (1993): 33–59.

Burckhardt, Jacob. *The Civilization of the Renaissance in Italy*. New York: First Modern Library, 1954.

Cahill, James. *The Painter's Practice: How Artists Lived and Worked in Traditional China*. New York: Columbia University Press, 1994.

Cai Runan 蔡汝楠. *Yudi lüe* 輿地略. 1543, manuscript. Rare Book Collection, Beijing University Library, Beijing University.

Cammann, Schuyler. "Presentation of Dragon Robes by the Ming and Ch'ing Courts for Diplomatic Purposes." *Sinologica: Review of Chinese Culture and Science* 3 (1953): 193–202.

Cao Guoqing 曹國慶. "Lun Mingdai de qingjun" 論明代的清軍. *Dierjie Ming Qingshi guoji xueshu taolunhui lunwenji* 第二屆明清史國際學術討論會論文集. Tianjin: Tianjin renmin chubanshe, 1993, pp. 500–509.

Cao Shuji 曹樹基. "Hongwu shiqi Hebei diqu de renkou qianyi" 洪武時期河北地區的人口遷移. *Zhongguo nongshi* 中國農史 14.3 (1995) 12–27.

————. "Yongle nianjian Hebei diqu de renkou qianyi" 永樂年間河北地區的人口遷移. *Zhongguo nongshi* 中國農史 15.3 (1996): 33–53, 61.

Cao Shumei 曹淑梅. "Tangshan Mingdai yimin dimingqun" 唐山明代移民地名群. *Diming zhishi* 地名知識 5 (1991): 20.

Cha Hye-wŏn 車惠媛. "Minmatsu chihōkan no ninji idō to chihō yoron" 明末地方官の人事異動と地方世論. *Shirin* 史林 79.1 (January 1996): 32–60.

Chan, Albert Chan. "Peking at the Time of the Wan-li Emperor." In *Proceedings of the Second Biennial Conference, International Association of Historians of Asia* (Taibei, 1962), vol. 2, pp. 119–148.

Chang Der-lang. "The Village Elder System of the Early Ming Dynasty." *Ming Studies* 7 (Fall 1978): 53–72.

Chang Pin-tsun. "Chinese Maritime Trade: The Case of Sixteenth Century Fuchien (Fukien)." Ph.D. diss., Princeton University, 1983.

Chang Sha 常沙. "Mingdai Jingji 'zhuangtian' xiaoyi" 明代京畿《莊田》小議. *Zhongguoshi yanjiu* 中國史研究 3 (1985): 108.

Chao Zhongchen 晁中辰 and Chen Fenglu 陳風路. "Mingdai de wuju zhidu" 明代的武舉制度. *Mingshi yanjiu* 明史研究 3 (1993): 52–58, 92.

Chen Baocheng 陳抱成. "Ming Wuzong cong lishi renwu dao wenyi xingxiang" 明武宗從歷史人物到文藝形像. *Zhengzhou daxue xuekan* 鄭州大學學刊 6 (1995): 54–60.

Chen Baoliang 陳寶良. "Mingdai de baojia yu huojia" 明代的保甲與伙甲. *Mingshi yanjiu* 明史研究 3 (1993): 59–66.

———. "Mingdai de mimi shehui yu Tiandihui de yuanyuan" 明代的秘密社會與天地會的淵源. *Shixue jikan* 文史集刊 1 (1994): 1–10.

———. "Mingdai de minbing yu xiangbing" 明代的民兵與鄉兵. *Zhongguoshi yanjiu* 中國史研究 1 (1994): 82–92.

———. "Mingdai xiangcun de fangyu tizhi" 明代鄉村的防禦體制. *Qi Lu xuekan* 齊魯學刊 6 (1993): 100–108.

———. "Wan Ming de shangwu jingshen" 晚明的尚武精神. *Mingshi yanjiu* 明史研究 1 (1991): 248–259.

———. "Mingdai wulai jieceng de shehui huodong ji qi yingxiang" 明代無賴階層的社會活動及其影響. *Qi Lu xuekan* 齊魯學刊 2 (1992): 91–97.

———. *Zhongguo liumangshi* 中國流氓史. Beijing: Zhongguo shehui kexue, 1993.

Chen Gaohua 陳高華. "Mingdai zhongye Liu Liu, Yang Hu qiyi de ji ge wenti" 明代中葉劉六楊虎起義的幾個問題. *Zhongguo nongmin zhanzhengshi luncong* 中國農民戰爭史論叢. Shanxi: Renmin chubanshe, series no. 1, 1978, pp. 305–350.

———. "Song Yuan he Mingchu de maqiu" 宋元和明初的馬球. *Lishi yanjiu* 歷史研究 4 (1984): 177–181.

———. "Yuandai de junhu" 元代的軍戶. In *Yuanshi yanjiu lungao* 元史研究論稿. Beijing: Zhonghua shuju, 1991, pp. 127–155.

———. "Yuanmo nongmin qiyijun minghao xiaoding" 元末農民起義名號小訂. *Nankai daxue xuebao* 南開大學學報 2 (1979): 95–96.

———. "Yuanmo qiyi nongmin de kouhao" 元末起義農民的口號. In *Yuanshi yanjiu lungao* 元史研究論稿. Beijing: Zhonghua shuju, 1991.

Chen Hongmo 陳洪謨. *Jishi jiwen* 繼世紀聞. Early sixteenth century. Reprint, Beijing: Zhonghua shuju, 1985.

Chen Quanzhi 陳全之. *Pengchuang rilu* 蓬窗日錄. 1565. Reprint, Shanghai: Shanghai shudian, 1985.

Chen Renxi 陳仁錫. *Huang Ming shifalu* 皇明世法錄. 1630. Reprint, Taibei: Xuesheng shuju, 1965.

Chen Wenshi 陳文石. "Mingdai weisuo de jun" 明代衛所的軍. *Zhongyang yanjiuyuan lishi yuyan yanjiusuo jikan* 中央研究院歷史語言研究所集刊 48.2 (July 1977): 177–203.

Chen Wutong 陳梧桐. "Nongmin zhanzheng yanjiu de zhongzhong zhenglun" 農民戰爭研究的種種爭論. In *Jianguo yilai shixue wenti taolun juyao* 建國以來史學問題討論舉要. Jinan: Qi Lu shushe, 1983.

Chen Zilong 陳子龍, ed. *Huang Ming jingshi wenbian* 皇明經世文編. Pinglu tang, 1638. Reprint, Taibei: Guolian chuban youxian gongsi, 1964.

Cheng Dong 成東. *Zhongguo gudai bingqi tuji* 中國古代兵器圖集. Beijing: Jiefangjun chubanshe, 1990.

Chiang, Siang-tseh. *The Nien Rebellion*. Seattle: University of Washington Press, 1954.

Chu Hung-lam. "Ch'iu Chün (1421–1495) and the *Ta-hsueh yen-i-pu*: Statecraft Thought in Fifteenth-Century China." Ph.D. diss., Princeton University, 1983.

———. "Huang Zuo's Meeting with Wang Yangming and the Debate over the Unity of Knowledge and Action." *Ming Studies* 35 (August 1995): 53–73.

———. "Intellectual Trends in the Fifteenth Century." *Ming Studies* 27 (Spring 1989): 1–33.

Chu Hung-lam (Zhu Honglin) 朱鴻林. "Mingdai zhongqi fangshe zhian chongjian lixiang zhi zhanxian" 明代中期方社治安重建理想之展現. *Chungguk hakpo* 中國學報 32 (1992): 87–100.

Chu Quan 儲巏. *Chaixu ji* 柴墟集. Photographic facsimile. Rare Book Collection, Gest Oriental Library, Princeton University. Original, Naikaku bunko.

Ch'u T'ung-tsu. *Local Government in China during the Ching*. Cambridge: Harvard University Press, 1962.

Cipolla, Carlo. *Before the Industrial Revolution: European Society and Economy, 1000–1700*. New York: W. W. Norton, 1980.

Clunas, Craig. *Superfluous Things: Material Culture and Social Status in Early Modern China*. Urbana: University of Illinois Press, 1991.

Cohen, Myron. "Lineage Organization in North China." *Journal of Asian Studies* 44.3 (August 1990): 509–534.

Cong Hanxiang 從翰香. "Shisi shiji houqi zhi shiliu shiji mo Huabei pingyuan nongcun fazhan de kaocha" 十四世紀後期至十六世紀末華北平原農村發展的考察. *Zhongguo jingjishi yanjiu* 中國經濟史研究 3 (1986): 11–26.

Cooper, Michael, ed. *They Came to Japan: An Anthology of European Reports on Japan, 1543–1640*. Berkeley: University of California Press, 1965.

Crawford, Robert. "Eunuch Power in the Ming Dynasty." *T'oung pao* 49.3 (1961): 115–148.

Dai Jin 戴金. *Huang Ming tiaofa shilei zuan* 皇明條法事類纂. Ca. 1531. Reprint, Tokyo: Koten kenkyūkai, 1966.

Da Ming huidian 大明會典. Shen Shixing 申時行, compiler. 1587. Reprint, Taibei: Dongnan shubaoshe, 1964.

(Zhengde 正德) *Da Ming huidian* 大明會典. Li Dongyang 李東陽. Early sixteenth century. Reprint, Tokyo: Kyūko shoin, 1989.

Danker, Uwe. "Bandits and the State: Robbers and the Authorities in the Holy Roman Empire in the Late Seventeenth and Early Eighteenth Centuries." In Richard Evans, ed., *The German Underworld: Deviants and Outcasts in German History*. London: Routledge, 1988.

Dardess, John. *A Ming Society: T'ai-ho County, Kiangsi, in the Fourteenth to Seventeenth Centuries*. Berkeley: University of California Press, 1996.

Davies, Natalie. *Society and Culture in Early Modern France*. Stanford: Stanford University Press, 1975.

Davis, Adrian. "Homicide in the Home: Marital Strife and Familial Conflict in Eighteenth-Century China." Ph.D. diss., Harvard University, 1995.

Dawson, Raymond. *The Chinese Chameleon: An Analysis of European Perceptions of Chinese Civilization*. London: Oxford University Press, 1967.

de Heer, Philip. *The Caretaker Emperor: Aspects of the Imperial Institution in Fifteenth-Century China As Reflected in the Political History of the Reign of Chu Ch'i-yü*. Leiden: E. J. Brill, 1985.

Dean, Trevor, and K. J. P. Lowe, eds. *Crime, Society, and the Law in Renaissance Italy*. Cambridge: Cambridge University Press, 1994.

Di Fusheng 邸富生. "Shilun Mingchao chuqi juzhu zai neidi de Mengguren" 試論明朝初期居住在內地的蒙古人. *Minzu yanjiu* 民族研究 3 (1996): 70–77.

Dingling 定陵 (*Imperial Tomb of the Ming Dynasty, Dingling*). Beijing: Wenwu chubanshe, 1990.

Ding Yi 丁易 (Ye Dingyi 葉丁易). *Mingdai tewu zhengzhi* 明代特務政治. Beijing: Zhongwai chubanshe, 1950.

Dray-Novey, Alison. "Spatial Order and Police in Imperial Beijing." *Journal of Asian Studies* 52.4 (1993): 897–902.

Dreyer, Edward. *Early Ming China: A Political History, 1355–1435*. Stanford: Stanford University Press, 1982.

Egmond, Florike. *Underworlds: Organized Crime in the Netherlands, 1650–1800*. Cambridge: Polity Press, 1993.

Elman, Benjamin. *A Cultural History of Civil Service Examinations in Late Imperial China*. Berkeley: University of California Press, 2000.

Esherick, Joseph. *Origins of the Boxer Uprising*. Berkeley: University of California Press, 1987.

Esherick, Joseph, and Mary Rankin. *Chinese Local Elites and Patterns of Dominance*. Berkeley: University of California Press, 1990.

Fan Zhongyi 範中義. "Lun Mingchao junzhi de yanbian" 論明朝軍制的演變. *Zhongguoshi yanjiu* 中國史研究 2 (1998): 129–139.

Fang Zhiyuan 方志遠. "Mingchao jundui de bianzhi yu lingdao tizhi" 明朝軍隊的編制與領導體制." *Mingshi yanjiu* 明史研究 3 (1993): 35–44.

———. "Mingdai de Yumajian" 明代的御馬監. *Zhongguoshi yanjiu* 中國史研究 2 (1997): 140–148.

———. "Mingdai de zhenshou zhongguan zhidu" 明代的鎮守中官制度. *Wenshi* 文史 49 (1994): 131–145.

———. "Mingdai de siwei, yongshi ying" 明代的四衛, 勇士營. *Dierjie Ming Qingshi guoji xueshu taolunhui lunwenji* 第二屆明清史國際學術討論會論文集. Tianjin: Tianjin renmin chubanshe, 1993, pp. 489–499.

Farmer, Edward. *Early Ming Government: The Evolution of Dual Capitals*. Cambridge: Harvard University Press, 1976.

———. "Social Regulation of the First Ming Emperor: Orthodoxy As a Function of Authority," in Liu Kwang-Ching, ed., *Orthodoxy in Late Imperial China*. Berkeley: University of California Press, 1990.

———. *Zhu Yuanzhang and Early Ming Legislation: The Reordering of Chinese Society following the Era of Mongol Rule*. Leiden: E. J. Brill, 1995.

Fei Hong 費宏. *Tai bao Fei wenxian Gong zhai gao* 太保費文憲公摘稿. 1555. Reprint, Taibei: Wenhai chubanshe, 1970.

Ferguson, Donald. "Letters from Portuguese Captives in Canton, written in 1534 and 1536. With an Introduction on Portuguese intercourse with China in the first half of the sixteenth century." *Indian Antiquary* 30 (1901): 421–451, 467–491. Reprint, Bombay: n.p., 1902.

Feuerwerker, Albert. *Rebellion in Nineteenth Century China*. Ann Arbor, Mich.: Center for Chinese Studies, 1975.

Fitzpatrick, Merrilyn. "Local Administration in Northern Chekiang and the Response to the Pirate Invasions of 1553–1556." Ph.D. diss., Australian National University, 1976.

Frank, Andre Gunder. *ReOrient: Global Economy in the Asian Age*. Berkeley: University of California Press, 1998.

Franke, Herbert, ed. *Sung Biographies*. Weisbaden: Franz Steiner Verlag GMBH, 1976.

Franke, Wolfgang. "Historical Writing during the Ming." In Denis Twitchett and Frederick Mote, eds., *The Cambridge History of China*. Vol. 7, *The Ming Dynasty, 1368–1644*, pt. 1. Cambridge: Cambridge University Press, 1988, 726–782.

———. *An Introduction to the Sources of Ming History*. Kuala Lumpur: University of Malaya Press, 1968.

———. "The Veritable Records of the Ming Dynasty (1368–1644)." In Edwin Pulleyblank and William Beasley, eds., *Historians of China and Japan*. London: Oxford University Press, 1961.

Fu Tongqin 傅同欽 and (Zheng) Ke Cheng (鄭)克晟. "Mingdai da taijian Liu Jin" 明代大太監劉瑾. *Gugong bowuyuan yuankan* 故宮博物院院刊 2 (1980): 25–28, 71.

Fu Yiling 傅衣凌. "Mingdai jingjishi shang de Shandong he Henan" 明代經濟史上的山東和河南. *Shehui kexue zhanxian* 社會科學戰線 3 (1983): 119–127.

Fuma Susumu 夫馬進. "Late Ming Urban Reform and the Popular Uprising in

Hangzhou." Translated from the Japanese by Michael Lewis. In Linda Cooke Johnson, ed., *Cities of Jiangnan in Late Imperial China*. Albany: State University of New York, 1993.

———. "Min-Shin jidai no shōshi to soshō seido" 明清時代の訟師と訴訟制度. In Kaoru Mamoru, ed., *Chūgoku kinsei no hōsei to shakai* 中国近世の法制と社会. Kyōto: Kyōto daigaku jinbun kagaku kenkyūjo, 1994.

———. "Shōshi hibon" *Shō Sō Ihistu* 訟師秘本蕭曹遺筆. *Shirin* 史林 77.2 (1994): 1–33.

———. "Shōshi hibon no sekai" 訟師秘本の世界. In Ono Kazuko, ed., *Min-matsu Shinsho no shakai to bunka* 明末清初の社会と文化. Kyōto: Kyōto daigaku jinbun kagaku kenkyūjo, 1996.

Gao Shulin 高樹林. "Hebei gudai renkou fazhan gaishu" 河北古代人口發展概述. *Hebei xuekan* 河北學刊 3 (1985): 68–72.

Gauvard, Claude. "Fear of Crime in Late Medieval France." In Barbara Hanawalt and David Wallace, eds., *Medieval Crime and Social Control*. Minneapolis: University of Minnesota Press, 1999.

Geiss, James. "The Cheng-te Reign, 1506–1521." In Denis Twitchett and Frederick Mote, eds., *The Cambridge History of China*. Vol. 7, *The Ming Dynasty, 1368–1644*, pt. 1. Cambridge: Cambridge University Press, 1988.

———. "The Chia-ching Reign, 1522–1566." In Denis Twitchett and Frederick Mote, eds., *The Cambridge History of China*. Vol. 7, *The Ming Dynasty, 1368–1644*, pt. 1. Cambridge: Cambridge University Press, 1988.

———. "The Leopard Quarter during the Cheng-te Reign." *Ming Studies* 24 (Fall, 1987): 1–38.

———. "Peking under the Ming (1368–1644)." Ph.D. diss., Princeton University, 1979.

Giles, Herbert. *A Chinese-English Dictionary*. 2d ed. Shanghai: Kelly and Walsh, 1912.

Goodrich, Carrington, and Chaoying Fang, eds. *Dictionary of Ming Biography, 1368–1644*. New York: Columbia University Press, 1976.

Great Qing Code. Translated from the Chinese by William Jones, with the assistance of Chen Tianquan and Jiang Yongling. Oxford: Clarendon Press, 1994.

Greenshields, Malcolm. *An Economy of Violence in Early Modern France: Crime and Justice in the Haute Auvergne, 1587–1664*. University Park: Pennsylvania State University Press, 1994.

Gu Cheng 顧誠. "Mingdai gengdishu xintan" 明代耕地數新探. *Zhongguo shehui kexue* 中國社會科學 4 (1986).

———. "Mingdiguo de jiangtu guanli tizhi" 明帝國的疆土管理體制. *Lishi yanji* 歷史研究 3 (1989): 135–150.

———. *Mingmo nongmin zhanzhengshi* 明末農民戰爭史. Beijing: Zhongguo shehui kexue chubanshe, 1984.

———. "Tan Mingdai de weiji" 談明代的衛籍. *Beijing shifan daxue xuebao* 北京師範學院學報 5 (1989): 56–65.

———. (Aramiya Manabu 新宮学, translation and commentary.) "Mindai no eiseki ni tsuite—jinbutsu likai no tameni" 明代の衛籍について — 人物理解のために. *Tōhoku daigaku Tōyōshi ronshū* 東北大学東洋史論集 7 (1998): 239–265.

Gu Yingtai 谷應泰. *Mingshi jishi benmo* 明史紀事本末. 1658. Reprint, Taibei: Sanlian shuju, 1985.

Guha, Ranajit. "The Prose of Counter-Insurgency." In Ranajit Guha and Gayatari Chakravotry, eds., *Selected Subaltern Studies*. New York: Oxford University Press, 1988.

Guo Tingxun 郭廷訓. *Benchao fensheng renwu kao* 本朝分省人物考. 1622. Reprint, Taibei: Chengwen chubanshe, 1971.

Guo Yunjing 郭蘊靜. "Ming-Qing shiqi Tianjin yuye" 明清時期天津漁業. *Tianjinshi yanjiu* 天津史研究 1 (1987): 1–5.

Guo Zizhang 郭子章. *Junxian shiming* 郡縣釋名. 1615 preface. Hishi copy held at Kyōto Jinbunken; original held in Naikaku bunko Collection.

Hale, J. R. *Renaissance Europe: Individual and Society, 1480–1520*. Berkeley: University of California Press, 1971.

———. "Violence in the Late Middle Ages: A Background." In Lauro Martines, ed., *Violence and Civil Disorder in Italian Cities, 1200–1500*. Berkeley: University of California Press, 1972.

———. *War and Society in Renaissance Europe: 1450–1620*. New York: St. Martin's Press, 1985.

Hall, John Whitney, Nagahara Keiji, and Kozo Yamamura, eds. *Japan before Tokugawa: Political Consolidation and Economic Growth, 1500–1650*. Princeton: Princeton University Press, 1981.

Halsall, Guy. "Violence and Society in the Early Medieval West: An Introductory Survey." In Guy Halsall, ed., *Violence and Society in the Early Medieval West*. Woodbridge: Boydell Press, 1998.

Hamashima Atsutoshi 浜島敦俊. "The City-God Temples (Ch'eng-huang miao) of Chiangnan in the Ming and Ch'ing Dynasties." *Memoirs of the Research Department of the Toyo Bunko* 50 (1992): 1–27.

Han Dacheng 韓大成. "Mingdai Beijing jingji shulüe" 明代北京經濟述略. *Beijing shehui kexue* 北京社會科學 4 (1991): 93–105.

———. *Mingdai chengshi yanjiu* 明代城市研究. Beijing: Zhongguo renmin daxue chubanshe, 1991.

———. *Mingdai shehui jingji chutan* 明代社會經濟初探. Beijing: Zhongguo renmin chubanshe, 1986.

Handlin, Joanna. *Action in Late Ming Thought: The Reorientation of Lü Kun and Other Scholar-Officials*. Berkeley, University of California Press, 1983.

Hanyu dacidian 漢語大詞典. Shanghai: Shanghai cishu chubanshe, 1986–1994.

Harrison, James. *The Communists and Chinese Peasant Rebellion: A Study in the Rewriting of History*. New York: Atheneum, 1969.

Hazelton, Keith. *A Synchronic Chinese-Western Daily Calendar, 1361–1661* A.D.

Ming Studies Research Series, no. 1. Minneapolis: University of Minnesota Press, 1984.

He Guanbiao 何冠彪. *Yuan Ming jian Zhongguo jingnei Mengguren zhi nongye gaikuang* 元明間中國境內蒙古人之農業概況. Hong Kong: Xuejin chubanshe, 1977.

Hebeisheng fenxian dituce 河北省分縣地圖策. Hebeisheng cehuiju, ed. Beijing: Zhongguo ditu chubanshe, 1992.

Heijdra, Martin. "The Socio-Economic Development of Rural China during the Ming." In Denis Twitchett and Frederick Mote, eds., *The Cambridge History of China*. Vol. 8, *The Ming Dynasty, 1368–1644*, pt. 2, Cambridge: Cambridge University Press, 1998.

Higgins, Roland. "Piracy and Coastal Defense in the Ming Period: Governmental Response to Coastal Disturbances, 1523–1549." Ph.D. diss., University of Minnesota, 1981.

———. "Pirates in Gowns and Caps: Gentry Law-Breaking in the Mid-Ming." *Ming Studies* 10 (1980): 30–37.

Ho, Pingti. *The Ladder of Success in Imperial China*. New York: Columbia University Press, 1962.

Hobsbawm, Eric. *Bandits*. New York: Delacorte, 1969.

———. "Introduction." *Bande Armate, Banditi, Banditismo: E repressione di giustizia negli stati europei de antico regime*. Rome: Jouvence, 1986.

———. *Primitive Rebels: Studies in Archaic Forms of Social Movement in the Nineteenth and Twentieth Centuries*. Manchester: Manchester University Press, 1959.

Hu Wenhuan 胡文煥. *Huayi fengtu zhi* 華夷風土志. 1613, preface. Hishi copy held at Kyōto Jinbunken; original held in Naikaku Bunko Collection.

Huang Bian 黃汴. *Yitong lucheng tuji* 一統路程圖集. 1570. Republished by Shang Jun 商濬 as *Shuilu lucheng* 水陸路程, 1617. Microfilm, Library of Congress.

Huang Liuhong 黃六鴻. *Fuhui quanshu* 福惠全書. 1694. Reprint, Tokyo: Kyūko shoten, 1973.

Huang Miantang 黃冕堂. "Lun Mingdai de jingying" 論明代的京營. *Shixue jikan* 史學集刊 3 (1992): 28–35.

Huang, Philip, C. C. *The Peasant Economy and Social Change in North China*. Stanford: Stanford University Press, 1985.

Huang, Ray. *1587, A Year of No Significance: The Ming Dynasty in Decline*. New Haven: Yale University Press, 1981.

———. *Taxation and Governmental Finance in Sixteenth Century China*. Cambridge: Cambridge University Press, 1974.

———. "The Grand Canal during the Ming Dynasty, 1368–1644." Ph.D. diss., University of Michigan, 1964.

Huang Wei 黃暐. *Pengchuang leiji* 蓬窗類集. 1526. In *Hanfenlou biji* 涵芬樓祕笈, ed. Sun Yuxiu. Reprint, Taibei: Taibei shangwu yinshuguan, 1967.

Huang Xun 黃訓. *Huang Ming mingchen jingji lu* 皇明名臣經濟錄. 1551. Photographic reprint of copy held in Naikaku bunko.

Huang Yansheng 黃燕生. "Mingdai de difangzhi" 明代的地方志. *Shixueshi yanjiu* 史學史研究 4 (1989): 56–70.

Huang Yunmei 黃雲眉. *Mingshi kaozheng* 明史考証. Beijing: Zhonghua shuju, 1979–1986.

Huang Zhangjian 黃彰健. "Lun *Huang Ming zuxun lu* suoji Mingchu huanguan zhidu" 論皇明祖訓錄所記明初宦官制度. *Zhongyang yanjiuyuan lishi yuyan yanjiusuo jikan* 中央研究院歷史語言研究所集刊 32 (1961): 77–97.

——— 黃彰健. *Mingdai lüli huibian* 明代律例彙編. Taibei: Zhongyang yanjiuyuan lishi yuyan yanjiusuo zhuankan, no. 75, 1979.

Hucker, Charles. *Chinese Government in Ming Times: Seven Studies*. Studies in Oriental Culture, no. 2. New York: Columbia University Press, 1969.

———. *A Dictionary of Official Titles in Imperial China*. Stanford: Stanford University Press, 1985.

———. "Hu Tsung-hsien's Campaign against Hsu Hai, 1556." In Frank Kierman and John Fairbank, eds., *Chinese Ways in Warfare*. Cambridge: Harvard University Press, 1974.

Imaminato Yoshinobu 今湊良信. "Mindai chūki no tōzoku ni tsuite" 明代中期の盗賊について. In Noguchi Tetsurō, ed., *Chūgokushi ni okeru ran no kōzu* 中国史における乱の構図. Tōkyō: Yūzankaku, 1986.

Inalcik, Halil. "Introduction: Empire and Population." In Halil Inalcik and Donald Quataert, eds., *An Economic and Social History of the Ottoman Empire, 1300–1914*. Cambridge: Cambridge University Press, 1994.

Inoue Susumu 井上進. "Hōshi no ichi" 方志の位置. In Mindaishi ronsō henshūiinkai, *Yamane Yukio kyōju taikyū kinen Mindaishi ronsō* 山根幸夫教授退休記念明代史論叢. Tokyo: Mindaishi ronsō henshūiinkai, 1990.

Ishida Hiroshi 石田浩. "Kaihōzen no Kahoku nōson no ichi seikaku—toku ni sonranku to byō to no kanren ni oite" 解放前の華北農村の一性格—特に村落と廟にとの関連おいて. *Kansai daigaku keizai ronshū* 關西大学経済論集, 32: 2–3 (1984). In Ishida, *Chūgoku no shakai keizai kōzō no kenkyū* 中国の社會経済構造の研究. Kyoto: Kōyō shōbō, 1986.

Ishihara Jun 石田. "Kahokushō ni okeru Min-Shin-Minkoku jidai no teiki-ichi—funpu, kaisō oyobi chūshin shūraku to no kankei ni tsuite" 華北省における明清民国時代の定期市—分布、解層、および中心集落との関係について. *Chirigaku hyōron* 地理学評論 46.4 (1973): 245–263.

Jiang Shoupeng 姜守鵬. "Mingmo Liaodong shizu" 明末遼東勢族. *Shehui kexue zhanxian* 社會科學戰線 2 (1987): 203–209.

Jiang Tingbi 蔣廷璧. *Guozi xiansheng Pushan Jiang Gong zhengxun* 國子先生璞山蔣公政訓 (1560). Reprinted in *Guanzhenshu jicheng* 官箴書集成. Hefei: Huangshan shushe, 1997.

Jiang Yikui 蔣一葵. *Chang'an kehua* 長安客話. Beijing: Beijing chubanshe, 1962.

Jiangsu shixian gaikuang 江蘇市概況. Jiangsusheng difangzhi bian weiyuanhui bangongshi. Jiangsu: Jiangsu jiaoyu chubanshe, 1991.

Jiao Hong 焦宏. *Guochao xianzheng lu* 國朝獻徵錄. 1594–1616. Reprint, Taibei: Xuesheng shuju, 1965.

Jin Ping Mei cidian 金瓶梅辭典. Beijing: Beijing shuju, 1991.

Johnson, Eric, and Eric Monkknonen, eds. *The Civilization of Crime: Violence in Town and Country since the Middle Ages.* Urbana: University of Illinois Press, 1996.

Johnston, Alistair. *Cultural Realism: Strategic Culture and Grand Strategies in Chinese History.* Princeton: Princeton University Press, 1995.

Kataoka Shibako 片岡芝子. "Minmatsu Shinsho no Kahoku ni okeru nōka keiei" 明末清初の華北における農家経営. *Shakai keizai shigaku* 社会経済史学 25.2–3 (June 1959): 77–100.

Kawagoe Yasuhiro 川越泰博. "Dai Min kaiten ni mieru Mindai eijokan no getsu-ryōgaku o megutte" 大明会典にみえる明代衛所官の月糧額をめぐって. *Kyūko* 汲古 15 (1989): 37–42.

———. "Mindai eisho no shajin ni tsuite" 明代衛所の舎人について. *Chūō daigaku bungakubu kiyō* 中央大学文学部紀要 31 (March 1986): 77–107.

———. "Mindai gunjishi ni kansuru kenkyūjōkyō o megutte" 明代軍事史に関する研究状況をめぐって. In Mori Masao, Noguchi Testsurō, and Hamashima Atsutoshi, eds., *Min-Shin jidaishi no kihon mondai* 明清時代史の基本問題. Tokyo: Kyūko shoin, 1997.

———. "Mindai hangun banjōkō" 明代班軍番上考. *Chūō daigaku bungakubu kiyō* 中央大学文学部紀要 22 (1977): 133–162.

———. "Tomoku no hen to shinseigun" 土木の変と親征軍. *Tōyōshi kenkyū* 東洋史研究 52.1 (June 1993): 24–55.

Kawakatsu Mamoru 川勝守. "Kōnan shichin no seisan, ryūtsū, shōhi no rekishiteki ichi—shukōgyōseisan to burai, konto, kyakufu" 江南市鎮の生産、流通、消費の歴史的位置—手工業生産と無頼、棍徒、脚夫. *Kyūshū daigaku Tōyōshi ronshū* 九州大学東洋史論集 26 (1998): 1–28.

———. "Minmatsu Shinsho ni okeru dakō to hōkō—kyū Chūgoku shakai ni okeru burai no shoshiryō" 明末清初における打行と訪行—舊中国社会における無頼の諸史料. *Shien* 史淵 119 (1982): 65–92.

———. "Minmatsu Shinsho no shōshi ni tsuite—kyū Chūgoku shakai ni okeru burai chishikijin no ichikeitai" 明末清初の訟師について—舊中国社会における無頼知識人の一形態. *Kyūshū daigaku Tōyōshi ronshū* 九州大学東洋史論集 9 (1981): 111–129.

Kishi Kazuyuki 岸和行. "Canton chihō shakai ni okeru buraizō—Minmakki no Shuchidō o megutte" 広東地方社会における無頼像—明末期の珠池盗をめぐって. In *Gen-Min-Shin ki ni okeru kokka shihai to minshū no saikentō-shihai no Chūgokuteki tokushitsu* 元明清期における国家支配と民衆の再討論—支配の中国的特質. Kyūshū daigaku tōyōshi kenkyūshitsu, 1983.

Kishimoto Mio 岸本美緒. "Sūtei jūnananen no Kōnan shakai to Pekin jōhō" 崇禎十七年の江南社会と北京情報. In Ono Kazuko, ed., *Minmatsu Shinsho no shakai to bunka* 明末清初の社会と文化. Kyōto: Kyōto daigaku jinbun kagaku kenkyūjo, 1996.

Kleeman, Terry. "Licentious Cults and Bloody Victuals: Sacrifice, Reciprocity, and Violence in Traditional China." *Asia Major* (third series) 8.1 (1994): 206.

Ko, Dorothy. *Teachers of the Inner Chambers: Women and Culture in Seventeenth Century China*. Stanford: Stanford University Press, 1994.

Kobayashi Kazumi 小林一美. "Chūgoku nōmin sensō shiron no saikentō" 農民戦争史論の再検討. In Mori Masao et al., eds., *MinShin jidaishi no kihonmondai* 明清時代史の基本問題. Tokyo: Kyūko shoin, 1997.

Kuhn, Philip. *Rebellion and Its Enemies in Late Imperial China: Militarization and Social Structure, 1796–1864*. Cambridge: Harvard University Press, 1970.

———. *Soulstealers*. Cambridge: Harvard University Press, 1990.

———. "The T'uan-lien Local Defense System at the Time of the Taiping Rebellion." *Harvard Journal of Asiatic Studies* 27 (1967): 218–255.

Kwan-wai So. *Japanese Piracy in Ming China during the Sixteenth Century*. Ann Arbor: Michigan State University Press, 1975.

Lach, Donald. *Asia in the Making of Europe*. Vol. 1. Chicago: University of Chicago Press, 1965.

Lamley, Harry. "Lineage Feuding in Southern Fujian and Eastern Guangdong under Qing Rule." In Jonathan Lipman and Stevan Harrell, eds., *Violence in China: Essays in Culture and Counterculture*. Albany: State University of New York Press, 1990.

———. "Hsieh-tou: The Pathology of Violence in Southeastern China." *Ch'ing-shih Wen-t'i* 3.7 (1977): 1–39.

———. "Lineage and Surname Feuds in Southern Fukien and Eastern Kwangtung under the Ch'ing." In Kwang-ching Liu, ed., *Orthodoxy in Late Imperial China*. Berkeley: University of California Press, 1990.

Langlois, John. "The Code and ad hoc Legislation in Ming Law." *Asia Major* (third series) 6.2 (1993): 85–112.

Lei Li 雷禮. *Guochao lieqing ji* 國朝列卿紀. After 1592. Reprint, Taibei: Cheng-wen chubanshe, 1970.

Li Dongyang et al. *Zhengde Da Ming huidian* (Seitoku Daimin Kaiten). Early six-teenth century. Reprint, Tokyo: Kyuko shoin, 1989.

Li Du 李渡. "Mingdai mubing zhidu jianlun" 明代募兵制度簡論. *Wen shi zhe* 文史哲 2 (1986): 62–68.

Li Guangbi 李光璧. "Ming zhongye Liu Liu Liu Qi da nongmin qiyi" 明中葉劉六劉七大農民起義. *Lishi jiaoxue* 歷史教學 4 (1951): 21–25. Later published in a slightly expanded version in Li Guangbi et al., *Zhongguo nongmin qiyi lunji*. Beijing: Sanlian shudian, 1958.

Li Heping 李和平. "Hebei de Huihui minzu" 河北的回回民族. *Ningxia shehui kexue* 寧夏社會科學 1 (1986): 34–39.

Li Jixian 李濟賢. "Mingdai mahu shulun" 明代馬戶述論. *Mingshi yanjiu* 明史研究 3 (1993): 10–20.

Li Jianxiong 李劍雄. "Yibu you jiazhi dan chongman le yiwen de Mingdai guji" 一部有價值但也充滿了疑問的明代古籍. *Lishi jiaoxue wenti* 歷史教學問題 1 (1987): 55–57, 63.

Li Kaixian 李開先. "Duishan Kang xiuzhuan zhuan" 對山康修撰傳. *Xianju ji* 閑居集. Reprinted in *Li Kaixian ji* 李開先集. Beijing: Xinhua shuju, 1959.

Li Longqian 李龍潛. "Mingdai junhu zhidu qianlun" 明代軍戶制度淺論. *Beijing shiyuan xuebao* 北京師院學報 1 (1982): 46–56.

Li Mengyang 李夢陽. *Kongtong ji* 空同集. 1531. Reprint, Taibei: Weiwen tushu chubanshe, 1976.

Li Shaoqiang 李紹強. "Shilun Ming Xiaozong de fushui zhengce" 試論明孝宗的賦稅政策. *Beifang luncong* 北方論叢 5 (1992): 62–66.

Li Wenzhi 李文治. "Mingmo de zhaibao yu yijun" 明末的寨堡與義軍. *Wenshi zazhi* 文史雜志 3.7–8 (1944). In Wu Zhihe, ed., *Mingshi yanjiu luncong* 明史研究論叢. Taibei: Dali chubanshe, 1984.

———. *Wan Ming minbian* 晚明民變. Shanghai: Zhonghua shuju, 1948.

Li Xun 李洵. "Lun Mingdai de li" 論明代的史. *Mingshi yanjiu* 明史研究 4 (1994): 51–59.

———. "Ming Wuzong he ta suo daibiao de fengjian guizu jieji" 明武宗和他所代表的封建貴族階級. In *Dierjie Ming Qingshi guoji xueshu taolunhui lunwenji* 第二屆明清史國際學術討論會論文集. Tianjin: Tianjin renmin chubanshe, 1993, pp. 604–613.

———. "Ming Wuzong yu zhujin" 明武宗與豬禁. *Shixue jikan* 史學集刊 2 (1993): 13–17, 48.

———. *Zhengde huangdi dazhuan* 正德皇帝大傳. Shenyang: Liaoning jiaoyu chubanshe, 1993.

Li Yuqing 李裕慶. *Jiangsu mingcheng lu* 江蘇名城錄. Beijing: Beijing lüxing, 1985.

Liang Fangzhong 梁方仲. "Mingdai de minbing" 明代的民兵. *Zhongguo shehui jingjishi jikan* 中國社會經濟史集刊 5.2 (1937): 200–234. In Wu Zhihe, ed., *Mingshi yanjiu luncong*, vol. 1. Taibei: Dali chubanshe, 1982.

Liang Fangzhong 梁方仲. *Zhongguo lidai hukou, tiandi, tianfu tongji* 中國歷代戶口田地田賦統計. Shanghai: Shanghai renmin chubanshe, 1980.

Liang Yong 梁勇. "Qianlun Mingdai Hebei de weisuo he juntun" 淺論明代河北的衛所和軍屯. *Hebei shifan daxue xuebao* 河北師範大學學報 2 (1987): 80–85.

Liao Xinyi 廖心一. "Liu Jin 'bianluan jiuzhi' kaolüe" 劉瑾《變亂舊制》考略. *Mingshi yanjiu luncong* 明史研究論叢 3 (1985): 139–166.

Liew, Foon Ming. *The Treatises on Military Affairs of the Ming Dynastic History (1368–1644)*. Hamburg: Gesellschaft Für Natur- Und Völkerkunde Ostasiens, 1998.

———. "Tuntian Farming of the Ming Dynasty." Ph.D. diss., University of Hamburg, 1984.

Lin Chunye 林春業 and Zhang Zengyuan 張增元. "Ming-Qing caoyun he yanye yu Tianjin chengshi de fazhan" 明清漕運和鹽業與天津城市的發展. *Tianjinshi yanjiu* 天津史研究 2 (1987): 13–24.

Lin Jinshu 林金樹. "Hongwuchao nongmin qiyi chutan" 洪武朝農民起義初探.

Zhongguo nongmin zhanzhengshi luncong 中國農民戰爭史論叢 4 (1982): 429–455.

Lin Zhisheng 林之盛. *Huangchao yingshi mingchen beikao lu* 皇朝應諡名臣備考錄. Late Ming. Photographic reprint of Wanli ed.

Ling Mengchu 凌濛初. *Erke pai'an jingqi* 二刻拍案驚奇. 1632; reprint, Shanghai: Shanghai guji chubanshe, 1983.

———. *Pai'an jingqi* 拍案驚奇. Late Ming. Reprint, Hong Kong: Youlian chubanshe, 1966.

Liu, James T. C. "Polo and Cultural Change: From Tang to Sung China." *Harvard Journal of Asiatic Studies* 45 (June 1985): 203–224.

Liu, Kwang-ching. "World View and Peasant Rebellion: Reflections on Post-Mao Historiography." *Journal of Asian Studies* 40.2 (1981): 295–326.

Liu Yusheng 劉玉生. "Fanying Mingdai Liu Liu Liu Qi nongmin qiyi zhangong de 'Shuangzhong ciji' bei" 反映明代劉六劉七農民起義戰功的雙忠祠記碑. *Zhongyuan wenwu* 中原文物 5 (1983): 115–118.

Lu Deyang 陸德陽. *Liumangshi* 流氓史. Shanghai: Shanghai wenyi chubanshe, 1995.

Lu Liang 路梁. "Mingchu yimin dui Hebei juluo diming de yingxiang" 明初移民對河北聚落地名的影響. *Diming zhishi* 地名知識 1 (1988): 28–30.

Luo Lixin 羅麗馨. "Mingdai jingying zhi xingcheng yu shuaibai" 明代京營之形成與衰敗. *Mingshi yanjiu zhuankan* 明史研究專刊 6 (1983): 1–36.

Ma Chujian 馬楚堅. "Mingdai de jiading" 明代的家丁. *Mingshi yanjiu zhuankan* 明史研究專刊 8 (Dec. 1985): 191–252.

Ma Deqing 馬德清 et al. and Zhou Chunhui 周春暉, comp. "Qinggong taijian huiyilu" 清宮太監回憶錄. In Zhongguo renmin zhengzhi xieshang huiyi quanguo weiyuanhui, Wenshi ziliao yanjiu weiyuanhui, eds. 中國人民政治協商會議全國委員會文史資料研究委員會, *Wan Qing gongting shenghuo jianwen* 晚清宮廷生活見聞.

Ma Mingdao 馬明道. *Mingchao huangjia xinyangkao chugao* 明朝皇家信仰考初稿. Taibei?: Zhongguo Huijiao wenhua jiaoyu jijinhui chuban, n.d.

Ma Shizhi 馬世之. "Liu Liu, Liu Qi qiyi jingong Shangcai wenti shitan" 劉六劉七起義進攻上蔡問題試談. *Xuchang shizhuan xuebao* 徐昌師專學報 4 (1985): 72–75.

Ma, Y. M. "The Knight-Errants in Hua-pen Stories." *T'oung-pao* 61 (75): 266–300.

Ma Zishu 馬自樹. "Mingdai jundui shuailuo de neizai yinsu" 明代軍隊衰弱的內在因素. *Gugong bowuyuan yuankan* 故宮博物院院刊 2 (1987): 11–17, 25.

Mackerras, Colin. *Western Images of China.* Hong Kong: Oxford University Press, 1989.

Maddern, Philippa. *Violence and Social Order, East Anglia, 1422–1442.* Oxford: Clarendon Press, 1992.

Mano Senryū 間野潜龍. "Kangan Ryū Kin to Chō Ei to no tairitsu" 宦官劉瑾と張永との対立. *Ritsumeikan bungaku* 立命館文学, 418–421 (1980): 273–289.

———. "Mindai rekichō jitsuroku no seiritsu" 明代歴朝実録の成立. In Tamura Jitsuzō, ed., *Mindai Man-Mōshi kenkyū* 明代満蒙史研究. Kyoto: Kyōto daigaku bungakubu, 1963.

Matsumoto Takaharu 松本隆晴. "Mindai bukyo ni tsuite no ichi kōsatsu" 明代武挙についての一考察. In *Yamane Yukio kyōju taikyū kinen Mindaishi ronsō* 山根幸夫教授退休記念明代史論叢. Tokyo: Mindaishi ronsō henshūiinkai, 1990.

McLaren, Anne. *The Chinese Femme Fatale: Stories from the Ming Period.* Sydney: Wild Peony, 1994.

McKnight, Brian. *Law and Order in Sung China.* Cambridge: Cambridge University Press, 1992.

———. "Urban Crime and Urban Security in Sung China." *Chinese Culture,* 29.4 (December 1988): 23–66.

Mencius. Translated from the Chinese by D. C. Lau. Penguin Classics edn. London: Penguin Books, 1970.

Meng Siming 蒙思明. *Yuandai shehui jieji zhidu* 元代社會階級制度. Beijing: Hafo Yanjing xueshe, 1937. Reprint, Hong Kong: Longmen shudian.

Mengcun Huizu zizhixian gaikuang bianxiezu 孟村回族自治縣概況編寫組. *Mengcun Huizu zizhixian gaikuang* 孟村回族自治縣概況. Shijiazhuang: Hebei renmin chubanshe, 1983.

Meskill, Johanna Menzel. *A Chinese Pioneer Family: The Lins of Wu-feng, Taiwan, 1729–1895.* Princeton: Princeton University Press, 1979.

Meskill, John. *Ch'oe P'u's Diary: A Record of Drifting Across the Sea.* Tucson: University of Arizona Press, 1965.

Miao Quanji 繆全吉. *Mingdai xuli* 明代胥吏. Taibei: Jiaxin shuini gongsi wenhua jijinhui, 1969.

———. "Qingdai mufu zhidu zhi chengzhang yuanyin" 清代幕府制度之成長原因. *Si yu yan* 思與言 5.3 (September 1967): 25–33.

Miki Satoshi 三木聰 . "Keishō zuraikō—toku ni 'ifuku' to no kanren ni tsuite" 軽生図頼考—特に威逼との関連について. *Shihō* 史朋 27 (1993): 1–18.

———. "Shigai no kyōkatsu—Chūgoku kinsei no zurai" 死骸の恐喝—中国近世の図頼. In Dōrōbo Kenkyūkai, ed., *Nusumi no bunkashi* 盗みの文化誌. Tokyo: Seikyūsha, 1996.

Ming Qing xiaoshuo cidian 明清小説詞典. Shijiazhuang: Huashan wenyi chubanshe, 1992.

Ming shilu 明實錄. 1418–Mid-Seventeenth century. Facsimile reproduction of *Guoli Beiping tushuguan cang hongge chaoben* 國立北平圖書館藏紅格抄本, 133 vols. Taibei: Zhongyang yanjiuyuan lishi yuyan yanjiusuo, 1961–1966.

Ming shilu leizuan: Beijing shiliao juan 明實錄類纂：北京史料卷. Wuhan: Wuhan chubanshe, 1992.

Mitamura Taisuke. *Chinese Eunuchs: The Structure of Intimate Politics.* Tokyo: Charles E. Tuttle Company, 1970.

Miyazaki Ichisada 宮崎市定. "Mindai So-Sho chihō no shidaifu to minshū" 明
代蘇松地方の士大夫. *Shirin* 史林 37.3 (1953): 1–33. Reprinted in *Miyazaki
Ichisada zenshū* 宮崎市定全集, 13:3–39. Tokyo: Iwanami shoten, 1992.

Mote, Frederick. "The Ch'eng-hua and Hung-chih Reigns, 1465-1505." In Denis
Twitchett and Frederick Mote, eds., *The Cambridge History of China*. Vol. 7,
The Ming Dynasty, 1368–1644, pt. 1. Cambridge: Cambridge University
Press, 1988.

———. "The T'u-mu Incident of 1449." In Frank Kierman and John Fairbank,
eds., *Chinese Ways in Warfare*. Cambridge: Harvard University Press, 1974.

Mu Dequan 穆德全. "Mingdai huizu de fenbu" 明代回族的分部. *Ningxia daxue
xuebao* 寧夏大學學報 3 (1987).

Muir, Edward, and Guido Ruggiero, eds. *History from Crime: Selections from
Quaderni Storici*. Translated from the Italian by Corrado Biazzo Curry,
Margaret A. Galluci, and Mary M. Galluci. Baltimore: Johns Hopkins
University Press, 1994.

Murray, Dian. *Pirates of the South China Coast, 1790–1810*. Stanford: Stanford
University Press, 1987.

Myers, Roman. *The Chinese Peasant Economy: Agricultural Development in Hopei
and Shantung, 1890–1949*. Cambridge: Harvard University Press, 1970.

Na Zhiliang, and William Kohler. *The Emperor's Procession: Two Scrolls of the
Ming Dynasty*. Taibei: National Palace Museum, 1970.

Nagasawa Kikuya 長沢規矩也. "Kō Min jōhō jirui o miru" 皇明条法事類纂を
観る. *Shoshigaku* 書誌学 15. 2 (1941): 27–32.

Nan Bingwen. "Mingdai liangji, Lu, Yu de minyang guanma zhidu" 明代兩畿魯
豫的民養官馬制度. In Ming-Qingshi guoji xueshu taolunhui lunwenji
mishuchu lunwenzu, *Ming-Qingshi guoji xueshu taolunhui lunwenji* 明清國際
學術討論會論文集. Tianjin: Tianjin renmin chubanshe, 1982.

Naquin, Susan. *Millenarian Rebellion in China: The Eight Trigrams Uprising of
1813*. New Haven: Yale University Press, 1976.

———. *Shantung Rebellion: The Wang Lun Uprising of 1774*. New Haven: Yale
University Press, 1981.

Needham, Joseph, Robin Yates, and Krzysztof Gawlikokowski, eds. *Science and
Civilization in China*. Vol. 5, *Chemistry and Chemical Technology*, pt. 6, *Military
Technology: Missiles and Seiges*. Cambridge: Cambridge University Press,
1994.

Ng, Vivien. "Ideology and Sexuality: Rape Laws in Ch'ing China." *Journal of
Asian Studies* 46.1 (1987): 57–70.

Ni Yue. *Qingxi mangao*. 青谿漫稿. Preface 1514. In vol. 1251 of *Wenyuange siku
quanshu* 文淵閣四庫全書, 1773–1783. Reprint, Taibei: Taiwan shangwu
yinshuguan, 1983.

Niida Noboru 仁井田陞. "Kyūshōhon Kō Min johō jirui san shiken" 舊鈔本皇
明事類纂私見. *Tōhō gakuhō* 東洋学報 27.4 (1940): 602–620.

Nimick, Thomas. "Ch'i Chi-kuang and I-wu County." *Ming Studies* 34 (July
1995): 17–29.

————. "The County, the Magistrate, and the Yamen in Late Ming China." Ph.D. diss., Princeton University, 1993.

Nishimura Genshō 西村元照. "Ryū Roku Ryū Nana no ran" 劉六劉七の乱. In Mori Masao and Tanigawa Michio, eds., *Chūgoku minshū hanranshi* 中国民衆反乱史, vol. 2. Tokyo: Heibonsha, 1979.

————. "Ryū Roku Ryū Nana no ran ni tsuite" 劉六劉七の乱について. *Tōyōshi kenkyū* 東洋史研究 32.4 (1974): 44–86.

Noda Tōru 野田徹. "Minchō kangan no seijiteki chii ni tsuite" 宦官の政治的地位について. *Kyūshū daigaku Tōyōshi kenkyū ronshū* 九州大学東洋史研究論集 21 (1993): 47–64.

————. "Mindai gaikangan no ichi keitai ni tsuite—chinshu kangan o megutte" 明代外宦官の一形態について — 鎮守宦官をめぐって. *Kyūshū daigaku Tōyōshi kenkyū ronshū* 九州大学東洋史研究論集 24 (1996): 25–54.

O Kŭm-sŏng (Oh, Keum-song) 吳金成. *Chungguk kŭnse sahoe kyŏngjesa yŏngu—Myŏng-dae sinsach'ŭng ŭi hyŏngsŏng kwa sahoe kyŏngjejŏk yŏkhal* 中國近世社會經濟史研究—明代紳士層의形成과社會經濟的役割 (Sŏultae tongyang sahak yŏngu ch'ŏngsŏ). Seoul: Ilchogak, 1986. Translated into Japanese by Watari Masahiro 渡昌弘 as *Mindai shakai keizaishi kenkyū—shinshisō no keisei to sono shakai keizaiteki yakuwari* 明代社会経済研究 — 紳士層の形成とその社会経済的役割. Tokyo: Kyūko shoin, 1990.

————. "Myŏng-Ch'ŏng sidae ŭi muroe: Yŏn'gu ŭi hyŏnhwang gwa gwache" 明清時代의無賴 : 研究의現況과課題. *Tongyang sahak yŏn'gu* 東方史學研究 50.4 (1995): 60–77.

Ocko, Jonathan. "Hierarchy and Harmony: Family Conflicts As Seen in Ch'ing Legal Cases." In Kwang-ching Liu, ed., *Orthodoxy in Late Imperial China*. Berkeley: University of California Press, 1990.

Ogawa Yōichi 小川陽一. *Nichiyō ruisho ni yoru Min-Shin shōsetsu no kenkyū* 日用類書による明清小説の研究. Tokyo: Kenbun shuppan, 1995.

Okuyama Norio 奥山憲夫. "Mindai chūki no keiei ni kansuru ichi kōsatsu" 明代中期の京営に関する一考察. *Mindaishi kenkyū* 明代史研究 8 (1980): 1–19.

————. "Mindai junbu seido no hensen" 明代巡撫制度の変遷. *Tōyōshi kenkyū* 東洋史研究 45.2 (Sept. 1986): 55–80.

Ōsawa Akihiro 大澤顯浩. "Minmatsu shūkyōteki hanran no ichi kōsatsu—kōto to shūkyō kessha no ketsugō keitai" 明末宗教的反乱の一考察 — 礦徒と宗教結社の結合形態. *Tōyōshi kenkyū* 東洋史研究 44.1 (1985): 45–76.

Ownby, David. *Brotherhoods and Secret Societies in Early and Mid-Qing China: The Formation of a Tradition*. Stanford: Stanford University Press, 1996.

————. "The 'Ethnic Feud' in Qing Taiwan: What Is This Violence Business Anyway? An Interpretation of the 1782 Zhang-Quan Xiedou." *Late Imperial China* 11.1 (1990): 75–98.

Parsons, James. *The Peasant Rebellions of the Late Ming Dynasty*. Tucson: University of Arizona Press, 1970.

Perry, Elizabeth. *Hideyoshi*. Cambridge: Harvard University Press, 1982.

————. *Rebels and Revolutionaries in North China, 1845–1945*. Stanford: Stanford University Press, 1980.

Perry, Mary Elizabeth. *Crime and Society in Early Modern Seville*. Hanover, N.H.: University of New England Press, 1980.

Peters, Edward. *Europe and the Middle Ages*. Englewood Cliffs, N.J.: Prentice-Hall, 1989.

Peterson, Willard. *The Bitter Gourd: Fang I-chi and the Impetus for Intellectual Change*. New Haven: Yale University Press, 1979.

Plaks, Andrew. *The Four Masterworks of the Ming Novel*. Princeton: Princeton University Press, 1987.

Qi Jiguang 戚繼光. *Jixiao xinshu* 紀效新書. 1526; reprint, Beijing: Renmin tiyu chubanshe, 1988.

Pomeranz, Kenneth. *Making of a Hinterland: State, Society, and Economy in Inland North China, 1853–1937*. Berkeley: University of California Press, 1993.

Qin Guan 秦觀. *Huai hai ji* 懷海集. Twelfth century. In vol. 1115 of *Wenyuange siku quanshu* 文淵閣四庫全書, 1773–1783. Reprint, Taibei: Taiwan shangwu yinshuguan, 1983.

Qiu Jun 丘濬. *Daxue yanyi bu* 大學衍義補. 1487; 1632 ed. Rare Book Collection, Harvard-Yenching Library, Harvard University.

————. *Daxue yanyibu* 大學衍義補. 1487. In vol. 713 of *Wenyuange Siku quanshu*. 1773–1783; reprint, Taibei: Taiwan shangwu yinshuguan, 1983.

Qiu Zhonglin 邱仲麟. "Cong jinli lüshen kan Mingdai Beijing shehui fengqi de bianqian guocheng" 從禁例屢申看北京社會風氣的變遷過程. *Danjiang shixue* 淡江史學 6 (1992): 67–88.

————. "Mingdai Beijing de shehui fengqi bianqian—lizhi yu jiazhiguan de gaibian" 明代北京的社會風氣變遷 — 禮制與價值觀的改變." *Dalu zazhi* 大陸雜誌 88.3 (1994): 28–42.

————. "Mingdai Beijing dushi shenghuo yu zhi'an de zhuanbian" 明代北京都市生活與治安的轉變. *Jiuzhou xuekan* 九州學刊 5.2 (October 1992): 49–106.

————. "Mingdai zigong qiuyong xianxiang zailun" 明代自宮求用現象再論. *Danjiang shixue* 淡江史學 6 (1994): 125–146.

Qufu shifan xueyuan lishixi 曲阜師範學院歷史係. "Cong Qufu yidai de jikuai beike kan lishishang nongmin qiyizhong de fan Kong douzheng" 從曲阜一帶的幾塊碑刻看歷史上農民起義中的反孔鬥爭. *Wenwu* 文物 213 (1974): 1–9.

Ricci, Matteo, and Nicola Trigault. *China in the Sixteenth Century: The Journals of Matthew Ricci, 1583–1610*. Translated from the Latin by Louis Gallagher. New York: Random House, 1953.

Robinson, David. "Banditry and Rebellion in the Capital Region during the Mid-Ming (1450–1525)." Ph.D. diss., Princeton University, 1995.

————. "Disturbing Images: Rebellion, Usurpation, and Rulership in Early-Sixteenth-Century East Asia—Korean Writings on Emperor Wuzong." *Journal of Korean Studies* 9 (2001).

————. "Notes on Hebei Eunuchs during the Mid-Ming." *Ming Studies* 34 (July 1995): 1–16.

————. "Politics, Force, and Ethnicity in Ming China: Mongols and the Abortive Coup of 1461." *Harvard Journal of Asiatic Studies* 59.1 (June 1999): 79–123.

————. "Korean Lobbying at the Ming Court: King Chungjong's Usurpation of 1506." *Ming Studies* 41 (Spring 1999): 37–53.

Ruggiero, Guido. *Violence in Early Renaissance Venice*. New Brunswick: Rutgers University Press, 1980.

Saeki Tomi 佐伯富. "Min Shin jidai no minsō ni tsuite" 明清時代の民壯につい て. *Tōyōshi kenkyū* 東洋史研究 15.4 (1957): 33–64.

Sakai Tadao 酒井忠夫. "Chūgokushijō no bō to ryūbō" 中国史上の氓と流氓. In Noguchi Tetsurō, ed., *Chūgokushi ni okeru ran no kōzu* 中国史における乱の構 図. Tokyo: Yūzankaku, 1986.

————. "Mindai zenchūki no hōkasei ni tsuite" 明代前中期の保甲制について. In Shimizu hakushi tsuitō kinen Mindaishi ronsō hensan iinkai, ed. *Shimizu hakushi tsuitō kinen Mindaishi ronsō* 清水博士追悼記念明代論叢. Tokyo: Shimizu hakushi tsuitō kinen Mindaishi ronsō hensan iinkai, 1962.

Sakurai Toshirō 桜井俊郎. "Mindai daisōhon seido no seiritsu to sono henyō" 明代題奏本制度の成立とその変容. *Tōyōshi kenkyū* 東洋史研究 51.2 (1993): 175–203.

Sansom, George. *A History of Japan, 1334–1615*. 7th printing. Tokyo: Tuttle Books, 1990.

Satō Fumitoshi 佐藤文俊. "Mindai chūki no gaiseki, Chōshi kyōdai" 明代中期 の外戚、張氏兄弟. *Tōyōshi kenkyū* 東洋史研究 49.3 (December 1990): 63–86.

————. *Minmatsu nōmin hanran no kenkyū* 明末農民反乱の研究. Tokyo: Kenbun shuppan, 1985.

Sawada Mizuho 沢田瑞穂. "Taikan Ryū Kin" 太監劉瑾. *Tenri daigaku gakuhō* 天 理大学学報 54 (1967): 1–31.

Serruys, Henry. "Foreigners in the Metropolitan Police during the Fifteenth Century." *Oriens Extremus* 8.1 (1961): 59–83.

————. "Landgrants to the Mongols in China: 1400–1460." *Monumenta Serica* 25 (1966): 394–405.

————. "The Mongols in China: 1400–1450." *Monumenta Serica* 27 (1968): 233–305.

————. "Remains of Mongol Customs in China during the Early Ming Period." *Monumenta Serica* 16 (1957): 137–190.

————. *Sino-Mongol Relations during the Ming*. Vol. 3, *Trade Relations; The Horse Fairs, 1400–1600*. In *Mélanges chinois et bouddhiques*, vol. 14, 1966–1967. Bruxelles: l'Institut belge des hautes études chinoises, 1967.

Shao Bao 邵寶. *Rongchuntang houji* 容春堂後集. First half of sixteenth century. Hua Ximin ed. Rare Book Collection, Harvard-Yenching Library, Harvard University.

————. *Rongchun tang ji* 容春堂集. Early sixteenth century. In vol. 1253 of *Wenyuange siku quanshu* 文淵閣四庫全書, 1773–1783. Reprint, Taibei: Taiwan shangwu yinshuguan, 1983.

Sharpe, J. A. *Crime in Early Modern England, 1550–1750*. New York: Longman, 1984.

———. "The History of Violence in England: Some Observations." *Past and Present* 108 (1985): 206–215.

Shaw, Brent. "Bandits in the Roman Empire." *Past and Present* 105 (Nov. 1984): 3–52.

Shek, Richard. "Sectarian Eschatology and Violence." In Jonathan Lipman and Stevan Harrell, eds., *Violence in China*. Albany: State University of New York Press.

Shen Defu 沈德符. *Wanli ye huo bian* 萬歷野獲編. 1619. 2d ed. Beijing: Zhonghua shuju, 1980.

Shen Dingping 沈定平. "Mingchao junzhi" 明朝軍制. In Liu Zhan 劉展, ed., *Zhongguo gudai junzhishi* 中國古代軍制史. Junshi kexue chubanshe, 1992.

———. "Mingdai qianqi jieji douzheng shulun" 明代前期階級鬥爭述論. *Mingshi yanjiu luncong* 明史研究論叢 3 (1985): 214–238.

Shen Shixing 申時行. *Da Ming huidian* 大明會典. Compiler. 1587; reprint, Taibei: Dongnan shubaoshe, 1964.

Shi Nai-an 施耐庵 and Luo Guanzhong 羅貫中. *Shui hu zhuan* 水滸傳. Beijing: Renmin wenwue chubanshe, 1985.

———. *Outlaws of the Marsh*. Translated from the Chinese by Sidney Shapiro. Beijing: Foreign Language Press, 1980.

Shi Yuan 石園. "Mingdai de hongpu" 明代的紅鋪. *Zhonghe yuekan* 中和月刊 2.3 (1941): 125–127.

Shimizu Taiji 清水泰次. "Jikyū kangan no kenkyū" 自宮宦官の研究. *Shigaku zasshi* 史学雑誌 43.1 (1931): 83–128.

Siku quanshu 四庫全書. 1773–1783; reprinted Taibei: Taiwan shangwu yinshuguan, 1983.

Sima Qian. "Harsh Officials." In *Records of the Historian*, translated by Burton Watson. New York: Columbia University Press, 1969.

Sima Qian et al. *Shiji*. Beijing: Zhonghua shuju, 1959.

Skinner, William. "Cities and Hierarchy of Local Systems." In William Skinner, ed., *The City in Late Imperial China*. Stanford: Stanford University Press, 1977.

———. "Regional Urbanization in Nineteenth Century China." In William Skinner, ed., *The City in Late Imperial China*. Stanford: Stanford University Press, 1977.

Smail, Donald. "Common Violence: Vengeance and Inquisition in Fourteenth Century Marseille." *Past and Present* 151 (May 1996): 28–59.

Sŏ In-bŏm 徐仁範. "Eijyo to eijyogun—gunshi no senjūhōhō o chūshin ni" 衛所と衛所軍—軍士の選充方法を中心に. *Mindaishi kenkyū* 明代史研究 27 (1999): 5–19.

———. "Minchūki no Hokuben bōei-ei to gunko—zaiei no yotei o chūshin toshite" 明中期の北辺防衛と軍戸—在営の余丁を中心とに. *Shūkan Tōyōgaku* 集刊東洋学 78 (1997): 81–103.

———. "Mindai chūki no Sensei no tohei ni tsuite" 明代中期の陝西の土兵について. *Shūkan Tōyōgaku* 集刊東洋学 74 (1995): 60–79.

———. "Tomoku no hen to kin-ŏhei—giyu to minso chūshin toshite" 土木の変と勤王兵―義勇と民壯を中心として. *Tōyō gakuhŏ* 東洋学報 82.1 (2000): 1–28.

So, Kwan-wai. *Japanese Piracy in Ming China during the Sixteenth Century*. Ann Arbor: Michigan State University Press, 1975.

Spence, Jonathan. *The Chan's Great Continent: China in Western Minds*. New York: W. W. Norton, 1998.

———. *The Memory Palace of Matteo Ricci*. New York: Penguin Books, 1984.

Spierenburg, Pieter. *The Broken Spell: A Cultural and Anthropological History of Preindustrial Europe*. New Brunswick: Rutgers University Press, 1991.

Staunton, George, trans. *Ta Tsing Leu Lee; Being the Fundamental Laws, and a Selection from the Supplementary Statutes of the Penal Code of China*. London: Cadell and Davies, 1810. Reprint, Taibei: Chengwen chubanshe, 1966.

Stone, Lawrence. "Interpersonal Violence in English Society, 1300–1980." *Past and Present* 101 (1983): 22–33.

Su Shi 蘇軾. *Su Shi wenji* 蘇軾文集. Late eleventh century. Reprint, Beijing: Zhonghua shuju, 1992.

Sun Xun 孫洵. *Huang Ming shuchao* 皇明疏鈔. 1584. Reprint, Taibei: Xuesheng shuju, 1986.

Suzuki Tadashi 鈴木正. "Mindai kahei kō" 明代家兵考. *Shikan* 史観 22–23 (1940): 1–26.

———. "Mindai katei kō" 明代家丁考. *Shikan* 史観 37 (1952): 23–40.

Takeuchi Teruo 竹内照夫. "Ketsuri no hibun ni tsuite" 闕里の碑文について. In *Uno Tetsujin sensei hakuju shukuga kinen Tōyōgaku ronsō* 宇野哲人先生白寿祝賀記念東洋学論叢. Tokyo: 1974.

Tallett, Frank. *War and Society in Early-Modern Europe, 1495–1715*. London: Routledge, 1992.

Tan Qixiang 譚其驤. "Shi Mingdai dusi weisuo zhidu" 釋明代都司衞所制度. *Yugong banyue kan* 禹貢半月刊 3.10 (1935): 459–464.

———. *Zhongguo lishi dituji* 中國地圖集, vol. 7. Shanghai: Ditu chubanshe, 1982.

Tan Qian 談遷. *Guoque* 國榷. Ca. 1653. Reprint, Beijing: Zhonghua shuju, 1988.

Tanaka Masatoshi. "Popular Uprisings, Rent Resistance, and Bondservant Rebellions in the Late Ming." In Linda Grove and Christian Daniels, eds., *State and Society in China: Japanese Perspectives on Ming-Qing Social and Economic History*. Tokyo: University of Tokyo Press, 1984.

T'ang Code. Vol. 2, *Specific Articles*. Translated by Wallace Johnson. Princeton: Princeton University Press, 1997.

Tani Mitsutaka 谷光隆. *Mindai basei no kenkyū* 明代馬政の研究. Kyoto: Tōyōshi kenkyūkai, 1972.

———. "Mindai no kunshin ni kansuru ichi kōsatsu" 明代の勲臣に関する一考察. *Tōyōshi kenkyū* 東洋史研究 29.4 (1971): 66–113.

Taniguchi Kikuo 谷口規矩雄. "Minmatsu kyōhei gihei ni tsuite—Minmatsu seikyoku hitokusari" 明末郷兵義兵について—明末政局一齣. (Kōbe daigaku bungakubu 神戸大学文学部) Kenkyū 研究 43 (1969): 99–122.

———. "Minmatsu Shinsho no hosai ni tsuite" 明末清初の堡寨について. [Hiratsuka] Tōkai daigaku shigakki 9 (1973): 1–15.

Taylor, Romeyn. "Ming T'ai-tsu and the Gods of the Walls and Moats." Ming Studies 4 (Spring 1977): 31–49.

———. "Official and Popular Religion and the Political Organization of Chinese Society in the Ming." In Liu Kwang-ching, ed., Orthodoxy in Late Imperial China. Berkeley: University of California Press, 1990.

———. "Yuan Origins of the Wei-so System." In Charles Hucker, ed., Chinese Government in Ming Times: Seven Studies. New York: Columbia University Press, 1969.

Teng, Ssu-yü. The Nien Army and Their Guerrilla Warfare, 1851–1868. Paris: Mouton, 1961; reprint, Westport, Conn.: Greenwood Press, 1984.

Teng Xincai 滕新才. "Ming Wuzong xinlun" 明武宗新論. Sichuan shifan daxue xuebao 四川師範大學學報 5 (1989): 85–89.

Tian Weiping 田衛平 and Liang Yong 梁勇. "Mingdai Hebei yimin wenti chuyi" 明代河北移民問題芻議. Hebei shiyuan xuebao 河北師院學報 2 (1988): 55–64.

Tiedemann, R. G. "The Persistence of Banditry: Incidents in Border Districts of the North China Plain." Modern China 8 (1982): 395–433.

Tilly, Charles. "War Making and State Making as Organized Crime." In Peter Evans, Dietrich Russchemeyer, and Theda Skocpol, eds., Bringing the State Back In. Cambridge: Cambridge University Press, 1985.

Tong, James. Disorder under Heaven: Collective Violence in the Ming Dynasty. Stanford: Stanford University Press, 1991.

Tsai, Shih-shan Henry. The Eunuchs of the Ming Dynasty. Albany: State University of New York Press, 1996.

Tsing Yuan. "Urban Riots and Disturbances." In Jonathan Spence and John Wills, eds., From Ming to Ch'ing: Conquest, Region, and Continuity in Seventeenth Century China. New Haven: Yale University Press, 1979.

Tsurumi Naohiro. "Rural Control in the Ming Dynasty." Translated by Timothy Brook and James Cole in Linda Groves and Christian Daniels, eds., State and Society in China: Japanese Perspectives on Ming-Qing Social and Economic History (Tokyo: University of Tokyo Press, 1984).

Twitchett, Denis, and Frederick Mote, eds. The Cambridge History of China, vols. 7 and 8 (pts. 1 and 2), The Ming Dynasty, 1368–1644. Cambridge: Cambridge University Press, 1988, 1998.

Udagawa Takehisa 宇田川武久. Higashi ajia heiki kōryūshi no kenkyū 東アジア兵器交流史の研究. Tokyo: Yoshikawa kōbunkan, 1993.

Ueda Shin 上田信. "Minmatsu Shinsho: Kōnan no toshi no burai o meguru shakai kankei, dakō to kyakufu" 明末清初: 江南の都市の無頼をめぐる社会関係、打行と脚夫. Shigaku zasshi 史学雑誌 90.12 (1981): 1619–1653.

Vale, Malcolm. *War and Chivalry: Warfare and Aristocratic Culture in England, France, and Burgundy at the End of the Middle Ages*. Athens: University of Georgia Press, 1981.

Von Glahn, Richard. "Municipal Reform and Urban Social Conflict in Late Ming Jiangnan." *Journal of Asian Studies* 50.2 (May 1991): 280–307.

Wada Masahiro 和田正広. "Minmatsu kahō no shūtsugen katei" 明末窩訪の出現過程. *Tōyōshi kenkyū* 東洋史研究 62.1–2 (1980): 71–98.

Wakeland, Joanne. "Metropolitan Administration in Ming China: Sixteenth Century Peking." Ph.D. diss., University of Michigan, 1982.

Wakeman, Frederick. *The Great Enterprise: The Manchu Reconstruction of Imperial Order in Seventeenth-Century China*. Berkeley: University of California Press, 1985.

———. "Rebellion and Revolution: The Study of Popular Movements in Chinese History." *Journal of Asian Studies* 36.2 (1977): 201–237.

Waldron, Arthur. *The Great Wall of China: From History to Myth*. Cambridge: Cambridge University Press, 1990.

Waltner, Ann. "Breaking the Law: Family Violence, Gender, and Hierarchy in the Legal Code of the Ming Dynasty." *Ming Studies* 36 (1996): 29–43.

Wanyan Shaoyuan 完顔紹元. *Liumang de bianqian* 流氓的變遷. Shanghai: Shanghai guji chubanshe, 1993.

Wang Ao 王鏊. *Zhenze changyu* 震澤長語. Early sixteenth century. In *Ming-Qing shiliao huibian* 明清史料彙編, *chuji* 初集. Taibei: Wenhai chubanshe, 1967.

———. *Zhenze chiwen* 震澤紀聞. Early sixteenth century. In Shen Jiefu, ed., *Jilu huibian*. 1617. Reprint, Taibei: Taiwan shangsu yinshuguan, 1969.

Wang Chunyu 王春瑜. "Mingdai liumang ji liuming yishi" 明代流氓及流氓意識. *Shehuixue yanjiu* 社會學研究 2 (1991): 122–126.

Wang Chunyu 王春瑜 and Du Wanyan 杜婉言, eds. *Mingdai huanguan yu jingji shiliao chutan* 明代宦官與經濟史料初探. Beijing: Zhongguo shehui kexueyuan, 1986.

Wang Hongxu 王鴻緒. *Mingshi gao* 明史稿. 1723. Reprint, Taibei: Mingwen shuju, 1991.

Wang Ling 王玲. *Beijing yu zhouwei chengshi guanxishi* 北京與周圍城市關係史. Beijing: Beijing Yanshan chubanshe, 1988.

Wang Qiong 王瓊. *Shuangxi zaji* 雙溪雜記. Mid-sixteenth century. In *Jinxian huiyan* 今獻彙言 and in *Baibu congshu jicheng* 百部叢書集成. Taibei: Yiwen yinshuguan, 1966.

Wang Shaoquan 汪少泉, ed. *Huang Ming zoushou leichao* 皇明奏疏類鈔. 1588. Photographic reprint, Hishi copy. Rare Book Collection, Gest Oriental Library, Princeton University.

Wang Shouren 王守仁. *Wang Yangming quanji* 王陽明全集. Shanghai: Shanghai guji chubanshe, 1992.

Wang Tingxiang 王廷相. *Junchuan zouyi ji* 浚川奏議集. Before 1572. Reprinted in *Wang Tingxiang ji* 王廷相集. Beijing: Zhonghua shuju, 1989.

Wang Xiande 王賢德. "Minmatsu dōranki ni okeru kyōson bōei" 明末動乱期に おける郷村防衛. *Mindaishi kenkyū* 明代史研究 2 (1975): 25–49.

———. *Mingmo xiangcun ziwei zhi yanjiu* 明末鄉村自衛之研究. Gaoxiong: Fuwen tushu chubanshe, 1992.

Wang Yinghua 王英華. "Mingdai guanfengzhi qianxi" 明代官俸制淺析. *Shixue jikan* 史學集刊 2 (2000): 82–89.

Wang Yuquan 王毓銓. "Huang Ming tiaofa shilei zuan duhou" 皇明條法事類纂 讀後. *Mingdai yanjiu luncong* 明代研究論叢 1 (1982): 1–28.

———. "Mingdai de junhu" 明代的軍戶. *Lishi yanjiu* 歷史研究 8 (1959): 21–34. Reprinted in his *Laiwu ji* 萊蕪集. Beijing: Zhonghua shuju, 1983.

———. *Mingdai de juntun* 明代的軍屯. Beijing: Zhonghua shuju, 1965.

———. "Mingdai de wangfu zhuangtian" 明代的王府莊田. In Wang Yuquan, *Laiwu ji* 萊蕪集. Beijing: Zhonghua shuju, 1983.

———. "Some Salient Features of the Ming Labor Service System." *Ming Studies* 21 (Spring 1986): 1–44.

Wanyan Shaoyuan 完顏紹元. *Liumang de bianqian* 流氓的變遷. Shanghai: Shanghai guji chubanshe, 1993.

Wei Lianke 魏連科. "Mingchu Hebei yimin shiliao jibu" 明初河北移民史料 輯補. *Hebei xuekan* 河北學刊 5 (1989): 75–77.

Wei Zuhui 韋祖輝. "Baofang yu Ming Wuzong: Jian yu Gai Jiemin, Ye Zufu xiansheng shangque" 豹房與明武宗：兼與蓋杰民，葉祖孚先生商確. *Gugong bowuyuan yuankan* 故宮博物院院刊 1 (1992): 29–33.

Weisser, Michael. *Crime and Punishment in Early Modern Europe.* Brighton: Harvester Press, 1982.

Wilkinson, Wade. "Newly Discovered Ming Military Registers." *Ming Studies* 3 (1976): 36–45.

Wills, John. "Maritime China from Wang Chih to Shih Lang: Themes in Peripheral History." In Jonathan Spence and John Wills, eds., From *Ming to Ch'ing: Conquest, Region, and Continuity in Seventeenth Century China.* New Haven: Yale University Press, 1979.

———. "Relations with Maritime Europeans, 1514–1662." In Denis Twitchett and Frederick Mote, eds., *Cambridge History of China.* Vol. 8, *The Ming Dynasty, 1368–1644,* pt. 2. Cambridge: Cambridge University Press, 1998.

Wong, R. Bin. *China Transformed: Historical Change and the Limits of European Experience.* Ithaca: Cornell University Press, 1997.

Wong, R. Bin, Theodore Huters, and Pauline Yu. "Introduction: Shifting Paradigms of Political and Social Order." In R. Bin Wong, Theodore Huters, and Pauline Yu, eds., *Culture and State in Chinese History: Conventions, Accommodations, and Critiques.* Stanford: Stanford University Press, 1997.

Wu Han 吳晗. "Ji Ming shi lu" 記明實錄, *Zhongyang yanjiuyuan lishi yuyan yanjiusuo jikan* 中央研究院歷史語言研究所集刊 18 (1948): 385–447. In *Dushi zhaji* 讀史扎記. 1956. Reprint, Beijing: Sanlian shudian, 1960.

———. "Mingdai de Jinyiwei he Dong-Xi chang" 明代的錦衣衛和東西廠. In

Dengxia ji 燈下集. Beijing: Shenghuo, dushu, xinzhi sanlian shudian, 1960; reprint, 1983.

———. "Mingdai de junbing" 明代的軍兵. *Zhongguo shehui jingjishi jikan* 中國 社會經濟集刊 2.2 (1937): 147–200.

———. *Zhu Yuanzhang zhuan* 朱元璋傳. Hong Kong: Zhuanji wenxue she, 1949.

Wu Lianzhi 吳連枝. *Goshi kaimon hachikyūken* 吳氏開門八極拳. Tokyo: Bei-subourumagajinsha, 1991.

Wu, Silas. "The Transmission of Ming Memorials and the Evolution of the Transmission Network, 1368–1627." *T'oung-pao* 54 (1968): 275–287.

Wu Xinli 武新立. "Xie Fen de *Hou jian lu* ji qi shiliao jiazhi" 謝蕡的後鑒錄及其史 料價值. *Zhongguoshi yanjiu* 中國史研究 1 (1980): 151–159.

Wu Yue 伍躍. "Administrative Costs of Local Governments during the Ming-Qing Period." *Transactions of the International Conference of Eastern Studies* 41 (1996): 105–113.

———. "Mindai no saishingin ni tsuite: yōeki to kanryō shūnyū no kankei" 明 代の柴薪銀について：徭役と官僚収入の関係. *Shirin* 史林 78.4 (July 1995): 98–123.

———. "Sōko o meguru saeki ni tsuite—Min-Shin jidai ni okeru yōeki to gyōsei no kankei" 倉庫をめぐる差役について — 明清時代における徭役と行政の 関係 (in three parts), *Ōsaka keizai hōka daigaku Higashi Ajia kenkyū* 大阪経済 法科大学東アジア研究, 11–13 (1996): 49–56, 39–54, 63–71.

Wu Yunting 吳云廷. "Tumu zhi bian qianhou de Menggu xiangren" 土木之變前 後的蒙古降人. *Hebei xuekan* 河北學刊 3 (1989): 106–111.

Wu Zhihe 吳智和. "Mingdai de jianghu dao" 明代的江湖盜. *Mingshi yanjiu zhuankan* 明史研究專刊 1 (1978): 107–137.

Xia Xie 夏燮, comp. *Ming tong jian* 明通鑒. Ca. 1870. Reprint, Beijing: Zhonghua shuju, 1959.

Xiao Lijun 肖立軍. "Mingdai de zhifa fanfa ji chengzhi cuoshi" 明代的執法犯法 及懲治措施. *Wenshi zashi* 文史雜志 5 (1994): 42–43.

Xiao Xu 肖許. "Mingdai jiangshuai jiading de xingshuai ji qi yingxiang" 明代將 帥家丁的興衰及其影響. *Nankai shixue* 南開史學 1 (1984): 102–122.

Xie Fen 謝蕡. *Hou jian lu* 後鑒錄. Early sixteenth century. In Xie Guozhen, ed., *Mingshi ziliao congkan* 明史資料叢刊, 1st series. Jiangsu renmin chubanshe, 1981.

Xie Guozhen 謝國楨. *Mingdai nongmin qiyi shiliao xuanbian* 明代農民起意史料選 編. Fujian: Fujian renmin chubanshe, 1981.

Xie Yucai 解毓才. "Mingdai weisuo zhidu xingshuai kao" 明代衛所制度興 衰考. *Shuowen yuekan* 説文月刊 2 (1940): 9–12. In Bao Zunpeng 包遵彭, ed., *Mingdai zhengzhi* 明代政治. Taibei: Xuesheng shuju, 1968.

Xin Xiuming 信修明. *Lao taijian de huiyi* 老太監的回憶. Beijing: Beijing Yanshan chubanshe, 1992.

Xu Daling 許大齡. "Mingdai Beijing de jingji shenghuo" 明代北京的經濟生活. *Beijing daxue xuebao* 北京大學學報 42 (1959): 185–207.

Xu Hong (Hong Hsu) 徐泓. "Ming Hongwu nianjian de renkou yixi" 明洪武年間的人口移徙. In Zhongyang yanjiuyuan sanmin zhuyi yanjiusuo, ed., *Diyijie lishi yu Zhongguo shehui bianqian (Zhongguo shehuishi) yantaohui* 第一屆歷史與中國社會變遷 (中國社會史) 研討會. Taibei: Zhongyang yanjiuyuan sanmin zhuyi yanjiusuo, 1982.

———. "The Internal Migration Policy During the Early Ming Period." *Guoli Taiwan Daxue wen shi zhe xuebao* 國立臺灣大學文史哲學報 36 (December 1989): 51–76.

———. "Mingdai houqi huabei shangpin jingji de fazhan yu shehui fengqi de bianqian" 明代後期華北商品經濟的發展與社會風氣的變遷. In Zhongyang yanjiuyuan jingji yanjiusuo, ed., *Dierci Zhongguo jindai jingjishi huiyi* 第二次中國近代經濟史會議, vol. 1. Taibei: Institute of Economics, Academica Sinica, 1989.

Xu Xueju 徐學聚. *Guochao dianhui* 國朝典會. 1601. Reprint, Taibei: Xuesheng shuju, 1965.

Yamane Yukio 山根幸夫. "Genmatsu no ran to Minchō shihai no kakuritsu" 元末の乱と明朝支配の確立. In *Higashi Ajia sekai no tenkai, 2: Sekai rekishi 12, chūsei 6* 東アジア世界の展開. Tokyo: Iwanami shoten, 1979.

———. "Kahoku no byōkai: Santōshō o chūshin ni shite" 華北の廟会：山東省を中心にして. *Tōkyō joshi daigaku shiron* 東京女子大学史論 17 (1967): 1–22.

———. *Mindai Yōeki seido no tenkai*. Tokyo: Tōkyō joshi daigaku gakkai, 1966.

———. "Minmatsu nōmin hanran to shinshisō no taiō" 明末農民反乱と紳士層の対応. In vol. 2 of Nakajima Satoshi sensei koki jigyōkai, ed., *Nakajima Satoshi sensei koki kinen ronshū* 中島先生古希記念論集. Tokyo: Kyuko shoin, 1981.

———. "Min-Shin jidai Kahoku ni okeru teiki ichi" 明清時代華北における定期市. *Tōkyō joshi daigaku shiron* 東京女子大学史論 8 (1960): 493–504.

———. "Min-Shin jidai Kahoku shishū to gakō" 明清時代華北市集と牙行. In *Hoshi hakushi taikan kinen Chūgokushi ronshū* 星博士退官記念中国史論集. Yamagata: Jigyōkai, 1978.

———. *Min-Shin kahoku teikishi no kenkyū* 明清華北定期市の研究. Tokyo: Kyūko shoen, 1995.

———. "Min-Shinsho no kahoku no shishū to shinshi to gōmin" 明清初の華北の市集と紳士と豪民. In *Nakayama Hachirō kyōju shōju kinen Min Shinshi ronsō* 中山八郎教授頌寿記念明清史論叢. Tokyo: Ryōgen shoten, 1977.

Yamane Yukio 山根幸夫 and Yu Zhijia 于志嘉. *Mindai keiseibun bunrui mokuroku* 明代経世文分類目録. Tokyo: Tōyō bunko, 1986.

Yang Guoxiang 楊國祥 et al. *Mingshilu leizuan: Beijing shiliaojuan* 明實録類纂：北京史料卷. Wuhan: Wuhan chubanshe, 1992.

Yang Hong 楊泓. *Zhongguo gubingqi luncong* 中國古兵器論叢. Rev. ed., 1985. Beijing: Wenwu chubanshe, 1980.

Yang Shaoyou 楊紹猷 and Mo Junqing 莫俊卿. *Mingdai minzushi* 明代民族史. Chengdu: Sichuan minzu chubanshe, 1996.

Yang Tinghe 楊廷和. *Shicao yulu* 視草餘錄. 1527. In *Yang wen zhong san lu* 楊文忠三錄. 1607. Reprinted in *Wenyuange siku quanshu* 文淵閣四庫全書 1773–1783; Taibei: Taiwan shangwu yinshuguan, 1983, vol. 423.

Yang Xianyi and Gladys Yang. *The Courtesan's Jewel Box: Chinese Stories of the Tenth to Seventeenth Centuries.* Beijing: Foreign Language Press, 1981.

Yang Yang 楊暘, Liang De 梁德, and Hong Yun 洪雲. "Mingdai zheyu Liaodong liuren yanjiu" 明代謫寓遼東流人研究. *Mingshi yanjiu* 明史研究 2 (1992): 122–131.

Yang Yiqing 楊一清. *Libu xianna gao* 吏部獻納稿. 1525. Microfilm. Rare Book Collection, Gest Oriental Library, Princeton University.

Yang Zhengtai 楊正泰. "Ming Qing shiqi Changjiang yibei yunhe chengzhen de tedian yu bianqian" 明清時期長江以北運河城鎮的特點與變遷. *Lishi dili yanjiu* 歷史地理研究 1 (1986): 104–129.

Ye Zufu 葉祖孚. "Xiyuan baofang ye yang bao" 西苑豹房也養豹. *Gugong bowuyuan yuankan* 故宮博物院院刊 2 (1989): 24–25.

Yin Junke 尹鈞科. "Mingdai Beijing jiaoqu cunluo de fazhan" 明代北京郊區村落的發展. *Lishi dili* 歷史地理 3 (1983): 121–130.

Yin Yungong 尹韻公. *Zhongguo Mingdai xinwen chuanboshi* 中國明代新聞傳播史. Chongqing: Chongqing chubanshe, 1990.

Yu Jideng 余繼登. *Diangu jiwen* 典故紀聞. 1601. Reprinted in Wang Hao, ed., *Jifu congshu* 畿輔叢書. Dingzhou: Wanshi kanben, 1879–1892.

Yu Zhijia 于志嘉. "Mindai gunko no shakaiteki chii ni tsuite: Gunko no kon-in o megutte" 明代軍戶の社會的地位について：軍戶婚姻をめぐって. *Mindaishi kenkyū* 明代史研究 18 (1990): 7–32.

———. "Mindai gunko no shakaiteki chii ni tsuite: Kakyo to ninkan ni oite" 明代軍戶の社會的地位について：科舉と任官において. *Tōyō gakuhō* 東洋学報 71.3–4 (1990): 91–131.

———. "Mingdai liangjing jiandu yu weisuo junhu qianxi zhi guanxi" 明代兩京建都與衛所軍戶遷徙之關係. *Zhongyang yanjiuyuan lishi yuyan yanjiusuo jikan* 中央研究院歷史語言研究所集刊 64.1 (March 1993): 135–174.

———. "Mingdai Jiangxi bingzhi de yanbian" 明代江西兵制的演變. *Zhongyang yanjiuyuan lishi yuyan yanjiusuo jikan* 中央研究院歷史語言研究所集刊 66.4 (December 1995): 995–1073.

———. "Mingdai Jiangxi weisuo junyi de yanbian" 明代江西衛所軍役的演變. *Zhongyang yanjiuyuan shiyusuo yanjiusuo jikan* 中央研究院歷史語言研究所集刊 68.1 (1997): 1–51.

———. *Mingdai junhu shixi zhidu* 明代軍戶世襲制度. Taibei: Xuesheng shuju, 1987.

———. "Mingdai wuzhi xuanbu yu weisuo wuguanzhi de yanjiu—ji Zhongyanyuan shiyusuo cang Mingdai wuzhi xuanbu canben jian ping Kawagoe Yasuhiro de xuanbu yanjiu" 明武職選簿與衛所武官制的研究 — 記中研院史語所藏明代武職選簿殘本兼評川越泰博的選簿研究, *Zhongyang yanjiuyuan lishi yuyan yanjiusuo jikan* 中央研究院歷史語言研究所集刊 69.1 (1998): 45–74.

———. "Mingdang de liyong yu Mingdai weisuo zhidu yanjiu" 明檔的利用與明代衛所制度研究, *Dalu zazhi* 大陸雜誌 99.5 (1999): 201–218.

———. "Shilun zupu zhong suojian de Mingdai junhu" 試論祖譜中所見的明代軍戶. *Zhongyang yanjiuyuan lishi yuyan yanjiusuo jikan* 中央研究院歷史語言研究所集刊 57.4 (1986): 635–667.

Yuan Liangyi 袁良義. *Mingmo nongmin zhanzheng* 明末農民戰爭. Beijing: Zhonghua shuju, 1987.

Yun Chŏng-bun 尹貞粉. "Myŏngdae kunhoche wa uisoche e taehayŏ" 明代軍戶制와衛所制에대하여. *Tongbang hakchi* 東方學志 43 (1984): 305–329.

Zeng Weihua 曾維華 and Yan Yaozhong 嚴耀中. "Cong Mingdai Shaolin si de ji fang beitamingwen kan Mingdai sengbing 從明代少林寺的幾方碑塔文看明代僧兵." *Shanghai shifan xueyuan xuebao* 上海師範學院學報 2 (1984): 75–77.

Zha Jizuo 查繼佐. *Zui wei lu* 罪惟錄. Ca. 1670. In Shangwu yinshuguan, ed., *Sibu congkan sanbian shibu* 四部叢刊三編史部. Shanghai: Shangwu yinshu guan, 1937–1938.

Zhang Gang 張岡. "Guanyu Mingchu Hebei yimin de kaocha" 關於明初河北移民的考察. *Hebei xuekan* 河北學刊 4 (1983): 141–148.

———. "Mingdai Beizhili diqu de nongye jingji" 明代北直隸地區的農業經濟. *Hebei xuekan* 河北學刊 1 (1989): 65–70.

Zhang Longxi. *Mighty Opposites: From Dichotomies to Differences in the Comparative Study of China*. Stanford: Stanford University Press, 1998.

Zhang Tingyu 張廷玉 et al., eds. *Mingshi* 明史. 1736. Reprint, Beijing: Zhonghua shuju, 1984.

Zhang Xuan 張萱. *Xiyuan wenjian lu* 西園聞見錄. 1632. Reprint, Taibei: Mingwen chubanshe, 1991.

Zhang Zengyuan 張增元. "Tianjin yanshang yikui" 天津鹽商一窺. *Tianjinshi yanjiu* 天津史研究 2 (1986): 12–19.

Zhao Lisheng 趙麗生. "Mingdai Zhengdejian jici nongmin qiyi de jingguo he tedian" 明代正德間幾次農民起義的經過和特點. *Wenshizhe* 文史哲 12 (1954). In Zhao Lisheng and Gao Zhaoyi, eds., *Zhongguo nongmin zhanzhengshi lunwenji* 中國農民戰爭史論文集. Shanghai: Xinzhishi chubanshe, 1955.

Zhao Ming 趙明. "Mingdai bingzhi liushinian zhi huigu" 明代兵制六十年之回顧. *Zhongguoshi yanjiu dongtai* 中國史研究動態 8 (1993): 14–20.

Zhao Zhongnan 趙中男. "Lun Mingdai junduizhong jiading de tedian yu diwei" 論明代軍隊中家丁的特點與地位. *Shehui kexue zhanxian* 社會科學戰線 3 (1988): 144–149.

———. "Lun Mingdai junshi jiading zhidu xingcheng de shehui jingji tiaojian jiqi fazhan" 論明代軍事家丁制度形成的社會經濟條件及其發展. *Shehui kexue jikan* 社會科學輯刊 2 (1991): 86–90.

Zheng Kecheng 鄭克晟. *Mingdai zhengzheng tanyuan* 明代政爭探源. Tianjin: Tianjin guji chubanshe, 1988.

(Zhengde 正德) *Da Ming huidian* 大明會典. Li Dongyang 李東陽. Early sixteenth century; reprint, Tokyo: Kyūko shoin, 1989.

Zhongguo kexueyuan Beijing tianwentai 中國科學院北京天文臺, ed. *Zhongguo difangzhi lianhe mulu* 中國地方志聯合目錄. Beijing: Zhonghua shuju, 1985.

Zhou Shunwu 周舜武. *China Provincial Geography*. Beijing: Foreign Language Press, 1992.

Zhou Xibao 周錫保. *Zhongguo gudai fushi shi* 中國古代服飾史. Beijing: Zhongguo xiju chubanshe, 1984.

Zhou Xun 周汛 and Gao Chunming 高春明. *Zhongguo fushi wuqian nian* 中國服飾五千年. Hong Kong: Shangwu yinshuguan, 1984.

Zhu Guozhen 朱國禎. *Huang Ming da shi ji* 皇明大事記. In his *Huang Ming shi gai* 皇明史概. 1632. Reprinted in *Yuan Ming shiliao congbian* 元明史料叢編, series no. 1. Taibei: Wenhai chubanshe, 1984.

———. *Yongzhuang xiaopin* 涌幢小品. 1621. Reprint, Beijing: Zhonghua shuju, 1959.

Zhu Honglin (Chu Hung-lam) 朱鴻林. "Mingdai zhongqi fangshe zhian congjian lixiang zhi zhanxian" 明代中期方社治安重建理想之展現. *Chungguk hakpo* 中國學報 32 (1992): 87–100.

Zhu Yunming 祝允明. *Jianghai jianqu ji* 江海殲渠記. Early sixteenth century. In *Congshu jicheng chubian* 叢書集成初編. Shanghai: Shanghai shangwu yinshuguan, 1936.

Gazetteers

Baoding fuzhi 保定府志. 1607. In *Riben cang Zhongguo hanjian difangzhi congkan*. Beijing: Shumu wenxian chubanshe, 1992.

Baxian xinzhi 霸縣新志. 1934. Reprint, Taibei: Chengwen chubanshe, 1968.

Bazhou zhi 霸州志. 1548. In *Tianyige cang Mingdai fangzhi xuankan*. Shanghai: Shanghai guji shudian, 1963; reprint, 1981.

Bozhou zhi 亳州志. 1564. Microfilm. Rare Book Collection, Gest Oriental Library, Princeton University.

———. 1775. Reprint, Taibei: Chengwen chubanshe, 1985.

Cangzhou zhi 滄州志. 1603. Microfilm. Rare Book Collection, Gest Oriental Library, Princeton University.

Dingzhou zhi 定州志. 1850; reprinted, Taibei: Chengwen chubanshe, 1969.

Dongchang fuzhi 東昌府志. 1600. Microfilm. Rare Book Collection, Gest Oriental Library, Princeton University.

Fuyang xianzhi 阜陽縣志. 1755. Reprint, Taibei: Chengwen chubanshe, 1985.

Guangping fuzhi 廣平縣志. 1549. In *Tianyige cang Mingdai fangzhi xuankan*. Shanghai: Shanghai guji shudian, 1981.

Guangshan xianzhi 光山縣志. 1556. In *Tianyige cang Mingdai fangzhi xuankan*. Shanghai: Shanghai guji shudian, 1981.

Gucheng xianzhi 固城縣志. 1594. Microfilm. Rare Book Collection, Gest Oriental Library, Princeton University.

Hejian fuzhi 河間府志. 1540. In *Tianyige cang Mingdai fangzhi xuankan*. Shanghai: Shanghai guji shudian, 1981.

Jining zhili zhouzhi 濟寧直隸州志. 1860. Reprint, Taibei: Xuesheng shuju, 1968.

Jining zhouzhi 濟寧州志. 1673. Microfilm. Rare Book Collection, Gest Oriental Library, Princeton University.

Laiwu xianzhi 萊蕪縣志. 1548. Microfilm. Rare Book Collection, Gest Oriental Library, Princeton University.

Liangxiang xianzhi 良鄉縣志. 1924. Reprint, Taibei: Chengwen chubanshe, 1968.

Lintao fuzhi 臨洮府志. 1605. Microfilm. Rare Book Collection, Gest Oriental Library, Princeton University.

Nanyang fuzhi 南陽府志. 1695 (1768?). Reprint, Taibei: Chengwen chubanshe, 1968.

Qufu xianzhi 曲阜縣志. Early sixteenth century. Reprint, Shandong: Shandong youyi shushe, 1989.

———. 1774. Reprint, Taibei: Chengwen chubanshe, 1968.

Shangcai xianzhi 上蔡縣志. 1691. Reprint, Taibei: Chengwen chubanshe, 1976.

Shanyin xianzhi 山陰縣志. 1551. Microfilm. Rare Book Collection, Gest Oriental Library, Princeton University.

Shuntian fuzhi 順天府志. 1593. Microfilm. Rare Book Collection, Gest Oriental Library, Princeton University.

———. 1884–1886. Reprint, Taibei: Chengwen chubanshe, 1965.

Suzhou fuzhi 宿州府志. 1537. In *Tianyige cang Mingdai fangzhi xuankan*. Shanghai: Shanghai guji shudian, 1982.

Tancheng xianzhi 郯城縣志. 1673. Microfilm. Rare Book Collection, Gest Oriental Library, Princeton University.

Tongzhou zhi 通州志. 1578. In *Tianyige cang Mingdai fangzhi xuankan*. Shanghai: Shanghai guji shudian, 1981.

———. 1755. Reprint, Taibei: Xuesheng shuju, 1968.

Tongzhou zhilüe 通州志略. 1549. Photostat reprint. Jinbun kenkyūjo, Kyoto.

Wenan xianzhi 文安縣志. 1629. Microfilm. Rare Book Collection, Gest Oriental Library, Princeton University.

———. 1703. Microfilm. Rare Book Collection, Gest Oriental Library, Princeton University.

———. 1922. Reprint, Taibei: Chengwen chubanshe, 1968.

Xiayi xianzhi 夏邑縣志. 1548. In *Tianyige cang Mingdai fangzhi xuankan*. Shanghai: Shanghai guji shudian, 1982.

Xuzhou zhi 徐州志. 1557. Reprint, Tianjin: Tianjin guji chubanshe, 1989.

Yexian zhi 葉縣志. 1542. Microfilm. Rare Book Collection, Gest Oriental Library, Princeton University.

Yingshan xianzhi 應山縣志. 1540. In *Tianyige cang Mingdai fangzhi xuankan*. Shanghai: Shanghai guji shudian, 1982.

Yongqing xianzhi 永清縣志. 1780. Reprint, Taibei: Xuesheng shuju, 1968.

Yuzhou zhi 裕州志. 1546 and 1717. Microfilms. Rare Book Collection, Gest Oriental Library, Princeton University.

Zhangde fuzhi 彰德府志. 1522. In *Tianyige cang Mingdai fangzhi xuankan.* Shanghai: Shanghai guji shudian, 1982.

Zhending fuzhi 鎮江府志. 1549. Microfilm. Rare Book Collection, Gest Oriental Library, Princeton University.

———. 1596. Microfilm. Rare Book Collection, Gest Oriental Library, Princeton University.

Index

aboriginal troops, 14, 145, 148, 149
administration: interstices, 164; local resources, 81–82
Altar of Heaven, 138–139
archery, 112
arms. *See* weapons

bandit, 22, 31, 41, 52, 67–68, 70, 82, 90, 96, 122, 129, 134, 140, 158
banditry, 3–4, 7, 11, 19–22, 32, 37, 45, 86, 99, 121, 135, 162, 167, 174n. 5, 215n. 68; causes of, 54, 56, 62, 83; definitions of, 47, 201n. 9; related laws, 47, 66–67
bare sticks, 21
Bazhou, 29, 33, 58, 61, 102, 103, 114, 126, 129, 138, 146, 153, 159–161, 190n. 45
Baoding, 30, 40, 46, 54, 57, 63, 66, 108, 129, 139, 147, 156, 157, 191n. 57
Beijing, 3, 13, 26, 27, 35, 40, 45; dominance of, 42–43; growth of, 47; population, 11–12, 47; security, 47, 155–156, 161
border generals, 149, 152
border troops, 14, 129–130, 132, 133, 136, 145, 148, 149, 152, 225n. 42
Bozhou, 136–137, 159
bravos, 7, 84, 97, 117
brothels, 49
brigands. *See* bandit

Calvo, Vasco, 9–10
Cangzhou, 30, 32, 62
Cao Jixiang (d. 1461), 86

Capital Garrisons, 14, 16, 18, 38, 62, 64, 75, 77, 80, 86, 91, 96, 102, 114, 123, 126, 129, 132, 136, 145, 158, 220n. 4
Capital Region, 3, 14; cities, 30–31; economy, 29–31; geography, 29–30; map of, 17; population, 31, 33; society, 31–33
cavalry, 18, 54, 91, 144, 197n. 105
Chen Kui, 53–54
Chen Quanzhi, 90
Chu Quan (1457–1513), 83–84
clothing: dragon robes, 133–134; status, 133–134
Confucian complex, 124
community, 20, 25, 82, 87, 100, 120, 121, 123, 133, 142
court intrigue, 15
crime, 23, 47, 79, 84, 163, 164, 170

dahang. See fighters guild
daozei. See bandit; rebel
Deng Maoqi, 91
Dingzhou, 115
dragon robes, 133–134
drought, 15

economy of violence, 2–3, 7, 96, 162, 169, 172, 174n. 1
elites: capital, 7, 50–52, 68, 120, 163, 164, 169; definition, 166–167; local, 19, 20, 33, 35, 84, 87, 88, 97, 98, 100, 103, 121, 123, 142, 144, 167, 172, 214n. 55; as patrons, 50–52, 90, 144, 163
emperors: Filial Ancestor (Xiaozong), 63, 104; Grand Progenitor (Taizu, Zhu Yuan-

279

About the Author

DAVID ROBINSON, who earned his doctorate in East Asian Studies from Princeton University, is currently assistant professor of history at Colgate University. He is the author of several articles on banditry, Sino-Korean relations, and the role of foreigners in China during the early modern period. *Bandits, Eunuchs, and the Son of Heaven* is his first book.